GRAND TRAVERSE
THE CIVIL WAR ERA

John C. Mitchell

SUTTONS BAY PUBLICATIONS

Published by Suttons Bay Publications, 301 St. Joseph Avenue, Box 361, Suttons Bay, MI 49682

info@greatlakeshistory.com

Printed and bound in the United States. First printing May 2011.

ISBN 978-0-9621466-4-0

Cover and book design by Saxon Design, Inc.

Contents

To My Father
James F. Mitchell
who served as a naval engineer in the
Atlantic, Pacific, and Mediterranean Theatres
during World War II.

Introduction

Grand Traverse: The Civil War Era is a story of contrasts. While the bonds uniting the North and South frayed under the weight of slavery, and then broke into the violence of the American Civil War, the wilderness harbors along the coast of Grand Traverse blossomed into booming port towns.

I have tried whenever possible to use first-hand accounts to tell the history of *Grand Traverse: The Civil War Era,* letting the reader experience the age of conflict through their eyes. Together the sources bear witness to diverse communities settling along the northern coast of Lake Michigan in an era that not only transformed Grand Traverse, but also radically altered the course of the United States.

Two extensive, first-hand accounts guide this book. The first is the diary of Reverend George Smith, a 40 year-long journal that is arguably the most comprehensive individual perspective of life along the coast of Lake Michigan in the mid-19th century. The diary only recently became available as a whole through the efforts of Avis Wolfe, whose late husband Bud was a descendant of the Native American Civil War hero Payson Wolfe and Reverend Smith's daughter Mary. I had the privilege of being the first author to mine the diary's vast storehouse of Grand Traverse Civil War history, and I knew almost immediately upon perusing its contents that the challenge of *Grand Traverse: The Civil War Era* would be to do justice to the epic story unfolding before me. The second driving source is the *Grand Traverse Herald,* the newspaper founded in late 1858 by the nationally recognized publisher Morgan Bates. The paper rolled off the presses just in time to capture the drama of the Civil War in Grand Traverse from a radical, anti-slavery point of view. A compendium of letters, photographs, and diaries from various sources round out the picture of life during this tempestuous time.

The Civil War history featured in this book evolved through four years of research. I found more Grand Traverse stories than I had expected, though I know I have missed at least a few. One of my goals for this book was to advance the discovery of other important Grand Traverse Civil War histories, and I look forward to hearing from everyone with a family story or photograph from the era to share. My email is printed on the back cover and I respond to all correspondence personally.

I began this project 50 years ago when I penned a little book on the Civil War – my first major work as an author. I must have been inspired by Civil War Centennial events of the time to take on the most sacred years of American history at the age of nine. Even then I sensed that something important happened during the Civil War that shaped the United States, something deeper than the wild charges and booming cannons and waving flags that fueled my boyhood imagination. This work, which attempts to give you a picture of the Civil War era in Grand Traverse from the eyes of those who lived it, completes my circle of exploration in the year of the Civil War Sesquicentennial. It is a sad yet beautiful story, and I hope I have told it well.

John C. Mitchell, May 2011

ACKNOWLEDGEMENTS

I extend my sincere thanks to the historians, editors, artists, and friends here mentioned who contributed their thoughts and expertise to this book. All played an important role at key moments during the long project. Avis Wolfe's efforts in transcribing the lengthy George Smith diaries will be appreciated by Great Lakes historians for decades, as I am now indebted to her for multiple editing, guidance, and access to Smith's work. Artist Tom Woodruff is back, drawing nine classic maps for this book. Three from the Stannard family deserve my thanks: Deb, for encouragement and a timely lead to the Smith diaries; Chris, for his reviews; and Eric, for his extensive and to the point analysis of the book in progress. Thanks also to the trio that is my family: son Matt for his interest and editing; son Drew for his role as a Kalamazoo College basketball player, providing four winters of entertainment while I wrote this book; and to my wife Ann Marie for patience and caring.

More thanks are due the Island House Hotel on Mackinac Island for the authentic historical setting and the fine hospitality and dining extended to this author during the past four autumns; L.G. Overmyer for Civil War expertise, especially in regard to the Lakeshore Tigers; to Skip Telgard for access to the Miller books and letter; to Mary Ellen Hadjisky for a thorough and honest edit; to Dr. Tim Keilty for twin edits, structural guidance, Civil War research, and encouraging phone messages; to Richard Hanson for technical work and advice on the use of photographs; to Susan Hanson for a thorough edit and historical knowledge; to the Northport Area Heritage Association, the Omena Historical Society, and the History Center of Traverse City for their cooperation; to veteran English teacher Donna Valente for deep double edits; to Keith Burnham for more great photographs; to Donna Allington for sharing her family's Civil War history; to Steve Stanton for repeated computer support; to Linda Broughton for computer skills and indexing; to Angela and Erik Saxon for their fusion of art, design, and technical excellence; to Dr. Will Thomas for editing: to Al Noftz for scanning and technical advice; to the late Ed and Virginia Ball for support in previous projects that prepared me for this book; to Civil War photographers Matthew Brady, James Gardner, William Marsh, George Barnard and dozens of anonymous pioneers in the field; and the hundreds of other people, books, and kindnesses than have made this book possible.

George and Arvilla Smith pictured with two of their daughters, Arvilla (standing) and Annie. *Leelanau Historical Society*

CHAPTER ONE

American Frontiers

The Smith family waited on the dock for the steamboat to emerge from the darkness. A damp spring wind whipped off Lake Champlain, adding a shine to the gray buildings and sending a chill through the would-be passengers. The couple ached from the long wagon ride to the harbor and the emotional turmoil of their impending departure. The young mother wrote: "My feelings were too big for utterance. We were soon to take our leave of beloved Father, the last friend. The roar of the boat was heard at a distance. The lamps were lighted about which had a very gloomy appearance. We went aboard about half past ten, leaving Father on the wharf, fifty miles from home."[1] The paddle-wheeled boat steamed away and the harbor lights faded into the distance. The family's journey to the Great Lakes frontier had begun.

Only months before, George and Arvilla Smith seemed destined to grow old among friends in northern Vermont, where they had both come of age. Then the headstrong George, in a series of bitter arguments over politics, alienated the Congregational minister he was studying to succeed, and his dream of securing a church in his hometown of St. Albans abruptly ended. Arvilla wrote of her husband's adversary: "Our hopes of future usefulness as a preacher of the blessed gospel were blasted by the conduct of one man." Determined to become a minister despite the setback, George Smith answered a call for missionaries to work in the wilderness Michigan Territory. For the dejected Smith, his new life among the Indians of the Great Lakes could not begin soon enough. With their prospects in Vermont in ruins, and an infant son to bind them, the Smiths set out on a course they had not planned for, and now they were leaving behind all they had known.

In May 1833, the unfolding scene repeated itself in one form or another throughout settled New England. Grandfather Smith would stay in a world of the familiar, while George, Arvilla, and child traveled west to their future. The 25 year-old Arvilla wrote: "We made up our minds to start the 8th of May from St. Albans…We were now greatly opposed by our friends on both sides. Stumbling blocks were thrown in our way, but all the world would not turn Mr. Smith from his object. He remained inflexible to entreaties. We accordingly started the 8th bidding adieu to all our beloved friends and native land. It was a day particularly distressing to us all."

Arvilla Smith had good reason to be concerned about the family's sudden change in direction. The distant Michigan Territory was then the northwest frontier of the United States, a place with few names on the map. A primordial forest darkened the countryside and the Indian people George Smith hoped to convert embraced a language and culture all their own. The village of Chicago - less than 100 miles by water from where the Smiths were headed – was a swampy outpost with a population of about 300 people. It had taken a century of hard work by determined Euro-American pioneers to wrest Vermont from the wilderness, and now the Smiths would face the same harsh realities of the frontier their forefathers had endured. In the eyes of established New Englanders, the risks seemed to far outweigh the potential rewards. However, the opportunity for her husband to preach, and a sense of familial duty, compelled Arvilla to embrace the bold move. She knew they would not be alone in their journey, for thousands of families like the Smiths were leaving New England to cast their fate to the Great Lakes, the young nation's newest coast of opportunity.

The Vermont couple benefited from the rigorous public educational system that then made New England one of the most literate regions in the world. The education came with a Yankee set of values in which the fruits of individual labor were highly valued. From an early age, New England children learned that slavery had no place within their code of conduct. Upon graduation, Arvilla and George worked as teachers in Vermont, where they honed a respect and command for the written word, and eventually met and married. While George would later keep the diary that serves as an invaluable record of Grand Traverse during the Civil War, it was Arvilla's journal that tells of the family's dramatic passage from Vermont to the distant Michigan Territory. The story of their adventure, written from a hard-to-find woman's perspective, detailed an early version of what would become a common experience among a generation of New Englanders heading west.

The Smith's trip unfolded aboard boats working their way towards the Great Lakes through a series of rivers, lakes, and man-made canals. Describing the first leg of the journey on Lake Champlain, Arvilla wrote: "Mr. Smith took deck passage, sister and myself took cabin. Eight o'clock next morning we were in Whitehall, having had a pleasant voyage." Whitehall lay at the southern end of Lake Champlain and marked the beginning of the 60-mile long Northern Canal.[2] At its terminus, the Northern joined the Hudson River at Albany - the state capital of New York and the start of the Erie Canal. Here passengers and freight converged from all directions and in particular from New York City, the largest city in the United States. Arvilla continued: "Took the Northern Canal, which carried us to the junction [at Albany] on the 11th day. In the afternoon, Saturday, we took the Western Canal[3]. Quite a contrast to this and the one we left; the former quite large and convenient, the latter contracted; inconvenient, the filthy hob this was…yet our captain and company were so pleasant…"

Despite Arvilla's poor first impression of the waterway, the Erie Canal would make the family's journey to the Great Lakes a far less tortuous affair than it had been only a decade ago. Before the canal, the Appalachian Mountains, rising from Maine to Georgia, stood as a formidable barrier to westward migration. The few roads through their peaks and valleys were a jumble of mud, rocks, and stumps that routinely destroyed wagons and the spirit of those who drove them. In addition, the forests hosted Native people who were desperate to halt further encroachment on their ancestral lands. With odds stacked against the traveler, only the most rugged New England pioneers ventured from the Atlantic coast. However, since the Erie Canal opened in 1825, passengers and cargo in horse-drawn boats could float the 360 miles west across the state of New York and enter Lake Erie at Buffalo. In only eight years, the canal had cut the cost of moving freight across the state by a factor of 25. The best the world had to offer was available all along the Great Lakes. Equally important, the freight and passengers embarking on the Erie Canal had a much better chance of making it to their destination intact than by braving the overland routes.

In a larger sense, the Erie Canal quickly transcended its material purpose as the gateway to the Great Lakes and came to symbolize the young nation's confidence in its own possibilities. The scale of the project was unprecedented - no other public endeavor this big had been attempted in the young United States. The canal was a huge gamble for the state of New York, whose citizens financed its construction and would have been bankrupt if it had failed. Instead, the many obstacles that stood in the way of the canal's completion were overcome by ingenuity and the labor of free people. The positive impact of the Erie Canal was realized almost immediately as villages along the route rose in the ranks of America's fastest growing cities. The canal became America's first expressway to the Great Lakes and cemented New York's dual positions as the United States number one city and state. The success of the vision built not only the Erie Canal, but also a monument to the American experiment in government by a free people.

As the Smith family approached the end of the Erie Canal, Arvilla reflected: "We saw some very fine places while passing through N.Y...Lockport is truly a very grand place in a Mountain, we go through five Locks in succession in this. We saw what the art of man could do to add grandeur and sublimity to the works of nature. We arrived at Buffalo after nine days voyage on the Western Canal." Having safely completed the first phase of their journey, the Smiths now faced the Great Lakes. Aside from the widely scattered harbors, there were few improvements or navigational aids along their thousands of miles of densely wooded coastline. The steam powered, paddle-wheeled passenger boats of the day were an experimental lot that had the bad habit of breaking down, or worse yet, blowing up. It did not help that they were often packed way beyond their capacity, as exemplified by the steamer the Smiths traveled on along Lake Erie. To add to the drama, every navigation season several of the hundreds of schooners working the Great Lakes sailed off into the horizon and were never seen again. Many passengers boarding boats in Buffalo for the voyage west felt the same apprehension their ancestors experienced when they left Europe for the New World. The excitement over future possibilities was tempered by the understanding of the danger and hardships that lay ahead.

Twelve days after leaving St. Albans, Vermont, Arvilla wrote: "We went on board of a Steam boat on Lake Erie Monday Morn. 20. She had on board about a thousand passengers. We took deck passage and during the voyage, we had not a place to lie down as it rained constantly; the lower deck was crowded... Arrived at Detroit Wednesday about noon...From the time we left our native land, we had just six pence left and a hundred forty miles from the place of our destination. Fortunately Mr Smith sold his watch for five dollars, but this did not much more than pay our expenses while here. But while we were despairing what to do, we found a man going with part of a load within of where we intended. He took our load and trusted Mr. Smith until he could pay him...Arrived...just a week after leaving Detroit...in town of Richland, Kalamazoo Co, a thousand miles from our native county, among entire strangers, and destitute of anything but ourselves and household goods."[4] Three weeks after boarding a steamboat on Lake Champlain, the Smiths had reached the east shore of Lake Michigan - penniless, without friends, and absolutely unsure of what their future might hold.

The hardships of the journey from Vermont to the Kalamazoo River Valley gave the Smiths a taste of the life that lay ahead in the Michigan wilderness. Soon after their arrival, Arvilla wrote: "We were by the hand of the Lord visited with the fever…most of the time for two or three months not one of us able to help ourselves…My little boy was attacked with it very violently, continued with him five weeks."[5] Following a winter spent in a town filled with bickering neighbors, the Smiths' second son died soon after birth. It was not the fresh start the Vermonters had hoped for.

Although a Congregationalist at heart, in 1834 Smith trained for the ministry with the Kalamazoo area Presbyterians, for the two churches worked together on the Michigan frontier. Smith's reputation as a dedicated preacher grew and by 1836 he traveled the region as a representative of the Kalamazoo County Bible Society. Arvilla described his duties, giving a glimpse of the solitary life pioneers experienced. She wrote: "He is to visit every family in the county and

The Smiths traveled on a series of canal boats, passenger steamers, and finally aboard a wagon on their three week journey from St. Albans, Vermont to the Kalamazoo Valley of Michigan. *Tom Woodruff*

present the destitute with Bibles...When he returns, I do not know. Stayed alone last night with my little ones; expect to until he returns. I shall be obliged to take my babe in arms and my little boy by the hand and go a half a mile after my cow, but this is but a trifle when compared to what others have done before me."[6] In his new role, Smith began a life-long tradition, and a quarter century later many Grand Traverse soldiers leaving to fight in the Civil War received a Bible from his hand.

The Odawa Indians Smith met in the Kalamazoo Valley, like all of the Native people of the Great Lakes, suffered from their 200-plus years of contact with Euro-Americans. Waves of disease and displacement, the fur trade, broken treaties, and the devastation of recurring wars had dramatically reduced the population and power of the previous masters of the region. While a godsend for Euro-American pioneers, for Great Lakes Indians the Erie Canal was more bad news. The rich and varied resources of the Great Lakes were now open to the world. The number of arriving settlers increased considerably every year, and Michigan Indians lost all ability to control the flow of immigrants onto their ancestral lands.

Farmers plowed and planted a wide swath of fertile land stretching west from Detroit and were now closing in on the Kalamazoo Valley, pushing the remaining Native bands steadily toward Lake Michigan. The rush of new farmers also drove Michigan's population past that of a mere territory, and representatives began to lobby hard in the halls of the United States Congress for statehood. Statehood would bring the ultimate upgrade in status for Michigan, a privilege that had not been bestowed on an American territory since 1820. One of the sticking points, however, was the fact that about half of the land in the proposed state still belonged to the Native people.

With the combined weight of Euro-American settlement, the United States government, and national destiny bearing down upon them, Michigan Indians had little alternative but to sell their remaining lands. In March 1836, they signed the Treaty of Washington, relinquishing title to their vast holdings in the Michigan Territory from the Grand River Valley north through the eastern Upper Peninsula. Now the Federal government had acquired all the land within the proposed boundaries of Michigan and statehood moved closer to reality. Although they were unsure of the consequences of the Treaty of Washington, the Michigan bands had seen the effect of previous government treaties on Native people, and in light of this dismal history, they sensed that their culture would be diminished by whatever they signed. One thing the young missionary

George Smith had in common with the Native people he hoped to help was that the way of life each was familiar with was at an end.

In October 1836, the Smith family moved into a rough cabin in the midst of the dark woods. Arvilla wrote: "My children have caught a very bad cold by coming into an unseasoned house. I suffer as much from smoke, having no fireplace, no door…we are obliged to put out the fire."[7] However, the New Year brought with it a procession of happier events. On January 13, Smith received a letter from the American Home Missionary Society stating their intentions to financially back his missionary work in the Kalamazoo Valley. On January 26, Michigan entered the Union as the nation's 26th state, lifting the Territory to a lofty new position. On April 7, Smith became the first Congregational minister ordained in the new state of Michigan, demonstrating his life-long propensity for having a part in the great events of the era.

The ascension of Michigan as a state closely followed the acceptance of Arkansas into the Union. The dual admissions were no coincidence but instead were the product of a political balancing act struck between the two rapidly diverging sections of the nation. Since joining together under the same Constitution a half-century before, the North and South had come to embrace two radically different social and economic systems within the shell of the United States, and the underlying friction between the two societies would eventually spark the fires of civil war. The great issue dividing the United States was slavery.

In the North, most citizens were farmers and tradesmen who lived and worked on the land they owned and advanced their positions through their labor. There was a consensus among them that all people had the right and ability to control their own destiny to at least some degree. The vitality of the North rested on the assumption that every citizen had a chance to share in the wealth of the nation. That assumption ceased when entering the South, where rights were reserved for whites, and success was defined by the number of African-American slaves a free man owned. Upon reaching the slave-holding South, visitors detected a tangible change in the atmosphere that went beyond the region's hot weather. The rural landscape, which in the North featured farms built and worked by their owners, now hosted the mansions of the planter class mixed with the shacks of slaves. By the time Michigan and Arkansas entered the Union, three out of ten Americans living in the slave states were the property of another American, and the ratio was steadily growing in favor of the slaves. The tremendous profits gained from slave-grown cotton made the distinct Southern way of life possible.

Since the year 1800, the yield of cotton in the United States had doubled every decade, spurred on by rising national and world-wide demand. During the harvest season, 500-pound bales of cotton crowded wharves all across the South. What had come to be known as King Cotton was at the core of a formidable economic engine whose tentacles extended well into the North and across the Atlantic Ocean, fueling an international industrial revolution. Most of the new factories in New England and Europe specialized in manufacturing cotton goods. By 1837, Lowell, Massachusetts was home to 26 cotton mills and 7,000 workers making cotton cloth. Throughout the rest of New England, an additional 50,000 people depended on slave-grown cotton for their livelihood. In England, King Cotton created another 85,000 jobs, most in the mills of Manchester, a city with the nickname "Cottonopolis." The United States then produced close to three-quarters of the world's cotton, which accounted for over half of all American exports. Plantation owners, buoyed by the fabulous wealth accumulated through the sweat of slave labor, assumed the mantle of American royalty. Though the nation's chief European trading partners, France and England, had both banned slavery from their empires during the decade, a world hungry for cotton now turned a blind eye as to how it was produced.

As the economy of King Cotton took root, the national government in Washington D.C. patched together landmark laws aimed at accommodating the diverging societies of the North and South. In considering what national laws should apply to territory gained by the Louisiana Purchase of 1803, a truce of sorts was hammered out in the Missouri Compromise of 1820. The bill prohibited slavery in all future states whose land lay above the southern border of Missouri. The exception to the rule was Missouri itself, whose request for admission to the Union as a slave state led to the pact.

The new line of demarcation split the nation into slave and free territory from the Atlantic coast to the Mississippi River and on to the Rocky Mountains. Thomas Jefferson, the author of the Declaration of Independence, railed against this line in the sand, correctly predicting it would define the borders between future combatants in war over slavery. It was no coincidence that the borderline matched the northernmost range of cotton, which required 200 frost-free days to bear a crop. Southern interests already envisioned an expanding empire based on slave-grown produce. However, the political balancing act in the 1820 bill required more than just the assignment of future state borders. The count of free versus slave states at the time was 11-11, and northern politicians insisted that Maine be admitted simultaneously with Missouri to preserve the tenuous balance of power.

The 12-12 division of free versus slave states created by the Missouri Compromise held for 17 years, until Arkansas joined the Union as a slave state and Michigan a free one. A half century after its founding, the republic they entered was a fragile entity of independent-minded states that lacked a strong sense of national identity, a unified economy, and common beliefs. The great distance between the two sections allowed the United States to evolve this way almost in secret, but by 1837, advancements in communication, transportation, manufacturing, and scientific inquiry began to radically change the nation and the world. The concepts of space and time were being redefined. Railroads and steamships accelerated the speed of transportation, telegraph wires linked distant areas through instant communication, machines powered by steam accelerated the pace of production, and scientific discoveries and theories challenged old ways of thinking. Numerous countries recognized human slavery as an abomination and passed laws against it. A new era was dawning. However, in the American South, King Cotton's planter class fought not only for slavery's preservation, but also for its expansion.

One of the most revered documents in the history of Western civilization is the United States Constitution, which promoted a revolutionary concept of government based on freedom and equality. However, the great document that gave birth to American democracy also fostered the apocalyptic divisions the United States faced as the nation began its decades-long tumble toward the Civil War. Its great fault, and the nation's original sin, was that the Constitution not only failed to prohibit slavery, but also contained a clause that made it a powerful ally of the institution's perpetuation and growth. The ultimate cost of the clause was three-quarters of a century more misery for American slaves and a catastrophic Civil War that claimed over 625,000 American lives.

The fault was found immediately following the Constitution's Preamble. Article One, Section 2, which determined the number of seats a state held in the House, said: "*Representatives…shall be apportioned…according to their respective Numbers, which shall be determined by adding the whole Number of free Persons, and…three fifths of all other Persons.*" As much as any three words in the Constitution, the phrase "all other Persons" caused the Civil War, for the "Persons" mentioned were slaves. The three-fifths clause gave nothing to slaves but rather increased a state's representation in Congress by three-fifths the number of its slaves. This constitutional manipulation of population numbers created what became known as the Slave Power. The clause created a self-feeding engine of inequity: the more slaves a state possessed, the more voting power it wielded in Congress. From the signing of the Constitution to the outbreak of Civil War, Northern politicians in the House of Representatives often found themselves outnumbered in crucial votes by the Slave Power.

The original debate over the three-fifths clause was intense and bitter. Pro-slavery representatives insisted on the statute, fearing that without it the more populous and faster growing North would vote to end the institution. Some of those opposed wryly asked that if the slaveholders claimed slaves were property in the manner of livestock, why couldn't Northern farmers count the animals in their barns and factor them into their Congressional representation. In the end, leaders at the Constitutional Convention who opposed slavery capitulated, knowing the southern states would not ratify the Constitution if this one clause was omitted. It was a terrible choice - to create an imperfect nation, one that immediately failed in its founding vision, or to create no nation at all.

The Constitution in its entirety never used the word slave. Avoiding the word brought to light the embarrassment many of the framers of the Constitution had in endorsing the archaic practice in what was otherwise an exceptional document. They could not have imagined the devastation their acquiescence would later inflict upon the nation.

Separated by distance, geography, and climate from the South, and consumed by the daily effort necessary to survive in the Michigan wilderness, few people in the Kalamazoo Valley had the time or inclination to fret over slavery. A laissez-faire attitude prevailed, and ignorance of the growing national divide hid the disease. As far as the newly-ordained Congregational Minister George Smith could see, the people in need he could actually help were the survivors of the decimated Indian nations who now gathered along the coast of Lake Michigan. His contemporaries agreed, and in 1837, leaders of the local Presbyterian and Congregational churches formed an organization called the "Western Michigan Society to Benefit the Indians" to minister to the Native bands. The decision turned out to be Reverend Smith's big break.

While preaching in the Kalamazoo Valley the previous year, Smith and the Odawa leader Joseph Wakazoo met and formed a lasting friendship. At Wakazoo's request, the Society appointed Smith to minister to the Black Lake

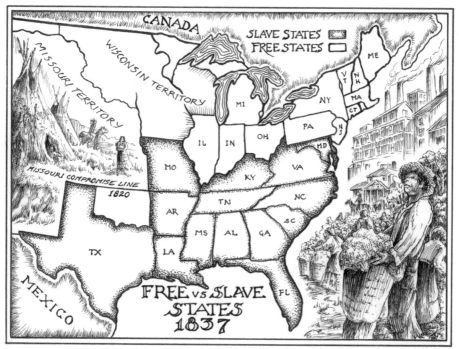

In 1837, three cultures lived within the United States and its Territories - the free states of New England and the Great Lakes, the Southern planting states, and the Indian nations to the west. *Tom Woodruff*

Band in the manner described in the 1836 Treaty of Washington. The treaty contained one of the nation's first experiments in social engineering, agreeing to fund Christian missionaries who would help educate and assimilate the Native people in the ways of western culture.

Reverend Smith started his diary as a means of recording the progress at Old Wing Mission with Wakazoo's Black Lake Band, which then numbered around 100 members. The mission was named after Wakazoo's late father Wing, an influential leader among Indians of the western Great Lakes. However, before going forward with the construction of Old Wing Mission, in 1839 Smith and Odawa companions left the area to explore potential mission sites along the north coast of Lake Michigan. Soon after the lake ice melted, George Smith wrote: "Began with ten Indians on prospecting trip to locate the site for the Indian colony. Went north as far as Petoskey." During the trip, Smith witnessed the beauty of Grand Traverse Country, where he would return to build another Indian mission exactly a decade later. In progressive notations, Arvilla Smith tracked his trip north, writing: "My husband started with ten Indians on the land expedition…intending to go…to Mackinac…All laid to their oars; such harmony in their movements I never saw before."[8] Arvilla stood at waters edge and watched the birch bark canoes disappear over the horizon. The Reverend planned to return in two weeks, but the time table for a journey on Lake Michigan was, at best, guesswork. The bark-skinned canoes were light, fast, and seaworthy, but in the end weather always dictated the travelers' schedule.

Four weeks later, Smith had yet to return, and Arvilla was tortured as she contemplated the fate that might await any traveler on Lake Michigan. She wrote: "My dear husband has not yet returned, O, the anxieties, fears; I have never known them to the extent that I do now. I throw myself down in my rocking chair to ruminate on my lonely condition. I can see him in my imagination in the lake struggling for life amid rolling waves, perhaps trying to repeat the name of his dear companion and little ones. Again I see him on the barren shore of the great Michigan lake almost dying with fever, calling for his dear wife…" A few days later, the travelers arrived in the company of 11 Indians from L'Arbre Croche, a collection of Native villages on the north coast of Lake Michigan. Smith announced his decision to stay in the Kalamazoo Valley and build Old Wing Mission near Black Lake. Arvilla contemplated the isolation of the new mission site, writing: "Husband left me again today to go to the Black river. He will be five miles from any living being."[9]

In August 1839, the preacher "purchased a cow, barrel of pork, flour nearly three barrels, and other necessary article so as to make us tolerable comfortable" when they settled at Old Wing. On the day of the move, Smith wrote: "We came up river in a boat to a point about 2½ miles north of here & then walked to this place bringing some provisions & the children on our backs…Now we are in a room only partly chinked. No window nor door and only part of a floor – but we are all well & comfortable & bless God for his goodness…may this mission field be a field of usefulness & though it be now a wilderness may it soon bud & blossom as the rose."[10]

Old Wing Mission did bud, but bore more thorns than flowers. The family's cabin provided little comfort and a week after moving in, George complained: "It has been very rainy the week past and the roof in this part of the house proves almost good for nothing, the rain coming down almost as hard as out doors."[11] By Christmas, with the snow mounting and supplies dwindling, Arvilla fretted about their lot, writing: "The care of my family takes my whole time. Our room is only twelve by seventeen, not a shelf or cupboard of any kind, two beds, a stove, chairs, table, trunks, etc., to fill, sometimes a half a dozen Indians also. I have all my sewing…knitting, housework, etc; not anyone to save me a step. All this with the care of three children…"[12]

At the mission, Reverend Smith found himself in a position of responsibility that multiplied the daily risks and hardships of frontier life. He noted taking quinine to combat the chills and fever of malaria and worked in harms way when treating the frequently lethal effects of smallpox, typhoid, and cholera – diseases all brought to the Great Lakes by Europeans. The common specter of infant death ignored racial boundaries, as Smith had seen, and would see again with brutal regularity. Like many North American Indians, members of the Black Lake Band proved dangerously vulnerable to alcohol, another European gift to the New World. After a service at Old Wing, Reverend Smith wrote: "Preached to the Indians on the subject of temperance. The chief and one other have been intoxicated within a few days. They obtained their spirits at the trader…on Black Lake…sent by Satan to break up our colony…The chief… expressed a strong desire that all might be free from it."[13]

Like most Great Lakes missionaries of the time, Smith believed the best way for Native people to succeed in the rapidly changing region was to learn the white man's ways. His job was to teach the Indians to read and write in English, settle in one place, and farm the land. The United States Government adopted these goals as policy in the 1836 Treaty of Washington, and the new wave of Protestant preachers in Michigan set out to achieve them. The mission Indians held a different view of Reverend Smith's job. They believed he should stand up for their rights in dealings with the government and the Euro-American community and help preserve as much of their traditional culture as possible. It was a mix of oil and water, one that often drove Reverend Smith to the brink of despair.

All the while, pioneer farmers descended upon Michigan. While the mission site was still a densely forested wilderness, there was no doubt that the axes and plows of settlers would soon make their way to this corner of the state's fabled grain belt. Driven by traffic streaming through the Erie Canal, Michigan's population had soared from 10,000 in 1820 to 30,000 in 1830, and now, in 1839, approached 200,000 - the fastest growth rate of any state or territory since the government began keeping figures in 1790. Every year more fence lines cut through the forests and defined another Euro-American farmer's dream. Their encroachment on the land and culture of Old Wing Mission was only a matter of time.

Settlers to date had avoided the northern half of Michigan's Lower Peninsula. The first Federal surveyors described it as a vast swamp, and lately Great Lakes shipping companies and land speculators, in order to lure pioneers further west, spread the word that the region was unusable for farming. However, as the land rush to the western Lakes gained steam, the reputation of Northern Michigan began to change. Many ship captains bound for Chicago chose to hug Lake Michigan's eastern shore after sailing up through the Straits of Mackinac, for the lee created by the 75 mile-long chain of islands offered relief from the prevailing west winds. The water highway tightened up as ships sailed south past the Beaver and Fox Islands and entered the Manitou Passage, the channel between the Leelanau Peninsula and North and South Manitou Islands. As passengers traveled through the Passage, they could not help but notice the exceptional beauty of the area, its towering hardwood forests, and its potential for growing crops. The word spread back east and settlers began to scout northern Lake Michigan's coastline.

While the west coast of the Leelanau Peninsula possessed only marginal harbors,[14] both North and South Manitou had good, deep-water anchorages. Schooners tacking their way through the Manitou Passage crowded the Islands' sheltered ports during storms. An ever growing fleet of sailing schooners and steam-powered ships cruised through the Manitou Passage on their trans-lake routes. The islanders sold cordwood fuel and other supplies to the passing ships. A decade before the first Euro-American pioneers settled on the Grand Traverse mainland, the Manitous were already well-known rest stops for boats traveling the Great Lakes water highway.

Crescent Harbor on South Manitou was a popular last stop for vessels preparing to sail the 200-mile stretch of open water between the Island and Chicago. Captains would anchor in the harbor and wait for good weather, then venture south on Lake Michigan. In 1838, the United States Congress recognized the importance of the Manitou Passage and Crescent Harbor when they approved funding to build a lighthouse on South Manitou Island. The new light, consisting of bright oil lamps set in a roof-top cupola, was one of only a handful on all of Lake Michigan at the time. That same year, Reverend Peter Dougherty established a Presbyterian mission for Indians at the tip of the peninsula that split Grand Traverse Bay, choosing the remote site largely on the basis of its great distance from the nearest white settlers. A decade later, Reverend Smith would follow Dougherty's lead and bring his Old Wing Mission community north, but for now he struggled to make his settlement work in the Kalamazoo Valley.

The challenges the Smiths faced at Old Wing's continued through the 1840's. George found that funds pledged by the Federal government for Indian education in the Treaty of Washington had already been committed, and the Mission had to scrape by on random gifts and donations. In 1841, Arvilla wrote: "The winter past has been one of trial and sickness. We have felt somewhat friendless, as we wrote for some necessary articles for our comfort, such as candles, groceries, but heard nothing from them for nearly four months. We are shut out from all civilized society...being nearly two months with no other light than that of the stoves."[15] In an 1843 report to superiors, George Smith said: "On the account of the small amount of funds annually received we have endured great privations, our hands have been in a measure paralyzed, our work impeded, and the small amount of individual funds we possessed is nearly expended; so that we shall not be able to continue in the field but a short time longer if the Govt does not lend its aid for our support."[16]

Then, within the space of a year, the Smiths lost three children, two in childbirth and one their beloved three year-old daughter. Arvilla wrote: "The coffin and grave hold the dust of my precious child, but I see yet the yellow locks pasted on that sweet and noble forehead and those lovely blue eyes...Darkness is on every side. Even the songs of the birds speak in tones of sorrow."[17] The Smiths' plight is worth noting not because of its individual severity, but because it reflected the common experience of many Euro-American pioneers on the Lake Michigan frontier.

In 1845, Old Wing Mission faced its greatest crisis to date. Smith's faithful supporter, Chief Joseph Wakazoo, fell "sick with lung complaint" and suddenly died. Smith lamented: "In the loss of our chief...our mission has lost much, in fact, almost all the influence among the Indians to bring them to meeting." The leader who kept band members within the Mission's circle was gone, and unity of the Odawa at Old Wing began to unravel. Then, in 1847, a colony of Dutch settlers bought land adjoining the mission and their farms began to encircle the site. A prolonged clash of cultures ensued. Once again, in a story that repeated itself since the first European sailing ships reached the Atlantic coast, Indians faced displacement. A decade after its founding, Reverend Smith and the remaining faithful at Old Wing Mission were looking for a new home.

Smith was now a very different man than the one who arrived on the coast of Lake Michigan 15 years before. He had faced with his family the many deprivations of the Michigan wilderness and survived. He had built several homes, raised crops, and made orchards bear fruit. He had cared for the sick and buried the dead, including four of his own children. Through his constant close contact with Native people, the Reverend had been transformed, adopting an Indian perspective of the evolving Lake Michigan frontier. Unlike many of his contemporaries, worldly gain at the expense of the Indians was not one of his goals. Though his work at Old Wing Mission had fallen short of the ideal, Smith was no quitter, and was ready to try again further north.

In 1848, Reverend Smith retraced his journey of a decade before searching for the right place to resettle. His party followed the annual migration route of the Black Lake Band north along the Lake Michigan coast. After paddling their bark canoes through a beautiful stretch of water lying in the lee of the Manitou Islands, and with the silhouette of the Fox Islands coming into view, they reached the mouth of the large bay named Le Grand Traverse. There was not a single building along miles of shoreline, nor a sign of a farm or sawmill anywhere nearby. For Smith, the search for a new home was over.

By the following spring, the exodus from Old Wing Mission to the wide-open Grand Traverse region had been planned and was gaining momentum. A friend of the Smiths, James McLaughlin, bought "a schooner lying in Chicago," the *Hiram Merrill*. The boat would soon carry the weight of the mission to Grand Traverse. Smith helped members of the Black Lake Band secure property near the future mission, noting he had "made out applications for 6 to buy each 40 acres of land at our new location." On June 1, the faithful abandoned Old Wing, and after ten days of battling stormy weather, the *Hiram Merrill* finally reached Grand Traverse. Smith wrote of the historic moment: "This morning passed Sleeping Bear. Wind blowing a gale from the South East…Saw our Indians' camps on the shore - 8 Oclk entered Grand Traverse Bay. Wind lulled to a calm…near night went ashore & examined a little."[18] At sunrise, the *Hiram Merrill* anchored in close and those aboard came ashore. The story of Wakazooville Mission had begun.

Smith founded his mission at the heart of one of Lake Michigan's last stands of wilderness. The primal beauty of the place had not changed much over the last 20 centuries. Away from the water, an ancient forest darkened the land for several days walk in any direction. There wasn't a road within a hundred miles and only sand and trees along the harbor's expansive shoreline. Wakazooville's nearest neighbor was Peter Dougherty's Presbyterian settlement six miles to the south by water, where Indian farmers had cultivated crops for a decade. Twenty-five miles down the Bay, a small, water-powered sawmill cut logs into boards in an otherwise deserted place called Traverse City. Except for the occasional trader's cabin and lumberman's dock, and the 1838 lighthouse on South Manitou Island, there were few other signs of Euro-American presence anywhere along the coasts of Grand Traverse. Within a week of landing at Wakazooville, the Smith family sowed their "plants & flowers & shrubs" and "began to clear a place for a house."[19] For the next 30 years, diarist George Smith recorded life from his perch at the tip of the Leelanau Peninsula and in the process provided a remarkable record of the Civil War as seen from a Grand Traverse perspective.

One of the key assets of the Wakazooville settlement was the *Hiram Merrill,* the schooner that supplied the mission throughout the critical first summer. Smith noted in July 1849, "our schooner arrived…made two trips from Black river to Chicago," confirming the seaworthiness and reach of the vessel. The *Hiram Merrill* made the mission's transition to the North Country much easier and by fall the schooner was making money for the Wakazooville pioneers by carrying tanning bark and other frontier products to towns along the southern lake. The importance of the schooner *Hiram Merrill* to the success of the pioneering venture was a preview of much bigger things to come. While isolated by land, the new-born Wakazooville settlement lay at a pivotal point on the Great Lakes water highway. The water route served as the conduit for almost all mid 19th century travelers heading west on the lakes, and ship traffic on Lake Michigan was increasing every year. In the ensuing decade, the many assets of the harbor at Wakazooville would make it the number one port on northern Lake Michigan, complete with the people and infrastructure necessary to service and supply ships. But for the moment, bark canoes and mackinaw boats and a few small schooners like the *Hiram Merrill* were the only craft to visit the remote spot.

The same problems that troubled Old Wing Mission followed Smith north. Peter Wakazoo, the leader of the Black Lake Band since brother Joseph's death, warned Smith that "the Catholics are doing all they can to break up our mission – even threaten his life."[20] The old rivalries between Christian faiths again stirred up bad blood on the frontier. By now, however, Smith was an old hand at the politics of religion and knew the danger from priests was only one of the threats to the Wakazooville community. On August 27, a Native courier arrived on an express steamboat from Mackinac Island bringing word that "the Indians must be there on the 30th." Work at Wakazooville Mission stopped and Natives paddled north to collect the annual payment prescribed by the Treaty of Washington. While on the Island, the travelers reunited with family members and reminisced with old friends, strengthening the bonds of the widespread Indian community. This year, however, the embraces shared at the Mackinac reunion brought with them deadly consequences.

Two week after the rendezvous, a panic spread along the shores of Lake Michigan. Reverend Smith wrote: "Morning 2 Indians came from Mackinaw. They started from L'Arbor Croche last night; rowed all night frightened by the cholera. Several Indians from Mr. Dougherty's Mission have died." A full blown epidemic was upon them. Soon after, a wretched survivor who had recently left Wakazooville to collect his annuity brought the gravity of the outbreak home. Smith said: "Prickett arrived from Mackinac…his wife died some days ago - his child died this morning of dysentery. He brought the corpse some distance in his arms." Fortunately, the plagues of cholera and dysentery did not strike Wakazooville this time. However, the Mission did lose most of its Indian inhabitants for the winter, for despite their promise to stay up north through the cold season, many chose to make their traditional passage back to their village on Black Lake. At Sabbath services Smith, "bid the Indians who are going to leave farewell. Only 5 or 6 families are going to stay."[21]

During the 1849 navigation season, Reverend Peter Dougherty's mission settlement was the hub of activity for the few Euro-Americans living in Grand Traverse. On a good day, it was an easy sail from Wakazooville, and Smith's diary recorded frequent contacts between the two places. In October 1849, Smith wrote of "a meeting of citizens at Mr. Dougherty's to petition for Post Office," the first one in the region. One cornerstone of modernity was about to be laid. Later, fall winds ripped west across Lake Michigan, driving ships to seek safe anchorage and presaging the upcoming transformation of Smith's mission site into the busy harbor town of Northport. Smith wrote: "The Schooner *Star of Youngstown* came into the Harbor with fore mast head carried away by a squall yesterday – another Schooner *Cherokee of Racine* came in with her fore peak block carried away – Both repairing."[22] Soon after, a letter arrived by way of Dougherty's post office bearing the news that the *Hiram Merrill* was marooned on a sand bar off Manitowac, Wisconsin, her fate unknown. As the winter snow began to fall, Smith could only pray that the second half of the century would be kinder to them all.

In 1848, former Michigan Territorial Governor Lewis Cass was nominated as the Democratic candidate for President of the United States. In the race, the Governor promoted a policy toward slavery called "popular sovereignty." To Cass, the concept seemed consistent with the tenets of democracy, for it allowed voters to choose whether to adopt or abolish slavery as new states and territories were defined. However, many saw popular sovereignty as a threat to the time-honored agreements contained in the Missouri Compromise, which permitted slavery in the South and forbid it north of the line drawn by the 1820 act. Heated arguments immediately surfaced as to how and where popular sovereignty would be employed, exposing the simmering anger about the issue of slavery that was building within the country. The stir created by the idea of popular sovereignty was a factor in Cass's defeat in the 1848 Presidential race, and for the moment the concept was shelved. Then gold was discovered in California.

In 1849, gold's allure cast a powerful spell across the American nation. Over the winter, citizens who thought themselves satisfied with their lot had time to stew on news streaming in from the Pacific coast, where every river reportedly glistened with the precious metal. Now hordes of the would-be prospectors prepared to abandon their labors and head for the western edge of the continent for their chance to strike it rich. As the days grew longer and the weather warmed, the '49ers crowded around bar stools and lamp-lit kitchen tables and plotted the best routes to the California gold fields. For many restless souls living along the Atlantic seaboard, where the population of the young nation was concentrated, the journey west began with the Erie Canal.

Gold fever spread across the Great Lakes as soon as the ice melted in the spring of 1849. Immigrants pouring into New York harbor mixed with second and third generation Americans and together they heeded the siren's call. Would-be prospectors swarmed through the Erie Canal to Buffalo on Lake Erie, where they crowded the docks looking for any berth up the lakes to Chicago. From there they traveled south to the Mississippi River, bought and outfitted wagons in St. Louis, and then headed west across the Great Plains. The California Gold Rush was on.

Prospectors streamed into California from all directions. Though few of the would-be millionaires made the big strike they came for, many easterners found the rich and dramatic country too compelling to leave. Others could not bear the thought of making the long journey back home in defeat. Prospectors turned into California settlers. Towns and farms emerged along roads leading to the rivers of gold. San Francisco's population swelled from 1,000 before the Gold Rush to 25,000 the year after. In an historical instant, the number of California residents soared past the requirement for statehood. The Territory began its quest to join the United States as a full-fledged member.

The population explosion in California caught the United States Congress by surprise. California petitioned for admission to the Union as a free state, a move that threatened to put slave state Senators at a numerical disadvantage. In terms of population, no United States territory in the South came close to qualifying for statehood, so no land-based balance to the admission of California was possible in the short run. If the nation really wanted California as a free-state, the Slave Power would have to get something big in return.

At the time, the belief prevailed among most Americans that increasing sectional tensions between the North and South could still be alleviated through compromise. For most of the lean and weathered pioneers settling along the western Great Lakes, slavery remained a vague and distant practice they may have disagreed with but had neither the time nor the inclination to fight about. However, in the decade ahead, the hope for continuing compromise would wither as a series of national laws aimed at settling divisions over slavery backfired, pushing the issue to the forefront of national politics and the United States to the brink of civil war.

From 1830 to 1850, the slave population of the United States grew by a half, from two to three million. Almost all the increase in the number of slaves took place in the South, where now one of every three residents enjoyed no freedom at all. At the same time, the nation as a whole swelled by three-quarters, from 13 to 23 million people. The vast majority of immigrants arriving in America – seven out of every eight who had a choice in the matter – settled in the North, where labor was respected and paid for.

At the time Michigan and Arkansas were admitted to the Union as a pair to maintain the balance of free and slave states, the two places were approximately equal in size and population. However, a dozen years later, the United States census revealed that Michigan's population had grown to over twice that of Arkansas. The free state had over 110,000 students in public schools, the slave state 8,000. Michigan libraries held 100,000 volumes on their shelves, while Arkansas had only 420. Michigan also had six times the number of manufacturing jobs and fifteen times more miles of railroad tracks than Arkansas. On a national level, slave-holding states claimed only 20 of the nation's top 100 most populous cities. New York City, with over half a million residents, was by itself larger than the sum of all Southern cities ranked in the nation's top 100. For most immigrants, the decision to debark at Northern ports was an easy one.

With little else to offer than their labor, the newcomers saw no opportunity in the closed Southern society that used slaves to perform its work.

Even with the three-fifths clause in the Constitution, which inflated Southern representation in Congress, the results of the 1850 national census found the Slave Power decisively outnumbered in the House of Representatives. Southern politicians fretted about losing the grip they had held over the legislative branches since the nation's conception. With two senate seats assigned each state no matter what the population, an equal number of Slave and Free states in the Union maintained an equal amount of votes in the Senate, a political position the Slave Power jealously guarded. Wisconsin had been admitted to the Union the year before without a corresponding slave state, and Southern politicians decided that if they were to give an inch on the admission of California, greater legal protection of slavery would be the price.

By 1850, cotton mills at home and abroad bought all the plantation cotton slaves could produce. Though both Great Britain and France abolished slavery over a decade before, their importers asked few questions as to how the cotton was grown. However, everyone knew slave labor was at the heart of it all. The profits and power flowing from cotton kept the status quo in place. In the era of King Cotton, a strong young slave was a valuable commodity, on par today with the cost of a new automobile. In the southern economy, slaves were both property and money, in essence savings accounts that paid interest with every pound of cotton harvested.

Cotton plantations were factories that used slaves as their machinery, often several hundred to a master. The institution of slavery was well-suited to the plantation system of growing cotton, for even the most recalcitrant slave could be whipped into shape to perform the menial and monotonous tasks associated with the cotton production. Although a number of slave owners may have felt empathy with their slaves, any attempt to gloss over slavery as benign and the plantation society as genteel ignored the refinement of cruelties owners could employ without consequence to keep their slaves in line. The obscure disciplinary practice called cat hauling illustrated the point. When the whip and the club failed to impress upon a stubborn slave the hopelessness of resisting their owner's will, the slave was stripped of his clothes and held face down on the ground while a leather-gloved overseer raked a feral cat across his back. During the gruesome ride, the wild animal tore into the flesh of the victim, and the screams of the slave warned all within earshot about the consequences of disobedience.

The wounds inflicted by the germ-laden cats often led to infection and death. Still, many slaves resisted submission and dreamed of eventual freedom.

The most valuable slaves - the young and healthy - were also the best at escaping. The hopelessness of a slave's life on the plantation made many risk the horrid consequences of a failed attempt and run. All through the 1840's, the number of fugitives fleeing north to Free States and onto the free country of Canada steadily rose. Too many slaves were stealing themselves from their masters and the problem was costing the Slave Power big money. The success of a few fugitives encouraged others to flee, undermining discipline on all plantations.

Slave catching was not a new legal concept in the United States - the practice was embedded in the U.S. Constitution. A clause titled Extradition stated that *"No Person held to Service or Labour in one State, under the Laws thereof, escaping into another, shall, in Consequence of any Law or Regulation therein, be discharged from such Service or Labour, But shall be delivered up on Claim of the Party to whom such Service or Labour may be due."*[23] The enlightened framers, wincing at the thought of the word slavery in their Constitution, chose the phrase "Persons held to Service or Labor" to soften the very hard condition of human bondage. Many grudgingly accepted the clause as a political necessity to forming a nation which included a slave-owning region.

Through the 1840's, the Slave Power became increasingly troubled by northern complicity in slave escapes. They resented the growing sophistication and success of the Underground Railroad, an informal yet widespread conglomeration of safe houses, transportation links, and sympathetic citizens that aided fugitive slaves in their flight from the plantations to freedom in Canada - a country which abolished slavery in 1834. The Great Lakes states shared a long, open border with its northern neighbor and its citizens often risked their own freedom and broke United States law by helping those escaping by way of the Underground Railroad. It further angered slave owners that their escaped property often lived relatively unmolested in northern towns. The figurative railroad pitted Northern values against the South's engine of profit and the United States Constitution and added another point of contention to the mounting number of sectional grievances. The tug and pull of free versus slave interests began to consume national politics. Congressional debates showed that rather than growing stronger as the nation aged, the diversifying economies, societies, and politics of the North and South had undermined the hope of maintaining a united nation made up of like-minded people. By 1850, Washington, D.C. was

100 DOLLARS
REWARD!

Ranaway from the subscriber on the 27th of July, my Black Woman, named

EMILY,

Seventeen years of age, well grown, black color, has a whining voice. She took with her one dark calico and one blue and white dress, a red corded gingham bonnet; a white striped shawl and slippers. I will pay the above reward if taken near the Ohio river on the Kentucky side, or THREE HUNDRED DOLLARS, if taken in the State of Ohio, and delivered to me near Lewisburg, Mason County, Ky. THO'S. H. WILLIAMS. August 4, 1853.

home not only to the nation's capital, but also the largest slave market in the United States.

With the auction blocks as a backdrop, Congress passed the Compromise of 1850 in the hopes of fostering an elusive peace within the nation. The Bill began with the admission of the free state of California and then defined the boundaries of two potential slave states, New Mexico and Utah. It envisioned a nation expanding to the west with alternate admission of free and slave states. However, trouble arose at the end of the bill, in the portion called the Fugitive Slave Act. This section allowed slave catchers to seize suspected fugitive slaves anywhere in the nation and carry them South without due process. African-Americans in the North, whether free or in flight, were presumed to be slaves on the run. All free citizens were compelled to aid slave catchers under penalty of law. The issue of slavery, long avoided in polite conversation, was now thrown in the face of Yankee sensibilities as slave catchers fanned out through the Free States. The reality of slavery was brought home to the big cities and small farms of the North as slaves were dragged away in chains. Rather than promote peace, the law destroyed what little middle ground was left between the two distinct societies. The fires of confrontation were now burning, and the nation began its decade-long slide toward Civil War.

In his memoirs, former Civil War General and President Ulysses S. Grant described how the Fugitive Slave Act of 1850 turned Northern sentiments sharply against slavery. He wrote: "The cause of the great War of Rebellion against the United States will have to be attributed to slavery. For some years before the war began it was a trite saying among some politicians that "A state half slave and half free cannot exist. All must become slave or all free, or the state will go down." I took no part in any such view of the case at the time, but since the war is over, reviewing the whole question, I have come to the conclusion that the saying is quite true.

"Slavery was an institution that required unusual guarantees for its security wherever it existed; and in a country like ours where the larger portion of it was free territory inhabited by an intelligent and well-to-do population, the people would naturally have but little sympathy with demands upon them for its protection. Hence the people of the South were dependent upon keeping control of the general government to secure the perpetuation of their favorite institution. They were able to maintain this control long after the states where slavery existed had ceased to have controlling power, through the assistance they received from odd men here and there throughout the Northern States. They saw their power waning, and this led them to encroach upon the prerogatives and independence of the Northern States by enacting such laws as the Fugitive Slave Law. By this law every Northern man was obliged, when properly summoned, to turn out and help apprehend the runaway slave of the Southern man. Northern marshals became slave-catchers, and northern courts had to contribute to the support and protection of the institution.

"This was a degradation which the North would not permit any longer than until they could get the power to expunge such laws from the statute books. Prior to the time of these encroachments the great majority of the people of the North had no particular quarrel with slavery, so long as they were not forced to have it themselves. But they were not willing to play the role of police for the South in the protection of this particular institution."[24] In the end, the divisive issue of slavery in the United States had to be settled by the devastating American Civil War.

Far from the turmoil of national politics, Reverend Smith continued the material work of building Wakazooville Mission. As soon as the ground thawed, he laid the foundation for the schoolhouse, and when the structure began to take shape, he "started for sawmill at head of Bay, 30 miles, to get lumber for school." The sawmill mentioned was Captain Boardman's modest works in the village of Traverse City, an operation he soon sold to Chicago lumberman Perry Hannah.

One of Smith's first ministerial acts of 1850 welcomed new members into the Wakazooville Congregational Church. The preacher wrote that he "received five members into our little Church" among them "Mary Jane Smith our eldest daughter…Payson Wolfe aged 16½ years."[25] Mary Jane Smith grew up with Indian children as her only companions, spoke the Algonquian language as fluently as English, and moved in both cultures with ease. Payson was the nephew of the late Chief Joseph Wakazoo and a young man who saw Mary Jane as more than a childhood friend.

In July 1850, Arvilla Smith and son George Jr., now 18 years old, left Wakazooville to visit relatives in Kalamazoo. They started the trip in their mackinaw boat by sailing to South Manitou Island, where they hoped to catch a steamboat to their final destination. Days later, Reverend Smith received a note from his son stating that "no boat had arrived & they could not get lodging on the island."[26] The travelers were forced to sleep on the beach in the midst of clouds of mosquitoes. The next day, Arvilla returned to Wakazooville, complaining that there was "no chance yet to go & the place was like Sodom," leaving her son to fend for himself.

That fall, Reverend Smith planted the first orchard in Wakazooville, "16 grafted apples, 7 grafted peaches."[27] Fruit trees - in particular the cherry - thrived in Grand Traverse, and became the foundation of the region's agriculture economy in the centuries ahead. Meanwhile, George Smith Jr. returned from a summer downstate in a boat captained by Ira Pickard, a Manitou Island lumberman. That same week, trader John LaRue visited Wakazooville and helped Reverend Smith seal the seams of his well-used mackinaw boat. These sporadic meetings between the few English-speaking settlers in Grand Traverse were welcomed occasions. The bonds of common experience and language made quick friends of Euro-American pioneers when their paths crossed. Smith believed that the chance for friendship between Euro-American settlers and Grand Traverse Indians would also be improving, for the new state constitution allowed "civilized

Indians" to become citizens, vote, and purchase designated pieces of land, including the entire Leelanau Peninsula.

When the harbor froze, a deep sense of isolation descended on Wakazooville. The first road north to Grand Traverse was a dozen years away, and primitive footpaths through the dense forests were now buried in snow. Though the area's first post office at Dougherty's Old Mission was open for business, the feeling of isolation was compounded by disappointment that winter when the mail failed to come through. After the snow melted in the spring of 1851, Smith was elated when a courier "brought about 3 months mail…this is the first full mail we have had since Dec. It did not arrive in Mackinaw until the first & 2nd of April – through the unfaithfulness of the contractor at Saginaw."[28] Irregular mail service would remain an aggravating aspect of life in Grand Traverse until the Northport-Newaygo road opened during the Civil War.

Reverend Smith made a landmark observation in Wakazooville that spring when he wrote: "Steam Boat…arrived. Mr Newbury the owner on board with provisions for sale – he sold none. The Steamer stopped scarcely one hour. It was quite cheering, probably the first one that ever landed here."[29] A vision of the rapidly approaching future had just shown itself in the remote wilderness harbor. The pace of settlement in Grand Traverse, driven by ship traffic, would intensify with each new year, changing not only the face of Wakazooville but the entire western Great Lakes.

In 1851, the imprint of local government on the region was a big step toward modernization. The Michigan Legislature passed a bill on April 7 to organize Grand Traverse County from an area originally mapped as Omeena. The region that had long been united by water now adopted a formal governmental structure. The unorganized counties of Antrim and Leelanau, including the Manitou and Fox Islands, were attached to Grand Traverse County to take advantage of its judicial and municipal services. A larger, more fluid concept of Grand Traverse Country began to take shape. Together the three counties added up to one of the most splendid assemblies of land and water along the Great Lakes.

The first Grand Traverse County election, including voters in Antrim and Leelanau, was held in August 1851. Twenty-eight votes were cast. The ubiquitous Reverend Smith was elected Probate Judge. The village of Traverse City was named county seat and became the administrative center of Grand Traverse Country, but it was Wakazooville – soon to be known as Northport - which rapidly grew into the population and transportation center of Northern Michigan.

In the summer of 1851, as the associated Grand Traverse counties worked to implement their legal arrangements, Reverend Smith blessed another union that would shake up the Wakazooville community. He wrote: "I solemnized the marriage of Payson Wolf aged 19 years & our oldest daughter Mary Jane Smith aged nearly 16 years. All the people of our settlement were present except Chief & family."[30] It was the first marriage between members of the Wakazooville settlement, and the discord it caused was a bad sign. While George Smith formalized the couple's vows in the spirit of racial harmony, his wife Arvilla was bitter about the marriage. Payson's Uncle Peter, the brother of the late Chief Wakazoo and current leader of the Wakazooville Indians, boycotted the wedding in protest of the mixing of races and cultures. The racial harmony Smith believed he helped foster at the mission proved to be an illusion.

A month later, Smith wrote: "We started for Mackinaw in Oshawun's bark [canoe]…were struck by a squall and went ashore, boats leaking." After repairing the vessels as best they could, the party continued on to Mackinac Island where "the Indians received $7.50 apeace," their annual payment under the terms of the 1836 Treaty of Washington. In a subsequent letter to a colleague, Smith expressed anger at the way white traders and government agents abused the Indians on the Island, and then explained his motivation for trying to help the Native people. He wrote: "The American people by their treatment of the Indians in past times have put themselves in the position of fearful responsibility. Those responsibilities must be cancelled or a blight awaits us…it remains for us…to redeem ourselves."[31] A decade later, the blight brought on by another branch of American racism would plunge the divided United States into civil war.

The winter of 1851 came in hard and the cold weather stayed on well into the spring. In April 1852, Smith complained: "The quantity of Snow continues the same. There is a threatening prospect of Suffering for provisions if the weather does not change soon. Many horses have already died. Many of the Indians…have nothing but Sugar to eat."[32] With no roads to the region, there was little chance of relief until the lake ice melted.

Across the Bay, settlers moved steadily up the Old Mission Peninsula toward Indians fields. Reverend Dougherty foresaw the inevitable results and decided to move his mission to Omena. After a meeting with his fellow preacher in May, Reverend Smith wrote: "Mr Dougherty…is preparing to build a new Mission establishment for a boarding and manual labor school." The Leelanau Peninsula would soon be home to two Protestant missions and a Catholic one as the centuries-old rivalry for Indian converts continued.

In July 1852, Smith began the long sail south along the coast of Lake Michi-

Grand Traverse County, 1851, with unorganized Leelanau and Antrim Counties attached for administrative purposes. *Tom Woodruff*

gan to the mouth of the Kalamazoo River. After spending the first night in John LaRue's trading post "at the mouth of the river in Sleeping Bear Bay," strong gusts battered Smith's boat and blew him ashore near Sleeping Bear Point.

Along the windswept dunes, Smith discovered a surreal scene from Michigan's past, a marker of those who lived along Lake Michigan for thousands of years. He wrote: "There are evident signs of there having been an Indian Village here before Europeans settled the country, at least before the Indians were supplied with Iron & Brass...we find here a great many pieces of the ancient Indian clay kettles apparently left on the fires & gone to decay...some of them we find on such stones arranged in circles to support them while heating, signs of the fires being under them also. All have doubtless been buried for ages under a Sand Bank & have recently been uncovered by the winds from their form & the ornamental figures on the borders around the Top."[33] Smith had stumbled upon a centuries-old Indian encampment in the dunes, opened now before him like an ancient Egyptian pyramid's hidden chamber.

It took Smith three weeks under sail to reach Black Lake, and he stayed away from Wakazooville for three months. While in southern Michigan, Smith lived at the home of his sister-in-law in Kalamazoo - then one of Michigan's most prosperous cities and a center of the state's abolitionist movement. The great increase in the national divide over slavery in the past two years must have surprised Smith, for his work at Wakazooville Mission had isolated him from the mood he encountered. From the streets to the pulpit, talk of slavery was everywhere. Southern slave catchers had invaded Northern cities. Citizens who had never paid much attention to the practice were appalled by the specter of shackled and chained slaves in their midst. Smith saw that while he had labored in the wilderness to lay a solid foundation for his mission, the rapidly diverging opinions on slavery between the two regions threatened the life of the country.

George Smith generally avoided discussing politics in his diary, preferring to record daily events transpiring around his missions. However, after returning to Wakazooville in the fall of 1852, Smith displayed his heightened awareness of America's number one problem when he wrote, "I sent...Mr Dougherty... *Uncle Tom's Cabin* to read."[34] While in Kalamazoo, Smith had obtained a copy of the sensational new book by author Harriet Beecher Stowe, who created the novel in reaction to the Fugitive Slave Act of 1850. The controversial work, which portrayed the dark side of slavery in the South, was having a profound effect on the conscience of the nation. Every time it was read it inflamed passions about slavery. The book quickly rose to the status of an international hit. In its first year, the book sold an unprecedented 300,000 copies in the United States and another 200,000 in England, on its way to becoming the best-selling novel of the 19th century.

World opinion of slavery in the United States took a dramatic turn for the worse due to the widespread circulation of *Uncle Tom's Cabin*. The novel helped further awaken the conscience of the North towards the cruelties of slavery, and aroused the anger of the South against its author and her fellow abolitionists. People who had never seen an African-American slave and knew little of their lot on the plantation were taken aback, while slave holders called the novel a lie. Southern booksellers were run out of town for stocking it and its readers were thrown in jail. Author Stowe received a stream of threatening letters, one containing the severed ear of a black man.[35]

The year after the novel's release, lumbermen Antoine Manseau and John Miller arrived by schooner at the mouth of the Carp River, the site of today's village of Leland. When the partners built a dam across the river to power their sawmill, they became the first Euro-Americans of record to settle at the Lake Michigan port. Future Civil War soldier John Miller brought with him his own 1852 edition of *Uncle Tom's Cabin*, a book recently discovered in the attic trunk of his antebellum homestead in Leland. The frayed edges of the novel testify to its wide circulation. At the time, books in the region were hard to find, especially one as in demand as *Uncle Tom's Cabin*.

No record exists of the effect Miller's copy of the book had on its readers in Grand Traverse, though it certainly influenced its owner, who backed the anti-slavery Republican Party years before it became popular in the region. However, Dr. Robert Kedzie, an 1851 graduate of the first class of the University of Michigan's medical school, described the reaction to the book in his downstate village of Vermontville. Kedzie wrote: "Food and sleep and earthly cares had little hold on us till wife and I, in tears and choking sobs, had read that wonderful book. Before we had read much it leaked out that we had a book of wonderful pathos, and Frances Mears…filed her application to read the book next, but before she got it seven other applications were on file, and before she had read it there were thirty who spoke for the book. After it left our hands we saw no more of it for two years, and it came back the most worn and tattered book I ever saw.[36] One can only guess at the number of local men and women who were touched by Smith and Miller's copies of the book, and how many Grand Traverse soldiers volunteered to fight in the Civil War due to their influence.

After the release of *Uncle Tom's Cabin*, the black abolitionist Frederick Douglass befriended Stowe and together they spoke and wrote against slavery during the tumultuous 1850's. An earlier autobiography by Douglass had helped form Stowe's view of the institution.[37] Although lost in the passions of the time, Stowe blamed both the North and the South for the national disgrace of slavery. In the midst of the Civil War, she reportedly said: "It was God's will that this nation—both North and South—should deeply and terribly suffer for the sin of consenting to and encouraging the great oppressions." Whether through the will of God or the product of human folly, every part of the nation did "deeply and terribly suffer" during the four catastrophic years of the Civil War that lay ahead.

As the bonds between the two distinct societies within the United States frayed, the concept of a greater Grand Traverse region solidified in 1853 when the state legislature acted to

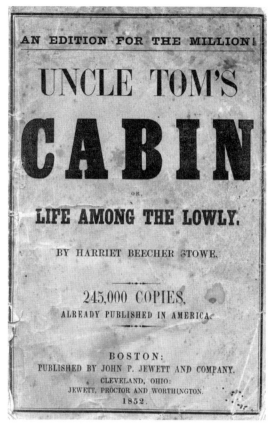

This well-worn 1852 copy of *Uncle Tom's Cabin* was recently found in a trunk belonging to Leland pioneer and Civil War veteran John I. Miller. *Courtesy Skip Telgard*

complete the organization of Grand Traverse County. The unorganized counties of Kalkaska, Missaukee, Wexford, and Manistee were added to the realm of Grand Traverse County government, in addition to the already attached counties of Antrim and Leelanau.[38] The total area now administered through Grand Traverse was vast and encompassed what would eventually become nine Michigan counties. Pioneer farmers settled almost exclusively along the Grand Traverse lakeshore, where there was access to supplies and markets. Inland the primeval forest prevailed. The evolving political entities united the region's growing port towns and began to create the perception of a distinct place along Lake Michigan - Grand Traverse Country.

The year 1854 marked a rapid acceleration of Euro-American settlement in Grand Traverse. The power of the pen proved to be a major factor in the region's discovery. That spring Reverend Smith noted: "Mr Dame wrote a letter last winter & published in the N.Y. Tribune. He is now receiving many letters of inquiry." The effect of Joseph Dame's words of praise for Grand Traverse appearing in the nation's most widely-read newspaper became clear as soon as the navigation season opened. Inquiries poured into the Old Mission post office from adventurous New Englanders who, like the Smiths a generation before, were ready to start over on the last of the Lake Michigan frontier. On July 1, 1854, Smith wrote: "A company of land lookers from York State came per Manito Islands." As summer progressed, *New York Tribune* readers arrived in increasing numbers, turning the fledgling town of Northport into a Euro-American enclave. The new Grand Traverse Lighthouse at the tip of the Leelanau Peninsula guided the land lookers south into the Bay. All newcomers shared the experience of arriving in Grand Traverse by way of the Great Lakes water highway.

Dame, who had moved from Mackinac Island in 1841 to join Reverend Dougherty on Old Mission as a teacher, had his own reason for promoting Grand Traverse. During the last few years, he had invested in a substantial amount of property around Smith's Wakazooville Mission and planned to develop his holdings into a village he named Northport. Dame drew up a plat divided with lots and laid out the town of the future. Now his letter to the *New York Tribune* created the Wakazooville-Northport land rush he hoped for.

Reverend Smith sensed that the rapid influx of settlers could mean more bad news ahead for the Native people. In concluding his diary note about Dame's promotional letter to the *New York Tribune*, Smith wrote: "How this movement will affect the Indians remains to be proved. Perhaps serious evils will grow out of it. The future only can tell."[39] Smith's 20 years on the Lake Michigan frontier had taught him that the mixing of cultures rarely went well for the Indians. He was justifiably concerned about how the influx of Western civilization would impact the Odawa settlement in Wakazooville. But like it or not, the land rush was on.

In one 1854 diary entry, Smith said: "To day a Mr Fisher came from Wisconsin to see the country – he is much pleased."[40] After reading Dame's letter, the John Fisher mentioned traveled from Wisconsin to scout the coast of Leelanau for a good stand of white pine. He found it 30 miles south of Northport at the present site of Glen Arbor, near the landmark Sleeping Bear Dunes. Pioneers John Dorsey and John LaRue met Fisher and showed him the extent of the local pinery, encouraging him to settle nearby. Pleased by what he saw, Fisher started to buy timberland and correspond with associates about the many resources of the area. The next summer, the steamer *Saginaw* brought 14 of Fisher's friends to settle in Glen Arbor. There was no dock on Lake Michigan at the time, and the newcomers were shuttled ashore in one of Fisher's lumber scows. One of the passengers, helped from the boat by John Dorsey, soon became the barrel-maker's wife. Dame's letter, aimed at promoting Northport, had also pushed settlement in Glen Arbor and other Grand Traverse harbor towns into high gear.

Natives along the coast of Grand Traverse again felt the pressure of Euro-American settlers in their midst. Reverend Smith wrote: "The Nagonabe Band have been settling with Peter today their interest in the village here with the intention of going to Canada."[41] A half decade before, the Nagonabe Band had welcomed Smith and the Black Lake Band to the area in hopes of building an Indian homeland at the tip of the Leelanau Peninsula. But now, like many Lake Michigan Indians, the Band had tired of white settlers and the government's broken promises and now moved on to Canada, a country where their prospects seemed brighter. The future of Smith's Wakazooville Mission as an Indian refuge dimmed as it became apparent Northport had been discovered.

More of the "serious evils" Smith feared would accompany the Euro-American land rush to Wakazooville-Northport began to appear later that summer. Smith wrote that Chief Pendunwan, also called Peter Wakazoo, "has been drinking & conducting himself badly for some time – and it is said he has bargained away…the rest of the Village that is not sold for $400.00 in goods…I am almost suspicious the liquor has been furnished to induce him to trade."[42] A week later the Reverend continued: "I called the Indians to Council PM that I may advise in relation to Pendunwan's intention to sell the Village – Pendunwan refused to come after being sent for twice. Others feared him & so did not come in."[43] The sudden Euro-American presence in Wakazooville was taking its toll and unsettling the Indians. The days of Smith's mission were numbered.

More than anything else, Grand Traverse Indians wanted secure title to their properties, knowing that a land base was essential to the health and welfare of their culture and traditions. Previous treaties had left issues of Indian ownership of land in question, which many Native leaders hoped to settle. During 1854, Smith's diary recounted events leading up to new treaty negotiations between the U.S. Government and the Natives of the region. He wrote: "Evening Pendunwan & Shabwasing came with a letter from Little Traverse's Chiefs to all the Chiefs here proposing a great Council on the 24th there, perhaps to send an embassy to Washington. It is presumed that some white man is at bottom."

Smith, the wary frontier missionary, was immediately suspicious of treaty talks, knowing any negotiations would eventually end in favor of the government. A month of debate among the Grand Traverse Bands brought the Indians to the same conclusion. Smith wrote: "Indians assembled in Schoolhouse to write to the Government that they are not in favor of the Little Traverse movement…I wrote for them. 8 Chiefs names were signed. Mr Dougherty & I witnessed & certified approval." However, the push for an Indian delegation to attend the summer negotiation in Washington continued. In June 1854, the preacher wrote that he "read the Treaty of 1836 to the Indians,"[44] for they wanted to better understand their current rights before any further talks took place.

Though in many places the Great Lakes wilderness was giving way to farms and towns, the same dreaded frontier diseases continued to plague Lake Michigan ports. Smith noted: "The *Edith* when here reported that while she lay in Chicago last Monday, 50 corpses dead of cholera were carried across 1 bridge in less than a day," later adding that "Deaths in Chicago by Cholera are 150 per day." In other bad news gleaned from the *Edith*, Smith learned that "15 died in a train of Cars on Central R. R. between Detroit & Chicago."[45]

During the 1850's, railroads were expanding as rapidly as the men and materials could be rounded up to build them. Economics worked strongly in their favor, for trains carried freight faster and at one-tenth the cost of sending it by way of the rough roads of the day. The growing national divide over slavery and the increasing amount of grain grown by Great Lakes farmers shifted the direction of trade in the United States away from north-south routes to an east-west orientation. Train tracks followed their lead. Most of the region's new railroads ran along the southern rim of the Lakes and headed toward the rising metropolis of Chicago. In 1850, there was only one railroad to the city, two years later there were five. Chicago's natural advantage as the terminal port on the Great Lakes was now greatly enhanced by the expanding web of railroad tracks emanating from the city. Unfortunately, like steam-powered ships, trains were in their early stages of commercial use and many problems had to be worked out. Deadly train accidents were frequent occurrences and lives lost were part of the cost of embracing the newest technology.

At the same time, a refinement in ship propulsion was rapidly changing the nature of steam-powered vessels on the Great Lakes. From the day the lake ice broke in 1854, Reverend Smith recorded an increasing number of boats anchoring at Northport harbor. This year, besides the sailing schooners and sidewheeled steamers, he wrote of a new type of steam-powered vessel frequenting the frontier harbor – the propeller.[46]

During the 1840's, almost all steam-powered ships serving the Lake Michigan trade were driven by side-mounted paddlewheels and referred to as steamers. The steamers, then the largest and fastest vessels on the Great Lakes, required stacks of energy in the form of cordwood to fire their boilers and power their extensive machinery. The boats attracted well-to-do passengers, for being independent of the wind, they kept a schedule better than the more prevalent schooners. But now the new propellers were taking over steam-powered lake traffic, accelerating the pace of settlement Grand Traverse was experiencing.

The first propeller on the Great Lakes was the *Vandalia,* which called at ports along Lakes Ontario and Erie. By installing stern-mounted propellers instead of sidewheels, the 1841 *Vandalia* was able to expand her cargo hold and still fit through the narrow Welland Canal that connected the lakes. Soon many other advantages of propeller propulsion came to light. The boats were easier and cheaper to build with far fewer moving parts. The machinery took up much less room, leaving more for cargo and passengers. Furthermore, propellers burned two-thirds to three-quarters less wood per mile than their paddlewheeled competitors. Reliability increased while ticket prices fell, and more and more people booked passage and freight by way of propellers.

The propellers reflected an evolving set of preferences for passengers traveling the Great Lakes. The old catch-as-you-can era of the luxury steamers was giving way to concerns about dependability, speed, and price. Smith noted that in mid-July the "Propellor *Pokahantas* at Grand Haven came direct to N. Manitou in 17 hours,"[47] a distance that had taken Smith three weeks to sail only two summers before. The quick and efficient propellers began to drive most of the graceful steamers into early retirement. But even the best of the Great Lakes fleet were at risk when gales swept across Lake Michigan.

One of the most dramatic accounts in Smith's 40-year long diary recounted an 1854 shipping disaster in the Manitou Passage involving the newest of the lake propellers. The year-old, 202 foot-long *Westmoreland* was the pride of the Cleveland shipyards, the latest version of the newest vessel technology. Her December demise was a reminder that late in the shipping season, no vessel was safe. Smith summarized his conversations with a few lucky survivors of the *Westmoreland* sinking, writing: "Today the Mate Polite & one passenger Mr Sattenstall of the Propellor *Westmoreland* arrived at Mr Dame's. She went down

3 Oclk PM...about 7 miles from ashore between Point Betsy & Sleeping Bear. 18 were lost, 16 saved.

"She was loaded with ice for many hours. She lay in the troughs, her fires out, her boilers tumbling from side to side, a fearful gale bearing upon them. While they were in working order they almost gained S. Manito but she leaked so fast as to put out their fires & left them at the mercy of wind and waves. Those who were saved were saved in 2 boats, one in command of Capt Clark, one under command of first mate. This boat, the metallic life boat, nearly filled twice, capsized once & lost two of her men before she reached shore. All suffered everything but death. The other 16 went down with the Propellor. They had the large boat but got tangled in the rigging & all sunk together."[48] That very summer, the United States Congress had appropriated money to equip the first life-saving stations on the Great Lakes - one built on North Manitou Island was just being finished when the *Westmoreland* went down. However, these volunteer stations were designed for near-shore rescues, and distance and weather made aiding the ill-fated vessel impossible.

The cargo hold of the *Westmoreland* was filled to the brim with barrels of flour. When the boat sank, the water-tight barrels scattered like seeds on the water, landing along the coasts of the Leelanau Peninsula and the Manitou Islands. Nothing went to waste on the frontier, and pioneers enjoyed a bounty of bread and cakes that winter by way of the *Westmoreland*.

In the early 1850's, the Fugitive Slave Act and *Uncle Tom's Cabin* severely damaged hopes for peacefully mending the national divide over slavery. A political culture born of compromise was becoming hard-pressed to find common ground. The next strike against national unity came in the form of the Kansas-Nebraska Act of 1854, whose passage was linked to the rapid rise of American railroads. Now, for the third time since the Missouri Compromise of 1820, debate over the admission of a new state from a frontier territory brought regional divisions over slavery to the boiling point. Once again, a national law helped destroy the old Union the would-be state hoped to join.

The Kansas-Nebraska Act started off with good intentions. Many of the nation's progressive leaders dreamed of linking the eastern states with the distant Pacific coast in the form of a transcontinental railroad. Statehood would bring a flood of settlers to Kansas, which was gaining fame for its deep, rich soil and the amazing per acre harvests of wheat and corn. The proposed railroad ran through the Territory for over 400 miles. More settlement meant riders and freight for the railroad and further fulfillment of the nation's perceived destiny to grow to the west.

Stephen Douglas, a United States Senator from Illinois and an influential leader of the Democratic Party, entered the debate promoting Chicago as the eastern terminus of the transcontinental railroad. The nation had witnessed how, during the last 30 years, the opening of the Erie Canal had built the premier Great Lakes cities of Buffalo and Chicago, and all harbor towns in between. Chicago, which at the dawn of the century was a swampy portage point with less than 100 residents, was now a top 20 American city, moving swiftly toward the 100,000-population mark. Senator Douglas had a strong argument for Chicago, given the railroads and shipping routes that already connected the city to all points east. But like everything in United States politics of the 1850's, the process of getting his way would require considerable arm-twisting and compromise.

The bill established new divisions of the vast Nebraska Territory and defined the borders of the two prospective states of Kansas and Nebraska. It proposed the standard mechanics by which the new states would function but also dragged back into the mix the provisions of the Fugitive Slave Act of 1850. The act refined judicial restrictions concerning the rights of slaves and increased the threat of prosecution for those aiding in their escape. By now these measures were old hat, and would probably have slipped by without causing much controversy if the bill had stopped there. However, in order to secure the future vote of the South in favor of the transcontinental railroad bill he backed, Douglas pushed through one last concession to the Slave Power.

The short-fused bomb lay in Section 14, which in essence voided the Missouri Compromise of 1820, calling it "inconsistent with the principle of nonintervention by Congress with Slaves in States and Territories." With the stroke of a pen, the Kansas-Nebraska Act destroyed the political foundation on which the North and South had built agreements for the last 34 years. The new law allowed slavery to take root in any section of the country and declared its regulation by the national government illegal.

The Kansas-Nebraska Act resuscitated the previously discarded concept of popular sovereignty that Michigan's Lewis Cass promoted in his unsuccessful run for President in 1848. Popular sovereignty allowed voters to determine the make-up of their state constitution and their position on slavery before admission to the Union. In a perfect world, letting states adopt their own laws through popular sovereignty may have proved a sound idea. The concept was consistent with the American and Democratic Party principle of self-determination by everyday citizens. However, in a perfect world, slavery would not have been a central part of the equation.

The popular sovereignty provision of the Kansas-Nebraska Act left voters "perfectly free to form and regulate their domestic institutions in their own way, subject only to the Constitution of United States..." The grand dreams of the Slave Power – the preeminence of states rights and popular sovereignty – were suddenly realized. By May 1854, the reaction against the Kansas-Nebraska Act had reached Northern Michigan, and Reverend Smith wrote: "I sent...to Post Office the Circular Petition against the Nebraska Bill signed by Mr. Dougherty and myself." The lines between church and state blurred as the two Grand Traverse ministers posted their opposition to the bill's expansion of slavery.

The passage of the Kansas-Nebraska Act immediately plunged the Kansas Territory into anarchy. People on both sides of slavery realized the national balance of power, and the future course of the country, were at stake. Pro-slavers crossed over the Missouri border to sway the Kansas vote in their favor, while New England and Great Lakes abolitionists arrived to tip the ballot their way. Many of the newcomers had no intention of settling in the proposed state. The clash of ideals quickly rose above the level of debate and turned bloody.

Just as the Fugitive Slave Act of 1850 dragged author Harriet Beecher Stowe into the anti-slavery fight, the 1854 Kansas-Nebraska Act pulled an obscure Illinois lawyer out of self-imposed political retirement. The lawyer's name was Abraham Lincoln. Like most people in the North, Lincoln grudgingly accepted slavery where it existed for the sake of the Union, but its potential extension throughout the United States was too much for him to bear. He spoke in favor of its containment as a member of the Anti-Nebraska Party, an organization that would soon be absorbed by the fledgling Republican Party.

By 1856, there had been two partisan elections, two sets of results, two separate state assemblies, and absolute chaos in Kansas. The conflict in the Territory was warfare at its worst, pitting neighbor against neighbor in fights that had no lines, no uniform, and no rules. In May 1856, a pro-slavery mob attacked the abolitionist town of Lawrence and burned it to the ground. In retaliation, John Brown - who would gain fame and the hangman's noose in 1859 for leading an unsuccessful slave revolt at Harpers Ferry, Virginia – led an attack on five pro-slave farmers and hacked them to death with swords. Pro-slavers countered with midnight raids and more killings. The Territory became known as "Bleeding Kansas," and all political discussions about statehood were suspended. Kansas was hosting the dress rehearsal for the Civil War.

The day after Lawrence was put to the torch, violence erupted within the inner sanctum of government in Washington D.C. Following a vehement anti-slavery speech by Massachusetts Senator Charles Sumner, South Carolina Senator Preston Brooks attacked the speaker and beat him with a metal-tipped cane. Sumner fell to his desk unconscious before fellow Senators subdued the attacker. The May 23 Albany *Evening Journal* accused Brooks of "brutally applying force to repress freedom of debate on the subject of Slavery" and noted "for the first time the extreme discipline of the Plantation has been introduced into the Senate of the United States." The Columbia *South Carolinian* countered that "Brooks had not only the approval, but the hearty congratulations of the people of South Carolina for his summary chastisement of the abolitionist Sumner." Brooks received dozens of canes from his constituents as a sign of solidarity. Across the nation, conflicts of opinion over slavery were escalating into violence.

Reacting to the Kansas-Nebraska Act, the Michigan Legislature took aim at the Slave Power by passing the 1855 Personal Freedom Act, directly defying national law by obstructing the slave catchers' work. Michigan's long border with slave-free Canada made the state an important last stop on the Underground Railroad, and since the passage of the Fugitive Slave Act, the state's citizens had grown tired of slave catchers in their midst. Under the new state law, Michigan county jails could no longer be used to imprison fugitive slaves. Officers of the court, rather than aid the slave catchers, were required to defend the rights of escaped slaves. Together the clauses of the Act were a slap at slave holders and national law. Yet, while most of the people in Michigan recoiled at the thought of slavery and slave catchers, abolition remained a radical concept. Few wanted to risk civil war over the issue. Support for abolition would evolve more slowly, and at a higher cost.

While the national condition deteriorated rapidly following the passage of the Kansas-Nebraska Act, pioneers continued to push their way west through the Great Lakes. Grand Traverse Country enjoyed its last years as a frontier of the United States and a Wild West atmosphere prevailed. In the spring of the event-filled year of 1855, Reverend Smith wrote: "Last night Mr. Beers had all his supplies taken at the light house by the Mormons,"[49] introducing one of the season's big stories. It wasn't the first time Mormons were accused of raids along the coast of Grand Traverse, but now it was Philo Beers, the keeper of the Grand Traverse Lighthouse, who was making the charges, and the stolen supplies belonged to the U.S. Government.

Trouble between the Mormons and their neighbors began soon after James Strang brought his congregation to Beaver Island in 1848. The colony grew quickly, and in 1850, Strang crowned himself king of the Mormon Church, establishing the only monarchy to exist within the United States. Later, Strang won a seat in the Michigan House of Representatives on the strength of the unanimous support of Mormon voters. The lawmaker set to the task of organizing Emmet County, which he accomplished in 1853. The Mormons acquired a base of power in Michigan county government and began to exert their influence from Little Traverse Bay to the Straits of Mackinac.

Mainlanders to the north of Grand Traverse grew weary of the Mormons in their midst. Among the disgruntled were Irish fishermen who had been forced off Beaver Island by the overwhelming Mormon presence. In 1855, Michigan lawmakers checked the kingdom's power when they united the seven islands of the Beaver Island archipelago with the Fox and Manitou Islands to create Manitou County, effectively isolating Mormon voting power offshore. St James, named in honor of King Strang, was selected as the county seat. In 1855, the religious settlement numbered around 2,000, and St. James on Beaver Island reigned as the largest town in Northern Michigan. Some of the faithful sailed south to the Fox and Manitou Islands to establish farms in honor of the Mormon kingdom, establishing their presence in Grand Traverse.

Despite the political reshuffling, conflict between the Mormons and their neighbors continued. Only months after complaining about items being stolen from the Grand Traverse Lighthouse, another incident involving Beers and Mormon mariners occurred. Smith wrote: "Near night…Mr Beers came…last Thursday the Mormans stole a gang of nets from him about 1PM. He started after them in his boat but they got up the nets & having much more sail, they out sailed him. There were 2 boats, 1 boat that took the nets toward Beaver Island, the other toward Pine river."[50] All along the coast of northern Lake Michigan, settlers kept an eye out for the alleged raiders, and anger toward King Strang and his island kingdom began to heat up.

The same summer, Reverend Smith noted several Indian leaders leaving for Detroit to attend negotiations for a new treaty with the Federal government.

The year before, the Grand Traverse Bands argued against such a meeting, but the Natives from Little Traverse and the eastern Upper Peninsula prevailed. Though they did not see eye to eye on all matters, the ties between the Grand Traverse and Little Traverse Bands ran deep. A canoe ride north from Waka-zooville to Little Traverse Bay was the same distance as the journey south to Traverse City, and transit between the two places was common. Many of the far-flung Odawa and Ojibwa considered the Little Traverse town of L'Arbre Croche their cultural center and counted close relatives and friends among the thousand-plus Natives who lived there. In addition, seasonal migrations along the Lake Michigan coast and the summer trip to Mackinac Island to collect treaty payments rekindled familial bonds between the Indian people. Eventually the Northern Michigan Bands came to a meeting of minds and decided to hold talks with the government.

The Indians gathered at Detroit believed that in signing the 1855 treaty, they had finally secured a way for their people to hold on to their land in the face of increasing Euro-American pressure. Indians were eligible to select parcels from within reserves defined by the treaty. Land set aside for Grand Traverse Bands included large swaths of the Leelanau Peninsula and land east across Grand Traverse Bay to Elk Rapids, including the Old Mission Peninsula. Since most of the Grand Traverse Band members lived within these boundaries, Na-tive leaders thought they had signed a fair deal. In practice, however, the treaty in time divested the Natives of most of their remaining holdings, and worked to further destroy what was left of their centuries-old culture.

As was the pattern with United States treaties with the Indians, there were plenty of loopholes and nuanced clauses within the 1855 document. Euro-Americans pioneers already living within the bounds of the reserves were al-lowed to stay. Swamplands in the reserves belonged to the state of Michigan, and defining those areas was in the hands of state agents, who did so liberally. All the while, more white settlers moved on to the reserve lands without inter-ference from authorities. Paperwork involving land selections made by Indi-ans often languished in the government bureaucracy. Individual Natives who eventually received title to their selections stood alone against many schemes to defraud them including liquor, taxes, harassment, and outright theft. Another round of nightmares had begun for Grand Traverse Indians.[51]

To the north, the Little Traverse Indians made the best of the rapidly evolv-ing political situation. The 1855 Treaty coincided with the creation of Manitou County, which concentrated the followers and political power of the Mormon

King Strang in an archipelago in the middle of Lake Michigan. Many Mormon citizens on the mainland – who now lacked the votes to control Emmet County politics – moved to the new island county, leaving the voting majority in the hands of the L'Arbre Croche Indians. With the Mormon block of voters gone, and far fewer white settlers to deal with than their Grand Traverse neighbors, the Indians seized the opportunity and through elections won many positions in Emmet County government. Under this political structure, Henry Graveraet, a Mackinac Island fur trader who lived among the L'Arbre Croche Indians, was elected Emmet County Probate Judge. Henry Graveraet and his son Garrett later fought in Company K of the 1ˢᵗ Michigan Sharp Shooters – the largest all-Native company from the Great Lakes region to serve in the Civil War. Indians had used their united Democratic vote to elect their own government leaders, and most stayed faithful to their historic party affiliation throughout the Civil War era.

In 1856, a harsh winter came early and stayed late. On January 7, Smith wrote in his dairy: "Snow fell last night eight inches. Gave an order of 10 dollars to the overseers of the poor…for the benefit of Kelsey Oliver who was lost between 3&4 days in the woods…& froze his feet, hands & thighs so badly that he is helpless." The next week, outfitting for the season proceeded when George and his son worked on their cutter, the two seat, horse-drawn sleigh most commonly used during a Grand Traverse winter. In late January, Smith drove his cutter along the frozen lakeshore and found that there was ice "as far as the eye can reach."[52]

Lake ice linked Grand Traverse harbor towns during the coldest winter months. Travel across the smooth Bay ice in a cutter was a faster and more pleasant trip than on the rough and snow-bound roads ashore. However, the ice roads came with an element of danger. In February, Smith wrote: "Yesterday a horse was drown about middle way between Mr Dougherty's and Old Mission," on its way across the Bay. Later, the preacher lent a Northport friend his "harness & cutter to go to Old Mission" along the same route. Smith also mentioned that "An Indian & 3 white men came yesterday from Le Arbor Croche on the ice,"[53] as year round communication between the two Lake Michigan towns continued.

On March 5, 1856, Smith noted: "A two horse team came from North Manito – returned Saturday. Sabbath a horse & ox team came over, these all to move families. The ice over the channel was 18 inches thick, solid ice. They came to Carp river." Exactly why the families mentioned left North Manitou that winter is unknown - isolation always made island life tough, and new ports along the mainland were cutting into the Island's cordwood business. But it was also true that Mormons now controlled Manitou County government. Those outside the church may have decided it was time to resettle on the mainland at Carp River, the site of present day Leland.

A month passed and the long-awaited start of navigation season edged closer. In mid-April, Smith wrote: "A Propellor was seen yesterday & today on the lake. Tonight a whistle was heard. She is not gone out of the bay yet." Soon the lake ice disappeared and a stream of ships followed. The Reverend frequently visited the suddenly busy Northport docks, hungry for the conversations and news he missed during the long winter. He wrote: "Propellor *Wisconsin* arrived...Isaac Pierce is aboard. I had a great discussion with him. He is a great Mormon. He contends for polygamy."[54]

Few white settlers were as open minded as Reverend Smith appeared to be when it came to the Mormons. Their endorsement of polygamy, their growing political power, and their alleged thefts of boats, nets, and other property along the coast of Lake Michigan had incited growing resentment against the islanders and their beliefs. This year, King Strang's edicts took on an increasingly dictatorial tone, and tensions mounted not only between pioneers and the inhabitants of Manitou County, but within the Mormon community itself. Strang's kingdom now had a dress code and numerous other rules that went well beyond church doctrine. Followers who balked as his orders were subject to a whipping or banishment from the islands. Some Mormons began to lose faith in their temperamental leader. An Indian friend of Smith's arrived in Northport in mid-June and reported that "a great many Mormons from Beaver Island are settling at Pine river"[55] in hopes of escaping Strang's increasingly harsh rule.

The Indian courier did not know that the day before he arrived in Northport, Strang had been shot in the back on a Beaver Island dock in an ambush by his own disgruntled followers. The U.S. Steamer *Michigan* had brought the conspirators to the island, not the last time the national government was entangled in a plot to remove an unwanted ruler. Reverend Smith wrote in his diary: "The *Northern Mich* came in here last night & brought word that Strang was shot last Thursday with three Pistol Shots & it is impossible that he should live." Now Smith called Strang "one of the worst of men" professing to be "King of the latter day Saints but was really the leader of a Band of Pirates of the worst kind."[56]

Another week passed and Smith wrote: "*Troy* reports Strang recovering – also that a large company has gone from Mackinac to drive the Mormans from

Beaver Island." The simmering anger toward the kingdom surfaced now that the king lay wounded. The Beaver Island faithful were rousted from their homes and farms and sent away aboard boats. On July 9 Strang died, leaving behind a crumbling island empire and five pregnant wives. Speculators joined the stampede to Beaver Island to divide the spoils. Smith wrote: "The *E Cushman & Eagle* were at dock this morning – they are going to Beaver Island. Mr Curtis of Old mission is moving there – when the Mormans broke up he bought considerable property."[57] Strang's flock scattered to the wind and by the winter of 1856, Manitou and Emmet Counties had lost almost all of their Mormon residents.

Despite the disappearance of the Mormons, the surge in lake traffic and numerous improvements along the coast during the mid-1850's began to transform the northern Great Lakes, bringing settlers and commerce to the previously unbroken wilderness. Wakazooville's sister settlement of Northport led the race to become the number one port in Grand Traverse, offering boats of all shapes and sizes safe anchorage, supplies, and cordwood. In May 1855, Reverend Smith wrote: "The Steamer *Britannia* came in early. She has been to Chicago & is on her return to Montreal. She took about 50 cords of wood."[58]

Wood was the fuel that powered the growing Great Lakes fleet of steamships. Paddle-wheeled steamers burned about 200 cords on the round trip from Buffalo to Chicago, the new propellers a third that amount. In the face of increasing demand for cordwood, captains of the trans-lake vessels sought a safe, deep water port near the shipping lanes where they could consistently buy hot burning fuel for their boilers - a search that led them to Northport and other harbor towns along the coast of Grand Traverse.

In addition to having plenty of cordwood to sell, the port of Wakazooville-Northport lay at the midpoint of a voyage through the western lakes and close to the well-traveled Manitou Passage. The sheltered harbor let vessels dock and load in almost any weather. Situated at the wide-open mouth of Grand Traverse Bay, the water here was the last to freeze and the first to thaw, extending the navigation season at Northport longer than any other harbor on northern Lake Michigan. These multiple advantages began to make Northport the harbor of choice in Northern Michigan. When the ice cleared this season, ships stopped there in unprecedented numbers. One carried the Reverend Smith's son and namesake George off to study at Oberlin College in Ohio; another took daughter Arvilla to Olivet College. The brand new, sidewheeled steamer *Sebastopol* stopped in Northport soon after her launch from a Cleveland shipyard. The propellers *Northern Michigan, Troy, Louisville, Wisconsin,* and *Ottawa* were also

The U.S. Steamer *Michigan*, built in 1844 to patrol the Great Lakes, brought treaty payments to Michigan Indians and in 1864 was the target of a Confederate raid on Lake Erie. *Bowling Green State University*

among the list of the Great Lakes best ships that loaded up with cordwood in Northport that summer. In one July morning alone Reverend Smith "saw on the lake 19 sail vessels and one Steamer."[59] Wakazooville-Northport harbor was no longer a quiet place on the Bay.

The infrastructure Northport needed to make it Northern Michigan's premier town was upgraded in several ways during the summer of 1855. A lumberman named Rose completed an expansive new dock where boats could load up with the best of cordwood. Pioneers and Indians were happy to supply it as a rare source of cash on the frontier. Millwright William Voice, who in 1853 accompanied Perry Hannah to Traverse City and built Hannah, Lay & Co.'s first steam-powered sawmill, now plied his trade in Northport. Reverend Smith wrote: "Mr Voice's sawmill started yesterday a little – I went today & saw it – it is a circular saw 4 feet diameter."[60] Soon piles of sawn lumber lay beside stacks of cordwood on the Rose dock, waiting for their turn to be loaded into passing ships. One of the millwright's sons, Joseph Voice, in time married Smiths' daughter Arvilla. Another son, William Voice Jr., would serve as a sergeant in a Union regiment nicknamed the Lakeshore Tigers.

The completion of another infrastructure project 100 miles north of Grand Traverse rapidly changed the nature of Great Lakes shipping and industry. To date, wild rapids in the St. Mary's River had prevented ships from traveling between Lake Superior and the lower lakes. Ships sailing east from Lake Superior's mining towns were forced to unload their heavy cargoes at Sault Ste Marie and carry it by wagon to ships waiting below the stretch of impassable water. But when the much anticipated Soo Locks opened in 1855, the rapids were circumvented, and boats could sail unimpeded throughout the Great Lakes. Vast deposits of copper, iron, and lead mined in Michigan's Upper Peninsula could now be delivered quickly and cheaply anywhere along their shores. With the bottleneck eliminated, vast quantities of metal began to flow south, sparking an industrial revolution along the Great Lakes.

The moment the Soo Locks opened, the South's chances of winning the rapidly approaching American Civil War were greatly diminished. The Civil War would define modern warfare as an exercise in propelling massive amounts of metal at the enemy with the hope of causing death and destruction. Now Michigan mines prepared to send as much metal as the fleet of Great Lakes ships could carry through the locks.

In the run up to the 1856 Presidential election, Pennsylvanian James Buchanan was chosen as the Democratic candidate over Illinois' Stephen Douglas. Delegates viewed Buchanan as the more centrist of the two men and able to carry more of the northern vote. At the time, Douglas's position as a prominent supporter of popular sovereignty made him unacceptable to New England states. They blamed him for igniting the conflict in Bleeding Kansas and pushing the nation closer to civil war. Eight years before, Michigan's Lewis Cass ran as the Democratic candidate for President on a platform that promoted popular sovereignty and lost, and the party was anxious not to repeat the mistake.

Another Illinois politician named Abraham Lincoln campaigned vigorously for candidates representing the new Republican Party during the 1856 campaigns. In this role, Lincoln made his first and only visit to Michigan, traveling to Kalamazoo to lend his support to Presidential candidate John Fremont of California. The Republican Party stood firmly against the Kansas-Nebraska Act and the principle of popular sovereignty. Although Fremont carried Michigan and a number of other Great Lakes and New England states, he lost the election to Buchanan. In the course of the campaign, Lincoln displayed his keen mind and oratory skills on the national stage, and the reputation he gained helped him rise through the ranks of the Republican Party during the next four years.

On Election Day 1856, Smith wrote that "every Indian except Payson voted Democratic out of fear of the Agent...it made me realize something about the

A Civil War era propeller steams through the Soo Locks. *Chippewa County Historical Society*

border ruffianism in Kansas." But it was more than fear that kept the Natives faithful to the Democratic Party. Generations of Michigan Indians negotiated treaties and collected annuities from Indian agents selected by Democratic politicians. Democrat Governor Lewis Cass had been the face of the United States Government in the Michigan Territory for 18 years. Cass hand-picked Indian Agent Henry Schoolcraft to write the 1836 Treaty of Washington and administer it from posts in Mackinac Island and Detroit. The Odawa and Ojibwa of northern Michigan came to see the party as the power behind the nation. More recently, the united vote by L'Arbre Croche Indians for Democratic candidates won them political control of Emmet County. Now, on the national level, Buchanan's victory in the 1856 Presidential Election reinforced the party's aura of power. Republican Smith found one bright spot in the election results, writing: "We unanimously declared Perry Hannah elected Representative to State Legislature."[61] Hannah represented the initial movement of voters in Grand Traverse to the Republican Party, and the base grew by the day as the national fight over slavery became increasingly divisive.

Violent November storms focused attention away from politics. A gale swept though Wakazooville and "water rose very high. Took off our old dock – rolled over our breakwater, washed boats from the shore." In between storms, Smith's Odawa son-in-law Payson Wolfe "caught 273 small whitefish this morning in

3 nets." Then a second gale swept the harbor and the trading schooner *Juliana* "parted her lines & cable & went ashore…a great deal of her cargo was underwater – some of my flour was wet."[62] Not long after, ice formed on the harbor, and the navigation season in Grand Traverse closed for the winter.

On a family foray to Traverse City several months later, the Smiths' horse and sleigh broke through the ice covering Grand Traverse Bay. For a moment the rig and its passengers were suspended above the freezing water, and then fell through the icy hole. This type of accident almost always caused the loss of equipment and horses and often the lives of the travelers. However, though far from shore, the water was shallow, and the Smiths were able to pull themselves and their horse and sleigh free. They walked to the nearby home of tannery owner Albert Norris, where they warmed by the fire and dried their clothes. Smith wrote: "We were much favored and very thankful that it was not very deep & it was near a house, if had been deep water or far away we must have perished."[63]

The opening of the 1857 navigation season again brought a swarm of boats to Northport. The sheltered port was gaining a reputation as the best place to buy boiler wood and other supplies on northern Lake Michigan, and many wood burning ships now made the place a scheduled stop. The assassination of King Strang and the collapse of the Mormon enclave on Beaver Island gave the title of Northern Michigan's most populous town to Northport. Settlers arriving at the harbor encircled the Wakazooville Mission and once again the Native people faced displacement. Seeing the writing on the wall, many Indians relocated to the village of Onumunese[64] on Lake Michigan, a few miles to the southwest. Reverend Smith continued to work with others to secure their selection of lands. The Congregational minister located their choices on the map, determined the legal description, and sent off the claims on departing boats to be registered with the United States government. Smith knew the faster the Indians received clear title to their selections, the less chance they had of losing it to one of the newcomers now arriving daily in Grand Traverse. Most of the applicants neither spoke nor wrote English with any degree of fluency, while a quarter century of practice had given the preacher a decent command of the Algonquian tongue. Other than missionaries like Smith, few settlers cared much about the plight of their Native neighbors, concerned instead with putting down roots and overcoming the obstacles of frontier life. If Native people stood in the way, the accepted solution was to ignore the treaties and drive the Indians further west.

That summer, Smith's observations of Northport swung from the raucous to the polished, capturing the many personalities of the rising frontier oasis. Northport showed signs of sophistication due to the quantity and quality of ships tying up at the docks, but in 1857, there were plenty of rough edges left. In May, Smith wrote: "Rev Mr Bailey & Brother…took tea with us. They are from Iowa, Ohio formerly, came by land from Glen Arbor, were looking for a location for a Colony (anti Slavery), also an institution of learning perhaps like Oberlin. They are Congregationalist."[65] Bailey, a former Oberlin College professor, would later establish Grand Traverse College in Benzonia, a liberal institution that accepted students of both sexes and all colors.[66] At the other extreme, Smith noted "a great appearance of drunkenness among whites & Indians. Screaming, Swearing & the like are indicative of great evil." The harbor town was rapidly growing beyond Smith's control, and at times he could only fret at the direction it had taken.

During August, hundreds of ships visited Northport, many dropping off new settlers. One day the preacher "saw 29 Sail vessels 1 steamer, 30 in all," from his home on the Bay. Next the propellor *Neptune* "came to land passengers," a Mr. Kater and his wife "moved here today on *Agate*," and the new propeller *Fountain City,* fresh out of the Cleveland shipyards, stopped at the harbor on her maiden voyage. Her captain, John Ball, hailed from St. Albans and paid a visit to his former Vermont neighbors. Other top of the line propellers including the "*Sciota, Michigan, Potomac & Iowa*" came to Northport and two of the captains took a tour of Smith's famous garden. The month ended with the return of the *Fountain City,* which "brought a great deal of freight" along with six passengers who intended to settle there. In less than a decade, on the strength of its harbor and location near the Great Lakes water highway, Wakazooville-Northport had grown from an uninhabited bay to Northwest Michigan's leading port. Other Grand Traverse harbor towns could only hope for the same success. It was hard to imagine while standing on the docks of the boom town of Northport in 1857 that the United States as a whole was falling apart.

Auction and Negro Sales. *Library of Congress*

Chapter Two

Separate Paths

The first ships to sail into Grand Traverse Bay in 1858 carried news of the widening divide over slavery. On a national level, Democratic President James Buchanan – who had been elected for his centrist views on slavery - began his slide toward the southern political camp. In a letter to his Secretary of State, former Michigan Governor Lewis Cass, Buchanan wrote that slavery was "an institution recognized & maintained by our constitution & productive of advantage both to the Master and the Slave as well as necessary to the existence of the Cotton Manufacturers of Great Britain & other countries."[67] For the rest of his term, President Buchanan expressed with increasing vigor the sentiments of the pro-slavery faction in the Democratic Party, creating a rift in the political organization that reflected the dismal state of the nation.

The common ground within the United States was quickly eroding as more people chose sides. There were few signs of a peaceful solution to the country's number one problem – slavery. Though the Territory had been quiet for a while, the opposing factions again stood ready to fight it out in Bleeding Kansas. Productive debate had ground to a halt. Northern Michigan residents, isolated from the outside world during winter, hungered for details about the nation's deteriorating state. On May 4, Smith wrote: "Mail came…two Speeches from the Senate. Charles E. Stuart's from himself, one Chandlers[68] sent by himself. Both against Kansas Bill." In these speeches, the two U.S. Senators from Michigan expressed their deep opposition to the expansion of slavery as prescribed by the ruinous Kansas-Nebraska Act. From the United States Capitol to the remote northern coast of Lake Michigan, all news took a back seat to reports of the growing turmoil created by slavery.

Though torn by fights over slavery to the point of paralysis, the United States Congress had recently agreed to fund a series of navigational aids along the busy Great Lakes shipping lanes, with replacement lighthouses on South Manitou Island and at the tip of the Leelanau Peninsula part of the spending bill. The meteoric rise in population along the western Great Lakes, and the growing commercial importance of the Lake Michigan ports from Northport to Chicago, gave new weight to the need for safe sailing on the water highway west. An observation in George Smith's diary recorded the progress of these improvements in Grand Traverse when he wrote: "This morning there was a Schooner anchored here loaded with bricks for the new light house."[69]

Three months later, with the bricks from the schooner now forming the outline of the Grand Traverse Lighthouse, George Smith wrote: "Midnight myself wife & Annie went on board the *Fountain City* to go to Chicago with a view of going to Oberlin to attend Commencement." Their son George was graduating from prestigious Oberlin College in Ohio, and the three Smiths planned to attend the commencement ceremonies. In addition to being one of

The Grand Traverse Lighthouse at the tip of the Leelanau Peninsula was built from bricks carried in a schooner that anchored in Northport harbor on May 6, 1858. *Grand Traverse Lighthouse Museum*

the region's best colleges, Oberlin was an abolitionist hotspot, and events were about to embroil the town in a nationally publicized incident involving slavery.

The *Fountain City* steamed out of Northport harbor at 1 AM - the next night the Smiths slept aboard the boat off Chicago. Later they sailed across Lake Michigan, traveled overland for a visit to Old Wing and Kalamazoo, and then traversed the state to Detroit. Here they boarded the steamer *Ocean* for Cleveland, followed by a train bound for Oberlin, where George Jr. waited at the depot.

Graduation ceremonies at Oberlin lasted a week. Reverend Smith noted that "21 young men & 1 young lady"[70] had earned their degrees. Professors, dignitaries, and graduating students gave speeches and Reverend Smith addressed a gathering and described his work as an Indian missionary. There were numerous meetings on campus about slavery, reflecting the college's lead role in the Ohio abolitionist movement. Oberlin took pride in its place as an important stop on the Underground Railroad, where escaped slaves waited for a boat to carry them across Lake Erie to Canada. Several blacks who fled the plantations lived openly in Oberlin in defiance of the Fugitive Slave Law. Throughout the South, slave holders viewed the college town as a den of thieves.

Following commencement exercises, Oberlin graduate George Smith Jr. "left for Urbana" where he was due to start a job teaching at the town's university. The rest of the Smiths boarded a train back to Cleveland where they waited for a steamship to carry them up the lakes. Smith gave details of the trip, writing: "Took ticket for home…on *Buckeye* tonight, all passengers came to office to go on board. Boat did not come till morning. All spent the night in Office. Took breakfast on board, left 10AM. At Detroit midnight, daylight St. Clair Flats, morning nearly across Saginaw Bay, sunset in Mackinaw. Reached the Dock 7 Oclk morning – very high sea all night."

At the same time the *Buckeye* carried the Smiths back home, Federal marshals arrested a fugitive slave named John Price in Oberlin. Price had escaped to Ohio from a Kentucky plantation years before and was now a familiar figure around town. Knowing the anti-slavery spirit of the college community and their hatred of the Fugitive Slave Law, the captors moved Price to the neighboring town of Wellington and waited for the next train south. Word raced through Oberlin of Price's arrest and townspeople rushed to Wellington to free their black friend. After failing to negotiate his release, a mob stormed the hotel where the slave catchers stayed and spirited Price back to Oberlin. Federal marshals descended on the town looking for the fugitive slave. A conservative

Oberlin College professor surprised his colleagues by agreeing to hide Price in his attic. As hoped, the marshals did not search his house. Price later escaped north across the border. All who had helped him had broken Federal law.

The citizens of northern Ohio now had the divisive issue of slave catching thrown squarely in their midst. While northern sentiment against the Fugitive Slave Law had risen dramatically since the bill's passage, the scale of the Oberlin incident and the open defiance of the slave catchers was unprecedented. President James Buchanan, now a friend of the Slave Power, recommended prosecutions against those who freed Price. The wheels of justice turned. An Ohio grand jury indicted 37 men for crimes against the Fugitive Slave Law, the majority from Oberlin. Their arrest made headlines in newspapers across the country, and another bloodless battle over slavery divided the United States. The Northern press named the jailed defendants the "Oberlin Rescuers' and made them overnight heroes in the anti-slavery movement. Had the incident occurred just two weeks earlier, chances are good one or more of the Northport Smiths would have shared a cell with the Oberlin Rescuers.

In Northport, the leaves began to change color when "the old Steamer *Michigan*...brought things for Indian payment" Yet for Smith, the government payments were tainted by the realization that life for his Indian friends was edging toward despair. Many of their land claims had been rejected due to faulty paperwork or sat languishing on bureaucrats' desks. There was a growing sentiment among the Indians that the Treaty of 1855 – a document they had pinned their hopes on - was only making their lives worse. Smith wrote: "I have never known the Indians to drink so hard as they have during & since the last payment. It is disheartening, sickening to witness it. What guilt rests upon the white who tempts them & supplies them with whisky? It is a horrid crime. It is like murder and robbery only it adds murder of the soul to that of body."[71]

On November 2, 1858, Smith wrote: "Today elections in our School house a pretty close affair. The Democrats use such low vile means with the Indians to get their vote that it is sickening." Liquor, and long ties to the Democratic Party, again delivered the Northport Native vote. The next day, however, Smith would have something to celebrate when the Grand Traverse region's first newspaper opened for business.

The first edition of the *Grand Traverse Herald* rolled off the presses on November 3, 1858, commencing publication just in time to record the unfolding drama of the Civil War. In unambiguous language, owner and publisher Morgan Bates announced his position and that of his weekly newspaper in the

Union soldiers patronize a roving newspaper vendor during the Civil War. *Library of Congress*

first editorial of Volume I. Bates wrote: "In politics we admit no such word as Neutrality. We hate slavery in all its forms and conditions, and can have no fellowship or compromise with it. We entertain no respect for any party or any religion which sanctions or supports it, we care not from what source they derive their authority, and regard that politician, minister, or layman who advocates its extension and perpetuity, as an enemy of the Human Race."[72]

Morgan Bates had just arrived in the village of Traverse City, continuing his professional habit of finding emerging edges of the American frontier and bringing his presses to them. In 1858, Grand Traverse was one of those places, and the veteran newspaperman again determined to create a viable weekly paper in a region that was coming of age. The debut edition of the *Grand Traverse Herald* displayed the skills Bates had honed during his long career as a journalist, one that dated back to the 1820's, when both he and the American newspaper business were young.

In the first half of the 19th century, apprentices learned the newspaper trade through the guild system, gradually acquiring the skills necessary to gather, write, print, and publish the news. Following this path, Bates spent his teenage years with various New York papers, including time in the state capital of Albany on the Hudson River, where the Erie Canal began. As a young journalist, Bates saw the ambitious canal project come to fruition through the strength of free labor, and then witnessed the rush of pioneers up the Great Lakes when the Erie Canal opened in 1825.

Bates had chosen a growing profession. At the time of his birth in 1806, there were some 250 American newspapers, by 1850 there were 2500. Inventors and engineers produced increasingly fast and reliable steam presses while a new breed of publishers followed the national migration west and started papers in frontier towns. Bates was a leader of this trend and saw local newspapers as a sign of an area's coming of age - a mark of distinction and culture. He knew that with a newspaper, communities gained not only a reliable source of information, but also a sense of identity. In 1858, he prepared to use his latest newspaper to shape the identity of Grand Traverse Country.

As a young newspaperman, Bates hired a teen-aged printer named Horace Greeley to work at a Pennsylvania paper he published.[73] Later, the men worked together in New York City, where Greeley founded the *New York Tribune* in 1841. The two journalists must have discussed the great national issues of the day, including slavery and its expansion. In their subsequent papers, both men embraced the radical positions of the Republican Party, an editorial position that ultimately affected, through their wide circles of influence, the course of the Civil War. By the time Morgan Bates pressed his first issue of the *Grand Traverse Herald* in 1858, Greeley's *New York Tribune* was already the most influential and widely-read paper in the North

Throughout his career, Bates displayed a restless spirit and a reporter's instinct to follow news in the making. These characteristics kept him on the move. After a few years in New York City, he left his job with Greeley and again struck out on his own. In his travels, he continued to rub elbows with the up-and-coming editors of American newspapers. In 1837, Bates journeyed to Louisiana to help fellow reporter George Kendall start the *New Orleans Picayune*.[74] Before heading back north, Bates came to know the South's largest city, the slaveholder port where bales of King Cotton flowed out to the world. Kendall stayed on in New Orleans to build the *Picayune* into the South's leading weekly. Bates later worked for the *Detroit Advertiser and Tribune,* a leading paper in the frontier river town that was the gateway to the western Great Lakes. Within a few years, he owned the *Advertiser* and advocated a liberal position on emancipation in the conservative Michigan city, preparing him for the reception he faced when he launched the *Grand Traverse Herald* decades later.

His career took another sharp turn in 1849 when, like so many of his fellow citizens, Bates fell victim to gold fever. From the Atlantic coast, he sailed around Cape Horn to California, joining the stampede of prospectors arriving on the western edge of the continent. Although failing to strike it rich, he gained invaluable knowledge about another emerging region of the nation, intellectual capital that would later serve him well at the helm of the *Herald.* On the return trip east from California, Bates trekked across the Isthmus of Panama, following the route of the future Panama Canal. Within a year he was back on the Pacific coast where he founded the San Francisco based *Alta California,* the first daily newspaper west of the Mississippi River.[75]

In 1856, the journalist returned to Michigan and worked as a government auditor in the state capital of Lansing. Chafing to start yet another newspaper, he moved to the wilderness village of Traverse City, a dot on the northeast coast of Lake Michigan. It was more than good luck that drew the veteran newspaperman to the sparsely populated region. In his debut editorial in the *Herald,* Bates wrote: "Why select such an out-of-the-world place as Traverse City, or the

Grand Traverse country for the theatre of your future labors? We answer, Because we like it better than any part of Michigan we have yet seen… The scenery around the Bay is delightful and the climate healthy and agreeable…the soil rich and productive… with no early frosts to injure the crops."[76] Though Traverse City was way behind Northport in its development, the experienced journalist had seen other regions emerge from the wilderness and believed the county seat would in time surpass its local rivals.

In a subsequent edition of the *Herald,* Bates elabo-

Together Reverend George Smith and Editor Morgan Bates (above) shaped and recorded the history of Grand Traverse during the Civil War era. *History Center of Traverse City*

rated on his decision to come north, writing: "Twenty five years of a life full of changes and vicissitudes have been spent in cities on both sides of the world, pushing and jostling and fighting our way through the reckless, selfish, and heartless crowd. We have seen enough of such existence – which cannot properly be called life – it became utterly distasteful, and we resolved to exchange its tinsel and its tainted atmosphere for the fine gold of God's pure, free country air."[77] Bates reasons for choosing Grand Traverse Country were timeless and mirror the mind of many who live in the region today.

Until the debut of the *Herald*, the printed news available in Northern Michigan arrived from distant cities, often aged and carrying little in the way of local stories or points of view. During the navigation season, Grand Traverse pioneers frequently congregated at the nearest harbor for a chance to talk with passengers and buy the latest papers from visiting ships. "You'll know more when the steamer comes in" was a common saying in Great Lakes ports of the time. When harbors froze shut, the sense of isolation in the Grand Traverse region grew especially acute, for with no roads leading to the area, almost all ties to the larger world ceased for at least three months. Many of the first Euro-American settlers lamented that the loneliness caused by the void of contact with the outside world was often harder to bear than the cold, hunger, and hard work of a wilderness winter.

Bates understood as well as anyone the power of a newspaper to unite and invigorate a region. For 40 years, he saw frontier newspapers transform scattered towns and homesteads into communities with shared perspectives. The editor set out to use the *Herald* to promote the concept of "Grand Traverse Country," attracting a readership well beyond its base in Traverse City. The unifying element of the extended community was the water, which included hundreds of miles of Great Lakes shoreline and the shelter of local bays, harbors, and islands. All Grand Traverse towns grew up along these waterways, and each was developing a unique, yet shared, perspective of Northern Michigan. While political boundaries in the region changed frequently in the decade leading up to and including the Civil War, in a larger sense, the common experience of life at the edge of northern Lake Michigan united the various communities. Bates knew that his paper's success depended on building a clear and shared vision of Grand Traverse Country.

In 1858 Traverse City, even a paper run by an experienced newsman was a challenge to publish profitably. Spare cash on the frontier was hard to come by and year-round distribution to a readership Bates hoped would stretch from

Manistee to Mackinac Island was problematic. His radical anti-slavery politics also worked against the venture, for eastern opinions on abolition were far ahead of local sentiment. Many Grand Traverse pioneers still viewed slavery as a distant, and somewhat irrelevant, issue – certainly nothing to fight about. Yet in his first words in the *Herald*, the editor called slavery "the enemy of the Human Race," valuing the abolitionist cause above the price of lost subscriptions.

A decade later, Bates reflected on the difficulties surrounding the *Herald's* launch. He wrote: "The first number of the *Herald* was issued …without a subscriber, and only one-fourth of a column of local advertisements. The undertaking looked more like a madcap freak than a sensible business enterprise. The county was then Democratic and all the county officers, and the register and receiver of the United States land office (which had just been established here) were bitterly hostile to us. The only word of encouragement we received was from the Hon. Perry Hannah, who welcomed our advent kindly, and who has proved a firm and steadfast friend."[78] In the face of long odds and determined opposition - and to the good fortune of the Grand Traverse historical record - Bates began to publish the *Herald*.

In 1858, the Republican Party was the most radical national political organization in the United States, and those Republicans who advocated the abolition of slavery occupied the party's far left wing. As Bates quickly found out, there wasn't much support at the time for a radical Republican in Grand Traverse Country. Here Democrats were in control, and they were a party that wanted to leave the hornet's nest of slavery alone. Rather than seek a compromise, Bates went on the attack. In an editorial titled "A Flattering Notice," the *Herald* reprinted a letter from the Democratic *Grand Rapids Enquirer* - written by the *Enquirer's* former editor and current Register of the Land Office at Traverse City – which criticized Bates and his debut, anti-slavery editorial. Bates had said: "We hate slavery in all its forms and conditions, and can have no fellowship or compromise with it." The *Enquirer* responded: "Mr. Bates…seems to have placed himself upon the black and rotten plank of Abolitionism alone; and only pledges his support to the present Republican organization in so far as they may devote themselves to the benefit of niggerism. From such a source we shall in the future expect little…" Bates shot back, mocking "the caustic pen" of the land office register by writing: "How unfortunate! In the very outset of our career we have offended…Mr. Buchanan's office-holders!"

The juxtaposition of the *Herald's* first editorial and results of the local vote in the previous day's elections provided another look at the political mindset the paper was up against. On Page 2, Bates wrote: "we shall support, with zeal and firmness...the Republican organization," while on Page 3 the *Herald* revealed that Grand Traverse voters chose Democrats in 20 of 22 state and local contests. Only Northport's Charles Holden, who won both the County Prosecutor and Circuit Court Commissioner seats, prevailed as a Republican candidate. Accentuating the positive, a *Herald* headline next to the local results cheered, "'Hurra!!! Republicanism Triumphed in Pennsylvania, Ohio, Indiana and Iowa. The People have Spoken!'"

Disgruntled Republican booster George Smith complained that on Election Day in Northport, the Indian vote had been tainted by liquor and Democratic fear-mongering. A month later, the preacher took a shot at Democratic politician Philo Beers – the former keeper of the Grand Traverse Lighthouse - suggesting that the "low vile means" Beers used to win his seat in the State Legislature had now ensnared him. Smith wrote: "Mr Beers...is going to Detroit. He is representative of this district chosen by the Democrats. His breath smelled of liquor."[79] The *Herald* in turn questioned Beers' victory by stating: "It is alleged that returns from Emmet [County] are a fraud, no election having been held at Little Traverse. There were 132 votes returned, all for Beers. We shall take some pains to investigate this matter. It seems that King Strang, "though dead, yet speaketh."[80]

Despite the immediate political setbacks, Smith found solace in the fact that a core of local Republicans was solidifying and now had a friend and voice in the weekly *Grand Traverse Herald*. In the region's harbor towns, a growing number of like-minded allies promoted a new American political philosophy rededicated to the founding principle that "all men are created equal." Subsequent editions of the *Herald* brought more good news to supporters of the fledgling Republican Party. Final election results showed that while the northern counties of Cheboygan, Emmet, Grand Traverse, and Mackinac voted Democratic, most of the rest of Michigan, in particular the populous farm districts, voted decisively Republican, carrying state contests in their favor. The same proved true throughout the Northern states, where Republicans won Governors' offices and U.S. Senate seats. In the pugnacious style characteristic of the radical abolitionist, Bates tallied votes under two columns - one labeled "Republicans," the other for "Slavery." While the election results in the North boded well for the Republican Party, national unity suffered as the South recoiled at the depth of the anti-slavery vote and the increasingly hostile rhetoric of Northern politicians. The election made it clear that in most of the northern United States, embarrassment over slavery had turned to anger.

In one of the 1858 contests, Abraham Lincoln challenged incumbent Stephen Douglas for his Illinois seat in the U.S. Senate. Though he lost the election, the Lincoln-Douglas debates established Lincoln's national reputation as a voice against the extension of slavery – a position at the heart of the Republican Party platform. The candidates in the 1860 Presidential Election began to emerge, and Lincoln and Douglas would meet again on a much larger stage.

Editor Bates understood that for many *Herald* readers, the paper was not only their primary source of information, but also one of their few contacts with the printed word. In a November 1858 article titled "Influence of a Newspaper," the *Herald* noted the benefits of subscription, stating: "scholars…with access to newspapers at home are better readers, excelling in pronunciation and…better spellers, and define words with ease and accuracy. They obtain a practical knowledge of geography…as the newspaper has made them familiar with the location of most important places, nations, their governments and doings, on the globe." [81] Bates was also mindful that the *Herald's* survival depended on more than a political audience. The paper added subscribers by presenting the written word in all its forms, in addition to presenting the news. A large part of the front page of the four-page weekly was dedicated to literary work – the center columns of the first issue featured poems, one titled *Nature* by William Shakespeare. The *Herald's* front-page formula also included the frequent use of fictional stories that explored topics of current interest and often concluded with a lesson in morals.

To help illuminate the *Herald's* objectives as a paper, Bates quoted a speech by Reverend Henry Ward Beecher – a nationally prominent Congregational minister and the brother of author Harriet Beecher Stowe - which praised the contributions of modern newspapers like the one Bates worked hard to create. Beecher said: "In no other way can so much, so varied, so useful information be imparted…as through a judicious, well-conducted newspaper. To live in a village, was once to be shut up and contracted. But now a man may…live in a forest, walking miles to a post office having a mail but once a week, yet he shall be found as familiar with the living world as the busiest actor in it. For the newspaper is a spyglass by which he brings near the most distant things…a museum full of real pictures of real life, drawn not on canvas, but with printer's ink on paper.

"Once a liberal education could only be completed by foreign travel. The sons of the wealthy could indulge in its costly benefit. But now the poor man's son can learn as much at home, as a hundred years ago a gentleman could learn by traveling the world over... The newspaper is a great traveler, a great lecturer. It is the peoples Encyclopedia – the lyceum, the college."

Large urban papers with extensive reporting staffs produced the core of world and national stories that ran in the *Herald*. The influence of these editions was substantial, for items contained in their columns rippled through a network of papers to the distant reaches of the country. Frontier editors like Bates picked through city journals as they arrived and recycled their stories to create their version of world and national events. In the second edition of the *Herald*, Bates acknowledged the process when he wrote, "We have changed our day of publication from Wednesday to Friday, as better suited to the mails," which brought the contributing newspapers to his Traverse City office. The distinct character of *Herald* came from this editorial sifting in addition to its coverage of local news.

Three months into his first Northern Michigan winter, Bates elaborated on the seasonal relationship between the mail delivery and the news. He wrote:

Jake Ta-Pa-Sah was Grand Traverse Country's first mail carrier. *History Center of Traverse City*

"From the closing of navigation in the fall until its opening in the spring, we are...completely isolated...and the only intercourse that we hold with the 'outside' world is through the medium of weekly mail, which is transported on the backs of 'Native Americans' from Grand Haven to Manistee, and from thence in the same manner over an Indian Trail...to this place. The arrival of the mail is a great event with us...As soon as it arrives and the contents are distributed, all business is thrown aside, worldly cares vanish, and we are lost in a huge pile of newspapers."[82]

A final bit of local news from 1858 was covered by both of Grand

Traverse Country's top writers – Northport's George Smith and Traverse City's Morgan Bates. Smith wrote: "Mr Dougherty came just after dark – wants me to aid in the Services at their new Church next Sabbath."[83] The Church Smith referred to was the just-completed Grove Hill Presbyterian Church on the shores of Omena Bay, a beautifully simple structure that continues to serve the faithful today. In turn, the *Herald* wrote of the new church: "Grove Hill, with its Mission building and high natural position, resembles a fortification in the distance, and stands out prominent in the panorama."[84] With the advent of the *Herald,* the history of the region would now be recorded by two distinct voices.

The most sobering article in all of the 1858 *Heralds* ran with the simple title "United States Army." It said: "The present military force of the United States consists of nineteen regiments of the line…making an aggregate of thirteen thousand rank and file of all arms. This little army covers the area of over two millions of square miles, being two thirds the area of all Europe."[85] During the Civil War, 50 times the total number of soldiers in the "little army" of 1858 would die in combat or of disease. By themselves, 19 Civil War battles would have eliminated the entire standing United States Army at that time. The Battle of Gettysburg alone claimed four times the number in killed, injured and missing.[86] As the 1850's pushed the nation steadily toward Civil War, no one could have imagined that settling the issue of slavery would exact such a catastrophic toll.

In the struggle to build their lives on the frontier, many pioneers had little contact with the world outside their immediate circle. They gathered news of their neighbors, the nation, and the goings-on in nearby villages in bits and pieces, and often from sources not blessed with the facts. When the *Grand Traverse Herald* began to circulate in November 1858, readers living in the region's harbor towns and on its isolated farms gained a weekly source of local information and world and national news, delivered by a skilled journalist. Their understanding of a shared sense of place was about to expand, for defining and describing the elements of "Grand Traverse Country" was one of the *Herald's* central themes.

In the debut edition, the *Herald's* Morgan Bates began his exposition of the region occupied by his immediate audience, writing: "The entrance from Grand Traverse Bay to Lake Michigan, is about seventy-five miles from the Island of

Mackinac, four hundred and twenty from Detroit, and two hundred and sixty from Chicago. Beaver Island (the Mormon kingdom of the late King Strang), the Fox Islands and the Manitous, are in fair view from its entrance. The Bay has an average width of ten miles, by forty miles in length, running north and south." The first town editor Bates mentioned was Northport, which in the last few years had become the transportation hub of Northwest Michigan. He wrote: "Ten miles from the north of the bay, on the west side, is the thriving village of Northport, a town of some three hundred inhabitants, separated only by a town-line road from the old Indian village of Waukee-zoo-ville. Many of the propellers running between the Lower Lakes and Chicago call here for wood. It has an excellent harbor, where vessels can ride out any storm in safety."[87]

In the late 1850's, it was hard to get to Grand Traverse Country without at some point docking at Northport. The finest to the least of the Great Lakes fleet made the harbor a regular port of call. Northport was a captain's best chance in Northern Michigan of attending to all his ship's needs in one stop. Hot burning beech and maple cordwood lined the docks, while local shipwrights stood ready to make necessary repairs. Northport merchants hawked outfitting supplies, meat and vegetables, salted fish, tanning bark, fresh cherries and apples, and other local produce. These commodities were available in varying measures on docks throughout Grand Traverse, which were all vying for their share of essential ship traffic. In the first edition of the *Herald*, however, Bates deferred comment on the region's other port towns, admitting that, as a newcomer, he had yet to visit them.

During the Civil War era, the *Grand Traverse Herald* regularly carried news of the comings and goings of ships, Grand Traverse Country's primary source of vitality and commerce. In 1858, there were over 1,600 vessels and 12,000 mariners working the Great Lakes, capable of moving half a million tons of cargo.[88] Articles in the inaugural paper found two boats passing through Grand Traverse late in the navigation season, trying to make a few more dollars before ice took back the lake. The two-sentence format Bates used to describe the vessels was common in the *Herald's* news briefs. One read: "The schooner *Telegraph*, Captain Herriman, sailed this morning for Chicago, with lumber, to Hannah, Lay & Co. She will make but one more trip this season."[89] Sailing schooners like the *Telegraph* far outnumbered their steam-powered counterparts on the Great Lakes. When speed of delivery was not essential, cargoes of lumber, bark, iron, and thousands of other non-perishables traveled in the holds of sailing schooners, due to their low cost of operation. At the time, many masters of

Great Lakes schooners owned their ships and hired their crews – generally five to seven men to a ship. The quality of a captain shaped the character of his vessel and the names of ship and captain often appeared together in the *Herald's* stories. Captain Herriman's *Telegraph* carried lumber from the mill of the area's largest employer - Hannah, Lay & Co. – to Chicago, where the boards helped build the fastest growing city on the Great Lakes. The article ended with the warning of "but one more trip" for the schooner, for soon winter ice would close all northern harbors to the outside world.

A second *Herald* article wrote of a steam-powered ship that stopped at Traverse City. It said: "The Propellor *Troy,* from Chicago and Grand Haven, arrived here on Monday last, and left the same day for Buffalo. O.A. Stevens, Esq., Receiver of the U.S. Land Office at this place, came passenger." The article referred to the *Troy* as a "Propellor," a ship driven by a stern-mounted, screw device that was revolutionizing Great Lakes shipping. In the last half decade, the faster, more reliable, and fuel efficient propellers drove most of the old style paddle-wheeled steamers into early retirement and took over their business of carrying passengers and freight on routes between Chicago and Buffalo. Both types of steam-powered vessels were the express boats of the Great Lakes, reserved for those who could pay the cost of arriving on schedule. The *Troy's* Traverse City passenger, O. A. Stevens, was boss of the region's powerful land office, where Grand Traverse real estate was purchased from the government.

The ante-bellum photograph of Northport harbor captured the 251' propellor *Globe* taking on cordwood. The tug *Leviathon* rests in the foreground, with a another half dozen schooners and mackinaw boats tied up along the freight-strewn docks. *Leelanau Historical Society*

Republican Morgan Bates was no friend of the Democrat Stevens, referring to the land office boss as "bitterly hostile to us." Several years later, after the *Herald's* editorials helped sway Grand Traverse voters to the Republican cause, Bates got his revenge when he was appointed by the Republican victors to take over Stevens' seat at the Land Office.

Advertisements in the *Grand Traverse Herald* rounded out a picture of life in the region. Perry Hannah bought space for an ad in the debut paper and continued to run it in various forms throughout the Civil War era. The extensive advertisements Hannah, Lay & Co. placed at the height of the conflict preserved important information about the prices and trends of a wide range of products sold in their store during the Civil War. One of the few other paid ads in the first edition, placed by an Elk Rapids farmer, offered fruit trees for sale – "Apple Trees, Peach Trees, Pear Trees, Plum Trees, and Cherry Trees" – a testimony to the early success of orchards in the region. In this manner, the premier edition of the *Herald* set the tone and format for all future volumes of the paper. Whether or not the paper's readers agreed with Bates' editorial opinions, there was no question they emanated from a capable and experienced journalist.

In subsequent editions, the *Herald* continued to sculpt its concept of Grand Traverse Country, running features on its landscapes, towns, people, and potential. Portraying the region's agricultural prospects in the best possible light was a high priority. Free labor farmers were the force transforming the Great Lakes wilderness and Bates founded the *Herald* in the region he believed would be the next place to feel the weight of their plows. In November, 1858, he wrote: "To the thousands of hardy and enterprising men, who will be seeking new homes in the Great West this Spring, we can confidently say that Grand Traverse country offers stronger and better inducements than either Illinois, Wisconsin, Iowa, or Minnesota. We have a Bay, 40 miles long and ten broad, with a dozen or more safe and commodious harbors. Twenty thousand farmers may settle in the counties bordering Grand Traverse Bay and not one of him have to carry his produce over ten miles to ship it to Buffalo or Chicago."[90]

Ready access to distant urban markets was critical to the success of frontier farmers. Without this link, farmers relied on a barter economy, which inhibited their prosperity. Anything grown beyond a community's ability to consume or trade it locally often went to waste, or was sold at distressed rates. Little cash could be raised to pay for taxes, supplies, or to buy more land. However, when a farmer was able to deliver his crops to growing port towns along the Great Lakes, demand was constant and a cash economy prevailed. A fleet of schooners bridged the gap, carrying bulk produce to market at a low price. Crops best suited to the local environment were sown and harvested to the extent of a farmer's ambition and ability and then distributed by water. With railroads still confined to the southern edge of the Great Lakes, a northern farm near a good dock was the ideal, and not hard to find in Grand Traverse Country.

In the first year of publication, Bates worked as the *Herald's* only employee, a common situation in frontier newsrooms. Letters to the editor served as correspondents for the weekly, adding local perspective and alternative points of view to the mix. The paper's use of the genre began with a December, 1858 letter titled "Elk Rapids and Vicinity," penned by A. W. Bacon of that town. Bacon was a well-known area surveyor who worked with many of the region's first settlers staking out their claims. His father, a prominent downstate judge, owned extensive tracts of timberland in Omena - a boat ride across the Bay from Elk Rapids. In his letter to the *Herald,* Bacon wrote of "numerous advantages of one of the many prominent points…of Grand Traverse Bay" not, as he said, to put it above others in the region, but because "the prosperity of one point adds value to the whole."[91] Bacon cited the town's position on the Bay, its extensive watershed, rich soils, and vast forests as reasons that "give the place much importance…among her sister towns now springing into existence on all parts of the Bay.[92]

A two line story in the same edition of the *Herald* titled "To the Woods," took a look at winter in the early days of Traverse City. It read: "The Lumbermen have nearly all gone to the Pineries to spend the winter, and our streets, in consequence, present quite a deserted appearance. We will visit the Pineries when the sleighing becomes good, and tell our readers something about them." Bates made good on his promise in a piece titled "A Visit to The Pineries," which described the tour lumberman Perry Hannah took him on through Hannah, Lay & Co.'s timber stands during the winter of 1859. It is one of the most beautiful portrayals of Grand Traverse Country to appear in the ante bellum *Herald,* penned just as rising sectional tensions and the issue of slavery began to consume all the editor's energies. Bates wrote of the sleigh ride with Hannah: "With a pair of fast ponies, we skimmed over the first two miles of level plain along the borders of Boardman Lake, before we had got fairly nestled under the buffalo robes…

"As we approach the region of pine, we suddenly find ourselves upon a ridge…just wide enough for a road, at an elevation of three hundred feet above the river. Our ascent over the table land has been so gradual and imperceptible that we are taken 'all aback' and thrilled with surprise and admiration at the magnificent panorama which is so unexpectedly present to view. On the right, at a distance of three hundred perpendicular feet below, the Boardman river, like a huge silvery serpent, winds its way through the narrow valley for miles… On your left, and at nearly the same distance below, is a chain of beautiful lakes, studded with small islands, and connected by liquid chains varying in width from ten to twenty feet…We could linger here for hours in gazing upon this sublime and magnificent scenery; but the ponies are impatient for their oats, and whirl us on to the Pineries.

"We were just in time to witness the descent of logs into the river. The loaded teams came in from the woods a few moments after our arrival…after the logs are measured…and the chains are tossed loose, they go thundering and crashing headlong down the steep plunge into the river, emerge and plunge again, like a school of huge porpoises on a frolic at sea…"

Returning to their sawmill in Traverse City, Bates wrote: "Hannah, Lay & Co. have their business so admirably systematised, that they can tell at any time just how many logs they have in the river, how much lumber they will make, what they have cost, and at what time they will arrive at their mill at Traverse City. They have five shanties, and employ this winter about 100 men in the Pineries. They will get out enough logs this season to make about nine million feet of lumber. Their two mills in Traverse City are competent to make 50,000 feet in twelve hours. The mills are situated on a narrow peninsula between the river and the bay, just wide enough for the mills to stand upon, and the logs are floated from the Pineries directly to the rear of the mills, where they are hauled by machinery into them, converted into lumber, and placed upon the wharf in front, ready to be loaded onto vessels which can lie alongside, and shipped to Chicago."[93]

A later *Herald* article titled "New Saw-Mill at Glen Arbor" noted the progress of another fast growing Grand Traverse settlement. It read: "John E. Fisher & Co…have just completed and put into operation…a saw mill, capable of sawing 5,000 feet per day. They have an excellent water power. This is the first mill erected at Glen Arbor, and will prove a very great convenience to the inhabitants of that thriving young town. The same Company intends to erect a Flouring Mill next season, to be propelled by the same power."[94] In his 1854 diary, Reverend Smith mentioned meeting Fisher on a Northport dock as he began to scout the Leelanau coast for a good stand of pine. He found it in Glen

John Fisher built his sawmill on the Crystal River in Glen Arbor. *Leelanau Historical Society*

Arbor, and a half decade later, Fisher's saw and flour mills were a big part of the town's draw.

A May 1859 piece in the *Grand Traverse Herald* titled "New Schooner *Perry Hannah*" recorded the specification of one of the quintessential worker-bee vessels that plied the Great Lakes. It said: "This new and beautiful schooner arrived here…on her first trip to Chicago. She was built at Newport, on the St. Clair river, last winter, and was launched only three weeks ago. She is 98 feet keel, 25 feet beam, 9 feet hold, will measure about 310 tons…and is built as stout as wood and iron could make her…Success and long life to the *Perry Hannah!*"[95]

The independently owned schooner guaranteed her share of cargo on the growing Chicago-Grand Traverse route by taking the name of the area's number one shipper of lumber and merchandise. It was a shrewd business decision. As proof, the schooner *Perry Hannah* sailed off on her maiden voyage to Chicago loaded with Hannah's Grand Traverse pine. A one-sentence note in next week's paper reported the vessel's return to Grand Traverse, "having made the trip to Chicago and back in one week."[96] The new schooner joined the ranks of over a thousand sailing ships that carried the weight of Great Lakes commerce across their beautiful but dangerous waters. The web of schooner routes bound together the port towns and the vast natural resources of the western lakes into a growing economic and industrial force.

Meanwhile, the work of the man Perry Hannah bore fruit in the competing field of land transportation. The civic booster knew that a Traverse City without roads would always be a backwater. He promoted the long-discussed Newaygo and Northport State Road for years, serving first as a commissioner in its planning stages. That spring, the State Road was coming off paper and surveyors staked its entire distance. The *Herald's* Morgan Bates interviewed the road work crew and reported: "The route surveyed is represented to be a very feasible one, and no serious obstacles exist to the construction of a good road."[97] Years of work lay ahead, but the mere possibility of a land link to the outside world was a local bright spot in the dark national mood of 1859.

The *Herald* continued to mix hard news about the declining national situation with descriptive reports of the region, sewing together a patchwork view of Grand Traverse Country. In January, the paper wrote: "The village of Leland is situated at the mouth of the Carp River, on the shore of Lake Michigan, in the township of Centreville, Leelanau County, and very near the geographical center of said county. It contains a population of about 100; and possesses one of the best water powers in the State of Michigan. Messrs. Cordes & Theis have built one of the best piers on the shores of Lake Michigan, with a water depth sufficient for the largest sized propellors and steamboats to lie at with safety.

"Carp River is about three-fourths of a mile long, and is the outlet to Carp and Traverse Lakes, which, together, are about seventeen miles long, with a average width of a half mile, abounding in fish and surrounded principally by good farming land…Settlers are coming fast. The land is mostly owned by the Government as yet, and can be bought for $1.25 an acre. The head of Traverse Lake is within ten miles of Traverse City, the county seat of Grand Traverse county. There is a sufficient depth of water the entire length of said lakes for boats of quite a large size to navigate."[98]

While Morgan Bates used his paper to enhance the image of the area, in 1859 his old friend Horace Greeley wrote a damaging portrayal of the Grand Traverse region in the *New York Tribune*. Greeley said: "I have spent the last week in traversing the State of Michigan, or rather the southern half of its lower peninsula to which its settlement and population have mostly been thus far confined. The northern half of this peninsula is colder, and in a good part uninviting to the cultivator, being diversified by vast swamps, by sterile, gravelly knolls, and by dense forests of but moderately valuable and not yet readily accessible timber, so that its settlement is likely to be slow, and its population sparse for generations."[99]

It was exactly this kind of bad reporting that had been the curse of Northern Michigan settlement for half a century. In the early 1800's, Federal surveyors spawned the negative image when they branded the entire state swampland. After the opening of the Erie Canal, shipping interests misled riders as to the quality of the region's soil in an effort to keep pioneer farmers aboard their boats all the way to Chicago. More recently, the financial collapse called the Panic of 1857 slowed commerce and settlement along the western Great Lakes. The effects of the national economic downturn reverberated through the region. Real estate values tumbled and paper currency issued through frontier banks lost much of its worth. Upon returning from a trip along Lake Michigan in August 1858, Reverend Smith complained: "My Wisconsin money is all depreciated – within three days I sold it at a broker in Detroit & lost on 40 dollars." Now, with the economy finally on the rise, Greeley had used hear-say evidence in his *New York Tribune* to diminish the area's prospects in the eyes of his 200,000 subscribers.

In response to Greeley's unflattering appraisal of Grand Traverse, Bates penned a column in praise of the region, hoping to undo some of the damage. The *Herald* wrote that the area's soil was "as rich and productive as that of Jackson, Calhoun, Kalamazoo, or in fact any other southern countries of this State; and it is equally well watered" and noted that Grand Traverse was "entirely exempt from frost until October... We have no swamps or marshes of stagnant water; no ague or sickness of any kind." The paper also argued that "Vessels of the largest class can enter any of the dozen or more excellent natural harbors on the Bay, and the farmer can ship his produce to Buffalo cheaper than it can be sent over the Railroad from Kalamazoo, Marshall or Jackson, to Detroit."

However, the exasperated Bates knew the start-up *Herald* had only so much reach, so he ended his editorial with a plea to his New York friend to set the record straight. Bates wrote: "But it would extend this article beyond our present limits to set forth all the natural advantages of our position, soil, timber and climate. Enough, we trust, has been said to convince Mr. Greeley that he has been misinformed in regards to the Grand Traverse country; and we ask him, as an act of justice, to copy this article. The circulation of his paper is so great that in no other way can we hope to correct the false impression which his letter is calculated to make. Do we ask too much?"[100] Apparently Bates did ask too much from his former friend Greeley, for he never printed the *Herald* article or any other retraction.

For Bates, the *New York Tribune* article must have been a low point in his newspaper career. His months of extolling the virtues of Grand Traverse Country seemed trivial in light of the damning comments made in the national paper. There was a deep irony to the *Tribune's* harsh words, for it was Joseph Dame's published letter of praise for Northport in an 1854 issue of the *Tribune* that brought the first mass migration of Euro-Americans to the area. Now, to add insult to injury, the negative press about his new home came from a friend, one Bates felt should have consulted him before the *Tribune* article was published.

Bates had already risked it all founding a paper on the edge of the Lake Michigan wilderness. His potential audience, even if generously supportive, would provide barely enough income to keep the paper going. Bates bet that the region would grow, and the *Herald* along with it. Now Greeley's *Tribune* undercut potential settlement throughout Northern Michigan as well as the prospects for the paper. The rift between the two editors widened when Greeley refused to retract his assessment of Northern Michigan, and their relationship later collapsed in conflict over Republican nominees for the President's race in 1860. The editor's long distant banter with Greeley and the *Tribune* over various issues during the great conflict helped illuminate the difference of opinions between the two noted abolitionists. Their friendship was just one more thing wrecked during the Civil War era. For now, however, the damage was done, and another issue of the *Grand Traverse Herald* was due off the presses.

The *Herald* resumed its regular survey of Grand Traverse harbor towns in a piece titled "Omenia and Vicinity." The paper said: "Omenia, better known to many as New Mission Harbor, is located nearly central on the west shore of Grand Traverse Bay, showing geographical features worth more than a passing notice... Much of the trade of the western slope will center here, when the harbor, which is commodious and perfect, and secure to trading craft at all times and in all weathers...is taken into consideration. Even in its natural state, vessels of the largest class lay alongside the shore, making fast to trees, remnants of the original forest, and discharging and loading their cargoes in perfect security. The depth of water, absence of shoals, and its horseshoe form, bid defiance to winds, and the finish which is soon to be put on in the way of docks, will make it a point that cannot fail to draw its full share of the steamer, wooding, as well as land trade.

"Ashore, nature has done no less, beautifully compounding its real and fancy finish, it completed a site unequalled for beauty in any land. The gentle slope at the head, displaying to great advantage the beautiful residence recently constructed,[101] giving in the same view that harbinger of progress, the Church, whose graceful spire indicates one point advanced in the religious, social, and even financial world. The entire surroundings are known as Grove Hill... From the eminence, far and near, the view is extensive and grand: covering the protruding Peninsula, the wild east shore...in the hazy distance Traverse City, with its highland background; the Round Island and Stoney Point; while nearer, the Indian settlements dot the shore for miles..."[102]

In the fall of 1859, the *Herald* reprinted a letter from the *Detroit Daily Advertiser*, which related a traveler's first impression of Grand Traverse Country. After spending the night on the Detroit waterfront, the downstate journalist wrote: "Early the next morning, Tuesday, we embarked on the propeller *Mendota*, paying five dollars each for our fare to Carp River, board included. About ten o'clock A.M. of Thursday following, we reached North Manitou Island, fifteen miles offshore from Carp River, where we were set onshore, a heavy sea (as the Captain supposed) preventing us from being landed at the place of our destination, which we reached in the afternoon in a "Mackinaw" belonging to some fishermen on the island. I would advise persons wishing to visit Grand Traverse to avoid being set ashore on this island, for it is a desolate looking spot, useful only as a wooding station, and it is impossible to reach the mainland without being subjected to an exorbitant charge. Be sure to land either at Carp River or Northport." The author warned readers away from the offshore ports which, since the assassination of King Strang and the subsequent contraction of population throughout the island archipelago of Manitou County, had never established a government and drifted toward lawlessness.

The journalist's letter continued: "The next day we set out from Carp River to Traverse City, going fifteen miles of the way in a sailboat to the head of Carp Lake, a most beautiful sheet of water abounding in fish and surrounded by a dense forest. From this point we made the journey to the Bay, a distance of some seven or eight miles on foot, packing our baggage on our backs and threading the intricate mazes of an Indian trail...over roots and logs, through brush, dodging around trees...until late at night we came to anchor three miles north of Traverse City... Early the next morning we set sail for Traverse City in a beautiful yawl, her canvas spread to a spanking breeze that sent the spray dashing from her bows.[103] It took the party more than a day's hard traveling to cover the distance from Leland to Traverse City, with most of the trip on water.

In a related article titled "How to Get to Grand Traverse," the *Herald* widened its lens and listed the ports and routes that linked the region to the outside world. The story advised: "Those living South and East, will take a Propellor at Buffalo, Dunkirk, Cleveland, or Detroit, and come directly to Northport, which is situated on Grand Traverse Bay ten miles from its mouth. The fare from Buffalo to Northport is about $8, and from Detroit $5. Those who wish to visit the western part of the county on the shore of Lake Michigan, will take a Propellor that will agree to land them at Glen Arbor or Leland. Those coming from the west will take one of Hannah, Lay & Co.'s vessels, at Chicago, which sail regularly between that port and Traverse City during the season of navigation; or one of Noble & Dexter's vessels, which will land them at Elk Rapids, on the eastern shore of Grand Traverse Bay at the mouth of Elk River. The fare from Chicago to Traverse City, by sail vessel, is $5. There are small boats running regularly between Northport, Traverse City, Elk Rapids and the Mission, which will take passengers to any point on the Bay. There is no land route to this place except an Indian Trail, on which the mail is brought once a week. In winter this is the only route to the outside world. A route for a State Road through the wilderness from Grand Traverse Bay to civilization, has been surveyed this season, and the time is not far distant when we shall have a good thoroughfare to Grand Rapids." [104]

A shared sense of Grand Traverse Country arose from local stories printed in the *Herald*. A common theme described life at the water's edge, where towns grew between good harbors and dense, original forests. Another recognized the area's seductive beauty, a special presence even among the spectacle of the wild, western Great Lakes of the late 1850's. The *Herald* stories documented the various cultures evolving along northern Lake Michigan with a depth and quality rarely found on the ante-bellum frontier. Editor Bates knew he was witnessing an extraordinary time and place in American history, watching Grand Traverse Country progress as the northern hub of the great water highway west, while the nation as a whole stumbled toward Civil War.

As the rift between rival sections within the United States grew, all attention focused on the approaching war. Grand Traverse readers viewed the national collapse from the perspective offered by the *Grand Traverse Herald*. From the start, the paper painted a desperate picture of the nation's downward spiral from divisive rhetoric to the agony of civil war. Two news shorts in the January 7, 1859 weekly presaged the division of the country as the rule of law steadily disintegrated.

An article titled "A Southern Confederacy" reported: "The Governor of South Carolina says, in his inaugural message, it is to be hoped that no occasion will arise requiring this State to call upon her sons for the defense of her rights and constitution, but believing this hope will prove fallacious he continues, "we should not only endeavor to unite the State, but the entire South, so that when we can no longer retain our place…we will be prepared to form a more perfect union, under the title of the *United States of the South.*"[105]

Reacting to sweeping Republican victories in the North in the 1858 elections, South Carolina again took the lead among Southern states in pressing for secession. South Carolina's hard line position was due in part to the make-up of the state's population, which at the time was 60% black, the highest ratio of slaves to whites in the nation. It took an uncompromising iron grip by the ruling South Carolinians to keep a majority of state's people in subjugation. The threat of secession echoed through the nation since the U.S. Constitution brought together divergent regions, but it had always been heard as a voice from the fringe. However, a nation united by constitutional compromise had evolved into a quarreling North and South, and by 1859, the United States of America was a very fragile entity. Now the cry for disunion carried with it the ring of possibility.

Following the secessionist speech of the South Carolina Governor, the *Herald* ran an article titled "The Slave Trade Revived." It read: "The Southern slaveholders have concluded not to wait for the repeal of laws against the slave trade by Congress, but have taken the matter into their own hands. They have already practically nullified the law, and are now driving a brisk business in importing slaves into the Southern States. Within a month, three cargoes have been landed in Southern ports, without obstacle from any quarter."[106] The Constitution banned the African Slave Trade in 1808, and since then, a fraternity of nations, including the world powers of France and England, abolished slavery throughout their empires. For many in the international community, slavery was the stigma of crude and brutal nations. The United States was a step behind in embracing the era's spirit of enlightenment and in the late 1850's fell further from grace when American slave ships again hunted the African coast looking for human cargo. The Constitution was losing its power to govern, for if its clearly stated, half-century old prohibition on the importation of slaves could be ignored, all the laws of the land were in peril. The rope of agreements that bound the nation together continued to fray under the weight of slavery.

Another *Herald* article taken from the *Albany Journal* came with specifics about the renewed African slave trade along the coast of Georgia. It warned: "With a strong sentiment at home in favor of the revival of the slave trade, and with officers in command of our ships along the African coast who deem that trade legitimate…it should be no matter of surprise if the trade now proscribed as piracy should very soon become as brisk as it is profitable."[107] The *Journal* noted that of the Southern papers that protested against the reopening of the African slave trade, none "place their objections on any higher ground than that it would cut down the price of the old stock."[108]

The article brought to light one of the convoluted economies arising from American slavery. In the 19th century, the South's 'peculiar institution' turned many border state farms into slave breeding pens, and in a tortured alliance with Northern abolitionists, made their owners vocal opponents of the African slave trade. Lacking the soils, terrain, and the 200 frost-free days necessary to grow the lucrative plantation crops of cotton and sugar, the profit from slavery in the Border States came from the raising and selling of dark-skinned human beings. Nothing chilled the heart of a border state slave more than being sold to a Deep South plantation, where life meant endless toil and death was often welcomed. Ships crowded with African slaves now arriving on the American coast flooded the slave markets and cut prices, and border state breeders reacted in protest.

Later in the year, the *Herald's* Morgan Bates penned an editorial that ridiculed this twisted aspect of the slave economy. He wrote: "Did it ever occur to those advocating the re-opening of the African Slave Trade that such an event would do more to hasten the downfall of the Slave power than all other causes combined? Were it not for its atrocity, we should certainly advocate this measure as the surest and speediest method of extirpating Slavery from the country. Look at it: In Virginia, Maryland, Delaware, Kentucky, and a large portion of Tennessee, slave-labor is unprofitable. The system is only continued because money can be made by raising negroes, as we of the North raise cattle, for a market. The sugar and cotton growing States are supplied with slaves by the abovementioned stock-raising States, and these will adhere to Slavery just so long as they can find a good market and make money by the operation. Re-open the African Slave Trade, glut the Southern market with slaves from abroad, and you will make Virginia, Maryland, Delaware, Kentucky, Missouri, and, perhaps, Tennessee, Free States, of their own will and by their own act." [109]

Hardliners in the South weren't buying the argument. The *Charleston Mercury* warned that "the laws against the slave trade cannot be enforced at the South, because public sentiment is favorable to the free traffic in negroes, whether brought from another State or Africa." The *Mississippian* added: "The agitation in favor of repeal of the slave-trade law is confined to no political party or class of our citizens, but is fast becoming the popular sentiment of the Southern people. The sooner our Northern fellow citizens are convinced of the fact, and make up their minds to accede to our just demand, the better for the peace and prosperity of our political Union."[110]

During the late 1850's, a revised edition of the book *The Impending Crisis of the South* further inflamed passions on both sides of the Mason Dixon line. The work took a different tack than most of the anti-slavery genre, for rather than attack bondage as a moral issue, the *Impending Crisis* cited a range of statistics that showed slavery to be an economic and social impediment to the advancement of the South as a whole. The book compared the progress of the two distinct cultures that arose during the first 75 years of the United States nation and concluded: "The commerce of the Free States is four times as great as that of Slave States; that the manufacturers of the Free States produce five times the value in fabrics, employ five times the capital, and five times the number of hands, that are employed in the Slave States; that there are twice as many miles of Canals, and twice as many miles of Railroads in Free States as in the Slave States; that the Banking Capital of the Free States is double that of the Slave States; that the Militia Force is likewise double and… nine Inventions are patented by citizens of Free States to every one patented by citizens of Slave States."

The *Impending Crisis* also revealed a significant gap between the educational standards of the two societies. It said: "There are three times as many Schools,

While the plantation system forced slaves to do the hard work of the South, free labor farmers explored mechanical means to accomplish difficult tasks, leading to inventions and patents. This stump-pulling device illustrated in the 1860 *American Farmers Almanac* presents an alternative to manual labor.

three times as many Teachers, and four times as many Pupils in the Free States as in Slave States; there are twenty times as many Libraries, with sixty times as many volumes in them, as there are in the Slave; that there are in the Free States twice as many Newspapers, issuing four times as many copies as in the Slave; that although the population of the Slaves States is less, the number of white men unable to read is one hundred thousand greater than Free;"[111] The book was a indictment of a culture living on borrowed time, and a catalyst that hardened sectional opinions about slavery.

While King Cotton created vast fortunes for plantation owners, the enterprise cut deeply into the future prospects of the South. The plantation system produced raw material but little else. Industry failed to materialize and education was for wealthy whites only. Economic, political, and social diversity was stifled. The *Grand Traverse Herald* would later write: "In the Planting States, the only standard of social position is the possession of negroes and land. Labor is dishonorable. Every poor white man aspires to own a slave. Every small slaveholder struggles to become a larger one."[112]

The reaction to the controversial book reflected the deep division in the country – Northern abolitionists championed it as proof of the evils of slavery, while producers of King Cotton branded the work as conjecture and banned it from their soil. The United States Congress bickered over its contents and a vote to elect the Speaker of the House in 1859 turned into a bitter referendum on the book. The hopes for the future of national unity took another turn for the worse. In the end, the uproar ignited by *The Impending Crisis* proved the book's central thesis - the United States was already two countries with distinct social and economic systems that could no longer be sustained under one roof.

While the *Herald* always took a stand against slavery in the South, the paper ignored - and sometimes encouraged - Grand Traverse Country's own brand of racism, especially in regards to treaties with the Indians concerning land. It was easier to rail against violations of human decency in the distant South than to take on the problem at home. A *Herald* article titled "Cheering Intelligence!" shed light on the prevailing Euro-American attitude toward Native American property rights. The story's long subtitle "*The Peninsula Lands Declared to be Part of the Public Domain – The Rights of the Settlers Respected – The 'Good Times' Coming*" revealed the news was anything but good for local Indians. Editor Bates wrote: "We are enabled this week to announce the cheering fact that all the lands lying in Townships 28, 29 and 30, heretofore held to be an Indian Reserve, are declared to be part of the Public Domain, and subject to pre-emption and settlement the same as other Government lands.[113]

Lake Michigan's Odawa and Ojibwa bands had come to the bargaining table in 1855 with the hope of finally gaining clear title to what remained of their ancestral lands. They were willing to renegotiate the 1836 Treaty of Washington with the understanding their rights to defined properties would be perpetually established, and left with a document they believed gave them that guarantee. Four years later, clauses within the Treaty of 1855 were being interpreted in a different light, and Indian land claims as provided through the treaty stalled within the Federal bureaucracy. The boundaries of the land set aside for Native selection under the Treaty of 1855 were ignored and white squatters put large sections under the plow. As had been the case for two centuries, each new treaty – no matter its provisions – cut deeper into the holdings of Native people. The *Herald* continued: "We most heartily congratulate the settlers upon these lands…This is the dawn of a brighter day for Grand Traverse county!" For the Natives, however, the news was a harbinger of darkness. Their hopes had been further diminished and their future as an equal people within a nation of unequally applied justice became all the more uncertain.

Days after the national elections in the spring of 1859, a passing schooner dropped off newspapers with the latest results. The *Herald* wrote: "By the arrival of a vessel at the East Bay from Chicago, we are placed in possession of papers a week in advance of those received by mail, and enabled to make the cheering announcement… Republicanism is everywhere triumphant in the North, and the Slave Democracy has no City of Refuge to flee to." Voters confirmed the hardening of Northern opinion against slavery by electing Republican candidates from Maine to Wisconsin. The article concluded with the prediction: "Coming events cast their shadows before, and we have an inkling of the result of the great contest in 1860."[114] The clock ticked on toward the momentous Presidential Election of 1860, and citizens began to choose sides in what was shaping up to be the final unified act of the United States.

There were only a limited number of seats up for grabs in the off-year election, but the balloting was enough to predict the deep divisions in the upcoming political drama. Hope for sectional reconciliation diminished as successful Republican candidates advocated the hard-line, anti-slavery positions that won them their seats. In Michigan, state and local elections also attested to the emerging power of Republicanism. Six months earlier, Democrats won 20 of

21 races in greater Grand Traverse County. Now voters changed their minds and chose Republicans for all 12 contested county seats, and the party that embraced free labor, preservation of the Union, and resistance to expansion of slavery gained a sizable foothold in the region. The *Herald* ended a column that tallied the local vote with the bold banner: "Grand Traverse is Redeemed!!"

Although the Presidential race was still a year and a half away, anticipation of the event began to nudge the election toward center stage. The field of presidential candidates gave little hope of finding a compromise figure who could unite the nation with a vision transcending sectional preferences. If anything, the approaching Presidential election of 1860 was already driving people further apart. The best friend of the young Republican Party was Democratic President James Buchanan, whose erratic leadership and scandal-ridden administration caused the fate of the United States to drift further toward self-destruction. Buchanan was poorly equipped for the high-stakes political game of the time and his effort to appease for the sake of national unity drove all parties from the negotiating table. It was the worst time in American history for a bad President and his administration wreaked havoc on the country's chances for conciliation, as well as his party's future. Buchanan was pulled from consideration as the Democrat's candidate for the 1860 Presidential race, and with Senator Stephen Douglas the party's frontrunner, the last national political machine broke apart along sectional lines.

Until recently Douglas, through his promotion of the Kansas-Nebraska Act and its theme of popular sovereignty, had been a hero in the South. Popular sovereignty as promoted by Douglas allowed each new state to choose whether to embrace or prohibit slavery, a position that nullified landmark national laws and expanded slavery's potential reach to every corner of the nation. Southerners had viewed Douglas as a Northerner who understood their minds, for he owned a large plantation with numerous slaves in Mississippi and placed accommodation of Southern interests at the top of his agenda. However, citizens in each of the increasingly hostile sections of the nation wanted total commitment from their candidates. When Douglas criticized some of the pro-slavery actions in Kansas, and called talk of secession treason, the South looked inward for a new Democratic leader. This was not unusual, for under the influence of the Slave Power, Dixie had been home to nine of fifteen United States Presidents to date.

The 1860 election was the Republican's first shot at the Presidency as an established party with a solid base of elected officials and committed voters. Looking ahead, a *Herald* editorial proclaimed: "To all republicans, a future opens, more bright and glorious than ever shed its luster upon the head of an Army. The campaign of 1860, to be made famous by the first full national demonstration for freedom and free labor, is upon us."[115] The problem was that Republican support was strictly confined to the North, and as such was a party of national division.

William Seward, New York's former Governor and current U.S. Senator, for years served as the spokesman for the eastern faction of the party and now reigned as the Republican frontrunner for President. In an 1858 speech, Senator Seward commented on the constant friction between the two systems of labor in the United States, saying: "It is an irrepressible conflict between opposing and enduring forces; and it means that the United States must and will, sooner or later, become entirely a Slaveholding nation, or entirely a free labor Nation.[116] In 1812, Virginian Thomas Jefferson advanced the same idea as Seward when he said: "Nothing is more certainly written in the book of fate than that these people (negro slaves) are to be free; nor is it less certain that the two forms of society cannot be perpetuated under the same government."[117] At the time of his speech, his words were taken as the intelligent musings of an enlightened American statesman. However, in these volatile years before the Civil War, Jefferson would have been branded a meddling traitor by the pro-slavery faction in the South for making the same statement. Seward's 'irrepressible conflict' became the byline of the North's resignation to the inevitability of civil war. Slaveholders saw Seward's speech as a Northern abolitionist's threat, and he had lost the South's vote before he became a Presidential candidate.

Seward was the pre-convention choice of Michigan Republicans and the long-time favorite of the *Herald's* Morgan Bates. In September 1859, the editor was able to boast: "All our readers know where we stand, the *Herald* having been the first paper in Michigan to break ground in favor of Mr. Seward." Ohio's Governor Chase, who was radicalized by the Oberlin incident and now embraced the abolitionist position, was also high on the list of Republican contenders. *New York Tribune* publisher Horace Greeley muddied the political waters when he cast his paper's support behind former Missouri Congressman Edward Bates, who represented the conservative wing of the Republican Party. This Bates had no quarrel with slavery, but opposed any expansion of the practice outside its current boundaries. Greeley's endorsement was a slap in the face of Seward, who had climbed the ladder of New York notoriety alongside Greeley, and helped the *Tribune* become the unofficial mouthpiece for the national Republican Party. Greeley thought Missourian Bates the ideal compromise candidate to unite the nation, but the *Tribune* editor overestimated the appeal of appeasement in light of the widening national divide.

Editor Bates mocked Greeley's choice for President. He wrote: "The idea of carrying a single Southern State with any man, Northern or Southern, who shall be nominated at the Republican Convention, is simply ridiculous. It cannot be done. We are equally well-convinced that no Slaveholder can carry...the Northern States."[118] A news story in the *Herald* citing the future Confederate President Jefferson Davis backed up the editor's assertions. It read: "Col Jeff Davis recently delivered a two hour speech in Jackson, Miss. in which he declared the Federal laws against the slave trade unconstitutional... He was in favor of an immediate dissolution of the Union if a Republican President was elected."[119]

In the 1858 Illinois Senator's race against Democrat Stephen Douglas, a country lawyer named Abraham Lincoln gave eloquent speeches in opposition to the extension of slavery that brought him national attention - and electoral defeat. Lincoln had recently completed a speaking tour in New England, culminating with an address at New York City's Cooper Union, which electrified the audience with its eloquent anti-slavery logic. Now Lincoln was Illinois' favorite son Republican candidate for President of the United States. In the fall of 1859, Illinois Republican papers, led by the influential *Chicago Press and Tribune,* enthusiastically embraced Lincoln, though at the time he held no office and lacked a political track record outside his home state. However, Lincoln's relative political obscurity shielded him against the sword the press always brought to bear against successful politicians. Unlike the seated candidates he came up against, having recently cast no votes, he had also made no enemies. There was just a chance, if the frontrunners deadlocked in the upcoming Republican convention, Lincoln would be positioned as the best second choice.

In the summer of 1859, the Oberlin Rescuers were back in the news. The Ohio Supreme Court upheld their convictions for crimes against the Fugitive Slave Law for freeing a runaway slave and guiding him to the safety of Canada. The Northern press railed against the Supreme Court verdict and again made heroes of the 37 defendants. While the Oberlin Rescuers languished in jail, abolitionist John Brown – whose father had been a trustee at Oberlin College - visited the prisoners and professed support for their defiance of the Fugitive Slave Law. Brown, like the Rescuers, felt the time for talk was over. He was

planning an abolitionist raid of his own and recruited two jailed Oberlin Rescuers to join in his future endeavor. In July 1859, after they exhausted all their
appeals without success, an Ohio court freed the Rescuers when they pledged,
upon their release, to leave Ohio forever.

The *Grand Traverse Herald* continued its abolitionist Republican drumbeat
in an article titled "Freedom and Slavery – A Contrast." The work examined
the progress of two of America's premier states since the signing of the U.S.
Constitution. It read: "Take New York and Virginia as an example: in 1790,
the population of New York was 304,120, and that of Virginia, 748,308. Both
were then Slave States. New York abolished Slavery and Virginia clung to it as
a heaven-born institution. Sixty years passed – and in 1850 the census showed
that New York had an active, enterprising population of 3,097,394 Freeman,
and Virginia only 1,421,661, including her slaves.

"What could have produced this immense disparity…The answer is obvi-
ous…One State regarded Slavery as a curse, and abolished it; the other as a
blessing, and clung to it…The one…establishes manufactures, fosters industry,
encourages arts and commerce, and creates a wholesome, permanent prosperity – while the other impoverishes, demoralizes, degrades. Yet, not withstanding
these stern facts, fortified by figure and statistics, the Democratic party labors
to spread and extend this curse that has brought Virginia down from her proud
estate to a disgraceful condition of poverty and negro-breeding, into and over
the territories of this fair land."[120]

Two days after the article ran in the *Herald,* a plot hatched in Virginia to
free slaves through violence divided North and South more than all the many
political battles to date. On October 16, 1859, abolitionist John Brown and
some two dozen followers launched their raid on Harpers Ferry, Virginia - the
site of a national armory and rifle manufacturing facility. Violent conflict over
the issue of slavery was no longer relegated to the distant Kansas Territory,
but instead took center stage in the heart of the original 13 states. Brown, accompanied by two sons, two Oberlin Rescuers, a few abolitionist friends, and a
handful of free and fugitive blacks, hoped to capture the Harpers Ferry arsenal
and spread the word to surrounding plantations of the start of a slave rebellion. Brown believed slaves would then rise up by the thousands, and an army
of blacks would purge the South of its sinful practice. The first part of the plan
worked well - in short order Brown's band commanded the lightly defended
armory grounds and waited for uprising slaves to pour in from the countryside.
However, the only force marching toward Harpers Ferry was made up of Vir-

ginia and Maryland militia and U.S. Marines commanded by the West Point graduate Major Robert E. Lee.

Brown's effort to hold the Harpers Ferry armory in the face of a superior force ended quickly. His two sons and four of his followers lay dead - one was a free black man he recruited from the Oberlin Rescuers. The other Oberlin Rescuer taking part in Brown's raid was later hung. Brown, like his Kansas foes in 1856, lay badly bloodied from the wounds of a sword, but survived. After his capture, a Virginia court brought him to a speedy trial, found him guilty of treason, and sentenced him to hang.

Fear swept the South as word spread that their worst nightmare – a massive slave rebellion – had come close to fruition. Fear turned to outrage when slaveholders witnessed the often tepid denunciation in the North of John Brown's actions, and boiled over when they found the raid had been financed by wealthy Northern abolitionists. Throughout the South, militias began to form, arm, and drill to protect against a slave uprising and to prepare for the increasing chance of armed conflict with the North. The seeds of the future Confederate Army germinated within these militias.

The *Herald's* Morgan Bates showed he was not inclined to soothe Southern tempers when he published an editorial on the incident titled, "John Brown, the Hero of the Tragedy at Harper's Ferry." He wrote: "Society cannot afford to justify such deeds of blood, although many of those who are loudest in their denunciation would be very ready to justify him if he had committed those wrongs in recovering slaves and attacking abolitionists...For his offence he is responsible. If there is any responsibility beyond him, it rests on those who first introduced and sanctioned the instrumentalities of violence, oppression and murder in the contest over the extension of Slavery; for they have taught him the game..."[121]

The condemned John Brown approached his fate with resolve, knowing the crusade of his life would now be best served by his upcoming death as a martyr. On the road from prison to the scaffold, he shared a wagon with an undertaker who said: "Capt. Brown, you are very calm and collected – much more so than I am; and yet your condition is much more critical." "I am cool," said Brown..."For thirty year I have been educated to look on fear as a myth, and now I do not know what it is."

On December 2, 1859, the scheduled date of John Brown's execution, Northport's normally terse George Smith gave a rare glimpse of his passionate side when he wrote in his diary: "Captain Brown, the brave the noble Deliverer of Kansas, the friend of humanity whether found in a white or colored skin - the friend of equal rights for all - who first having seen several sons sacrificed on the altar of Liberty, has today himself been made a Sacrifice for conceiving the thought that the Negro has a soul & the same right to liberty that the white man has.

"If there is one magnanimous thought in the Democratic party...he has been pardoned. But I think – I feel sure - it has no such redeeming quality, but rather the more noble the Spirit – the more worthy, the severer the penalty; and on the other hand...the viler the crime, the greater the reward – such is the character of the present administration in these U[nited] States. May the Lord deliver us. If his blood be shed, what woes await the slave oligarchy, nay what woes hang over our land." [122] Shortly before his execution, Brown penned a hasty note and handed it to a nearby witness. It read: "I am convinced that the great iniquity which hangs over the country cannot be purged without immense bloodshed."[123] Minutes later Brown was dead.

As was the pattern in the late ante bellum years, South Carolina led the attempt to rally Southern fear and anger over John Brown's raid around the flag of secession. A *Herald* news brief titled "Treason" said: "Resolutions have been offered in the South Carolina Legislature that the State is ready to enter, with other Southern States, into the formation of a Southern Confederation." An article in the paper's last edition of 1859, titled "Let Us Arm," pointed in the direction the United States was going. It read: "Under this startling head, the *Charleston (S.C.) News* advocates the expenditure of $100,000 by the State in the purchase of cannon, rifles and revolvers! The excuse is that "no one knows what a twelvemonth will bring forth."[124]

The year ended quietly for Northport's George Smith. He repaired the family piano, delivered his daughter by sleigh to her singing lessons, and wrote letters to family and friends. The final entry in his diary on New Year's Eve, however, betrayed a darker mood, one that had enveloped the nation. He wrote: "O Lord, when shall my sorrows have an end?" he asked, "My joys when shall I see?"

Northport harbor, 1860's, with three propellers taking on wood. *Northport Area Heritage Association*

CHAPTER THREE

The Southern Scare-Crow

1860 was the last full year of peace in a United States with slavery, but peace only in the sense that shots between opposing armies had yet to be fired. Every nerve in the nation tensed at the dismal prospects ahead. News focused more and more on the "irrepressible conflict" and the *Grand Traverse Herald's* first editorial of the decade began to weigh the equations of war. It said: "This disunion cry is a Southern 'scare-crow' which has been hung up in every Northern cornfield for the last thirty years, whenever the South has wished to make aggression upon the rights of the North. But it has lost its power to terrify. The North has made all the concessions that it will ever make to the Slave Power; and if the Disunionists in the South are serious in their threats, they had better undertake to put them in execution at once...

"Suppose a war should occur between these Republics. The South cannot manufacture a cannon, a musket, a sword, a revolver, a cannon ball, or a grain of powder...While the North could easily raise an army of a million men, the South could not raise over two hundred thousand; and that force would be required to keep their three million slaves in subjection. Gentlemen of the South, we do not think you will dissolve the Union this spring. You can't afford it."[125] Even for the radical abolitionist Bates, war was still an unimaginable consequence of regional divisions over slavery.

Throughout the nation, attention increasingly focused on the upcoming 1860 Presidential race and political parties worked to define their platforms. In an address to Congress, President James Buchanan attempted to cool passions inflamed by slavery by announcing that the legal questions pertaining to the institution had already been addressed and answered. He proclaimed: "I cordially congratulate you upon the final settlement by the Supreme Court of the

United States of the question of slavery in the Territories, which had presented an aspect so truly formidable at the commencement of my administration. The right has been established of every citizen to take his property of any kind, including slaves, into the common Territories belonging equally to all...and to be protected there under the Federal Constitution. Neither Congress or a Territorial Legislature, nor any human power has any authority to annul or impair this vested right"[126] Buchanan's position was premised on the Supreme Court's decision in the 1857 Dred Scott Case, in which Chief Justice Roger Tawney summed up the majority opinion by stating that blacks were "so far inferior that they had no rights which the white man was bound to respect." Buchanan's oration was a desperate attempt to end by decree the rage building on both sides of the Mason-Dixon Line. However, as was the pattern with Buchanan's speeches, rather than help matters, the President's words brought an escalation of political strife into the New Year.

The Republican *Albany Evening Journal* summed up the essence of President Buchanan's message, writing: "The Democrats proclaim as to Slavery in the Territories, that it can neither be kept out by Congress, nor kept out by the inhabitants. They declare it goes wherever the Federal Government goes; that wherever we plant the American flag, there we plant Slavery; that wherever we carry the Constitution, there we carry the auction block and the Slave Pen!"[127]

President Buchanan's latest position went well beyond popular sovereignty's potential to expand the range of slavery in the United States. According to Buchanan, owning slaves was an individual choice protected "under the Federal Constitution." The choice, he claimed, could be exercised anywhere in the national territory as a "vested right." Buchanan hoped he had put the slavery debate to rest, and encouraged "north and south to cultivate their utmost feelings of mutual forbearance and goodwill toward each other, and try to allay the demon spirit of sectional hatred and strife now alive in the land." Instead of making peace, however, Buchanan's words underscored the hopeless disparity of political positions, not only between North and South, but within his own party.

Most northern Democrats wanted to leave slavery alone in the existing slave states, for although they might deplore the practice, they felt the issue was not worth national division, and certainly not civil war. Others supported the concept of popular sovereignty, as embodied by Illinois' Democratic Senator Stephen Douglas. Respect for the right to choose the specifics of local government followed the Democratic Party's traditionally populist platform. Douglas, once the favorite of the South due to his support of popular sovereignty, now found himself stuck in the middle of the increasingly polarized nation and party. His support of slavery was not ardent enough for most Southerners and too obliging to the Slave Power for many Democrats and almost all Republicans. After failing to reach a consensus at the Democratic nominating convention in Charleston, Douglas was chosen as the presidential candidate by Northern Democrats, while Southerners picked Kentucky's John Breckenridge. The Democratic Party dissolved as a national institution.

Across the nation, the conflict over slavery grew increasingly personal. The *New York Evening Post* interviewed travelers arriving from Southern ports and wrote: "Among passengers of the *Columbia,* which arrived in this city, from Charleston…were several who were driven out of the State, on suspicion of entertaining anti-slavery sentiments. None of them…have violated any law of the State; but the excitement is so great there that the bare suspicion of feelings hostile to Slavery, is deemed sufficient ground for expelling men from the State, no matter how honest or industrious their habits of life." The *Albany Evening Journal* commented: "Were such outrages on personal rights and liberty perpetrated at the North upon men who hold Pro-Slavery opinions, there would be a tremendous outburst of indignation. But when perpetrated in the South upon men who hold Anti-Slavery opinions, they are treated as being all right and proper."[128]

Six years of fighting over statehood for Kansas served as a glaring example of the inability of the United States government to function in the overheated political atmosphere. The Territory had settled into an uneasy truce, the Kansas territorial government represented a majority of fulltime Kansas residents, and all other requirements for statehood had been met. However, now the extremes ruled, and by the time Kansas voted through the framework of popular sovereignty to prohibit slavery, the Southern standard had shifted to the one put forward in Buchanan's speech. Now the slaveholders held that slavery could not be forbidden in national territory under any circumstances.

The *Herald* reported: "The struggle in Kansas is not yet over. It is now a nearly settled fact that the Democracy at Washington intend to resist her admission to the Union with the Constitution and boundaries agreed upon by the people. Foiled in their purpose to make it a Slave State, they intend, if possible, to have it a Democratic state, which is about the same thing."[129] With the South's representation bolstered by the three-fifth clause of the Constitution, the Slave Power had enough votes in Congress to prevent the margin required for statehood, and the bill for the admission of Kansas stalled. A great national wound remained unhealed.

In 1860, the Republican Party's "Land for the Landless" platform was "against any view of the Free Homestead policy which regards the settlers as paupers." *History Center of Traverse City*

In February 1860, the Republican Party published a series of position papers called *Political Tracts.* An advertisement for *Political Tracts* in the *Herald* promised to expose "Frauds and Expenditures of the present Administration for party purposes," and the "marked deterioration of moral sentiment at the South in regards to the African Slave Trade." One of the platforms promoted "Land for the Landless" and accountability for Congressional votes on the most recent Homestead bill.

The Homestead Act was another nation defining law that lay dead in Congress due to the cultural conflict between North and South. The proposed Homestead Act, which gave up to 160 acres of land to settlers who lived on their claim and made improvements to the property, directly rewarded free-labor farmers for their efforts in wresting a life from the wilderness. It embraced a theme contrary to slavery by elevating the value of manual labor and sought to extend the privilege of owning a landed estate beyond the limits of class structure. Class structure, however, was the basis of the Southern plantation society. In the inflamed environment, there was little productive debate on this proposed use of national territory. Plantation owners knew that every successful Homestead Act farmer, who earned his property through his own labor, was likely to be one more person opposed to slavery. Republicans promoted individual ownership of land as one of the ultimate expressions of personal freedom. The party took a populist position which was "against any view of the Free Homestead policy which regards the settlers as paupers or supplicants."[130] As in the case of Kansas statehood, the Slave Power resisted the bill, and another important piece of legislation stalled in Congress. As much as any event in the 19th century, the passage of the Homestead Act two years later accelerated the settlement of Grand Traverse Country.

A letter to the editor of the *Herald* in the spring of 1860 gave insight into the rationale of one Grand Traverse resident's opposition to slavery. The letter said: "For one class or community of man to unite and combine together to deprive another class of men of their natural rights of life, liberty and the pursuit of happiness is to violate the law of God... The principle or idea that man can be the property of man...is not entertained by one-forth the inhabitants of the world. All enlightened and intelligent Christian nations consider Slavery contrary to the law of God. It can exist only through violence, force or fraud... warfare between master and slave. Witnessed the burning tortures and cruel punishments inflicted on the slave; the severe and rigorous laws enacted; the constant watchfulness and vigilance necessary to keep them in obedience and subjection; and the fears and anxieties of slaveholders at any rumored rising or rebellion of their slaves."[131] Religious groups themselves were not immune to the fracturing effects of slavery. Like the nation, the Baptist Church, and the Presbyterian Church of Reverend Peter Dougherty, broke in two along sectional lines at the approach of Civil War. The Presbyterians remained divided into Northern and Southern churches for a century after the conflict ended.

In Northport, a battle of a different sort shaped up between Reverend George Smith and local government officials, one that defined his love of cultivation. He wrote: "Mr Porter was here to dinner. He has today surveyed a shore road with the Commissioners to run through my garden through my best fruit trees - Dwarf pears, Cherrys &c. I told him it should never pass" At a time when people were begging for improved roads, the contrarian Smith took the commissioners to court to stop one from running through his cherished orchard. He pressed his case and a month later reported the results of his resistance, writing: "The Jury have decided unanimously against the road designed to pass through my garden."[132]

In politics, however, Smith wasn't as lucky. Unable to break the Democrat's hold on Indian voters, he lost the April 1860 race for Leelanau Township

Supervisor. The Democratic Party had deep roots in Northern Michigan, and for many voters – especially the Indians - generational loyalties were hard to shake. However, in 1860, the demographics of Grand Traverse were rapidly changing, and new settlers with different points of view were diluting the old power base of the Democrats. Politician Smith would make another run for office that fall.

Acknowledging the growing population and influence of the western Great Lakes states, the Republicans chose Chicago as the site of their 1860 national convention. The *Herald* noted: "We have over eight millions of people in the seven North-western States, a number equal to the white population of the fifteen slave States. It is a population nearly equal to New York, Pennsylvania and New England all combined! Westward the star of empire takes its way."[133] In the last decade alone, the population of Chicago had quadrupled to over 100,000 residents, with the pace of growth increasing daily.

Preservation of the Union stood on the top rung of the Republican Party platform heading into the 1860 Presidential race. The platform said that "to the Union of the States this nation owes its unprecedented increase in population, its surprising development of material resources, its rapid augmentation of wealth, its happiness at home, and its honor abroad; and we hold in abhorrence all schemes for disunion, come from whatever source they may."[134] The Republicans branded the reopening of the African Slave Trade "a crime against Humanity, and a burning shame to our country and age," and blasted "the new dogma that the Constitution, of its own force, carries slavery into any or all of the Territories." However, the party stopped short of endorsing the abolition of slavery, knowing that popular sentiment was not yet in favor of this radical position. Preventing the expansion of slavery was their stated goal. To broaden their appeal, the Republican Party also pledged its support for the admission of Kansas as a free state, backed a national policy that welcomed immigrants, promoted river and harbor improvements, embraced the Homestead Act, and pushed for a transcontinental railroad.

New York's William Seward appeared to have the nomination wrapped up when the convention began to vote on May 18, 1860. Michigan delegates wholeheartedly supported Seward – future Governor Austin Blair seconded his nomination. On the initial ballot, Seward led all rivals by a substantial margin, but failed to garner a majority, due in a large part to the traditional first round votes for each state's favorite son candidate. However, a number of Seward's staff were troubled that several New England states they thought would go unanimously for their candidate cast some of their votes for Abraham Lincoln.

In the days leading up to the vote, the Lincoln campaign avoided confrontation with any rival candidate, deciding instead to position themselves as the best second choice vote. "Make no enemies" was at the core of their strategy. Lincoln men knew that with every indecisive ballot, the chances for his nomination increased. As it turned out, the work to undermine Seward was taken on by *New York Tribune* editor Horace Greeley, who promoted the conservative Missourian Edward Bates for President. The newspaperman believed Bates had the best chance in the upcoming election to reunite the country. Gree-

Republican Presidential candidate Abraham Lincoln in Springfield, Illinois, two days after he won his party's nomination. *Library of Congress*

ley brought influential citizens and politicians from the western states to meet with the convention delegates and warn them that Seward's abolitionist politics were too radical to carry their states. Seward had recently tried to soften his reputation as a radical but succeeded only in losing some of his constituents. While Greeley's aggressive campaign against Seward caused many delegates to question their support of the Republican frontrunner, those who changed their minds often shifted their votes to the centrist Lincoln rather than the conservative Missourian politician Bates. Lincoln also held the advantage of hosting the nominating convention in his home state. His backers inundated Chicago and raucously supported their favorite son. Their loud and constant cheering for Lincoln inside and out of the convention hall helped convince delegates of his widespread appeal. The second ballot would be crucial.

The next tally reflected a shift from favorite sons to the two leading candidates. While Seward gained 11 votes over the first round and now led with a total of 184, Lincoln closed the gap by gaining 79, with his tally standing at 181. Though neither candidate garnered a majority, momentum had shifted in Lincoln's favor. The noisy hall fell silent as delegates cast their third vote. The counting ended with Lincoln in possession of 231½ votes, 1½ short of the majority. Before the vote was announced, the leader of the Ohio delegation stood up and in a trembling voice said: "I arise, Mr. Chairman, to announce a change in four votes…to Abraham Lincoln." The hall erupted in deafening cheers, so loud that the thundering ceremonial cannonade outside could be noticed only by the smoke pouring out of the gun barrels.

When news of the nomination reached Lincoln's home of Springfield, Illinois, he was in the office of the *State Journal,* the town's Republican newspaper. The *Grand Traverse Herald* wrote: "A boy came headlong into the room where he was sitting, with a sealed dispatch, which he placed in his hand. Mr. Lincoln opened it and a sudden pallor came over his features. He gazed upon it intently for over three minutes. Then his customary smile returned and he rose, saying: "Well, boys, there is a little woman down at our house who is interested in this business," and he walked away without any further appearance of agitation, to inform Mrs. Lincoln of the joyful news."[135]

For Michigan Republicans, the news was anything but joyful. All the major Republican newspapers and party operatives had cast their support behind Governor Seward. They had expected the Chicago convention to rubber stamp his nomination. So unlikely was Lincoln's nomination that many newspapermen were unfamiliar with his given name, including Morgan Bates of the *Grand Traverse Herald.* In the three editions following Lincoln's triumph as the Republican candidate for President, the *Herald* misstated his first name as Abram rather than Abraham, a mistake repeated in papers throughout the country.

In his first editorial following Lincoln's nomination - a piece titled "The Result" - Bates was unable to hide his consternation. He wrote: "We will not disguise the fact that we were sadly disappointed at the results of the Chicago Convention. But this disappointment is confined exclusively to *men,* not to *measures.*" By the end of the editorial, however, Bates had decided to put the vote in the best possible light, and said of candidate Lincoln: "We accept him as our standard bearer and go into the contest with strong courage and hope."

On the very day Abraham Lincoln celebrated his nomination in Springfield, the all too familiar grim reaper visited George Smith and family. The preacher's namesake and grandson George - the seven year-old son of Payson and Mary Wolfe – lost a ten-day battle with typhoid fever and died. The Smiths, who had agonized over the untimely deaths of six of their ten children, now bore the loss of their oldest grandchild. Later Smith reflected: "Oh how sad that so many children should suffer and die before they have passed through life's destinies."[136] During Lincoln's four tumultuous years in the White House, 625,000 more young Americans would die "before they passed through life's destinies" in the fight to settle the issue of slavery.

After his initial disappointment in the nomination of Lincoln over his favored candidate Seward, the *Herald* worked hard to build an everyday man image of "Honest Old Abe." The paper pieced together a picture of Lincoln from national newspapers and wrote: "Mr. Lincoln stands six feet and four inches high in his stockings. His frame is not muscular, but gaunt and wiry; his arms are long…He walks slowly and deliberately with his head inclined forward and his hands clasped behind his back…In manner he is remarkably cordial, and at the same time simple. His politeness is always sincere but never elaborate and oppressive. A warm shake of the hand and a warmer smile of recognition are his method of greeting his friends.

"In his personal habits, Mr. Lincoln is as simple as a child. He loves a good dinner and eats with an appetite which goes with a great brain, but his food is simple and nutritious. He never drinks intoxicating liquor of any kind, not even a glass of wine. He is not addicted to tobacco in any of its shapes. He was never accused of a licentious act in all his life. He never uses profane language…He never speculates. The rage for sudden acquisition of wealth never took hold of him… While others have dreamed of gold, he has been in pursuit of knowledge."[137]

Simultaneously, the *Herald* continued to hammer away at the policies of the opposition. An article titled "Misnamed Democracy" said: "The Democratic Party was organized to defend the rights of the People, to maintain the equality of men who labor for their bread with those who in other countries assume superior privileges, because of the advantages of wealth and birth. But it has sadly lapsed from its ancient faith and practice. "Democracy" is now a misnomer. It is the party of all others which opposes the interests of the laboring man and denies privileges to the poor. Witness its resistance to Homesteads for actual settlers, its persistent attempt to shut Free Industry out of the Territories for the benefit of a Slaveholding Aristocracy, its unjust discriminations against the American artisan in all its tariffs, and the insults which its Congressional leaders seem to delight in heaping upon all who work for their own living."[138]

Another story titled "Facts for the Northern People" chronicled more of what editor Bates saw as the Democratic candidate's shortcomings. On the critical issue of trans-lake navigation, the life blood of Grand Traverse Country, the paper stated: "Douglas is opposed to all appropriations by Congress for improving our lake navigation…and for rendering secure our numerous lake harbors… He opposed any protection of American industry, where Michigan might supply iron for the whole American continent, give employment to tens of thousands of men…and establish a system of manufacturing that would soon make her one of the richest and most populous States in the Union." As Bates predicted, in the century following the Civil War, Michigan would rise to the position of the manufacturing center of the world. Finally, the paper scorned the Democrat's position on the use of national land, an issue dear to the great majority of Northern Michigan residents. It said: "They should never forget that he is opposed to a homestead act by which every landless man in the Union, whether native or adoptive citizen, could secure a homestead of 160 acres from the public domain."[139] The long, heated Presidential Campaign of 1860 was underway.

Throughout the summer of 1860, the harbor at Northport swarmed with the latest ships of the day, with over 20 of the newest propellers visiting at the docks on each leg of their trans-lake trips. Boats named the *Adriatic, Buckeye, Prairie State, Nile, Tonawanda, Ogdensburg, Susquehanna, Potomac, Niagara,* and *Sun* - and dozens of other prominent steam-powered vessels - regularly called at the port for wood. The frenetic activity of ships on the Bay was an indicator of the growing vitality of the western Great Lakes, and the Grand Traverse region in particular.

The premiere of two boats on Grand Traverse Bay marked the further coming of age of Grand Traverse Country. The *Herald* wrote: "Hannah, Lay & Co.'s Propellor *Alleghany*…has now commenced her regular weekly trips between Traverse City and Chicago. She is as staunch, steady, safe and pleasant a boat as we have ever traveled on; her passenger accommodations are good; her table-fare excellent, and her captain, officers and crew courteous and attentive. The trip to Chicago, instead of being a terror, a dread, and often a ten day voyage, as it was in sailing vessels, is now a pleasant pastime." The boat quickly became a point of pride for Grand Traverse and a standout on the Great Lakes. An article the following week noted: "*Alleghany* made her last trip from Chicago to this place in 29½ hours, including all stoppages. The distance is over 300 miles, and her detention by stoppage at least three hours. She is, unquestionably, one of the fastest and best Propellors on the Lakes, and performs her trips as regularly as clockwork. A Herald report on a subsequent trip enhanced the ship's reputation for speed when it said: "The ever reliable propellor *Alleghany* arrived here from Buffalo on Wednesday noon, having made the trip there in eight days…this is believed to be the fastest passage ever made."[140]

Further up the Bay, Reverend Smith of Northport documented the debut of a second passenger vessel operated by Hannah, Lay & Co. He wrote: "*Little Eastern* came early and left for Traverse City – She is a little steamer to run on the Bay."[141] The *Little Eastern* introduced reliable, scheduled service between the port towns of Grand Traverse, uniting settlements along the Bay and the Lake Michigan coast. Together the locally-owned *Alleghany* and *Little Eastern* linked neighboring and distant Great Lakes harbors and fostered a sense of community among the people of Grand Traverse. In the process, the boats improved the Grand Traverse region's status and standard of living. The *Herald* noted: "Among the many luxuries that we derive from a regular steam communication with Chicago, not the least is an indulgence in the luxuries of the Chicago market, which are brought into us fresh and green by the Propellor."[142]

Meanwhile, Hannah, Lay & Co. worked to build Traverse City into a well rounded, mercantile town that was worth the trip down Grand Traverse Bay. The *Herald* wrote that the firm had "moved into their new Store and are greatly extending their business in that line. Their new building is 20 by 100 feet, entire glass front, finished internally in the neatest modern style, and is unquestionably the best building north of Grand Haven."[143] Throughout the Civil War years, Hannah, Lay & Co. owned the region's largest store and was the *Herald's* biggest advertiser, and the market updates and recurring price lists contained in the ads documented the war's effect on a wide range of commodities. The new store, in combination with the *Alleghany* and *Little Eastern*, began to make Traverse City a serious rival to Northport.

Continuing refinements in transportation and infrastructure further encouraged people to settle in the Grand Traverse region. The widely-read *Detroit Tribune* wrote: "Emigration is pouring rapidly this season into the embryo city of Northport…The Propellors *Wisconsin* and *Prairie State*, which passed up a few days since, had some fifty or sixty passengers who designed locating at that place, and about as many more since. Northport has a fine harbor, and is contiguous to a fine agricultural region, whose beautiful climate has been the theme of frequent comment."[144] In May 1860 alone, the Northport area added over 100 people to its number. While the United States as a whole was dissolving, Lake Michigan ports between Grand Traverse Country and Chicago were emerging as a strong and united entity that would stand behind the Union in the national struggle ahead.

When the Grand Traverse portion of the 1860 U.S. Census was completed, the *Herald* built the data into a comprehensive survey that defined the culture, politics, and economics of the region only six months before the outbreak of the Civil War. The *Herald* wrote: "Grand Traverse and its attached territory, which includes the entire surrounding of the Bay, and over 80 miles of Lake coast, contains nine organized townships and a population of 3,627, of which 544 are Indians. Traverse City, at the head of West Bay, is the county Seat, and contains about three hundred inhabitants. It has one gang saw mill which turn out 8,000,000 feet of lumber per annum; a Steam Flouring Mill, three stores, two Hotels, one Printing-office, a Court-House, one School House, three Shoe Shops, one Blacksmith shop, one carpenter and Joiner's Shop, one Physician, one Lawyer, and no whisky shop. The United States Land Office for the Traverse City District is located here. Hannah, Lay & Co…own the mills and nine-tenths of all other improvements…The site commands the Bay and its charming and romantic scenery for twenty miles, while in the rear of town, partly embraced within its limits, we have the beautiful Boardman Lake…clear as crystal, and filled with trout, pickerel, pike, bass, perch, and many other varieties…

"The township of Traverse…is settled sparsely for twelve or fourteen miles south of Traverse City, and four or five miles east. In the neighborhood of Silver Lake there is a considerable settlement of farmers, and the land in that immediate vicinity is almost all taken up. But still further south…choice farming lands are open to actual settlers at fifty cents an acre…The timber is primarily hard maple and beech…the country is well-watered with small clear lakes, running brooks and rivers, and there are no stagnant pools or marshes to cause ague or bilious fever. The soil is admirably adapted to wheat…corn…oats…"[145]

The article described the 16-mile long Peninsula Township with Dougherty's venerable settlement of Old Mission at its tip, and then commented on neighboring Whitewater Township's low population. It said: "These lands, like those of the Peninsula, were kept out of the market until last year, and the early settlers have been subjected to all the vexations and annoyances incident to such a state of uncertainty; but they struggled nobly and manfully, and will soon reap the reward of their energy and perseverance. It is settled almost exclusively by

A look north through Traverse City and into West Grand Traverse Bay, with two schooners at dock near the Hannah, Lay & Co. sawmills, circa 1860. *History Center of Traverse City*

farmers, of the right stripe – just the men wanted in a new country to make the wilderness blossom like the rose - and they will do it."

The *Herald* article, while sympathizing with the travails of white settlers, again exposed the type of prejudice the Indians had endured for two centuries in treaty agreements with Euro-Americans. The latest dose came as lands reserved for the Grand Traverse Band under the Treaty of 1855 were encroached upon by farmers, then removed from the reserve and put up for general sale. The "vexation and annoyances" the *Herald* referred to were in fact the provisions of the recently enacted United States treaty with the Indians. Those who would "soon reap the reward of their energy and perseverance" were illegal squatters who had staked out farms within the Indian reserves the 1855 Treaty created. Meanwhile, the paperwork Natives submitted to secure their land selections often stalled within the government bureaucracy.

For the *Herald's* Morgan Bates, it was easier to condemn sin in the distant South than to see racial injustice in his own backyard. On one hand, Bates decried slavery and the culture that sustained it, while on the other, the editor encouraged the manipulation of treaty agreements with the Indians that diminished their holdings and undercut their traditional way of life. The double standard was not confined to Grand Traverse, but followed the course of contact between Native people and Euro-American settlement throughout the western Great Lakes. Seemingly unaware of the underlying conflict in editorial policy, the *Herald* continued with its description of the region.

"The unorganized counties of Kalcasca, Antrim and Leelanau, are attached to Grand Traverse for judicial and municipal purposes." The paper described Kalcasca as "an unbroken wilderness, with the exception...of a few settlers in the Northwest corner." In Antrim County, "the soil and timber are of the very best quality for farming purposes, and...There is a chain of beautiful lakes some seventy miles in extent, Elk, Torch, Intermediate and Branch. There are two organized Townships, Megeezee and Milton. Megeezee contains, by the last census, 179 inhabitants, and Milton 90, making the entire population of the county 269. Elk Rapids is the principle business point in the county, at the confluence of Elk Rapids with the Bay. Dexter and Noble have a new saw mill at this point, which manufactures some 3,000,000 feet per annum. When Antrim shall become more densely populated and the material resources developed, the village of Elk Rapids will grow into a busy and prosperous town." [146]

According to preliminary census figures, the unorganized County of Leelanau claimed nearly two-thirds of the region's population with 2157 residents, including over a 1000 living at the tip of the peninsula around Northport. This concentration of people was now unrivaled in Northern Michigan. Leelanau continued to be governed as part of Grand Traverse County, though it had recently been divided into four townships – Leelanau, Centreville, Glen Arbor and Crystal Lake - in preparation for its anticipated organization. The *Herald* listed their statistics: "Leelanau contains a population of 720 whites and 317 Indians; Centreville, 414 whites and 237 Indians, Glen Arbor, 252 – no Indians; Crystal Lake 217, no Indians. Total, 1603 whites and 554 Indians – Grand Total, 2157."

The *Herald* continued: "The County of Leelanau embraces the entire Peninsula formed by Lake Michigan and Grand Traverse Bay...it has 86 miles of Lake and 40 miles of bay coast...The old Indian village of Wau-ka-zoo-ville and Northport are now one in the same...and the largest village on the Bay, containing four hundred inhabitants...It is an important wooding point for the Propellors trading between Chicago and the Lower Lakes, and has two extensive wharves, five stores, three hotels, several saloons, one saw mill, and a number of mechanic shops. The largest hotel in the county was erected here last year by Deacon Joseph Dame, one of the early pioneers." The article also mentioned the "New Indian Mission, under the charge of Reverend Dougherty...delightfully situated on a commanding eminence of the bay, six miles south of Northport."

The Centreville Township summary contained an ad-lib who's who list of Leelanau pioneers. Businessmen Cordes & Theiss harnessed the water power of the Carp River for their mills, sawed lumber and ground flour for the local market, and linked the people and products of Leland to the outside world through their dock. Republican activist John I. Miller was the son-in-law and partner of lumberman Antoine Manseau - together the Leland pioneers had dammed up the Carp River in 1854 to create the giant mill pond that today bears the name of Lake Leelanau. The Lee Brothers farmed the rich soils along Lee Point on West Bay, while pioneer Sutton lent his name to another Bay settlement a few miles north. Farmer Cumberworth sent the *Herald* "samples of new potatoes which are superior in size and quality to any we have ever seen,"[147] many weighing half a pound each. Mr. Grylick founded a firm near the head of the Bay that sent lumber, doors, and wood trim to Chicago for over half a century. Norris the tanner, who would lose a son in the Civil War, welcomed Reverend Smith and family into his home the winter their sleigh broke through ice on Grand Traverse Bay.

Less is said in the *Herald* about the most westerly of Leelanau's townships – Glen Arbor and Crystal Lake – for their distance by water from Traverse City made them less accessible to Editor Bates. He wrote that "Glen Arbor is at the cove formed by Sleeping Bear Point, and is a wooding station for Propellers," while the township's other village, North Unity, is described simply as a

The idealized vision of a homestead being worked by its owner appeared in the *American Farmer's Almanac* of 1860. The book was part of the library of Leland resident John I. Miller, who then served as the region's Probate Judge. The sketch looks remarkably similar to Miller's original estate in Leland.

"German settlement." Bates acknowledged "he cannot speak from actual observation" about Crystal Lake, but noted that "the settlement...known as Baily colony...is in contemplation to build a College." Further south, a Detroit company was opening a business at the mouth of the Betsie River on Lake Michigan – today's Frankfort. The Fox and the Manitou Islands were then part of the late King Strang's Manitou County and escaped the article's attention altogether. Thus was the state of Grand Traverse Country as the nation approached the Presidential Election of 1860 and its epic Civil War

On August 20, 1860, Northport's Reverend Smith wrote: "*Pittsburg* came to Union Dock sunrise left 8 Oclk. Wife and Annie went on her for Milwaukee...She is going to Grand Rapids to visit George & attend his wedding next Sabbath." Smith lingered at the harbor as the *Pittsburg* steamed north toward the Manitou Passage, with his wife Arvilla and daughter aboard. He stayed to feel the morning temperature creep toward 70 and saw the trans-lake propellers *Tonawanda* and *Nile* come and go. Later, Hannah & Lay's *Allegheny* made her scheduled stop at the Northport docks. Smith, apprehensive over the departure of his loved ones, "sent a letter to Mrs Smith and Annie on the *Erie,*" then turned to the work of the day.

A harbor town man like George Smith knew a voyage on Lake Michigan was never a sure thing - the possibility of disaster came with the ticket to board. Predicting the weather was a guessing game, and the scarcity of lighthouses and other navigational aids on the western lake tried the limits of even the best captains. The season of gales was still a month off, but in late August, there was always a chance the weather could suddenly turn vicious. Smith witnessed the comings and goings of families who faced this reality everyday, but it was different now that his wife and daughter were part of the human cargo. He watched the *Pittsburg* fade into the horizon and wondered when he would see them again.

With his family's fate consigned to Lake Michigan, Reverend Smith's attention focused expectantly on the harbor. He had time to note in detail the demand for one of Northport's chief exports – cordwood fuel. On August 23, Smith wrote: "*Niagara* came to Union Dock took 22¼ cords wood & left for Port Sarney with corn." On the 28th, the *Niagara* returned, and along with the *Cleveland,* and "both took above 70 cords."

A scene at the Northport docks on September 1, 1860 presaged a terrible week ahead on Lake Michigan. Smith wrote: "*Nile* came to Union Dock towing *Niagara* with her shaft broke. She broke it between Milwaukee and Manito yesterday about noon." After lunch onboard the *Nile*, Smith handed a letter addressed to Arvilla to the ship's captain and said his goodbyes. The *Nile*, along with the captain and broken shaft from the *Niagara*, steamed off toward the next port of call. On September 6, with two weeks gone and no word from his wife, Smith began to worry in earnest about the fate of his family. He wrote: "*Adriatic* came to Barton's Dock, then to Rose's Dock for passengers & 2 AM left down. I went on horseback to Mr. Barton's to see if Mrs S. & Annie had come, but they had not. The boat was three days in Milwaukee so that they could have come, but perhaps they were left in Chicago..."[148] During the next 24 hours, the two Lake Michigan port cities Smith mentioned would play a central role in the largest offshore shipping disaster in Great Lakes history – an accident set in motion by divisions over slavery.

On the morning of September 7, 1860, the venerable steamer *Lady Elgin* cruised out of Milwaukee harbor. On board, members of a Wisconsin militia group named the Union Guard looked forward to a day in Chicago, paid for by Democratic Presidential candidate Stephen Douglas. The Presidential Election of 1860 was only two months away, and Douglas wanted to make political capital of the controversy that had recently enveloped the Union Guard. He saw their case as a warning of the danger posed by radical Republican abolitionists like Wisconsin's Governor Alexander Randall. Randall hated the Fugitive Slave Law, obstructed its enforcement, and threatened to secede from the Union if the federal statute was not repealed.

The Fugitive Slave Law required state militias – along with every able bodied citizen "properly summoned" – to assist slave catchers as needed. Governor Randall asked the three Wisconsin militia regiments to ignore the Fugitive Slave Law and pledge their support for the abolitionist position. Two militias did so voluntarily, but members of the Union Guard, composed mainly of Milwaukee Democrats, supported enforcement of national law and were ambivalent about abolition. Randall reacted by disarming the Union Guard and sacking its commander. The incident attracted the national spotlight, demonstrating that the conflict caused by American slavery not only divided North and South, but the North itself.

The steamer *Lady Elgin* was a familiar sight on the waters of Lake Michigan, a survivor of the once-elite fleet of side-wheeled vessels called "palace steamers."

When launched at Buffalo in 1851, the *Lady Elgin,* at 252 feet, ranked among the largest and fastest vessels afloat – a marvel of modern machinery. The beautiful steamer became a symbol of progress on the western lakes and crowds regularly showed up at harbors to see her. However, not long after the *Lady Elgin* entered service, new railroad lines gutted the Great Lakes passenger trade on key routes between south shore cities. At the same time, propellers were proving to be considerably more efficient and reliable than sidewheel propulsion, and many shipyards stopped building the old-style steamers. Only years after being put into service, most of the genre were converted into propellers, or pulled out of water and left to rot. A notable exception was the *Lady Elgin,* which through a combination of nostalgic charm and extraordinary reliability, escaped the damnation of premature obsolescence that plagued the paddle-wheeled fleet.

A change in ownership of the *Lady Elgin* coincided with the opening of the Soo Locks in 1855. The steamer joined the Chicago & Lake Superior Line and began to service the booming iron and copper district along the north shore of Michigan's Upper Peninsula. During the navigation season, the ship averaged two round trips per month between Chicago and Lake Superior, each 11 days long, and also hired out for excursions.[149] During her first voyage north from Chicago the previous year, the ship stopped at the Northport docks. Smith wrote: "Steamer *Lady Elgin* came AM, left 1:30 PM for Lake Superior. Bought on the boat Chicago and New York papers of the 9th also *Harpers Monthly.*"[150]

George Smith's diary confirmed that after leaving Northport in the spring of 1859, the *Lady Elgin* was scheduled to continue on toward Lake Superior. In this time of approaching national conflict, rumors arose that the roving vessel was in league with the Underground Railroad and shuttled runaway slaves from Chicago to the free soil of Canada. On this trip, three weeks passed from the time the *Lady Elgin* left Northport until she steamed through the Soo Locks on May 3. Records at the Soo confirm the *Lady Elgin* was the first vessel of the season to enter Lake Superior through the locks that year. Perhaps in the intervening weeks she ran down to Detroit with a shipment of cargo, or, as rumor would have it, carried on clandestine abolition work along the Canadian coast of Lake Huron.

While visiting the Northport docks, Smith bought "New York and Chicago papers" aboard the *Lady Elgin* and mentioned by name *Harper's Monthly,* a New York literary magazine. The success of the *Monthly* recently spawned the more news orientated *Harper's Weekly,* whose circulation was skyrocketing due in part to its pioneering use of printed images. Increasingly, words found

The *Lady Elgin* at the Northport docks in 1859, the year before her demise. *Leelanau Historical Society*

themselves in competition with sketches and photographs for space in columns of the nation's newspapers.

The first known photograph of a Grand Traverse harbor scene captured the *Lady Elgin* at the Northport docks in the same period Smith wrote of the boat in his diary. In the years leading up to the Civil War, photography's ability to portray the visual history of an exact moment in time was changing the way people viewed the present and experienced the past. Scenes were no longer subject to interpretation by the writer's pen or artist brush, but came frozen in black and white. Only recently, technological advances in imaging allowed pioneer photographers to venture outside of their studios and expand the scope of their work beyond staged portraits. However, during the late 1850's, very few photographers practiced their art on the frontier. Even the most up-to-date equipment was heavy and temperamental and required an experienced technician to keep it operational.

The frontier photographer who took the picture of the *Lady Elgin* in Northport was most likely a man named King. In October 1858, Reverend Smith noted the presence of "Mr King the picture (portrait) man" on the wharf. In October 1859, he wrote: "Mr King the Artist came up with us…I had let Mr King have the school house to take pictures."[151] Smith mentioned helping clear the old school of desks to make room for the photographer's equipment.

The pre-Civil War image of the *Lady Elgin* at dock is a pioneering example of the documentary power of the new medium and also reveals its potential as fine art. The photograph stands as one of the finest ante-bellum images of a harbor scene taken in Northern Michigan. The composition and clarity of the shot suggests that King or some other accomplished photographer took the photo. Besides a good eye, the photograph required considerable staging to achieve its bird's eye perspective from above the harbor. As a bonus to posterity, nature on this day cooperated by lending an exceptionally calm aspect to the Bay.

The *Lady Elgin's* presence in Northport reaffirmed the town's standing as the leading harbor in Grand Traverse Country - the port ships could rely on. Using the ship's 252 feet as a reference gives an idea of the size of the docks that united the busy harbor with the outside world. The packed wharves strained under the weight of the freight and cordwood, while a two-masted schooner took on cargo. Across the way, a single-masted mackinaw boat stood ready to carry fishermen to their nets or ferry cargo and passengers around Grand Traverse Bay. The photograph forever linked the *Lady Elgin* and Northport to this extraordinary moment in time, as the antebellum United States and the vessel marked their final months of existence. While the photograph proved the medium's power to capture the present, it had no ability to foresee or forestall the *Lady Elgin's* tragic end a year later on Lake Michigan.

When the steamer docked at Chicago on September 7, 1860, she was greeted by marching bands and crowds of well-wishers who joined with the Milwaukee Union Guard in a parade through downtown. The day continued with parties and fundraisers hosted by the Democratic Party with the aim of helping the Union Guard buy new arms. Following a late dinner, the Milwaukee militia, along with some 50 general passengers, boarded the ship for the return trip home. Captain Jack Wilson – the same master who brought the *Lady Elgin* into Northport harbor the year before – saw that weather was turning and seas rising. He ordered up fire in the boilers and soon the ship was underway.

Captain Wilson held course against the gathering storm. In their half-dozen years together, the master and his vessel had steamed through far worse weather on the 90-mile voyage north to Milwaukee. There was late night laughter in the salon and cabin lights glistened off the spray from the waves. Suddenly the schooner *Augusta*, packed with lumber for Chicago and her sails taut with wind, broke through the darkness and smashed into the side of the *Lady Elgin*. The *Augusta's* heavy load made her a battering ram and the collision left a deep gash in the *Lady Elgin's* hull. As the two vessels parted, Captain Malott of the

Augusta checked the damage to his schooner. He found broken rigging, but his ship was watertight, and he resumed his course south. Later, after narrowly escaping lynching by a Chicago mob, Malott told authorities the *Lady Elgin* was under steam when he last saw her, and believed his schooner had imparted only a glancing blow.

The scene on board the *Lady Elgin* was disastrously different than Malott's appraisal. Captain Wilson surveyed the damage to his ship, recognized the wound as mortal, and turned the steamer toward shore. Rising water soon drenched the boiler fires and left the *Lady Elgin* at the mercy of the storm. None was coming. The *Grand Traverse Herald,* citing Chicago papers and first-hand accounts, detailed the wreck of the *Lady Elgin* and scenes of chaos on Lake Michigan in the early hours of September 8. The paper wrote: "...when informed by Captain Wilson that the steamer was sinking, none of the passengers seemed to realize the awful fate impending, and there was consequently comparative quiet, until the moment she was swallowed up, when an awful scream of despair went up from the scene of appalling death."

Milwaukee firemen from the Union Guard chopped loose a section of the upper deck as the *Lady Elgin* slipped below the waves. Hundreds of passengers clung to the make-shift raft and other pieces of the doomed steamer. By dawn, the mass of survivors and wreckage was in sight of shore, having drifted eight miles from the site of the collision. The *Herald* continued: "The work of rescue began about 5 A.M., a little north of Waukegan, where the earliest intelligence was received by survivors who came ashore in the Steamer's yawl. Parties of men were soon on the alert and ready for the work of rescue. Attention was soon directed to a large raft coming steadily but bravely over the waves, upon which were standing a large group of human beings, since known to be some *fifty* in number. Around and beyond it on all sides were single survivors and groups of two or three or more, but painful interest centered about the fate of that larger raft. It neared the seething line of surf. With a glass, those on shore could see that the company on board seemed to obey the orders of one. The ladies and children were there – hearts on shore forgot to beat for an instant, then saw the raft break apart and disappear into the sea. Of the entire number on board, only fifteen were saved. Of those lost was the brave heart who tried to save those committed to his charge...*Captain Jack Wilson,* the commander of the unfortunate steamer."

One Northern Michigan survivor of the wreck - a Lieutenant Hartsuff posted at Fort Mackinac on Mackinac Island - recorded the tragedy from a passenger's point of view. He wrote: "I was on board the *Lady Elgin* when she collided with the schooner *Augusta* asleep in my berth and…soon discovered that the steamer was settling. I…ran toward the pilot house where I found Capt. Wilson on the hurricane deck. He told me where there were life preservers… and I went and passed them down to the passengers…From a quarter to a half hour after she was struck, she broke up, the hurricane deck floating off, and the hull going to the bottom with a tremendous noise.

"As she broke, I jumped with my life preserver – a board six or eight feet long and about one foot wide in to the water…and pulled with all my might to escape the mass of the wreck. I heard the voice of Capt. Wilson cheering and encouraging the people on the wreck, telling them that the shore was but a few miles off…All around me were numbers of persons floating on pieces of the wreck…I was several times buried deep under the waves. When close in to the shore, I was thrown from my preserver and went to the bottom, and although the water was not more than three or four feet deep, I was so exhausted as to be unable to rise, and crawled for some distance under water until I reached dry land…Under one piece of the wreck which was floating near us were four dead cattle fastened to it. On this were two or three persons. The buoyancy of the dead bodies of the cattle kept this piece of wreck almost entirely out of the water, and when last seen, this peculiar life-boat was very near the shore, and the persons on it were doubtless saved."

Lieutenant Hartsuff concluded: "When I reached the shore, every attention which heartfelt sympathy could suggest, was paid to me and the other survivors. One gentleman pulled off his coat and gave it to me, and another his boots." The *Herald* added: "No accurate list of persons on board can be given, but it is estimated that there were about four hundred and eighty, of whom only ninety-eight were saved." The Union Guard of Milwaukee, compelled by an issue involving slavery to board the *Lady Elgin*, had been decimated, a casualty in a cold war that was about to turn hot. A debate continues today about the number of lives lost, but all figures put forward confirm that the sinking of the *Lady Elgin* was the worst offshore disaster in the history of the Great Lakes.

News of the wreck of *Lady Elgin* did not reach Northport for another two days, but on September 9, Smith felt the effects of the far-reaching storm, noting that the "wind blew hard through the night." Nearly three weeks after Arvilla and Annie's departure, worry over his family had driven George Smith close to despair. He wrote: "*Allegheny* came…I met her as she struck the dock & took her lines, but Mrs Smith was not on board. What a disappointment &

almost agony seized me…I have watched night & day till I am almost exhausted – I began to write to her on the boat but it started and I had to leave – I slept almost none through the night, what could be the matter? Will she ever return?" If he had known about the wreck of the *Lady Elgin,* Smith's state of mind would have been that much darker.

On the morning of September 11, 1860, Reverend Smith awoke to a "furious gale" sweeping across Lake Michigan. He lamented: "May be my wife & daughter are being tossed on the billows. May be they will find a watery grave. Why could they not come when the weather was good?" The day grew worse when news of the *Lady Elgin* disaster finally reached Northport. Smith wrote: "The *Allegheny* brought the account of the wreck of the *Lady Elgin…* a few only were saved. Oh what if my Dear wife & daughter should meet such a fate. I cannot bear the thought of their absence. May the Lord keep them." The fact there was no accurate manifest for either victims or survivors tortured many whose loved ones traveled on Lake Michigan at the time, including George Smith. The questions loomed – who were the 50 passengers aboard the *Lady Elgin* with no ties to the Union Guard, and were Smith's wife and daughter among them? The only sure thing was that Arvilla and Annie were still at large, their location unknown. Smith spent another sleepless night, noting the *Acme* left the docks at three AM, and then he worked through his Sabbath duties. He closed the day with the plaintiff cry, "When will my Dear wife and daughter get home? Oh that they would come!"

September 13 brought an end to the drama. Smith's demeanor regained its usual reserve by the time he wrote: "*Prairie State* came to the Union Dock near sunset, took 12 cords wood & left down. Through the Lord's goodness wife & daughter came on her…I was happy - the Lord be praised." Smith was all business later that evening when he said: "*Nile* came dark, made fast to *Niagara* - brought her to get her shaft aboard – wooded & left midnight." The *Niagara's* propeller shaft, shattered off the Manitous on September 1, had cost the ship two weeks of down time, but now she too would soon be on her way. However, the bodies of victims of the *Lady Elgin* disaster continued to wash up near Chicago for months, and Lake Michigan was by no means finished extracting its toll for the year.

In the weeks before ice closed Northport harbor, Reverend Smith wrote: "*Globe* came to Barton's [dock]," documenting one of the last moments of another fabled palace steamer in Northport harbor. A photographer also captured the *Globe* at the Northport docks, possibly the same artist who had earlier caught the *Lady Elgin* at the frontier port. The images the *Lady Elgin* and the *Globe* are the only two known ante-bellum shots of ships in Northport, and are arguably the best pre-Civil War harbor scenes taken in all of the northern Great Lakes. As it turned out, the extraordinary coincidence of being mentioned in Smith's diary as well as photographed in Northport harbor was a death sentence for the two historic steamers. On November 8, 1860, exactly two months after the *Lady Elgin* disaster, and less than a week after leaving Northport, the *Globe* blew up on the Chicago River when workers dumped cold water into her red-hot boilers. Sixteen of her crew died in the explosion, and the *Globe* settled to the bottom of the river within miles of the *Lady Elgin*. However, the story of the *Globe* disaster was lost in the excitement as results of the 1860 Presidential Election rippled across America.

In the first issue following the election, the *Grand Traverse Herald* could only confirm local results. All nine townships administered through Grand Traverse County - except Leelanau - gave Republicans substantial victories. The following week, in the lead article titled "The Victory!!" the *Herald* proclaimed: "With unspeakable joy and full of glory, we announce the election of Abraham Lincoln to the Presidency of these United States, and the complete and overwhelming triumph of the Republican Party...The dominion and the power of Slavery are crushed forever, and the Flag of Freedom waves in triumph over a land consecrated to Liberty and Equal Rights by the blood of the heroes of the Revolution. Every Northern State...has wheeled into line and declared for Lincoln and the Right."[152]

Though a bright moment for the Republicans, Southern reaction to the election results made it clear it was likely the last presidential election in the *United States of America*. In South Carolina, "An effigy of Mr. Lincoln was hung and burnt," while "ladies...waved handkerchiefs from the windows as it passed." The Governor of Georgia labeled Northern states "unfriendly" and proposed a tariff of twenty-five per cent on the importation of their manufactured goods, as if the North was a foreign country. Meanwhile, a Georgian county passed a resolution that the election of Lincoln "ought not and will not be submitted to."[153]

In his year-end message to Congress, an addled President Buchanan, alarmed by widespread threats of Southern secession, bowed again to the slaveholders and blamed the North for the national discontent. He said: "The long continued and intemperate interference of the Northern people with the question of Slavery in the Southern States, has at length produced its natural effect.

The different sections of the country are now arrayed against each other, and the time has arrived…when hostile geographic parties have been formed."

Buchanan then advised Lincoln: "It will be the duty of the next President, as it has been my own, to act with vigor in executing the Fugitive Slave Law… Should this be refused, the injured States, having first used all peaceful means to obtain redress, would be justified in revolutionary resistance to the Government of the Union." With these words, the President of the United States, James Buchanan, committed treason by encouraging armed rebellion. The *Herald* countered: "And now again, through the President, we are told that the only condition on which Slavery will consent to the continuance of the Union, is such a change in the fundamental laws as will accord to human chattels all the attributes of common law property, and will provide a Slave Code for its protection in all our Territories. We tell the President that the price demanded this time will not be paid – that the people of the free States, Democrats as well as Republicans, have grown tired of this thing, and have concluded that a Union which cannot be maintained without paying for its existence every time it suits three hundred thousand slaveholders to set a price upon it, is scarcely worth preserving."[154]

The temper of Lake Michigan's weather reflected the foul national mood following the Presidential election. In late November, Smith wrote: "Furious gale …through last night, it would seem all boats on the lake must perish." He later noted: "*Hunter* reports between 70 & 80 Schooners & Props lost during that storm a week ago…how shocking." The *Herald* added "some sixty sail vessels and three Propellers were lost in the Lakes in the severe gale…and that over two hundred lives were lost. The first class Propeller *Dacotah*, went down…and every person on board, some sixty in number, were drowned."[155]

On December 13, 1860, Lewis Cass, the Secretary of State in the Buchanan Administration, resigned in protest over the lame duck President's neglect in protecting United States interests in the South. The old general was outraged by Buchanan's failure to mobilize the military and secure Charleston Harbor, where threat of armed revolt now reached a fevered pitch. On December 20, 1860, South Carolina seceded from the Union, and the United States as envisioned by the founding fathers ceased to exist. Though 1860 had been a very rough way to start the new decade, it would soon seem like the good old days.

American armies prepare for battle. *Library of Congress*

CHAPTER FOUR

1861
Civil War!

The first big news of 1861 came out of South Carolina. The *Grand Traverse Herald* wrote: "The Steamer *Star of the West*, chartered by General Scott to take troops and supplies to Fort Sumter, was fired upon by the rebels in entering Charleston Harbor, and four balls took effect. She put out to sea again… Maj. Anderson sent a flag of truce to Governor Pickens, to inform him that if any further attempt was made by the rebels to prevent the entrance of U.S. vessels into the Harbor he would shell Charleston and burn it to ashes in 24 hours…The crisis is at hand."[156] The same day, Mississippi seceded from the Union, followed by Florida on the 10th and Alabama on the 11th. In short order, Georgia, Louisiana, and Texas joined the rebel states. Before President-elect Lincoln ever took office, the seven Deep South slave states that excluded him from their ballots left the United States and now made plans to form a Southern confederacy.

For the first three weeks of the New Year, the wrangling over the bill to admit Kansas as a free state wore on, with pro-slave Senators blocking the vote. The break came, literally, on January 21, when ten Senators from southern states resigned their seats to protest Lincoln's election, effectively ending the 75-year reign of the Slave Power in Congress. The Kansas bill then passed quickly, and the disastrous fight over statehood was over. However, if Southern states were allowed to secede, the Union Kansas entered would be greatly reduced in both size and prospects.

Representatives of the Border States met to make one last attempt to save the Union through compromise. They constructed a plan that recommended the repeal of all Northern personal liberty laws, balanced by an amendment to the Fugitive Slave Law that would prevent kidnapping, and equalized the amount judges were paid in fugitive cases regardless of their verdicts. In exchange for a Northern promise not to interfere with the interstate slave trade, they urged the South to back the perpetual prohibition of the African slave trade. Finally, they recommended that as each territory "shall apply for admission as a State, it shall be admitted, with or without Slavery, as its Constitution shall determine," in ef-fect promoting popular sovereignty. However, as the *Herald* had recently stated, "the people of the free States, Democrats as well as Republicans, have grown tired of this thing," and the time for compromise had passed.

On March 4, Abraham Lincoln was inaugurated as the 16th President of the United States, though the word United now came with an asterisk, dimin-ished as it was by secession of seven states. Reverend Smith wrote: "Mr Lincoln was inaugurated with great style on the 4th and appears to promise great energy to the Government – May the Lord preserve his life & give him wisdom & success."[157] Early in his acceptance speech, in attempt to reassure the South, Lincoln quoted the Republican platform, saying: "…the maintenance inviolate of the rights of the states, and especially the rights of each State to order and control its own domestic institutions according to its own judgment exclusively, is essential to the balance of power on which the perfection of our political fab-ric depends." From the start, the centrist Lincoln made it clear he would leave the existing slave states alone if they stayed in the Union, and concluded with an appeal to the seceded states for peace. He said: "In your hands, my dissatis-fied fellow countrymen, and not in mine, is the momentous issue of civil war. The government will not assail you. You can have no conflict without being yourselves the aggressors. You have no oath registered in Heaven to destroy the government, while I shall have the most solemn one to "preserve, protect, and defend it."

President Lincoln continued: "I am loath to close. We are not enemies, but friends. We must not be enemies. Though passion may have strained, it must not break our bonds of affection. The mystic chords of memory, stretching from every battle-field, and patriot grave, to every living heart and hearth-stone, all over this broad land, will yet swell the chorus of the Union, when again touched, as surely they will be, by the better angels of our nature." After the speech, Lincoln was asked if he was frightened by numerous threats of assassination made against him. He replied that "he had no such sensation, and that he had often experienced much greater fear in addressing a dozen Western men on the subject of temperance."[158]

Although no exchange of fire between the gathering armies had commenced, the hot spot in the nation continued to be Charleston Harbor. Lincoln promised at his inauguration "to hold, occupy and possess the property and places belonging to the government," which included Fort Sumter. The supplies at the Federal garrison were nearly exhausted, and the Lincoln administration searched for a way to reach the fort while preventing war. Editor Bates gave his view on the conundrum, writing: "The Traitors, in collusion with the Traitors in Washington, have had three months time for warlike preparations at Charleston. The Harbor is obstructed. Batteries have been erected and defenses perfected…the President says that a successful effort to relieve Fort Sumter would require double the force of the active United States Army." In this time of false peace, the Michigan Legislature prepared for the inevitability of civil war, passing a resolution in February 1861 which recognized the supremacy of the Union and pledged the resources and military strength of the state to it, declaring that "concession and compromise" with the South were no longer possible.

The Lincoln administration found itself outgunned for the present in Charleston Harbor, but the release of the final version of the 1860 Census figures gave an idea of the long odds the South was up against. The census found that the total United States population topped 31 million, with nearly 12 million in the slave states, 4 million of whom were slaves. In the approaching Civil War, 20 million free people of the North would face 8 million whites in the South. The census figures also revealed a radical change in the two sections from the time the country was founded, when the populations of slave and free states were about equal. Since then the South, where a landed aristocracy ruled, had grown fitfully except for the steady importation of involuntary immigrants from Africa. All the while, opportunities in the North continued to attract 7 out of every 8 immigrants with the freedom to choose where to live and pursue work.

While the nation waited for the drama in Charleston to play out, the Michigan Legislature voted to keep greater Grand Traverse County intact. Although the Leelanau Peninsula was home to more people than any other county in Northern Michigan, a bill to organize an independent Leelanau County was defeated. Perhaps the Republican state legislature was hesitant to grant independence to a county with Northport as its largest town – a town that had recently voted overwhelmingly for the Democrats. The *Herald* wrote: "Our Leelanau friends must be content to travel with us two years longer, at least; and we hope by that time they will be so well pleased with our company that they will not wish to leave us."[159]

In April, ice cleared from Northport harbor, opening another welcome navigation season. On land, Reverend Smith assisted a frontier woman in an agonizing, three day delivery, in the end losing the baby and almost the mother. On April 11, a day the preacher described as "pleasant," Smith called on a sick friend, "put the bell on my cows & let them out," and "set a few Siberian grape grafts." In his last diary line of the day he noted that "the Robins & other summer birds are as merry as larks." By the time Smith took the temperature reading in Northport the next morning – 40 degrees – Confederate batteries opened fire on Fort Sumter, and the epic American Civil War had begun.

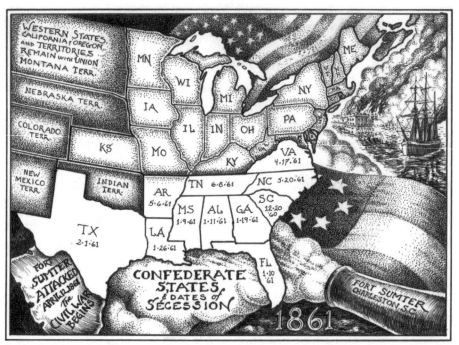

On April 12, 1861, Rebel batteries in Charleston opened fire on Fort Sumter to begin the Civil War. *Tom Woodruff*

It was no surprise the Civil War began in South Carolina, the only state where slaves outnumbered the white population. Nowhere in the South was the landed aristocracy more vocal about the need to protect the institution from the intrusion of abolitionist ideas, for theirs was the most to lose. Fear was the tool that made slavery possible, and South Carolinians understood the importance of keeping their property in line. If slaves began to think that one day they might be free, the whole plantation way of life might collapse, and slaveholders could find themselves in the embarrassing position of working their own fields. South Carolina had incited talk of secession since the United States was founded, and used that threat and the Slave Power to have their way in politics. Faced with the changing values of the nation, and the future as embodied by President Abraham Lincoln, South Carolina was the first state to secede from the Union. When the first shots of the Civil War were fired, Charleston residents took to the streets, cheering on the cannonade against Fort Sumter.

A wave of indignation swept the North when citizens heard the national flag had been fired upon. The radical Republican Governor Alexander Randall summarized Northern sentiment toward the cradle of rebellion in a speech to the Wisconsin State Legislature. He said: "The people will never consent to any cessation of the war, forced so wickedly upon us, until the traitors are hung or forced into an ignominious exile. This war began where Charleston is – it should end where Charleston was."[160] In turn, the *Grand Traverse Herald* minced no words when announcing the news of Confederate aggression. Under the banner "A Great National Struggle" the paper said: "A Civil War has been inaugurated by the South, and hostilities have commenced! The contest is between the Slave Power and the Government of the United States - between Despotic Rule and the Freedom of the People to govern themselves.

"Mr. Lincoln, for refusing to surrender Fort Sumter to the Southern traitors and robbers…will receive the plaudits of every true friend of Constitutional Freedom, North and South, and they will sustain him in the end. The South has forced this unnatural drama upon us, and there can be no more hesitation in the mind of any Patriot as to the duty which this emergency imposes. The Stars and Stripes must be sustained at all hazards and at every sacrifice…Michigan must not be behind her sister States in rendering efficient aid to the General Government in this great struggle for Freedom, and the right to sustain itself on the principles upon which it was founded."[161]

Since its first edition in November 1858, *The Grand Traverse Herald* had grown to be the dominant source of news in Northern Michigan, a position of considerable influence. Many citizens who initially thought Editor Bates too radical now embraced the politics he promoted in his paper. With shots fired against the national flag, Bates filled almost all the columns in the *Herald* with war news and editorially supported President Lincoln as Commander in Chief.

Following the fall of Fort Sumter, Lincoln called on all states to send soldiers to help end the rebellion. Leaders of the Border States, which had yet to secede, scoffed at the idea. Governor Magoffin replied: "Kentucky will furnish no troops for the wicked purpose of subduing her sister Southern States." Governor Ellis of North Carolina said: "I can be no party to this wicked violation of the laws of the country, and to this war upon the liberties of free people." Governor Harris wired: "Tennessee will not furnish a single man for coercion, but fifty thousands, if necessary, for the defense of our rights or those of our southern brethren."[162] However, in the North, Union men poured in to join up, quickly filling Lincoln's request for 75,000 volunteers. There was no doubt where Michigan stood in the fight. The state, which was required to raise one regiment of 780 or more soldiers, petitioned the War Department for permission to raise four more due to the overwhelming response of volunteers. Michigan railroads carried soldiers to the front for free, and steamship lines ferried troops along the coast of the Great Lakes at no cost. All through the North and South, armies were organizing for a fight.

Patriotic fever swept through Grand Traverse and inspired the Smith family to action. The Reverend wrote: "Annie has made Union Colors 4 by 8 feet. Payson painted the Stars. He & I got a pole and raised the flag on the N. end of our house over 40 feet high. Our country is rousing against the rebels of the South who are seeking to destroy the government – the object is to extend and perpetuate Slavery."[163]

The opposing American armies assembled and trained in mass following the attack on Fort Sumter. Most Union recruits signed up for 90 day stints, expecting a quick end to the war. The *Toronto Globe* wrote: "It is not the refuse of the population who are volunteering, but mechanics, shop-keepers, and professional men. Some in high position serve in the ranks as an example."[164] By the end of May, the *Herald* reported that more than 300,000 Union men had enlisted nationwide.

In the quiet months following the bombardment of Fort Sumter - before the casualty roles began to build beyond all expectations - war was still a glorious concept and people hungered for action. Every skirmish made the headlines. A *Herald* article titled "First Victory" stated: "The first actual success on the side of the United States in this war was achieved at Alexandria, Va. A party of fourteen went from Washington and seized a steamer there with several thousand stands of arms belonging to the rebels, compelled the engineer to fire up, and brought her in triumph to Washington." Another article said: "A reconnoitering force of two regiments was sent in the western direction, from Alexandria, early this morning. The men comprising it took up the rails of the Alexandria and

Virginia railroad, and took down the wires of the telegraph as they went along. All advance troops of the Federal army were instructed to answer the challengers of the rebel pickets – Who goes there? with this: "*The Advance Guard of the Grand Army of the United States!*" This answer in all instances made the rebels beat a precipitate retreat…"[165] The scale of the war was still very small, and patriotic bravado seemed enough to carry the day. Widespread death and destruction within the divided United States would soon change that perception.

In the spring of 1861, the town of Glen Arbor received a big boost to its prospects when the Northern Transportation Company chose the port as its northern Lake Michigan wooding station. The company owned eight propellers that ran the entire distance of the Great Lakes, including the *Buckeye, Prairie State, Michigan,* and *Ogdensburg* - ships which had previously called at Northport for cordwood fuel. With scheduled stops of the NTC fleet guaranteed, Glen Arbor began to grow in earnest, and Northport harbor faced its first serious competition on the Leelanau Peninsula. In other local shipping news, Hannah & Lay's ship the *Alleghany* commenced service for another season, "thoroughly overhauled, repaired, and newly painted…one of the fastest and best propellers on the Lakes."[166]

The *Grand Traverse Herald* expanded its audience and sphere of influence when the *Mackinac Herald* closed its doors in the summer of 1861. After the paper folded, the *Grand Traverse Herald* took over as the publisher for Mackinac, Cheboygan, Emmet, Manistee, and Manitou Counties, in addition to current duties with Grand Traverse and its attached counties. The concept of Grand Traverse Country, and the *Herald's* circulation, took on new dimensions. Whether or not they liked the paper's politics, the *Grand Traverse Herald* was now the only journal serving Northern Michigan, and every county official in the northern third of the state had no choice but to print their legal notices in it. Overnight the paper became more financially viable, for as Editor Bates wrote: "Our main reliance for support is upon legal advertising and the tax lists."[167] Bates and the *Herald* had survived two tough years in Grand Traverse, but now events began to swing in their favor.

With the summer in progress, the *Herald* wrote: "The wheat crop throughout this country is looking remarkably well. A much greater quantity has been sown than in any previous year. Indications are now favorable to crops of all kinds. Summer has fairly set in." All through the North, farmers' fields teemed with record breaking crops, with wheat and corn abundant. New types of farm implements produced in Great Lakes factories helped farmers plant more acreage, and the sun and rain this season graced the fields in ideal proportions. Across the Atlantic Ocean, the forecast for the harvest was just the opposite. The *Herald* wrote: "Accounts from Europe report that the weather since March has been extraordinarily cold, with drought and sharp frosts, which have checked, and in many cases injured, vegetables."[168] There was a surplus grain available in the North just as crops in Europe failed. For the first time in decades, the North had the upper hand over the South in the politics of international farm exports.

Rebel leaders understood that recognition by the European powers of France and England was essential to their cause. Confederate status as an independent nation was at stake. Most European industry depended on cotton as their raw material, and the South saw this fact as a weighty bargaining tool. In order to emphasize the importance of the plantation's star product, the South decided to withhold their cotton from European buyers during the first months of the Civil War. The Rebels believed that hardship caused by cotton shortages would drive England and France firmly into their camp. The decision proved to be an ill-timed and costly mistake.

In the previous two years, Southern planters enjoyed record harvests and European warehouses overflowed with 500-pound bales. The abundant supply in reserve could spin a good deal of cloth, and in consequence the Confederate embargo of their own chief export had little immediate effect on European cotton mills. A correspondent for the *London Times* wrote: "The present stock of cotton in the English warehouses...leaves no doubt that the Manchester mills will be able to run full time for an entire year without touching a pound of the new crop"[169] Concurrently, the North had grain, and starvation in Europe was a real possibility. Cotton was important, but food was essential. Faced with the choice, the European powers were not prepared to jeopardize the flow of grain by embracing the Confederate cause.

By the fall of 1861, the cotton economy faltered and bales stacked up on Southern docks. The fledgling Confederate war machine had lost the chance to acquire European weapons and supplies in exchange for cotton before Northern naval superiority locked their harbors in a tight blockade. Meanwhile, the North's wheat and corn arrived at European docks in ships flying the Union Stars and Stripes. The *Grand Traverse Herald* reported: "A bright stream of gold which for several months has been setting in upon us in England, still continues to reach our shores, and with the prospect of a short supply in Europe, gives us assurances that it will not cease for many months to come."[170] During the next two years, exports of wheat from northern ports to Europe would double, helping avert starvation on the continent. The Confederacy's first attempt at international cotton diplomacy had been a failure.

The raw armies facing each other in the summer of 1861 awaited their first great battle. Union recruits poured into Washington D.C. to protect the capital against invasion from neighboring Virginia, the heart of the Confederacy. During the next fours years, in the lethal 100 miles between the warring capitals of Washington and Richmond, the lives of hundreds of thousands of American soldiers were lost in the deadliest military engagements in the history of the United States. The *Grand Traverse Herald* predicted the suffering that lay ahead for the South's most populous state. It said: "Her soil is to be made the battle ground of the impending struggle; and in addition to the horde of secession traitors who are quartered upon her, she is to be overrun with the armies of the U.S. and compelled to furnish of her already scanty store subsistence for her enemies. Already there are thirty thousand Federal troops within the limits of the State, and before another week the number will be doubled. The whole weight of the struggle is to fall upon Virginia, and her soil is to be the scene of bloody strife which, she…has brought upon the nation."[171] The *Herald* had foreseen the essence of the upcoming struggle before the first major battle occurred.

Virginia papers painted the future in a completely different light. The *Richmond Whig* wrote: "We are not enough in the secrets of our authorities to specify the day on which Jeff Davis will dine at the White House…We should dislike to produce any disappointment by naming too soon or too early a day; but it will save trouble if the gentlemen will keep themselves in readiness to dislodge at a moment's notice…They must know that the measure of their inequities is full, and the patience of outraged freedom is exhausted. Among all the brave men from the Rio Grande to the Potomac…there is but one word on every lip: "Washington," and one sentiment in every heart: Vengeance on the tyrants who pollute the Capital of the Republic!"[172]

As the summer heated up, there was still very little fighting except for the verbal jousts. Each side waited for the other to make a move. Here the pressure was on the North, whose forces were compelled to invade to quell a rebellion on what had become enemy soil. During this false peace, the *Herald* ran an article that assessed the substantial damage to the nation to date, even though few shots had yet to be fired. It read: "Six months ago…the Rebel Flag was first unfurled at Charleston. Let us glance over the field and see what the conspirators against American Liberty have accomplished.

Military camps convert the rural American landscape into "tented fields." *Library of Congress*

"They have inaugurated civil war. They have plunged the most prosperous nation on earth into the horrors of Revolution. They have driven twenty-six millions of people into the bloody arena of fratricidal conflict. They have let loose the furies of passion, and stimulated all the baser instincts of man into preternatural activity. They have arrayed peaceful communities against each other; set brothers to cutting each other's throats, and reproduced in this free land the sanguinary spectacles of semi-barbarous times. They have converted prosperous cities into barracks, and fruitful plains into "tented fields." They have paralyzed commerce, suspended business, brought bankruptcy and ruin to thousands of American homes and converted a land that was the envy of Christendom into the scene of the most unnatural struggle the world ever beheld."[173]

Far from the building armies, Northport enjoyed the bustle of a new navigation season. Workmen "began to drive piles in the extension of Union Dock," to satisfy demand for space on the wharf. The *Susquehanna* arrived in the night and "took 2400 bushels of potatoes," then one of Grand Traverse Country's chief agricultural exports. Republican Solomon Case was named keeper of the Grand Traverse Lighthouse, announcing that a new party was in power in the North. On the Fourth of July, Reverend Smith wrote: "Early in the morning the Union Flag was raised. It is large and very beautiful. At 10AM all met at the school house…the Declaration of Independence read…then singing Down the traitor's Serpent Flag – very appropriate."

On July 25, ships arriving in Northport carried the news from Virginia of the first great battle of the Civil War. A rattled Reverend Smith wrote: "The

Hunter brought awful news…the Union army in the battle of Manassas has been conquered by the rebels & driven back with immense loss. The rebels, whose loss is unknown but said to be very great, were 90,000 strong. It is said that the low estimate of our loss was 4 to 5,000. Shocking! Shocking! Col. Wilcox of the Michigan 1ˢᵗ regiment was killed."

The first intelligence from almost every Civil War battle was full of factual mistakes, as was the case with information gleaned from the *Hunter* in Northport harbor. Colonel Willcox, whose name Smith had misspelled, was alive but wounded and held prisoner by the Rebels. The real size of the Confederate Army fighting at Manassas was 30,000, only a third of the number reported. Union soldiers killed, wounded, or missing stood at 3,000 while the Rebels lost 2,000, again considerably less than what Smith heard. However, even the adjusted figures revealed a scale of battle unprecedented in North American history. In all, 75,000 Union and Confederate soldiers fought at Bull Run Creek near the railroad town of Manassas Junction.[174] Together the armies fielded five times the number of men in the entire United States Army only two years before. For the first time, green American troops fought against each other in great numbers and witnessed the destructive force of flying metal and the terrible vista of friends cut down beside them. During a day of chaotic clashes, the momentum of the battle changed by the hour, and victory and defeat were hard to judge among the carnage. Many volumes have detailed the fighting along Bull Run creek that day and by its end, the Union Army was in full retreat. The Army's mad scramble back to Washington ended all hope this would be a short war.

The *Grand Traverse Herald* later wrote of the battle: "Our County was represented at Manassas and Bull Run by Curtis Fowler Jr., son of the honorable Curtis Fowler, Judge of Probate, who fought bravely in the ranks of the gallant First, and was wounded at the Battle of Bull Run."[175] All four Michigan regiments fought in the battle, with the 1st Michigan Infantry the most heavily engaged, and Fowler one of its many wounded. The first blood of a Grand Traverse soldier had fallen on Virginia soil. Curtis Fowler Jr. returned to Grand Traverse to convalesce from his wounds, and his younger brother would later enlist to replace him.

The *Milwaukee Sentinel* recorded an unusual scene at the Battle of Manassas – Bull Run involving Great Lakes industrialist Eber Ward, whose business ventures helped shape Grand Traverse Country. Starting with a small schooner on the Detroit River in 1823, Captain Ward had sailed the far corners of the Great Lakes and knew Grand Traverse from these voyages. By 1861, Ward owned a shipyard and metal works near Detroit that was the largest in Michigan. His Great Lakes fleet of schooners, steamers, and propellers carried hundreds of tons of ore from Upper Peninsula mines to his foundry, where it was made into train tracks, boilerplate, and a variety of other metal products advertised for sale in the *Grand Traverse Herald*. Some of Ward's metal may have been used to make the musket and minie balls he fired in the scene described in the following *Milwaukee Sentinel* story. Under the title "Cool Courage Displayed by a Citizen at the Battle of Bull Run," the paper wrote: "Capt. E.B. Ward, a well known and highly respected citizen of Detroit, who went purposely from there over a week ago to witness the anticipated battle at Manassas, displayed great coolness and courage during the disgraceful retreat of a portion of our troops. Seeing a panic stricken soldier throw down his musket, he deliberately picked it up, ran to where a wounded soldier lay writhing in the agonies of death, tore off his cartridge box, and loaded and fired at the enemy eight times, remaining cool as an oyster throughout."[176]

Beyond his reported moment of bravado, Ward's contribution to the North's manufacturing capacity during the Civil War was considerable. Ward was one of the first Michigan industrialists to bring the vast natural resources that lay along the shores of the Great Lakes together under one roof. There he transformed the raw materials into finished goods, writing the script for a century of the state's manufacturing dominance to come. Ward continued in industry after the war, and in the 1870's owned and operated the Leland Iron Works, Leelanau County's largest employer at the time.

Both armies reeled from the massive collision at Manassas and began to refit for more inevitable battles. Across the country, the reality that there could be years of bloodshed ahead began to sink in. The days of bravado and posturing were over. Recovering from the shock of losing the first major engagement of the war so close to the nation's capital, President Lincoln resolved to build the demoralized Union Army into a professional force capable of engaging the Rebels for as long as it took to defeat them. He summoned General George McClellan, who had recently won several skirmishes with Confederate forces in western Virginia, to mold the green Union regiments assembled in Washington into the Army of the Potomac. The escalation of the Civil War had begun.

In August 1861, volunteers formed four more new regiments of Michigan Infantry, bringing the state's total to eight, with nearly 10,000 men enlisted. To date, all Michigan regiments originated from the populous farm communities in the south of the state where the ten, 100-man companies in each regiment often filled up with neighbors. In the more isolated regions of the state like Grand Traverse, volunteers found their own way to the Union Army. Many recent settlers left the area in groups to enlist in their home state's regiments, cheered on by friends and loved ones. War was still a glorious concept, and young men signed up for what they hoped would be the time of their lives. In a September article titled "Volunteers from Grand Traverse," the *Herald* wrote: "Fifteen or twenty of our best citizens have volunteered for the war within the past ten days, and have gone to fight the battles of their country. Five stalwart and noble hearted young men as ever shouldered a musket, left here Friday evening to join Captain Busteed's Chicago Light Infantry. Their names were Martin A. Hopper, Andrew McKillup, Isaac Winne, James Nicholson and James Fitpatrick. They had long been in the employ of Hannah, Lay & Co; and on settling with them, Mr. Hannah made each a handsome present, and told them if they were ever in distress, or in need of funds, to draw on him at sight, and their drafts would be honored."

The paper continued with a list of area men heading to Chicago to volunteer together, writing: "Among others...are Wm. E Sykes, Sheriff of the County, Samuel A. McClelland, E.J. Brooks, Lewis Steele, Frank May, and Aaron Page of Northport; Orelus Evans, of Whitewater; and the son of Thomas Lee of

A Union Army ambulance corps practices the removal of wounded from the battlefield. *Library of Congress*

Centreville. God speed them all, and give them the victory!"[177] The volunteers did not know they faced four terrible years of fighting in the worst battles of the Civil War, at the end of which all would be heroes, both living and dead.

The *Herald* followed the progress of the first group of Grand Traverse volunteers, publishing a letter dated October 13 from volunteer William Sykes, who had made his way to Washington. He wrote: "There are about 400,000 men on both sides of the Potomac; we are ordered to keep our horses harnessed and saddled day and night, to be ready at a moments warning; we heard heavy guns last night, and had orders to march across the river; but, before we had our cannon ready, the firing ceased, and the order was countermanded. We remain in camp – expecting a call every moment." The story ended with this note about the author: "Mr. Sykes was elected last fall Sheriff of this County; he enlisted in Company C, Chicago Light Artillery, commanded by Captain Bustud, of which company he is now 2d Lieutenant. He has seen service before, and having an ardent desire for liberty and welfare of his country, he is patronizing it again."[178]

The *Herald's* published list of volunteers grew longer as fall progressed. Editor Bates wrote: "Considering our isolated position and scarce population, Grand Traverse is furnishing its full quota for the War. There may be, and doubtless are *some* among us who are traitors at heart, and would be glad to see the Government overthrown; but the masses are loyal and patriotic."[179] As the stream of volunteers left the area to become soldiers, a river of newcomers who sought to become farmers replaced them. The *Herald* noted: "Grand Traverse County is filling up rapidly with the right sort of citizens, who are availing themselves of the opportunity now offered to secure first-rate farming lands, in a healthy locality, for fifty cents an acre. More lands were sold to actual settlers at the Traverse City Land Office, in September, than in any previous month since it established here. The country around Glen Arbor is attracting a good deal of attention, and as a daily line of Propellers is running there this season, that desirable point is easy of access."[180]

The great asset that Grand Traverse and all the Northern states possessed was the promise of opportunity. Even in the throes of a rebellion, the world looked on the North as a place of hope and freedom, and immigrants kept pouring into its harbors. In the South, however, every man who joined the fight created a hole in society, for there was no one arriving to replace him. Few immigrants wanted to start a new life in a place where labor was owned, not paid for.

Throughout the fall of 1861, problems aboard the region's flagship, the *Alleghany*, reminded Grand Traverse residents of their dependence on water transport. The *Herald* wrote: "Hannah, Lay & Co.'s Propeller *Alleghany*, met with a serious accident on Sunday morning last off the Manitous, on her trip from Chicago to Traverse City and Sarnia. Her cylinder was entirely destroyed and the engine otherwise badly injured. She was towed into Northport on Monday morning. Her engine will have to be taken out and sent to Cleveland for repairs, or the vessel towed down to that place. In any event the accident will cause a detention of three to four weeks, and the damage by delay, and the cost of repairs, will be heavy. She is loaded with wheat for Sarnia, together with a large amount of merchandise for this place." Reverend Smith provided another view of the incident, writing: "*Susquehanna*...towed in *Alleghany* from this side Sleeping Bear. She lies at the Union Dock with her cylinder broke to pieces. She laid at the mercy of the waves over thirty hours."[181]

The scene Smith described sounded similar to the sinking of the *Westmoreland* in 1854. If the waters off the Manitous had been riled, the *Alleghany* may have shared the *Westmoreland's* fate, complete with a scattering of flour barrels along the coast of Lake Michigan. With the *Alleghany* laid up, the *Herald's* Bates soon complained: "During the season of navigation we rely upon the regular trips of the Propeller *Alleghany* for news, rather than Uncle Sam's slow coach, the Mail: but the accident that has happened to that boat deprives us of these facilities, and we are thrown back upon old resources."[182]

Smith continued to record the news from Northport harbor. He wrote that the "*Free State* came to Rose's dock. Some 18 volunteers from Elk Rapids went out on her," and mentioned seeing Morgan Bates and his wife on the boat. In the next edition of the *Herald* Bates wrote: "Rev. Geo. N. Smith of Northport, has sent us some fine specimens of Apples grown in his garden. Among them are Rhode Island Greenings and blue Pearmian of last year's growth, in a fine state of preservation, retaining their flavor. His is strong proof of the purity of our climate."[183]

As the Great Lakes region mobilized for prolonged war, a tremendous amount of cargo moved across their waters, making the temporary loss of the *Alleghany* all the more dear. In an article titled "An Extraordinary Advertisement," the *Herald* gave a hint of the amount of freight now being hauled on the lakes. It said: "The Detroit papers contain an advertisement of the Western Transportation Company, soliciting patrons of the North shore line of propellers to ship as much as possible by the Great Western Railway to relieve the pressure upon their line for freight room." The bitter transportation rivals – railroads and steamships - had brought out the fig leaf to propel the Union war machine forward. Then, just after the Grand Traverse icon *Alleghany* reentered service, she was waylaid by another accident. The *Herald* wrote: "On Friday evening last, when within about ten miles of Traverse City, the Propeller broke her connecting rod, and came into port on Saturday morning under sail."[184]

In his capacity as the doctor of Northport, Smith often wrote of the dreaded diseases that were part of life in Grand Traverse - the same illnesses that would devastate the barracks of both armies during the Civil War. In October 1861, Smith lamented: "There is so much whooping cough and measles it is said it is hardly proper for children to come out." Later he visited his sick friend William Voice, the Northport lumber mill owner, and concluded: "His case appears to be typhoid,"[185] a disease that always tortured and often killed. For a week, Smith tended to the gravely ill Voice, and "found him in a bad state passing a good deal of blood…prescribed increased portions of quinine, laudanum and sweet oil injections." With Smith's help and good luck, the lumberman William Voice Sr. eventually recovered from his bout with typhoid, but the disease was not finished with his family.

While the fighting between armies cooled with the approach of winter, the war continued to exact its toll. The winter camps concentrated volunteers from widespread communities in tight quarters, and various diseases spread from bunk to bunk with ease. As the snow began to fall on the nation's capital during the first winter of war, the *Herald* noted: "There were twelve hundred sick soldiers in the hospitals at Washington, Alexandria and Georgetown."[186] All told, during the next four years, disease killed nearly twice the number of American soldiers than died on the battlefield. Of the 625,000 who gave their lives, nearly 400,000 fell to disease.

All across America, people chose sides in the war, and many families were torn apart. The *Herald* told of one Border State's experience, writing: "The statement made in Gen. Thomas's report, that the young men of Kentucky had in considerable numbers been misled to take part in the revolt, is too true. At this moment Gov. Wickliffe, one of the most thorough friends of the Union, has a son in the Confederate's service. The Rev. Dr. Robert J. Breckenridge, one of the most distinguished divines in the Union, has another. The editor of the Louisville *Journal,* whose loyalty is unshaken, has another. In one county that gave a large majority for the Union, two hundred young men entered the rebel service."[187] The Border States by their location had divided loyalties, but nowhere in the United States was there agreement as to why the war was being fought, or which cause was right. The political lines that ran east-west across the nation gave a general idea of the sympathies of local citizens, but the lines that divided extended into neighborhoods and households, creating more personalized scenes of destruction.

Near the end of 1861, a familiar name resurfaced in a *Herald* article. The paper said: "John Brown, Jr., son of "Old Ossawatamie" Brown, was in Grand Rapids on Tuesday, en route for Grand Traverse. His business seems to have been recruiting for his regiment of Sharp-shooters from the hunters of Michigan."[188] John Brown Jr. had raised a Sharp-shooting regiment in New York and came west in the hope of coaxing some of Lake Michigan's riflemen from the woods. Brown knew that frontiersmen who hunted for their dinner proved to be the best shots. Though no account was given of Brown's success in recruiting volunteers from Grand Traverse for the New York regiment, later in the war a number of area men volunteered in the 1st Michigan Sharp Shooters, and these "hunters of Michigan" would fight and die in some of the bloodiest battles of the war.

In his December 3, 1861 message to Congress, President Lincoln spoke of the great Civil War that was consuming the land. The President recognized that the issues that brought on the conflict transcended the usual motives of armies at war. This was not a fight over land or riches or religion but for principles set forth in the nation's founding document, the Declaration of Independence, with its revolutionary phrase "all men are created equal." Lincoln said: "The struggle of today, is not altogether for today – it is for the vast future also. With a reliance on Providence, all the more firm and earnest, let us proceed in the great task which events have devolved upon us." Lincoln resolved that the United States he was elected to lead would stay the course, stay together, and settle the great issues of slavery and union through war.

On the final day of the year, Northport's George Smith counted his family's blessings. He wrote: "Thus ends the record of 1861. All of us who lived at the beginning have lived to the end of the year." As the Smiths' 28 years on the Lake Michigan frontier had demonstrated, 12 months without the death of a child, a grandchild, or a loved one was a record to celebrate. However, the Civil War was about to escalate beyond what anyone had imagined, and the grief caused by death would become the last common element of experience shared by families throughout the divided nation.

Supplies for the Peninsula Campaign cover the docks of Yorktown, May 1862. *Library of Congress*

CHAPTER FIVE

1862
Gone to War

O n the 2nd day of January, 1862, Glen Arbor lumberman John Fisher wrote to friend John Boizard, a quartermaster in the Union Army stationed in Chicago. Fisher's letter preserved the thoughts of a leading Grand Traverse Republican as the gravity of the Civil War sunk in. He wrote: "How often it is that the history of Nations is but a parallel to the history of Families. We have often seen the favorite son or daughter in a family, the very ones that give the Parent the most trouble. So with our Nation. The Government had paid more of its means, given more of its appointments, more of its patronage. In fact, that portion of the Nation now in Rebellion has itself administered the government for four fifths of the time since we commenced our National existence. So they had but to help themselves to all they wanted, and they did.

"Now, friend Boizard, when I think of all these things and many more connected with the history of our government, my blood boils with anger, while a deep, deep grief burdens my mind to think that so large a portion of our People should be so ungrateful as to attempt to destroy, tear down, and annihilate so good a government…I feel a deep and earnest solicitude that the God of Battles will preserve you and those with you till this Rebellion is crushed, and History shall engrave your name on its brightest page, and millions and millions shall point to that page and say, There are the names of the Preservers of the Great Republic."[189]

Fisher was a solid Union man, but he mentioned nothing about slavery in his letter. His words reflected the fact that in early 1862, most northern support for the fight was based on holding the country together. At this point in the war, many Unionists would have agreed to leave the institution of slavery intact if Southerners laid down their arms and quit the rebellion. Slavery had brought sectional differences to a head and incited war, but it was preserving the Union – not freeing the slaves – that motivated most Northerners. This fact did not stop Fisher's friend and fellow Republican Morgan Bates from beating his abolitionist drum.

The *Grand Traverse Herald's* first editorial of 1862 went beyond advocating freeing the slaves and promoted a radical new position concerning African-Americans in the Union Army. Bates wrote: "There is a mass of population in the United States amounting to about four millions, friendly to the government, and ready to fight for it, from which the Government has not called for nor accepted a single soldier. These people, it is true, are more or less black…But black men fought under Washington, and fought well. They fought well under Jackson. They are not prone to insurrection, or secession, but will fight if well-armed and disciplined. They have the best reason in the world to fight well in this war. The same insolent traitors who have for so long insulted us have still longer robbed them of liberty…Those traitors would now use them to fight against the Government if they could trust them, but they cannot. By the same token we can. Why don't we?"[190]

A Union company stands guard in front of "Price, Birch and Co. Dealers in Slaves" in 1862 Virginia. *Library of Congress*

The answer to the editor's question was as complex as the varied issues that divided North and South. Despite the war in progress, many in the fractured United States hoped some miraculous settlement of the conflict was still possible, one that would allow the country to get back to normal. Any major change in the status of blacks in the nation would end this hope for good. Bates wrote of the conundrum: "These four million are held as property by a few other people of the Southern States, now mostly rebels. Out of regard to this property, and from the fear of spoiling it entirely, we abstain from enlisting black soldiers, and thus throw away about one-fifth the loyal fighting force of the country, and what is immensely worse, that part of it which is key to the situation."[191]

The northern mindset had changed dramatically in the years leading up to the war, as witnessed by the election of the Republican President Lincoln. However, the idea of abolition and equal status for African-Americans on any field was for the moment a hard thing for most Americans to accept. The majority in the North rallied behind preservation of the Union and did not necessarily see the fate of slavery as a central part of the fight. The Confederate bombardment of Fort Sumter eight months before had signaled the South's commitment to the old ways, but the North had yet to fully commit to "the new birth of freedom" Lincoln would later speak of in his Gettysburg Address.

Blacks were not the only ones forbidden in the Union Army - Native Americans were also denied the chance to serve in the ranks. On several occasions since the outbreak of war, recruiters turned away contingents of Michigan Indians who attempted to enlist - another sign of the North's incomplete vision of equality. During the first year of his presidency, Lincoln commanded an all-white army. However, as the year 1862 unfolded, the growing intensity of the war shattered all hope of reviving the old Union, and Congress considered how to best employ all races as soldiers. Once again, the *Herald's* Morgan Bates proved to be a seer.

In January 1862, Reverend Smith received a letter from his sister, informing him that three of his nephews had joined the Union Army. "May they be noble supporters of the Government," he prayed. Every American's stake in the Civil War was rising as two massive armies prepared for the long fight ahead. Though still in its innocent stages in January 1862, the war was already a monstrous affair. The *Albany Journal* noted: "The magnitude of the scale upon which the war now raging in this country is conducted is appalling...The war of the Revolution was relatively a mere succession of skirmishes. The war of 1812, measured both as regards numbers and field of operations, shrinks into...insignificance beside the gigantic operations that are going on at the present hour."[192] The "magnitude of scale" the *Albany Journal* described was only the start of a conflict that would engage two of the largest and hardest fighting armies ever assembled. In the fight at Manassas-Bull Run the previous summer, 4,700 American soldiers were casualties in the largest battle of the Civil War to date. Before the war was over, 44 battles would exceed that gruesome toll. However, as the divided nation moved into its first full year of bloodshed, the cold weather brought a pause in the fighting.

With the Great Lakes frozen shut, the overland delivery of the mail to Grand Traverse became the area's sole link to outside world. The weekly mail always contained a bundle of national newspapers addressed to Morgan Bates, who would digest their articles and reassemble them for his northern audience. Local residents looked forward to every Wednesday's mail delivery and each subsequent edition of the *Grand Traverse Herald,* which published on Fridays. With the war putting friends and loved ones and the fate of the United States in peril, the hunger for news grew fierce. However, as had been the case since the first post office opened on Old Mission a decade before, the winter mail often failed to make it to Grand Traverse. The Northport-Newaygo road had yet to be completed, and the only way to reach Northern Michigan during the snow-covered months was by Indian trails. The delivery of goods, including the mail, remained a hit or miss proposition.

The New Year of 1862 was a case in point. The first mail bags were delayed a week in Manistee, causing Bates to dig through old issues of papers to fill his columns. The second mail of the year, traveling north on a rough wagon road from the Muskegon Post Office, met with disaster. The *Herald* wrote: "When crossing the Ferry at Pentwater, the horses jumped off the scow, carrying the Mail wagon and all its contents with them. The horses were drowned and the wagon lost. The Mail Bag floated on the surface and was rescued, but all the Mail matter was thoroughly soaked. In this condition we will probably receive it Saturday night."[193]

At a time when the Civil War consumed the resources and energy of the nation, the influx of settlers into Grand Traverse Country was transforming the region's lakeshore villages into boom towns. The *Herald* wrote: "There are now, besides the Steam Flouring Mill of Hannah, Lay & Co., four grist mills in this county: one at Whitewater, one at Leland, one at Sutton's Bay, and one at Norris's, three miles from Traverse City, on the west side of the Bay. Three years ago there was only one in the county, that of Hannah, Lay & Co., which was then

Grand Traverse pioneers deliver pine logs cut to make way for their crops. *History Center of Traverse City*

propelled by water power. These improvements are the surest indications of our growth and prosperity."[194] In addition, mail delivery to the region doubled from once to twice a week, pushing Grand Traverse a step closer to modernity. By spring, fast-growing Traverse City added a layer of sophistication by building wood plank sidewalks throughout its downtown and separating its citizens from the mud. The *Herald* wrote: "The moral effect of this sidewalk will be equal, at least, to one year's preaching, for cleanliness is allied to godliness."[195]

Closer to the battle lines, General George McClellan spent the early winter near Washington, D.C. molding the Army of the Potomac into an impressive fighting force. This was no longer an army of 90-day soldiers, but instead consisted of two and three-year volunteers in regiments representing dozens of states, preparing to fight it for as long as it took to suppress the rebellion. The army would remain in training along the banks of the Potomac until the General judged they were ready for battle. The Grand Traverse volunteers who left in the fall of 1861 to join the Chicago Light Artillery were among the 100,000 plus soldiers in the Army of the Potomac, and their regiment had already incurred General McClellan's wrath over an incident involving stolen horses. In a letter from Camp California, Virginia, dated February 7, 1862, former Northport schoolteacher and current artillerist E.J. Brooks explained the volunteers' situation, writing: "Knowing that you, in common with all the Friends at home, are deeply interested in the welfare of the Traverse Boys now in the Grand Army, I commence to-night…writing for the columns of the *Herald,* informing all of the past and present situation of the little bands of twenty…who left the Bay in August and Sept., last, to join Busteed's Battery C, Chicago Light Artillery.

"After encountering the usual number of difficulties, the first of October found the Company numbering one hundred and twenty-eight men…uniformed according to law, and ready to march. Never did a company feel more the strength inherent in them than did the Busteed Boys; and a better company of men never went forth to defend their country's flag then ours, which left Chicago by way of the Pittsburgh, Fort Wayne and Chicago Railroad, on the eve of the first day of October, bound for Washington, where we arrived the morning of the 4th and…encamped at…the Artillery reserve and Camp of Instruction…

"The 2nd of November…we were placed under marching orders…The Battery was sent to the Arsenal the same day for ammunition, all highly elated at the prospect of soon treading the sacred soil. But, alas, for human calculation; on our return we were met by Capt. Smith of the N.Y. Parrott Battery, with an order from Gen. Barry, for the immediate delivery of all government arms and property, in our possession, to the said Captain Smith. In the afternoon of the same day, Gen. Barry, in person, delivered to us the orders of General McClellan, which were, that the company he declared were without competent officers, and the men, unless they chose within thirty-six hours some regiment or company of artillery that they preferred to join, should be transferred to the regular Artillery. All but fourteen men…decided to go into Col. Bailey's First N.Y. Artillery Regiment; and then…we packed knapsacks, broke up camp, and joined the said regiment…November 9, we were permanently assigned to companies; forty-six with Lieut. Rogers…the remaining sixty-five, nearly all hailing from Mich., with S. A. McClelland as Lieut., now form the most efficient, manly, best drilled section – having the center in Captain Frank's Battery G, the star company of 14 in the regiment."

The mystery of why the Busteed's Boys had been abruptly disbanded came to light when Brooks wrote: "I have learned by letters to the boys that many false statements are in circulation at home, regarding the unfortunate cause of our dismemberment; and herewith I give you the truth. About October 12, a Government horse was missed from the picket rope, and again another about the 24th of the same month. Words spoken by Lieut. Cudney and Sergeant Baker caused them to be suspected by Captain Busteed; one horse was found where it had been left by them for sale, and proof found that they had sold the other and received eighty dollars for it. Busteed immediately preferred charges against them, stating that he had good cause to believe Lieut. Parker had received part of the purchase price from the sale of the first horse; Cudney and Baker were arrested, and Parker applied for a Court of Inquiry. About the same time, some of Busteed's defalcations were discovered, and that, with his physical disability, caused him to be deposed and his resignation quickly following, we were thus then left without any senior officers and no course remained, only to give us new officers, or transfer us; and the latter course was adopted. Cudney, after acknowledging all to myself and others, left Washington late in Nov. and has not been seen since. At a court of inquiry, held last month, Lieut. Parker had his trial and was acquitted, no evidence being adduced against him, and the fact being established that the only cause for the charge was Busteed's hatred, caused by Parker's unsparing reproof of his dishonesty. Baker, at his trial, acknowledged his theft, and claimed Cudney as his only auxiliary. His sentence has not yet been made public. No other member of the company have been arrested, imprisoned, or even suspected."

Brooks, who would rise through the ranks as an artillerist during the war, wrote of his Northport friend and current battery commander: "Lieut. McClelland, who took a more prominent part in company affairs than any other person, is deserving in all commendation for his untiring effort in recruiting, and his constant labors after our dismemberment was ordered, to procure a reconsideration and rescinding of the order…the boys bought and presented a very fine sword to him, as a slight mark of their appreciation, and I believe I speak the sentiments of all the men, when I say that his actions, so far as the old company were concerned, were…for the good of all."

In his letter, Brooks shed light on a problem that plagued Union artillery through the war – bringing their heavy cannon to bear in rough southern countryside. He continued: "The 7th of December we broke up camp, at the regimental head-quarters, crossed long bridge and tread, for the first time, the sacred soil of Old Dominion. We are…two and a half miles from Alexandria…Here we shall probably stay for some time, the state of the roads precluding all possibility of movement of Artillery."

Discouraged by events during his short time in the Army of the Potomac, Brooks concluded: "As for our present situation, though it is not what we hoped for when we entered the service; yet, our hearts are with our country's cause, her star spangled banner is as dear to us as ever. We are engaged in the work and our lives, if need be, are a ready sacrifice to be offered for the stability of our good old institutions, the loved constitution of our country, and the blood bought liberties of the Father land, the glorious old Union; and if we ever meet the enemy, be sure…that foremost among them, the sons of Michigan, looking back to the loved Northern homes with hearts full of love, will walk truly, strike manfully for the dear ones there, for liberty, for God, and for their country.[196] The reputation of the Grand Traverse volunteers had been soiled by association with the incident of horse theft, but the hard start was soon forgotten as the artillerists proved themselves in the heat of the summer's battles.

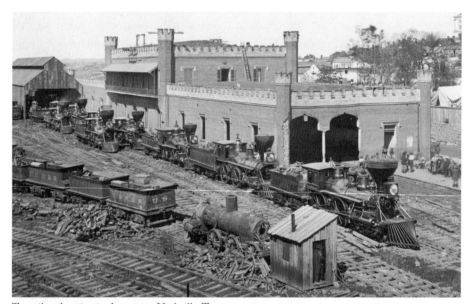

The railroad station in downtown Nashville, Tennessee. *Library of Congress*

On the western front, Union forces attacked Confederate Fort Donelson on the Cumberland River in Tennessee. Possession of the fort was the key to military success in the Border States, where citizens remained terribly split in their loyalties. For the Rebels, control of the nearby manufacturing city of Nashville depended on holding Fort Donelson. For three days, Federal gunboats shelled the outpost while a Union army of 20,000 men sealed off the Rebel garrison. On February 16, 1862, the Confederate commander of the fort sent a message to his Union counterpart asking to discuss terms of a possible surrender. A previously unknown general, Ulysses S. Grant, replied that "No terms except an unconditional and immediate surrender can be accepted." The next day, 15,000 Confederate soldiers laid down their arms, and throughout the North, the victorious general was hailed as "Unconditional Surrender" Grant.

The Union needed a warrior general to cheer in victory - a bright spot in the dark business of civil war. The *Herald* wrote: "A special dispatch, Washington 19th, says Gen. Ulysses S. Grant, the hero of Fort Donelson, has been unanimously confirmed as a Major-General by the Senate, an honor conferred in testimony of his gallant conduct in battle.[197] Supporting Grant during the Donelson campaign was fellow General William Tecumseh Sherman. By 1864, the two friends would command the two Union armies that won the war – armies that included most of the fighting men from Grand Traverse.

Due in a large part to the success of General Grant's initiatives, in 1862 it appeared the western half of the Confederacy was near collapse. In Grant, the Union Army possessed a West Point trained leader who was ready to fight, and true to form, he continued his relentless push through Tennessee as the weather warmed. The strategic Mississippi River town of Memphis prepared for a Yankee invasion. A *Grand Traverse Herald* article quoted a Tennessee paper, writing: "No troops at Memphis. Many persons were leaving the city. Cotton, molasses, sugar and other articles of merchandise are being shipped down the river. The policy of burning the city was being discussed. Speeches were made every night, and all means were used to check the increasing demoralization and excite a war spirit."[198]

Before the war, there was little mixing of the peoples of the North and South, especially the working classes. Now, thrown together in combat, distinctions between the two versions of America stood out. In an article titled 'What Slavery Does" the *Grand Traverse Herald* wrote: "Out of sixty-eight Confederate prisoners, taken…in Jackson county, Missouri, only fourteen could write their names…The large portion of prisoners from Fort Donelson, who cannot read, is notorious. This is one of the saddest fruits of slavery…A free and popular government cannot prosper with an uneducated people, and the tendency in slavery is to enshroud them in ignorance."[199]

Soon after the capture of Fort Donelson, Nashville fell into Union hands. Three influential, pro-Rebel citizens of Nashville were arrested for treason under orders from Tennessee Senator Andrew Johnson when they refused to pledge allegiance to the Union. Johnson was the only seated U.S. Senator from a southern state to remain loyal to the Federal government and now served as military governor of his home state, where the Union was riding a wave of victories. Johnson had the three prisoners spirited out of Tennessee to stop them from stirring up anti-Union sentiment in Nashville. The three Tennessee prisoners

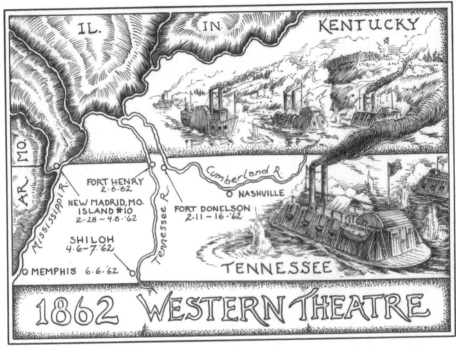

IL.   IN.   KENTUCKY

AR.   MO.

FORT HENRY
2.6.'62

NEW MADRID, MO.
ISLAND #10
2.28 ~ 4.8 · '62

Cumberland R.

NASHVILLE

FORT DONELSON
2.11 ~ 16 · '62

SHILOH
4.6~7.'62

MEMPHIS 6.6.'62

Mississippi R.

Tennessee R.

TENNESSEE

1862 WESTERN THEATRE

Tom Woodruff

wound up behind bars in Mackinac Island's Fort Mackinac, 75 miles north of Grand Traverse.

In April 1862, a company called the Stanton Guard was organized to watch over the three Tennessee men, who were in essence political prisoners. The 50 members of the Guard, recruited in Detroit, arrived at Mackinac Island aboard the propeller *Illinois* soon after the winter's ice cleared from the Straits. The Rebels they guarded served easy time, especially in light of the horrible treatment prisoners of war on both sides experienced later in the Civil War. The three captives moved freely about the fort and made escorted trips around town. Despite their liberal treatment, two of the Tennessee prisoners soon grew tired of their confinement. They signed an oath of allegiance to the Union and were allowed to travel back home. The third was shipped to a conventional prison on Johnson Island in Lake Erie, where he too was later parolled. With no prisoners to watch, the Stanton Guard was disbanded in September only six months after being formed, and Northern Michigan's sidebar to the Civil War ended.[200]

Throughout the spring, the northern press hailed General Grant as a hero for his victories in the western theatre of the war. Meanwhile, outside the nation's capital, General George McClellan continued to drill his stationary army along the banks of the Potomac River. In response to increasing pressure to engage the enemy, McClellan began to ship his 120,000 man Army of the Potomac and their great mass of equipment down the Chesapeake Bay to Yorktown beginning the first phase of the Peninsula Campaign. Here General McClellan penned an open letter to his men, saying: "Soldiers of the Army of the Potomac: For a long time I have kept you inactive, but not without a purpose. You were to be disciplined, armed and instructed. The formidable artillery you now have, had to be created. Other armies were to move and accomplish certain results.

"I have held you back that you might give the deathblow to the rebellion that has distracted this once happy country. The patience you have shown and the confidence in your General are worth a dozen victories. The preliminary results are now accomplished...The Army of the Potomac is now a real army, magnificent in material, admirable in discipline, and excellently equipped and armed...The moment for action has arrived, and I know I can trust you to save the country...It shall be my care – it has ever been – to gain success with the least possible loss, but I know, if it is necessary, you will willingly follow me to your graves for our righteous cause."[201]

McClellan proved his ability to organize a great army, which was now fitted with the best the North had to offer, and drilled to precision. After distributing the letter to his troops, he began to move up the Virginia peninsula toward the Confederate capitol of Richmond. Having committed the great Army of the Potomac to action, the nation braced for carnage along the Atlantic seaboard. People in the North believed the culminating battle they had hoped for was at hand. However, it took McClellan a month to organize an attack on Yorktown – a harbor town only miles from where the army had landed. As quick and decisive as the action had been under Grant in Tennessee, it was conversely slow and ponderous under McClellan in Virginia. With the temperature rising, so did the question - When would McClellan use his creation to crush the Confederates? By the time the general did attack, the Rebel army had withdrawn from their Yorktown trenches, leaving behind rows of black painted logs, the counterfeit artillery batteries that had kept McClellan at bay for so long. The northern press berated the commander for cowering before the "Quaker Guns." For McClellan, caution was the operative word, and the phrase "least possible loss" he used in his letter to the Army of the Potomac proved to be the one he took most seriously. He repeatedly overestimated the size of Confederate forces he faced and justified his hesitation on the lack of reinforcements.

Quaker guns held the Army of the Potomac at bay in the spring of 1862. *Library of Congress*

While General McClellan and his Army of the Potomac laid siege to York-town, Grant's Army of the West chased Confederates south across Tennessee. As Union troops rested and prepared to attack the nearby railroad town of Corinth, Mississippi, the Rebels surprised them in a charge near the log church called Shiloh. General Grant described the scene in his memoirs, writing: "The Confederate assaults were made with such a disregard of losses on their own side that our line of tents soon fell into their hands. The ground on which the battle was fought was undulating, heavily timbered with scattered clearings, the woods giving some protection to the troops on both sides. There was also considerable underbrush. A number of attempts were made by the enemy to turn our right flank, where Sherman was posted, but every effort was repulsed with heavy loss. But the front attack was kept up so vigorously that, to prevent these attempts to get on our flanks, the National troops were compelled, several times, to take positions to the rear nearer Pittsburg landing. When the firing ceased at night, the National line was all of a mile in rear of the position it had occupied in the morning."[202]

The casualties inflicted on both sides during the April 6 fighting at Shiloh were unprecedented in American history. Although the Confederate Army had won the field, they lost their leader, General Albert Sidney Johnston, who was struck in the leg by a Federal minie ball and bled to death in the saddle. Grant continued with a gritty description of the aftermath of the day's battle, writing: "During the night rain fell in torrents and our troops were exposed to the storm without shelter. I made my headquarters under a tree a few hundred yards back from the riverbank...Sometime after midnight, growing restive under the storm...I moved back to the log-house under the bank. This had been taken as a hospital, and all night wounded men were being brought in, their wounds dressed, a leg or an arm amputated as the case might require, and everything done to save life and alleviate suffering. The sight was more unendurable than encountering the enemy's fire, and I returned to my tree in the rain."[203]

Union reinforcements arrived through the night aboard steamships at Pittsburg Landing on the Tennessee River. At dawn on April 7, Grant's forces were 25,000 stronger than the day before. The swollen Union Army charged across lost ground and drove the Rebels south toward the Mississippi border. For a second day the two armies fought with "disregard of losses." Today the Union could claim victory, but nothing had been settled at Shiloh.

Michigan regiments whose ranks included Grand Traverse soldiers suffered in the bloodiest battle of the war to date. The *Grand Traverse Herald* reported: "The 12th, 13th, and 15th Michigan Regiments were in the battle at Pittsburgh Landing. The 15th went into the fight with 800 men, and came out with only 400. The 12th and 13th were badly cut up."[204] Northport's John Leikman, a corporal in company C of the 15th Michigan Infantry, lay among the wounded. His friends and fellow Company C volunteers, Walter Palmer of Suttons Bay and Robert Moore of Northport, had been killed in action. Nearly a quarter of the 100,000 soldiers engaged at Shiloh were casualties. The list of dead heroes from Grand Traverse was growing.

There was little celebration on either side following the bloodbath at Shiloh. The 23,000 American casualties suffered during the fight outnumbered those of the Revolutionary War, the War of 1812, and the Mexican-American War combined. The size of the armies engaged, and the will to fight and die displayed by both armies, killed all hope that the war might soon end. Grant shared the bitter insight he gained in the fight, writing: "Up to the battle of Shiloh I, as well as thousands of other citizens, believed that the rebellion against the Government would collapse suddenly and soon, if a decisive victory could be gained over any of its armies. Donelson and Henry were such victories. An army of more than 21,000 men was captured or destroyed. The Tennessee and Cumberland rivers, from their mouths to the head of navigation, were secured. But when Confederate armies were collected which not only attempted to hold a line farther south…but assumed the offensive and made such a gallant effort to regain what had been lost, then, indeed, I gave up all idea of saving the Union except by complete conquest."[205]

In addition to the battlefield deaths, the soldiers' common enemy - disease – continued to kill nearly twice as many men as the exchange of fire. The *Grand Traverse Herald* wrote: "There are seven thousand sick soldiers in Nashville, two thousand of these are from the rebel army, taken prisoners at Donelson, Bowling Green and Nashville."[206] The North had secured through combat two significant Border States, but the price had been unexpectedly dear. A cloud of gloom hung over the nation as its citizens realized there would be no quick end to the war.

In the same week that 23,000 American soldiers fell at Shiloh, the citizens of Northport fought their own Civil War battle. On Election Day, as people lined up to cast their vote at the schoolhouse, pushing and name-calling broke into fistfights that pitted Democrats against Republicans. Emotions had been running high in the town now that many families had a son serving in the Union Army. Reverend Smith suspected that liquor had fueled the altercations, writing: "The Democrats seemed determined to bully down the Republicans – for a while the whole mass was in a riot."[207] After the brawl, tempers cooled, and Smith worked in his role as town doctor to patch up the injured.

Republican candidates won almost all the contests in the Grand Traverse elections that day. The partisan *Herald* proclaimed "Grand Traverse county is sound to the core." The glaring exception was Leelanau Township, anchored by Northport. The *Herald* reported: "The entire Democratic ticket elected by a slightly increased majority over last year. Philo Beers is elected Supervisor over Geo. N. Smith, by 66 majority. Last year his majority was 56…The Indians voted the Democratic ticket. There is a Republican majority of the white population of that town."[208]

The *Herald's* editor Bates, riled at Democratic charges that he mishandled funds in his position as Grand Traverse County Treasurer, and spurred on by overwhelming Republican victories at the polls, lashed out against the last seat of opposition in Grand Traverse. He wrote: "There is, at Northport, a little clique…of whiskey politicians of the Bogus-Democracy stripe, composed of men who have grown fat upon the drippings of unclean things under former Democratic Administrations. Having nothing to do, they are restless, dissatisfied, meddlesome, and, when under the influence of an extra head of steam, malignant and devilish."[209] What little tolerance Bates had for the Democrats decreased as lives lost in the Civil War mounted. In the year since the war had commenced in Charleston Harbor, the *Herald* had changed as a paper, and now almost all news stories focused on the war. Space for local stories was being squeezed by the weight of reports coming from the battlefields.

The Northport vote must have been humiliating for Smith, having again been badly beaten in his home town. In the end, it was the united Indian support for Democrats that cost Smith the race. The election raised questions about the Congregational minister's influence with the Indians, for if Smith was unable to bring the Natives to his side in politics, was he really reaching their souls? Grand Traverse Indians looked at the election differently. They had witnessed the power of the united Indian vote in Emmet County - where Natives won numerous elected positions - and that vote had been unanimously Democratic. The Little Traverse Bands had gained a rare power base in government, and now their Leelanau brethren followed suit. The voter solidarity showed there was still some hope among northern Lake Michigan Indians of building a local community with the political muscle to maintain their hard-pressed culture. In the midst of Civil War, however, the political parties were being defined solely by their stand on slavery and the Union, and many whites saw the Indian's affiliation with the Democrats as unpatriotic. In Grand Traverse, as in every corner of the nation, peace was hard to find.

Reports from the western front made it appear that part of the South might soon collapse. A flotilla of Union gunboats steamed up the Mississippi River and captured New Orleans, the largest city in the Confederacy. Reverend Smith wrote: "*Alleghany* came…I went to her, got a Free Press of Day before yesterday with Washington news of 29 April – this is pretty good. New Orleans has lately been taken by Govt forces."[210] The next week Memphis fell to Federal troops and in the battle the Confederate Navy on the Mississippi River was all but destroyed. In quick succession, the South had lost a key city on each end of its vital river highway. However, rather than give up, the battered Confederates formed new battle lines and held on.

The superiority of the Union Navy, which began to shutter Confederate ports along the Atlantic coast in a tight blockade, and now dominated much of the Mississippi River, was a testament to the North's ability to mobilize for the war. The *Herald* wrote: "On the 4th of March, 1861, when President Lincoln was inaugurated, the government vessels available for service were only four in number, carrying 25 guns. Our Navy now consists of 264 vessels of all sizes, carrying 2,157 guns…The number of seamen now employed is 22,000."[211]

As the spring military campaigns progressed, the Union Congress worked to change the old national order for good. The worst had already happened – a Civil War had ripped the nation asunder. Too much blood had now been shed to ever go back. To start, legislators passed a bill that abolished slavery in the District of Columbia, which only a dozen years before hosted the largest slave market on earth. The *Herald's* editor Bates rejoiced over the news, writing: "Thank God! the Slave Power has been crushed in the District of Columbia, and the National Capitol is free!" The waters had been tested and a national law of abolition, though limited, was now on the books. The Federal government had inched closer to its founding declaration that "all men are created equal."

After abolishing slavery in the Capital, Congress looked to the west to further define its concept of the new United States through legislation. The *Herald* wrote: "The bill prohibiting slavery in the Territories of the United States...reads as follows: "To the end that Freedom may be and remain forever the fundamental law of the land...there shall be neither slavery nor involuntary servitude in any of the Territories of the United States." Reflecting on the legislative process, Bates reviewed the cost of the country's original failure to act against slavery. He said: "Had this act been passed in 1784 - when Mr. Jefferson proposed one essentially the same – the fratricidal war which we are now involved would never have existed."[212] Several weeks later, the House passed a law "permitting our armies to subsist off the rebels along the route of their march." Union soldiers were now encouraged to forage for supplies during advances through Rebel territory, cutting miles from the cumbersome wagon trains that usually trailed the armies. The Federal government had taken off the kid gloves and brought modern warfare to the divided nation.

Not finished with their new agenda for the nation, Congress passed the long-debated Homestead Act, which President Lincoln promptly signed into law. The *Herald* wrote: "The Republican party has been true to its pledges...and the passage of this bill will infuse joy and hope into the hearts of thousands of poor but industrious and worthy families. Every man can now have a *home*."[213] The Homestead Act served as the catalyst that sparked a land rush to the last pockets of wilderness on the western Great Lakes, including the north coast of Lake Michigan, where good acreage was still available, and now free. The requirements of the Act were simple - file a claim, live on and improve the property, and it was yours in five years. All that was needed to become a landowner was labor. The political message contained in the bill was clear. The North valued labor, the South enslaved it. Soldiers who left Homestead Act farms for Civil War battlefields knew exactly what they were fighting for.

Even before the Homestead Act became law, would-be farmers poured into Grand Traverse to buy the best parcels. In June 1862, the *Herald* noted: "There were sold in the Traverse City Land Office, during the last month, 4,400 acres of land – the most of which is in Grand Traverse County. It was purchased, mainly, in tracts of 80 and 160 acres, by those who intend to settle upon and improve it immediately."[214] The Erie Canal carried the first wave of Euro-American pioneers into the western Great Lakes, where they inhabited a thin line between ancient forests and fresh water. In the ensuing years, good ports grew into prosperous towns and the woods began to fall to the ax and saw. Fleets of schooners and modern, propeller-driven ships carried passengers and cargo around the lakes with relative ease. The stage was set for a new era. By the summer of 1862, the rooflines of homesteads and stump-filled fields radiated away from the lakeshore and deeper into the surrounding forest. The Homestead Act now shifted the land rush in Grand Traverse into high gear, and the frontier days on the Great Lakes were rapidly coming to an end.

The Union Army also helped steer the United States in a new direction. General David Hunter, while fighting along the coast of South Carolina, brought fundamental change to the ranks when he commissioned the First Regiment of South Carolina Volunteers, comprised of recruits from the area's recently freed slaves. The *Herald* reported: "Gen Hunter finds all the white men in South Carolina rebels of the very worst description. He finds all colored men loyal and true to the Government. The only class of people who are attached to the Union and Constitution are slaves. He invites them to help defend the National flag. The Secretary of War has given his consent to Gen Hunter to receive the services of all loyal men in South Carolina, irrespective of color, who are willing to work or fight for the Union."[215] Hunter, acting on his own, had allowed slaves to enlist, demonstrating that in this time of great turmoil, an individual act could push the national agenda forward. When, after wavering, the U.S. Government backed General Hunter's move, the Union Army not only took its first step toward racial integration, but also boosted its prospects for victory in the Civil War. The escalating conflict had opened the door to change faster than anyone expected. White soldiers soon learned that former slaves shot and caught bullets as well as any men. South Carolina planters lived their worst nightmare as their human property lined up to fight against them.

In another personal initiative, the author of *Uncle Tom's Cabin*, Harriet Beecher Stowe, traveled to Washington to urge President Lincoln to act to abolish slavery. Upon meeting the author, the President reportedly said: "So you're the little lady who wrote the book that started this great war." A short time after Stowe's visit, Lincoln composed the first drafts of the Emancipation Proclamation, which he discussed in secret with his cabinet during a July 1862 meeting. Following their advice, Lincoln tabled the Proclamation and waited for the right moment - a Union Army victory - to present the momentous document to the Northern public in a positive light. As a political move, the Emancipation Proclamation would certainly be controversial, but Lincoln believed it would lift the Union's position in the Civil War to a new and higher moral ground and lend a sense of purpose to the terrible carnage.

While the Union moved forward with a new national agenda, General McClellan continued to avoid battle with the Confederate Army despite considerable prodding from the President. With Rebels on the western front battered, Lincoln argued that decisive action against Richmond might well end the war for good. Instead, McClellan embraced caution and gave the Army of the Potomac little opportunity to fight. The General's failure to use the army turned many in the North against him, and whispers of his sympathy for the patrician South were now spoken aloud. After praising the Union victories at New Orleans and Memphis, the *Grand Traverse Herald* derisively reported: "All is quiet before Richmond, Gen. McClellan having made no further demonstration."[216]

By the end of May, however, Confederates in Virginia were backed up against their capital, with the Army of the Potomac unscathed. Union momentum, though slow, seemed irresistible. Perhaps General McClellan had a plan that would work after all. The Confederate commander in Virginia, General Joseph E. Johnston, knew Richmond could not survive a prolonged siege. Rather than succumbing to McClellan's glacial advance, Johnston attacked Union forces on May 31. For three days at a battle called Fair Oaks, the two opposing American armies fought the first major engagement of the Peninsula Campaign.

Fair Oaks, also known as Seven Pines, was the first chance for the 20 Grand Traverse men who had been tainted by association with Busteed's disgraced Chicago Light Artillery to prove their worth on the battlefield. Lt. Sam McClelland of Northport, now the commander of a 1st New York Artillery battery manned by the Grand Traverse volunteers, wrote: "We have just fought, and won, a hard contested battle...None killed and wounded in our battery. The Grand Traverse Boys are all safe that are with me. We have been standing by our

Tom Woodruff

guns all night, expecting an attack from some other quarter, but we learn from a reconnaissance made by our cavalry this morning, that they have fallen back and formed another line which they are preparing to defend. We are confident of success whenever we advance. I would like to give you a more detailed account of the battle, if I had convenience to do so, but I have not; I am writing this on part of my gun carriage, with a borrowed pen and paper, and I hear firing on our right, which is probably our skirmishers, but we shall have to prepare for any emergency; you will therefore excuse anything more at this time." McClelland concluded: "Every Grand Traverse Boy, without exception, stood up manfully at his post without flinching, throughout the whole battle."[217]

Of the 30,000 soldiers engaged at Fair Oaks, nearly half were killed, wounded or missing – there was no victor. Although all of Lt. McClelland's s men had been lucky enough to avoid injury in their first engagement, at least one Grand Traverse family lost a husband and father that day in Virginia. Reverend Smith later wrote: "Mrs Wadsworth came with…Children. She is sick - her husband killed at Battle of Fair Oaks."[218] Among the seriously wounded was Confederate General Johnston, whose command fell to West Point graduate Robert E. Lee.

Although Lt. Samuel McClelland, like most soldiers in the Army of the Potomac, "was confident of success whenever we advance," General McClellan was leery of any more action. His army had driven the Confederates back to Richmond, and they were now close enough to hear church bells ringing in the Rebel capital, but the General's will to fight was gone. He ordered the troops to dig in and called for reinforcements, though he had at his command twice the number of soldiers he faced. The Army of the Potomac languished outside Richmond for nearly a month while General Lee prepared for an attack.

Late in June, Governors of the Northern states sent a letter to President Lincoln requesting permission to raise another 300,000, three-year troops for the Union Army. The Governors designed the move to take some of the heat off Lincoln for what would be an unprecedented call to arms. On July 1, the President responded to the Governors' request as planned, bringing about a dramatic escalation of the Civil War. The action recognized the desperation of the struggle and affirmed that the end of the fighting was a long way off. In spite of the rising costs, all remaining states in the fractured United States again committed to pursue the war to its conclusion. One of the first volunteers to fill Lincoln's quota was the right-hand man at the *Grand Traverse Herald*. Editor Bates wrote: "John Lewis Patrick, who has been in our employ as an apprentice for two years past – a pure and noble-hearted youth – has left us and gone to the war. We loved that boy, and could not let him go without a severe heart-pang. But he was eager to respond to the urgent call of his country, and we sent him out with a blessing. God shield him in the day of battle, and nerve his arm to strike terrible blows for freedom."[219]

July 1, 1862 was a landmark day in American history in numerous other ways. President Lincoln signed the Pacific Railway Act, which used land grants to finance the laying of tracks across America. The new rails would run from Nebraska to California and connect to the vast network of railroads serving Chicago. The Railway Act would have pleased the late Illinois Senator Stephen Douglas, who introduced the 1854 Kansas-Nebraska Act to achieve exactly this result. In a statement of confidence amidst the growing fury of the Civil War, the Union government committed to a vast, nation-building project for the future. To add to the drama of the day, the national debt reached a half a billion dollars on July 1 - an all-time high. War expenses were decimating the Treasury, and the record public debt had only started its rise. To make matters worse, all the expenses to date had yielded little progress in the course of the war. A half year of battles on the eastern and western fronts left the opposing armies in a stalemate. The 100,000 casualties and the fortunes spent on death and destruction seemed in vain. Many now predicted that in addition to the bloody military

A spotter in a hot air balloon relays information on troop movements and the effect of artillery fire during the Battle of Fair Oaks, 1862. *Library of Congress*

cost, the conflict would soon bankrupt the country. On this day in Virginia alone, the armies of the divided nation clashed at Malvern Hill, and another 8,500 Americans fell in battle.

William Sykes, the former Grand Traverse Sheriff now serving in Lt. Mc-Clelland's 1st New York Artillery battery, described the action at Malvern Hill in a letter to W.E. Powers of Northport.[220] W.E. was the father of Albert Powers, who fought beside Sykes during the battle. The sheriff turned soldier began his missive by praising Northport, writing: "It is a long time since I heard from you till to-day. Your son has just read a letter, which has put me once more in the humor of writing, in hopes of hearing once more from that Elysian, Northport. I mean what I say, for it [Northport] far exceeds anything I have seen, since I left, in health and beauty; and I often think how you are luxuriating on vegetables, a thing we seldom get here. Our living is mostly dry salt provisions, except for what we buy of the sutlers at exorbitant prices. Onions cost five cents apiece, and other things in proportion."

"We have been resting here some two weeks, after about two weeks hard fighting. We left our position before Richmond, and are now some thirty miles from there. It can hardly be called a retreat; it was a flank movement, in order to save the army – as we could not get sufficient supplies for the army, and could not conveniently be reinforced. We are now being reinforced, and there will be a forward movement sometime. For my part, I am in no particular hurry until it gets cooler. I have just dined on ham and fruit pudding, and am too lazy to write much now, but I must try and tell you something about the two days' fight we had before we reached here.

"There were probably more killed here than at any previous battle. Our force was small compared to that of the enemy; but still we drove the rebels from the field at every attempt they made to dislodge us. Tuesday, the 1st day of July, I shall never forget. We fought the rebels almost hand to hand for over three hours. They marched up in full brigades – one after the other – upon our small band, but we never gave one inch of ground. Sometimes they were not more than eight or ten rods from us. We mowed them down by the thousands with cannister; the destruction was terrible; they seemed determined to take our battery, but could not. At 10 o'clock p.m. there was not a rebel to be seen; they actually piled up their dead as a breastwork before our battery: the balls flew around our heads like raindrops. Why we were not killed God only knows; we had only one killed, and seven wounded in our company. Eight of our horses were wounded. Your son was a driver on my gun, and I called him to act as number 4 – I being shorthanded. He performed his duties with most admirable coolness, he could not be beat in the army. I was twice complimented by our Colonel during the action, for the coolness and precision with which I handled my gun."

Lt. Samuel McClelland, the commander of the artillery battery Sykes and Powers brought to bear on Confederates at Malvern Hill, also described the fight, writing: "About 5 o'clock, after throwing shell all day at long range, the enemy commenced to drive in our pickets, and a brisk musketry fire commenced, with one battery of artillery. It continued about half an hour, when Gen Meagher, whose brigade lay immediately in and protecting our front, was ordered to the scene of action, and our battery was immediately ordered to follow – which we did as fast as the horses can run, and as we passed the brigades of our division

Guns of the 1st New York Light Artillery stand ready for battle on the Peninsula, June 1862.
Library of Congress

who were going on the double quick, they gave us three hearty cheers. On arriving on the field of battle, we…immediately opened fire amid a perfect storm of grape and cannister and musket balls, which flew around our heads thick and fast, and it was a mystery to all - after we came out at the close of the battle – how any of us lived ten minutes after we entered it, but our men, (Michigan men in particular) fought like heroes and exhibited a degree of coolness and bravery that exceeded by far the anticipation of their most intimate friends…

"All Grand Traverse boys, by their conduct in the battle of Malvern Hill, on the 1st of July, established their reputation here of brave and worthy soldiers. Our Captain says he never saw better. The battle ended about nine o'clock P.M. when the enemy withdrew, and left us masters of the field." Lt. McClelland failed to mention he had been wounded twice in the battle but instead continued with his story. "We then took about three hours sleep, when an order came, ordering us to be ready to march in two hours. The Captain then packed all the munitions that remained in the battery…and started at the appointed time. After marching about three miles, an aide overtook us, and said the rear was left unprotected by artillery…Our Captain ordered a left about, and moved at a double quick to the rear, where we arrived in time…the rebels seemed rather shy, since the severe lessons taught them, on the march from Fair Oaks.

"As we took our position to guard the rear, we could see their skirmishers… examining our rear guard to see what chance there was of taking us to Richmond [prison], but thanks to our own watchful commander, who disposed of his forces to such advantage that they appeared to be three or four times their actual strength, which effectually held the enemy at bay. This was so well carried out, that the enemy did not come within range of our guns. The guns were moved so rapidly from place to place, appearing at different points in such quick succession, supported by the cavalry, that it must have appeared as a heavy force, at least. These maneuvers were so effectual, that the whole army was conducted to its present position from Malvern Hill, without an attack. We could see the enemy hovering around our rear, all day. We had two guns placed in each opening as the enemy came up, which would lead them to believe we had a large force of artillery there, which completely baffled them. The army all arrived here safe, and have been placed in such a position that our General thinks we can defeat any number of troops they are able to bring against us.

"President Lincoln was here last night, and made an inspection of the army. The soldiers all express great confidence in an ultimate success and are all eager for the time to come when they can march upon Richmond and take it, as they then expect to go home. In conclusion I ask this favor, I wish you would tell all the friends of those that are with me that have friends in Grand Traverse, that their friends are all well, and are heroes every one of them. [221]

Despite being beaten in battle at Malvern Hill, suffering casualties on a two to one basis, Confederate General Lee had achieved a strategic victory by keeping the Union Army away from of Richmond. Though in command of a superior force, General McClellan failed to take any initiative. President Lincoln and many in the Union Army despaired at his inaction. McClellan eventually withdrew the Army of the Potomac back to Washington, and another two years passed before the Union would again bring the fight this close to the Rebel capital. A long and lethal stretch of time would pass before the Grand Traverse soldiers in Lt. McClelland's artillery battery could "expect to go home," and for a number of the men it came too late.

One of the factors that made Civil War battles like Malvern Hill so deadly was a recent technical improvement to the inside of gun barrels that greatly increased the accuracy of the weapons. In previous wars, soldiers used smooth bore muskets, good to a range of about 100 yards. By 1862, most American infantry regiments carried weapons with rifled barrels, featuring an inner spiral groove running along their length. The groove caused passing bullets to spin, raising the accuracy of "rifles" to 400 yards. There was now four times the distance where a soldier in the trenches could accurately fire on an advancing enemy. Unfortunately for soldiers on the field, infantry tactics remained as they had been for a century. Generals were slow to react to the bloody consequences of attacking entrenched positions, as reflected by the unprecedented casualty figures that followed every engagement.

Another advance in lethal weaponry used by both American armies came in the form of cannister, which essentially turned artillery pieces into giant sawed-off shotguns. The cannister consisted of hundreds of iron balls packed into a thin-walled artillery casing and attached to a gun powder charge. When the balls were in short supply, nails, hinges, and other pieces of metal scrap that could tear through the enemy made do. When fired from cannon, the casing disintegrated, and the contents spread out in a lethal cloud, opening gaping holes in the charging lines where moments before there had been soldiers. The effectiveness of this weapon had nothing to do with accuracy but instead created a crude wall of metal that killed in wide swaths. At close range, multiple cannister were often loaded in one charge, making the wall all the more dense and deadly. Civil War artillerists told of the cloud of red mist that often rose above the battle lines when concentrated cannister fire was applied to charging soldiers. Cannister killed more men on both sides of the conflict than any other form of artillery shell used in the Civil War.

During the summer of 1862, the *Grand Traverse Herald* squeezed local stories in between the volume of news arriving from distant battlegrounds. In one, the paper attacked Philo Beers, the former keeper of the Grand Traverse Lighthouse, reminding readers that the region, like the nation, was at war with itself. The article said: "Philo Beers, of Northport, is the supervisor of Leelanau Township. He is a Democrat of the Hard-shell persuasion, and encourages all Republicans to enlist and Democrats to stay home. The law makes it his duty to return to the County Clerk, on or before the first day of June, a list of ALL men in his Township subject to military duty, and to certify that the list is *correct*, under penalty of one hundred dollars. He has two sons residing in that Township who are subject to military duty, *but he has omitted the names of both*, in his returns to the County Clerk, and they thereby escape all risk or chance of being drafted! Now we ask the good people of Leelanau Township if they are not heartily ashamed of their Supervisor?"[222] A story about another one of Northport's leading citizens identified Rev. George Smith as President of the Grand Traverse County Bible Society, an organization whose mission was to put a Bible in the

Fish shanties on the Carp River in Leland, with a sailing mackinaw boat at the dock and Lake Michigan in the background. *Leelanau Historical Society*

hand of every soldier leaving the region to fight in the Civil War. Distributing Bibles was old hat for Smith, a habit he began in his first missionary job in the Kalamazoo Valley of Michigan over a quarter century before.

In a rare, upbeat story from this war-torn year, Bates added a patriotic spin to his coverage of a well-attended boat launching on the Lake Michigan side of the Leelanau Peninsula. He wrote: "A singular circumstance occurred at the village of Leland on the 31st day of July last, which augurs well for our enterprising citizens Messrs. Cordes & Theis, who have had a tow-boat built at Milwaukee, by the name of *August Julius*, to ply on the waters of Carp Lake. She arrived at Leland on the 30th day of July, and had to be taken across a narrow neck of land to be put in Carp River. The next day, just as she was launched in Carp River, with the Stars and Stripes waving to the breeze, and while the spectators were yet cheering, a large Eagle came flying along the shores of Lake Michigan until directly opposite where the boat was launched from, when she turned and passed over the peoples heads and lengthwise over the boat, then whirled and went back towards Lake Michigan again, when she was directly over the American Flag, and but a few feet above it, she seemed to poise, and as it were to say to the inhabitants of Carp Lake and vicinity – "Success to the progress of improvement, and to the persevering proprietors of the *August Julius*, go on and prosper."

The week's *Herald* also published news of the presence of nearly 10,000 Confederate soldiers at the south end of Lake Michigan, prisoners-of-war in a camp run by the Union Army near Chicago. The paper said: "The whole number of rebel prisoners received at camp Douglas amounts to 9,472, of which 510 have died, 8,962 are who still in confinement." The Chicago area prison was built on land received from the estate of the late Senator Stephen Douglas, who died less than two months after the Civil War began. The Senator had given the property to the Union Army to use as a training base for soldiers. Instead, the 80-acre parcel now held Confederates captured during Grant's spring offensive through Kentucky and Tennessee. Disease, starvation, and lingering battlefield wounds had already killed over 500 of the Rebel prisoners, and Chicago's cold weather had yet to descend on the cramped barracks.

Local news that summer focused on the growing number of Grand Traverse volunteers. To date, Union recruiters had concentrated their efforts on the more populous areas of Michigan. Lincoln's massive new call for volunteers now forced them to scour more remote regions of the state, and they reached Grand Traverse in force a month after President's 300,000 soldier mandate. In an August article titled "Grand Traverse Company" the *Herald* wrote: "We understand that Lieut. Charles H. Holden, who has been enlisting volunteers for Captain Knapp's Company of "Lake Shore Tigers," has received a commission from Gov. Blair to raise a Company of Volunteers in this county. As Capt. Knapp's Company is doubtless full, Mr. Holden will probably transfer the 50 Grand Traverse Boys, which he already enlisted, to his own company; and with a little extra effort he will be enabled to fill up his Company with volunteers from Grand Traverse Bay. Should he succeed before the 1st of September, there will probably be no drafting here, as that would be our full quota."[223]

Editor Bates had his own plan to help meet the quota, suggesting that "those who are too old to enlist, or whose business is such that they cannot possibly leave it to go into the army, contribute liberally of their substance to support the families of those who can leave, and are willing to respond to the urgent call of their country...I will give two hundred dollars to that fund." The *Herald* also made note of nickname of the 26th Michigan Infantry – the Lake Shore Tigers – a regiment in which many Grand Traverse soldiers would fight and die during the next three years.

Recruiter Charles Holden was a successful Northport lawyer and politician – the right man to recruit a company from Grand Traverse. In 1858, Holden became the first Republican elected to a post in Grand Traverse County when he won the race for Prosecuting Attorney. His victory broke the Democrat's monopoly over local government and initiated the region's dramatic swing to the Republican Party in the ensuing war years. Now Holden took the lead in the fight to bring the governing concepts he introduced as a pioneering Republican to fruition through war. That is what the great divide in beliefs within the nation had come to – the time for talk was over.

Holden's method of enlisting neighbors to fight together in one company - standard procedure during the Civil War - demonstrated how any battle had the potential to decimate an individual American community. When a company of friends fighting shoulder to shoulder was hit with concentrated fire, a community could lose a good many of its best men in an instant. In this case, Holden's volunteers were not only from the same place, but of the same mind. The *Herald* noted: "Holden enlisted 60 volunteers in Grand Traverse...*fifty-nine* of whom were Republicans." One of Holden's recruits was 19 year-old Melville Palmer, who left his parent's farm in Suttons Bay to join the 26th Michigan Infantry. Four months earlier, his older brother Walter, a volunteer in the 15th Michigan, had been killed at the battle of Shiloh.

A *Herald* article put the scale of local commitment to the Union cause in perspective. It said: "Grand Traverse County polled 600 votes in the last General Election and has sent, in all, about 100 Volunteers to the war. When taken into consideration that our population is composed mostly of farmers, who are struggling against all the hardships and privations incident to clearing up new farms in the wilderness, it must be conceded that our infant county has sent forth her full quota to the war." As the Grand Traverse volunteers boarded a schooner in Traverse City, Perry Hannah "made an eloquent and patriotic speech," and Editor Bates exclaimed, "God bless them, and give them victory."

In its next edition, the *Herald* published a list of Grand Traverse volunteers who joined Holden's Company A of the Lakeshore Tigers. The Leelanau Peninsula, home to two-thirds of the region's population, sent the lion's share off to fight. William Voice, the son and namesake of the Northport lumber mill owner, was one of eight men who enlisted from Leelanau Township. Recruit Herman Dunklow and 15 others came from Centreville, a township that stretched from Leland on Lake Michigan east to Suttons Bay. Within the month, fate brought Voice and Dunklow together in one of the great stories of the Civil War.

In August 1862, Grand Traverse volunteers in the Lakeshore Tigers began to gather near the tip of the Leelanau Peninsula. It was no accident the soldiers would leave for the war from Northport, currently the busiest port on northern Lake Michigan. Reverend Smith made a special effort to spend time with volunteer William Voice Jr., a personal friend and member of the family through marriage. In 1861, Smith had risked his life to care for William Voice

Sr. during his bout with typhoid and in turn his son William Jr. helped the preacher with his garden this spring. Now the young soldier was about to leave Northport for the war.

The dog days of August passed while Reverend Smith and friends "practiced some pieces of Music to sing when the Volunteers leave. Mr Holden & Mr Voice were here for tea & staid with us." Smith's two guests would soon be chosen as the lieutenant and sergeant of Company A by their fellow soldiers. On August 27th, Smith wrote: "Volunteers arrived... last night with Mr Holden - part on *Olga*, part on foot. A box of Bibles from the County Society for the Volunteers came on *Olga*. I got them home noon." Soon after, the boat that would take the Grand Traverse re-

Lt. Charles Holden of the Lakeshore Tigers.
Grand Rapids Public Library

cruits off to their training camp arrived. The men of the 26th Michigan said goodbye to their loved ones, a few for the last time.

Smith witnessed the scene from the Northport docks as he pushed his way through the crowd, a box of bibles in his arms. The Reverend wrote: "*Mendota* came, Capt Knap on her. Mr Holden to be first Lieutenant. Boat agreed to wait awhile for them all to get in. I gave them their Bibles, in all 36, then addressed them briefly. Mr Holden replied - he did well...we sang Brave Boys Are They. After varied cheering, shaking of hands, bidding farewell &c., they went aboard and the Boat started. It was a solemn time. Lord preserve them...perhaps half will never return. Some have left large families, Mr Budd & Nash, others smaller families. One, James Lee, has been married but a short time, but our country is in danger & they have bravely gone to the rescue. O Lord, keep them." Temperance advocate Smith could not ignore another aspect of the soldiers' departure and the last lines of his diary entry said: "One vile thing was done. Rose & Store gave all liquor who would take it – I felt that was wicked." On September 1, two more Northport volunteers left the harbor town to join the Lakeshore Tigers.

TRAVERSE CITY.

THE GRAND TRAVERSE HERALD is the Official Paper for the organized Counties of Grand Traverse, Manistee, Manitou, Emmet, Cheboygan and Mackinac. The Tax Lists, and all Legal Advertisements for these counties, are published therein in pursuance of law.

Grand Traverse Volunteers.

We publish below a partial list of the volunteers from this County who went out with Mr. Holden last week.— We have been promised a complete list, which we shall publish, when received.

WHITEWATER.—P. D. Greenman, Francis Hopper, C. R. Tookey, Horace Phillips, John A. Brainard, Milton Stites, John Duncan, Henry Odell, Oscar Eaton, George Allen.

TRAVERSE.—Elias Langdon, jr., Thomas Bates, Giles Gibson, Asa V. Churchill, George Moody.

PENINSULA.—Gilbert Lacnor, John A. Thayer.

LEELANAU.—Wm. Voice, Mortimer Boyes, Henry Budd, George W. Bigelow, Charles H. Holden, William W. Nash, Henry Holcomb, Charles E. Lehman.

CENTREVILLE.—George H. Ramsdell, Joseph Warwick, Melville Palmer, Wm. Lawson, James Lee, Frederick Cook, Jacob Hans, Deidrick White, Geo. W. Miller, John Egler, James Adameson, L. Grant, H. Dunklow, Thomas McCreary, Charles E. Clark, George H. Mills.

Grand Traverse Herald, September 5, 1862.

Smith wrote: "*Evergreen City* came…G.W. Bigelow and Mortimer Boyes, Volunteers, left on her. Gave Mortimer a 50 cts. Bible."

Reverend Smith's guess that "perhaps half will never return" was not far from the truth. The frontiersman from Grand Traverse, who along with most of the Lakeshore Tigers possessed the skills of stealth and marksmanship associated with hunting, would soon be selected as skirmishers at the head of the Army of the Potomac - one of the most dangerous assignments a regiment could receive. Before the war ended, Confederate fire and the scourge of disease killed 16 of 41 men on the *Herald's* fall list of 26th Michigan Infantry volunteers - a staggering 40% mortality rate.

The Grand Traverse volunteers arrived at Camp Jackson in southern Michigan and began training. Back home, news reached Northport that sent a chill through the community that had just sent over 60 of its best men off to fight in the Union Army. Reverend Smith wrote: "*Kenosha* came…got a paper of the 2nd: terrible news from the war."[224] The Union had lost a second battle at Manassas – Bull Run, this time at the hands of General Robert E. Lee. The 22,000 casualties the two American armies suffered were five times as high as the first engagement. In the finale of the encore performance, the larger northern army again staggered back toward Washington in chaos. The price of invading the most populous Confederate state was on the rise, with the Union capital of Washington D.C. now at risk.

A *Grand Traverse Herald* article titled "Sad News" carried notice of the death of a well-known Traverse City soldier in the battle. It said: "The *Detroit Advertiser and Tribune* of the 12th, brings us the melancholy tidings of the death of our young friend Francis Z. Fowler, son of Hon. Curtis Fowler, Judge of Probate of this county. He was killed at the recent battle near Bull Run. He was a most estimable young man, and the news of his death will cast a gloom over this community. Curtis Fowler Jr., brother of the deceased, was wounded at the first battle of Bull Run, and on his discharge and return to his home, his brother entered the army, and has nobly fallen in defense of his country. He is the first Martyr from Grand Traverse county to this Slaveholder's Rebellion."[225]

The news got worse when word trickled into Grand Traverse about a massive Indian revolt in Minnesota, the most western of the Great Lakes States. Another war involving issues of race and equality was suddenly raging in the United States, this time along its northernmost boundaries. A force of Sioux Indians, desperate after decades of displacement and facing starvation, attacked settlers on a broad front across the plains. Farm families were being massacred and Minnesota towns were in flames. Hundreds of settlers were killed in the raids. Under intense pressure to commit every possible soldier to the secessionist war, President Lincoln was now forced to dispatch Federal troops to the Minnesota Plains. It was the worst of times for the fractured United States.

Tensions mounted between Indians and Euro-Americans all along the western Great Lakes. Settlers in Grand Traverse were frightened by the gruesome details coming from neighboring Minnesota and were unsure how their Indian neighbors would react. In Northport, Reverend Smith worked to cool passions. On September 14, when the conflict in Minnesota was at its height, Smith recorded his meeting with a local Odawa leader, writing: "I talked to the man about the fright – Akosa said the Indians all felt bad about it, would have a Council…to assure the Whites of their friendship." Two days later,

Smith's efforts paid off. He wrote: "Had a large Council at our school house in which the Indians gave the whites every possible assurance of their friendship."[226] Though terrible accounts of the fighting continued to pour in from Minnesota, it appeared that the bloodshed would not jump to the shores of Lake Michigan. By the end of September, the fighting was over, with another 1,000 Americans killed. Over 300 Sioux Indians were put on trial for murder. In 1862 America, the spirit of brotherly love was hard to find.

General Lee's summer of victories had transformed the Army of Northern Virginia into a formidable fighting force. The Confederate commander reasoned that the South's best chance was to keep the war short. With the Federal armies in disarray, he decided to strike North, with an eye on capturing Washington D.C. By mid-September, the Rebels had marched into Maryland, where Lee expected the citizens of the border state to both welcome and join his army. In reality, the reception was much cooler, for Maryland was becoming progressively more pro-Union as the national conflict wore on. For the first time, Southern troops felt the hate-filled atmosphere that accompanied a march through enemy territory.

In a stroke of amazing good luck, a soldier in the Army of the Potomac found a mislaid copy of Lee's battle plans wrapped around three cigars, just as the opposing forces closed in for a fight. The discovery changed the course of the war. The normally hesitant General McClellan was compelled to act, engaging a Rebel army that Lee had for the moment strategically divided. What followed was the deadliest single day of combat in American history – the Battle of Antietam.

Word from Antietam arrived at the Northport docks only two days after the September 17 battle in Maryland, setting a record for speed of delivery of news from the front. Reverend Smith wrote: "*Edith* came PM. She brought word that a fearful battle with great slaughter had been fought at Hagerstown, M'd in which the rebels were conquered and some 50,000 were taken prisoner. When will the rebels desist? I fear not until half the land is desolate. I hope not until slavery is abolished."[227] Two weeks later, the *Herald* had yet to receive official reports from Antietam in its Traverse City office. Editor Morgan Bates wrote: "We have delayed the publication of our paper beyond the usual hour, in expectation of news by the *Alleghany,* which is now two days past due from Sarnia. We can wait no longer, and go to press without any news. A rumor, however, has reached us from Northport, that McClellan has fought another battle, gained a great victory, and taken 40,000 rebel prisoners."[228]

Confederate dead along the Hagerstown Road near Antietam, September 17, 1862. *Library of Congress*

Only parts of the stories arriving in Northport and Traverse City aboard ships were true. On September 17, the Union Army had gained a great victory at Antietam, stopping the Confederate invasion and sending Lee's Army of Northern Virginia back home. The 40,000 to 50,000 rebels reportedly captured, however, was an exaggeration - as was often the case with initial battlefield reports – but the truth proved to be good enough news. The battle had been a disaster for Lee, as the invincible General lost one-quarter of the soldiers fighting in his fabled army. The 23,000 combined American casualties suffered at the battle of Antietam matched the two-day losses at Shiloh, a battle whose carnage had stunned the nation only six months before. The scale of the war kept growing, with no end to the violence in sight.

Had General McClellan taken advantage of his battlefield gains and used the Army of the Potomac's two-to-one superiority in numbers, Lee's army may have been crushed and 40,000-plus prisoners actually taken. As it was, the battered Rebels were allowed to escape South without as much as a chase. For the second time in as many months, McClellan let a chance for the Army of the Potomac to bring the war to a quick end slip through his hands. Lincoln ordered the dormant general to pursue, but McClellan had halted his army in Maryland and would not move.

Although the Union Army lost the chance to deal the Confederates a fatal blow after the battle, Antietam was the victory Lincoln had been waiting for. On September 22, the President unveiled the Emancipation Proclamation to the nation. It said: "On the 1st day of January, A.D. 1863, all persons held as slaves within any State…in rebellion against the United States shall be then, thenceforward, and forever free." Though the imperfect Proclamation failed to emancipate all American slaves, over 3,000,000 captives held in the South would be free by decree on New Year's Day. The *Grand Traverse Herald* called Lincoln's work "the most important document ever penned by a mortal and proclaimed to the world…Slavery and Rebellious War – the Cause and the Effect – will perish together, and man will accord to man the right that God gave, to life, Liberty, and the pursuit of Happiness."[229]

The Emancipation Proclamation brought a clearer focus to the American Civil War, one that began to alter the world-wide perception of the combatants. Now the North had committed to a second revolutionary war in which victory would eventually make the abolition of slavery universal in the United States – a policy European nations had made into law decades before. The South, meanwhile, appeared to be far behind the times as its armies desperately fought to save what was widely considered an uncivilized institution.

While September 22, 1862 carried tidings of emancipation to the nation, it would be remembered as a sad day in Grand Traverse Country's lead town. On that date, Northport's favorite son, Sgt. William Voice Jr. of the 26th Michigan Infantry, died of disease in Camp Jackson, where he had been training with his fellow volunteers. Smith chronicled the moment the news reached the harbor four days later, writing: "*Buffalo* came to Union Dock…I was at once called to the boat to see to arrangements about the remains of Wm. H. Voice. He died in hospital last Monday 22 of lung fever after 5 days sickness. The Company paid 50 dollars for a Metallic Coffin & 4 soldiers were sent home with him viz Mr Budd & Mr Nash and 2 young men from Old Mission. I went and informed Mr. Voice's family – Mrs Voice was almost distracted. I went to the dock and had the coffin opened & the corpse was so badly injured I made up my mind the family must not see it. The coffin was some way defective. I conducted the funeral at the school house…it was the largest meeting I ever saw in the place & most feeling manifest. On a silver plate on the breast was engraved Sgt. Wm H Voice died Sept. 22, 1862 aged 20 years."

The next week the *Grand Traverse Herald* published a letter from Reverend Smith concerning his young friend's death. He wrote: "Our Village was thrown into great distress this morning, by the arrival of the Propellor *Buffalo,* bringing the remains of Sergt. Wm H. Voice, oldest son of William Voice of this place, accompanied by four volunteers, who left this place with him but a short time since. He died at Camp Jackson, on the morning of the 22nd, after an illness of five days. It may be said of him that he never did an unworthy deed, and that he was inspired by a noble patriotism that led him promptly to offer his life for the defense of our glorious Union. His companions in arms generously raised fifty dollars to purchase a metallic coffin for him, which, with the expenses of bringing him home for interment, will amount to over one hundred dollars – this shows how highly he was esteemed. His funeral exercises were attended at half past ten A.M. to-day, by the largest collection of people ever assembled at this place. His family is deeply and almost inconsolably afflicted, and all who knew him greatly mourn his loss..”[230]

The sudden passing of the vibrant, 20 year-old William Voice Jr. was made all the worse because neither the town nor his family were prepared for his death. As the Smiths' experience had tragically demonstrated, the specter of infant mortality was all too common in mid-19th century America, especially on the frontier. However, if children survived the difficult early years, they were expected to live at least until middle age. Voice's death marked a shift in how the people of Grand Traverse, and in a larger sense the nation, confronted death during the Civil War. Young men in their prime were now the reaper's chief target. The notion of who and how people died was being radically altered, and due to the ever increasing scale of the war, almost every family would face the new and unwelcome reality.

Smith's letter to the *Herald* was accompanied by one from the soldiers of 26th Michigan Infantry. It said: “…in the death of Sergeant William H. Voice, our fellow soldier and comrade in arms, we deeply mourn his loss, knowing, as we do, his uprightness of character and many manly virtues.” In a war where military casualties were often buried in trenches by the dozens, it was rare when a fallen soldier was shipped back to his hometown, all the more so in an expensive metal casket with an accompanying honor guard. Reverend Smith failed to mention that secured to the top of the coffin was an unexplained item – a box containing the head and shoulders of a fine porcelain doll. None of the honor guards knew anything about the package or the beautiful doll within it. Over half a century would pass before the secret of the doll was uncovered.

Sgt. William Voice's death at Camp Jackson at the hands of typhoid fever illustrated how one of the war's main killers operated. All across the country,

young men from isolated farm communities and distant towns were thrown together by the thousands in army training camps. In the close quarters of the barracks, germs spread quickly and disease took a terrible toll on the recruits. Three
weeks after leaving the docks of Northport aboard the propeller *Mendota,* Sgt.
Voice of Northport lay dying of typhoid fever. While wracked by the full fury of
the disease, Voice told hospital attendant and fellow Grand Traverse volunteer
Herman Dunklow about a promise he had made to his baby sister before leaving Northport. Dunklow had enlisted from Centreville and shipped out with
Voice and was now the dying soldier's last link to home. From his hospital bed
at Camp Jackson, Voice described the day of their departure and how his three
year-old sister Abbie wept inconsolably, frightened she would never see her beloved brother again. The only way he could persuade her to stop crying, Voice
told Dunkelow, was to promise to bring her a beautiful doll upon his return, or
send one back if he was not home soon.

In the ensuing days, the sergeant's condition worsened until the outcome
became certain. Rallying on occasion from delirium, Voice begged Dunklow to
find a doll before the disease claimed him. With desperation in the dying man's
pleas increasing, and the end of the young soldier's life in sight, Dunklow took
what little money he had and scoured the nearby town. At one store he found a
fine porcelain doll's head and shoulders which he bought and carried back to the
bedside of his Leelanau friend. As the sun set over Camp Jackson, Voice drifted
between life and death. During a moment of awareness, Dunklow presented the
dying sergeant with the doll, and the soldier's ravaged face broke into a smile.
Dunklow propped the doll at the foot of the bed, and after receiving assurances
it would be delivered to his sister Abbie in case the worse happened, Sgt. William Voice relaxed into sleep. By morning he was dead.

Northport's meeting house overflowed with people who came to pay their
respects at Sergeant Voice's funeral. After the local hero was put to rest, area
women made a body for the doll they had found on his casket and fitted it with
a dress and a pair of knit stockings. On Christmas Eve 1862, the townspeople
presented the china doll to the child Abbie Voice, who cherished the remem-
brance of her brother from that day forward. The late William Voice had kept
his promise to his sister. However, the story of the doll was far from over.

After the Civil War, Abbie married Northport merchant Norman Morgan
where for years they ran a prosperous mercantile store. Later, the couple moved
to Traverse City. Soon after World War I, a friend asked her to call on a lonely,
90 year-old Civil War veteran who lived in her Traverse City neighborhood.

The Northport doll rests at the grave of Sgt. William Voice in Northport Cemetery. *Keith Burnham*

Abbie, who felt a strong bond to Civil War soldiers since the death of her brother William, was happy to oblige. She paid the old man a visit and they talked about their lives. Like many Civil War veterans, the one-armed man began to reminisce about his war experiences. He remembered one soldier in particular, a fellow Leelanau volunteer he helped nurse in the army hospital at Camp Jackson, Michigan. The soldier kept raving about a doll for his sister. The old man said he was so touched by the dying man's pleas that he went and bought him a doll. This was over a half century ago, he explained, in September, 1862. Abbie listened to the soldier's story with growing astonishment. When the old man finished, she asked if he remembered the soldier's name.

"His name was William Voice," the veteran answered. Abbie excused herself and hurried home to retrieve her doll, and then returned to the old man's bedside. "This is the doll you bought," she told him, "and I am William Voice's baby sister." The old man, whose name was Herman Dunkelow, took in the news slowly. "I'll never forget the look on your brother's face when he saw that doll," he said. "He died a happy man."[231] Now, for a second time, the Northport doll gave a Civil War hero a measure of peace.

The first Hannah, Lay & Co. store opened in 1860 and for each of the next three years the Traverse City business added a new wing. *History Center of Traverse City*

The six months of war from Shiloh to Antietam were the worst the country had ever experienced. The opposing armies together suffered 150,000 casualties, with no end to the bloodshed in sight. The continued escalation of the conflict without a sign of either side wavering made it clear there was still a lot of blood yet to be shed on the battlefield. However, as the old United States crumbled and died, Grand Traverse sprang to life as never before. Every harbor town bustled with activity as new settlers, drawn by the Homestead Act, converged on the region.

Perry Hannah continued to develop the village of Traverse City, expanding his business ventures beyond pine lumber. Under the title "A Mammoth Store," the *Herald* wrote: "Hannah, Lay & Co. have built another addition to their store, 30 by 90 feet, and they now have the largest store in Michigan. It is ninety feet square and divided into three equal compartments. The centre is devoted to Dry Goods, the East wing to Groceries and Provisions, and the West wing to Hardwares, Crockery, Stoves, Tinware, Iron, Nails, Saddles' Harness, &c. &c. They have the largest and best assortment of Goods ever brought into Northern Michigan, and from a recent comparison of prices with Detroit and Chicago, we are satisfied that they sell goods cheaper than they do at either of those places."[232]

As October 1862 progressed, George Smith recorded a series of events that measured the increasing human cost of the Civil War to his family and friends.

On the 13th, he wrote: "Joseph Wakazoo came AM took dinner, left near night - little over 3 weeks since he left the army at Potomac." Smith's long-time Indian friend – a boy he had taught to speak and write in English - was now a Union Army deserter. The next week Smith "Got mail - 1 letter from niece Mary Stearns. Her brother Erastus was killed at Baton Rouge August by the bursting of one of our own shells as it left the gun, by the concussion, without being marked at all." A few days later, Smith wrote of more bad news. "Mail came - 1 letter from Sister Jane McMartin. Her son D.E. McMartin was killed at the battle of South Mountain on Sabbath, Aug. 14, by a musket ball through his head. She is greatly afflicted."[233] Smith's all too regular notations of soldiers' deaths, which now included his nephew, testified to the expanding reach of the conflict. McMartin's death was a cruel reminder that every bullet or germ that struck down a soldier also carried misery back home to loved ones. The extended Smith family, like so many other Americans, was paying the price of the Civil War in blood and grief.

With the 1862 elections at hand, Morgan Bates once again used the *Herald* to vigorously support the Lincoln Administration and promote the radical Republican platform. In October, he cited the party's accomplishments, writing: "The Republican party was formed in this State in 1854…It laid down its platform in clear and distinct terms…It overthrew its enemies in a fair, bold struggle, and came to power in the State and Nation…It has secured the freedom of the Territories of the United States from negro slavery…It has driven the institution from the Capitol of the Nation. It has established the homestead policy…In 1860 it proved itself stronger than any other political organization, by bringing into power the present Administration. It must show itself stronger than any other party in 1862, in *aiding* that same Administration in crushing the rebellion." Another article in the *Herald* warned of the alternative, saying: "The Northern Democratic party is taking a position against the war in favor of the Southern Confederacy. "These men are our allies," says a rebel paper in Georgia, "and will in time effect the overthrow of the Lincoln Government, and pave the way to Southern independence." The *Herald* warned: "Let those who desire to enable these "allies" of the traitors…vote with and for the "Democrats" next Tuesday."[234]

The strident Republican Bates said little about the sizeable rift and defections that were occurring in his party throughout the state and the nation. The failure of the Peninsula Campaign in Virginia that summer, the monetary cost of the Civil War, and its unprecedented and mounting casualties, dulled the enthusiasm of many voters in the North. In addition, a considerable percentage of conservative Republicans who embraced the idea of fighting to preserve the Union now balked at the loud voice of radicals who were gaining ground in the party's ranks and expounding their uncompromising positions on emancipation, integration of the Army, and annihilation of the southern way of life. The disgruntled Republicans and pro-Union Democrats formed an alliance called the Fusion Party, which claimed to represent a more centrist point of view. Bates could only wait and see what effect they would have on the upcoming mid-term elections.

On November 1, 1862, a boat load of Grand Traverse volunteers arrived home on furlough. Smith captured the historic scene unfolding in Northport harbor, writing: "*Galena* came noon…between 30 & 40 volunteers came home to attend. It was a joyous occasion." Soldiers in uniform crowded every sidewalk and wharf in the port town, happy to have returned alive to family and friends. It was the first time most had been back since their enlistments. The influx of soldiers wearing Union blue left its impression on area citizens, presenting a constant reminder that many of the town's young people now staked their lives on the Union cause.

The presence of the volunteers may have been enough to sway some of the town's voters, for on November 4, after years of humbling defeats at the hands of his neighbors, Smith finally enjoyed an Election Day in Northport. The Reverend wrote: "We have given up the day to election matters & we have gained a glorious victory over the semi secession Democrats. The Indians came up like men and voted the Republican Ticket…apparently without any fear of their old masters who have ruled over them with an iron hand. We gave them a rich and abundant dinner where there was served to them baked pig…cakes pies coffee - our average majority over 30 votes." An exuberant Morgan Bates wrote: "Every Township in the County has given a Republican majority. Even Leelanau, hitherto the Gibraltar of Secession-Democracy, has wheeled gallantly into line, and rolled up a handsome majority for freedom."[235] For the first time, the Democratic grip on Grand Traverse Country's lead town had been broken - Northport had gone Republican. Voters throughout Michigan also supported Republicans in national races, but their margins had fallen since 1860. The real impact of the Fusion Party was felt in the state legislature, where they captured 51 of the 132 contested seats.

Two days after the elections, Reverend Smith recorded a bitter sweet moment during the pause in the war. He wrote: "The Citizens gave a fine Pic Nic to the Volunteers at the Dame House – there were perhaps 100 people in attendance – we carried in a baked pig & Mary a large Chicken pie – it was a joyous occasion." As was the habit of the Civil War years, the moment's tenuous hold on happiness was suddenly broken by the intrusion of outside events. Smith continued: "Just in the midst the *Galena* came…how cruel it is…over 40 volunteers go on the Boat."[236] The party in Northport was suddenly over and the hard business of Civil War resumed.

As local soldiers in the 26th Michigan Infantry steamed off aboard the *Galena*, another regiment that would fill with Grand Traverse volunteers began to take shape. In response to yet another call by President Lincoln for more troops, Michigan's Governor Austin Blair authorized the raising of several new state regiments, including the "First Regiment Michigan Sharp-shooters." Recruiters for the Sharp Shooters were ordered to make a special effort to seek out woodsmen who displayed skill with a rifle. That mission sent them north, where people living on the edge of the wilderness still relied on hunting for much of their food. Blair saw the Sharp Shooters as a good place for Native Americans soldiers, and reserved one company for Indian volunteers. Within the year, Company K of the 1st Michigan Sharp Shooters, composed mostly of Indians recruited along Lake Michigan, became the largest all-Native force in the Union Army fighting east of the Mississippi River.

However, in the wake of the Sioux uprisings in Minnesota, relations between Indians and Euro-American settlers along the western Great Lakes were clouded by suspicion and fear. A thousand people had been killed, some in gruesome ways. In mid-November, Reverend Smith wrote: "A large meeting was held …to discuss the subject of organizing home guards & asking the governor to furnish arms & equipment & ammunition. I was chairman of committee to notify the Indians of our feeling of confidence in them & kindness toward them." The message, it seemed, was delivered with the proverbial gun in hand, for the next day Smith noted that the "Indians held a council at our School house to express their friendliness to the Whites."[237]

In late November, the *Herald* published news of the fate of Sioux combatants in Minnesota, writing: "Over three hundred Indians have been convicted by Military Commission, at the Lower Sioux Agency, as participators in the late horrible massacres, and condemned to be hung. Whether they live or die rests with the authorities in Washington. The people of Minnesota, to a man, are in favor of their immediate execution."[238] That same week at Camp Jackson, William Remar, a soldier in the 26th Michigan, succumbed to disease in the same hospital Sergeant Voice had died in a few weeks before. Now two Grand Traverse men had given their lives to the Union cause without leaving Michigan.

Following the November elections, Lincoln relieved General McClellan of all his duties, effectively ending his military career. The General's failure to pursue Lee after the Confederate defeat at Antietam proved to be his undoing. In a letter recalling McClellan to Washington, Lincoln wrote: "If you don't want to use the Army, I should like to borrow it for a while." Upon learning of McClellan's downfall, the *Grand Traverse Herald* said: "Every loyal man in the County will rejoice to learn that the President has removed Gen McClellan from the command of the Army of the Potomac…When the rebel army was allowed to cross the Potomac after the battle of Antietam, with all their baggage and plunder, and were not immediately pursued in Virginia, the whole country became amazed and disgusted at what was so plainly a lack of energy and good military management. This feeling has been growing with each day that our army has been lying inactive on the north bank of the Potomac, while the enemy was concentrating and recuperating his strength only a few miles southward. The opinion is almost universal that a most precious opportunity was allowed to pass unimproved by not following up and making the most of advantages we had gained at South mountain and Antietam."[239]

Command shifted to General Ambrose Burnside, who aimed to restore the martial reputation of the Army of the Potomac. The new commander was determined to end 1862 with a significant Union victory. He set his sights on Fredericksburg, the railroad town where the Army of Northern Virginia refitted after being beaten at Antietam. General Burnside submitted his battle plan to Lincoln in mid-November, emphasizing the need for its speedy execution if the attack was to succeed. Cursed by a series of misfortunes that delayed the 100,000 man Army of the Potomac's march on Fredericksburg, Burnside's attack did not begin until a month later, long after the necessary element of surprise was gone.

In a repeat of every invasion of Virginia to date, superior Union forces took a terrible beating. For three days, waves of men in blue were mauled when attacking fortified Confederate positions near the city, and the stone wall they were ordered to charge became another symbol of Federal military incompetence. The Union Army lost three times as many soldiers as the Rebels and once again limped back toward Washington. After being briefed on the disaster at Fredericksburg, Lincoln wrote: "If there is a worse place than hell, I am in it."[240] Despite overwhelming on-paper advantages, the North seemed determined to lose the war. At this stage in the conflict, Grand Traverse volunteers were engaged all along the battlefronts, including Fredericksburg, and suffered from the Union Army's poor leadership in the Virginia campaigns. The *Herald* later reported: "We deeply regret to learn that Andrew McKillip, of this place, who was one of the first to volunteer from Traverse city, was killed at the battle of Fredericksburg." McKillip quit his job as a lumberjack with Hannah, Lay & Co. in 1861 and joined a score of local volunteers who ended up in the 1st New York Light Artillery. Later, Reverend Smith wrote that McKillip's friend and fellow artillerist Albert Powers "lost one of his legs in the Battle of Fredericksburg & is in the hospital in Baltimore...I carried the word to his parents."[241] The New York battery had beat the odds and survived several bloody engagements in the summer's Peninsula Campaign virtually unscathed, but now Virginia began to take its toll on the unit, as it would with regularity over the balance of the Civil War.

1862 had been a terrible year for the United States, one no nation could possibly survive intact. Epic battles had been fought within its borders, with the casualties, collateral damage, and costs escalating with each engagement. Yet the bloodshed was not over for the year or the war; on the contrary, it would compound itself as the conflict escalated toward a conclusion over the next 30 months. On the day after Christmas 1862, 38 Sioux Indians were hung for their involvement in the Minnesota uprisings. Though President Lincoln commuted the sentences of most of the 306 condemned by military trial, the December 26 hangings stand as the largest mass execution in American history. So ended the first full year of war, whose passing few mourned.

President Lincoln meets with General McClellan following the Battle of Antietam. *Library of Congress*

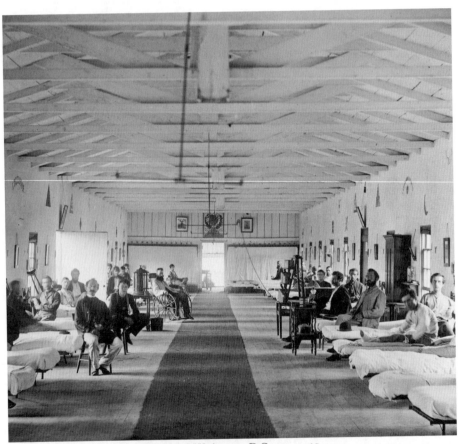

A soldiers' ward in a Union Army hospital, Washington D.C. *Library of Congress*

Chapter Six

1863
Whip or Get Whipped

January 1, 1863 was a momentous day in American history, a standout date even among the Civil War years, when almost every turn of the globe carried with it another nation-defining moment. July 4, 1776 is revered as the birthday of the nation, the day the founding fathers signed the Declaration of Independence. The revolutionary document championed the infant nation's promise that "all men are created equal," an idea that cracked the foundations of monarchy and stirred the hopes of people all over the world. Now, on New Year's Day 1863, as the fractured nation engaged in suicidal conflict over the meaning of "all men are created equal," the founding promise was given force of law when President Lincoln issued the Emancipation Proclamation. Preparing to put his pen to the document in the Executive Mansion, Lincoln said, "I never, in my life, felt more certain that I was doing the right thing than I do in signing this paper."

Four hundred miles to the northeast, the black orator Frederick Douglass, in the company of *Uncle Tom's Cabin* author Harriet Beecher Stowe, mingled with the crowd on the steps of a Boston church. All waited for news from Washington. Although highly anticipated, Lincoln's release of the Emancipation Proclamation on this day was anything but a sure thing. Abolitionists worried that the President might back off a document that would radically alter the nature of the war. Those who admired Lincoln's conciliatory nature feared he might, in the final moment, pocket a law that would irretrievably destroy any chance of ending the conflict without the total dismantling of the Southern way of life. As New Year's Day turned to evening, then surrendered to the cold January darkness, tensions mounted. Speakers the likes of historian Francis

Parkman and the poet Henry Wadsworth Longfellow tried to calm the crowd with their eloquent orations.

Frederick Douglass recalled the high-strung drama of the moment, writing: "A line of messengers was established between the telegraph office and the platform of Tremont Temple, and the time was occupied with brief speeches... But speaking or listening to speeches was not the thing for which the people had come together. The time for argument was passed. It was not logic, but the trump of jubilee, which everybody wanted to hear. We were waiting and listening as for a bolt from the sky, which should rend the fetters of four million slaves; we were watching, as it were, by the din of the stars, for the dawn of a new day; we were longing for the answer to the agonizing prayers of centuries. Remembering those in bonds as bound with them, we wanted to join in the shout of freedom, and in the anthem of the redeemed.

"Eight, nine, ten o'clock came and went, and still no word. A visible shadow seemed falling on the expecting throng, which the confident utterance of the speakers sought in vain to dispel. At last, when patience was well-nigh exhausted, and suspense was becoming agony, a man with hasty step advanced through the crowd, and with a face fairly illuminated with the news he bore, exclaimed in tones that thrilled all hearts, "It is coming!" "It is on the wires!" The effect of this announcement was startling beyond description, and the scene was wild and grand. Joy and gladness exhausted all forms of expression, from shouts of praise to sobs and tears...It was one of the most affecting and thrilling occasions I have ever witnessed..."[242]

As January 1, 1863 gave way to midnight, Douglass and friends embraced and wept, stunned by the nation's historic affirmation of its founding promise. Through the explosive power of words, the Emancipation Proclamation announced the North's secession from the values of the old Union in as thunderous a manner as the Confederates cannonade on Fort Sumter. The Proclamation recognized that the condition of the United States nation as established by George Washington's generation was terminal, and a new nation – or nations – would have to rise from the ashes of the Civil War. Now, from all perspectives, the lines between North and South were indelibly drawn, with one cause doomed to fail.

An article in the first issue of the 1863 *Grand Traverse Herald* said: "The 26th Regiment of Michigan Infantry has gone to Dixie's land. Before leaving Jackson, the officers of the Regiment, wishing to express their appreciation of the untiring efforts of Mrs. Gov. Blair in relieving the sick and otherwise contributing to their comfort, purchased and presented to her a beautiful black horse, with silver plated harness, an elegant side saddle, and a blanket of the most costly kind. They marched to the Governor's residence, where the presentation was made by Lt. Col. Wells, after which they were invited in, and partook of a sumptuous repast."[243]

Several weeks later, a letter to the *Herald* from Lt. Charles Holden of the 26th Michigan described the Grand Traverse volunteers' journey to the battle lines in Virginia. He wrote: "Friend Bates – We are in one of the most God forsaken, desolate regions of earth - far beyond the comprehension of one unused to such scenes. We left Camp Jackson Dec. 13 for Washington, via Toledo, Cleveland, Dunkirk, Elmira, N.Y; thence to Williamsport, Harrisburg and Baltimore; arriving in Washington on the 19th. Our route was a perfect ovation for the most part, the citizens hailing us at various stations where we stopped with the good things of life, "coffee included." We marched through the very street at Baltimore where the lawless mob assailed the Massachusetts boys on their way to defend the Capitol a little more than a year before. How changed are matters now! We were greeted with cheers and the glorious Flag was displayed as we marched

through…While there I took occasion to visit the Capitol, White House, Patent Office and Post Office – all magnificent structures built of white granite and limestone. I also visited both Houses of Congress, which were in session, and beheld the seats once occupied by Webster, Clay, Douglas and others, whose "names were not born to die."

"Michigan troops rank A No.1, and it is very seldom that a Michigan Regiment is ordered to garrison a fort, but are generally sent into the

President Lincoln. *Library of Congress*

field; and thus it has been with us. We are located, for the present, 25 miles from Washington, near Manassas, and two and a half miles from the last battlefield of Bull Run. We drink and wash out of Bull Run creek, and occupy the old forts held by Beauregard last winter and until recently held by Gen. Lee...The Blue Ridge is seen in the distance and a Rebel fort and flag are to be seen. We are the farthest in the advance, having a force of five Regiments and two batteries all told. The boys are all well and spoiling for a fight."[244]

A subsequent letter written by one of Lt. Holden's men gave a Grand Traverse private's view of the war, one quite different from the officer's. John Brainerd of Whitewater wrote: "After arranging our tents in nice style for winter quarters we received marching orders; Dec. 28th marched till sundown, when we camped for the night. Between 10 and 11 was roused from our slumbers by the startling news *"Fall in! – To Arms!* The Rebels are upon us."* After standing in line of battle an hour or two we marched one quarter mile across a bridge and formed another line, stacked arms, built fires in front and waited for the enemy; 8 a.m. shouldered guns and knapsacks; reached Alexandria about noon; pitched tents and layed on the ground during the night. Our camps is on a clay plat near town; we are tolerable comfortable all things considered, but straw is very scarce in the barren country.

"Camp soldiering is all very well, but fighting soldiers tell me they have had enough of war, privation and suffering. Oh, that we had wide-a-wake, go-ahead leaders that would wake up our sleepy, lazy army and pitch into the enemy with such fury as to put them all to flight in a month, we have seen enough of a few men fighting at a time, but want to see every soldier called out to face the music – whip or get whipped, this is past an age for such slow ox movements.

"Judging from all appearances we will stay here till spring; our business is guarding this filthy looking city [Washington, DC], our army finds plenty to do guarding without fighting. It is a general time of health in camp. Whitewater boys are all well; imagine yourself sitting on the ground, paper on your knee, ink in hand, crowded into a very small room with 15 men, and you can correctly judge my situation while writing this letter; soldiers are not supposed to need much room, particularly privates.

"The 26th have received only one month's pay and 25 dollars bounty for five months service, which is only a drop in the bucket toward supporting a family. In behalf of my fellow soldiers from Grand Traverse, may I be permitted to state that if you will have the kindness to wake up some of those sleepy Supervisors with a sharp needle and tell them they must do something for the needy families of the Volunteers that are spending their time, health and may be their lives to sustain this government, by doing so you will do more practical christian good than all the preachers in Grand Traverse will do in a year. All the Traverse boys believe that Mr. Hannah and Bates are soldier's true friends. What can be more discouraging to a man than to know their families are suffering while their hands are tied, and unable to assist them. A human man thinks more of his family than he does of his country."[245]

For year-round Grand Traverse settlers, winter was a time of deep isolation, a stretch of long weeks when the spirit and body hunkered down and waited for the tree sap to flow. With the harbors frozen shut, supplies ran short, money was tight, and the weekly mail and news were often stranded 'outside.' True to form, 1863 began with a series of blizzards, one that Northport's Reverend Smith described as "a tempest…wind blowing and drifting so you could not see."[246] A book was a treasure for those locked in by winter's cold, and in this state Reverend Smith pored through a hard-to-get copy of the latest anti-slavery novel, *South in Secession Time* by Edmund Kirke. He described the book as "a most stirring thing and ought to be read by every man in the north. It would open the eyes of some who do not or will not see the facts of Slaving."

Though the outcome of the war was anyone's guess at the time, there was no doubt which side held the advantage in terms of resources. In an article titled "Rebel Visions Vanishing," the *Grand Traverse Herald* summarized an interview with a Georgia merchant who recently fled his home state. It said: "The people of the South have been grossly deceived by their leaders in regard to the strength, resources, determination and endurance of the people of the North…They were told that our Northern towns and cities were all depopulated, our agricultural interests suffering, travel and commerce stagnating; that our manufacturing establishments are lying idle for want of operators. He was disappointed finding everything the reverse of this. He heard the busy hum of industry at every hand, saw the golden grain being gathered in, and marked the life, vigor, and activity of our commerce. He was, in fact, surprised at the recuperative energies of our people, remarking that the stranger visiting us could see no evidence that a mighty rebellion was raging on our Southern borders."[247]

The Confederate establishment spoke of a collapsing Union, but the opposite was true, especially along the Great Lakes. An article in the first *Grand Traverse Herald* of 1863 documented the rampant growth occurring in the region. It said: "A carefully taken census of the city of Chicago, just completed, shows the populations during the last two years has increased 27,768 – in 1860 it was

109,262. Now it is 137,030."[248] Thirty years before, Chicago had been a village with 300 residents - now it was larger than any city in the Confederacy. The continued boom in Chicago was another indicator of the vitality of the Great Lakes, demonstrating that even in a nation ravaged by war, a vast region of the North grew and prospered while supporting the Union cause.

The story of Chicago was repeated in port cities and towns all along the Great Lakes, including those in Grand Traverse. Jobs in expanding industries and free Homestead Act farms promised opportunity and drew people from around the world. Nowhere were the benefits of a self-governed society of free people so evident, and so attainable. The *Herald* said that in January 1863 alone, "there were 128 entries made at the Traverse City Land Office under the Homestead Law…averaging 135 acres to each man…in Grand Traverse and its attached territories. There are still lands enough in the Grand Traverse Bay country, of the very best quality, to accommodate thousands of families, and we expect a great rush in the Spring."[249] Many of the homesteaders who held the

Building the Newago and Northport State Road in Grand Traverse. *History Center of Traverse City*

gift of free land in their hands now stood ready to fight for the country in which they were given a stake.

In a further sign of progress in Grand Traverse, the contract to complete one of the last sections of the Newaygo and Northport State Road, the 16-mile stretch between Traverse City and Suttons Bay, had been awarded, with the work to begin as soon as the snow melted. Editor Bates wrote: "This road will open up some of the richest farming lands on Grand Traverse Bay. Steadily and surely our beautiful Bay country is emerging from a wilderness to a garden." [250] The contractor performing the road work was the surveyor Albert W. Bacon, whose father owned timberland on the Leelanau Peninsula, and whose sister would soon be the wife of General George Armstrong Custer. The paper assured readers the project would be completed by its June 1864 due date, for Bacon's "well known promptitude and energy are sure guarantees of this." Even the prescient Morgan Bates could not have imagined the fate that awaited Bacon in the terrible month of May, 1864.

This winter, Reverend Smith was instrumental in reviving the effort to make the Leelanau Peninsula a free standing, organized county. On January 6, 1863, he wrote: "Meeting held at District School to petition Legislature to organize this county. I was chosen...to draft petition." Ten days later, Smith "got together the Petitions for organization containing 193 names...put them in a large En-velope, wrote a letter to accompany & directed them to Mr. Dixon," the Grand Traverse region's representative in Lansing. From Northport, the parcel was car-ried over snowy footpaths to the state capital, where it awaited action by law-makers. In the meantime, the Reverend looked after the loved ones of soldiers who had gone off to fight in the war, in one instance helping "get some wood drawn for Mrs. Biggelow & other volunteer families." [251]

In late February, Smith decided to break the monotony of winter in North-port by taking his family on a ride to visit friends. He wrote: "10 Am started for Traverse in double sleigh – wife and Sissy with me...we arrived at Traverse about 4PM. Went to Mr Hannah's, where we were received and entertained very kindly." The Smiths most likely traveled on the smooth Bay ice to Traverse City, for the road south had yet to be improved beyond a rugged two-track and was now banked high with snow.

Perry Hannah and George Smith had the knack of being together when big things happened in Grand Traverse - meetings between the two friends often marked significant moments in the region's history. From the beginning, Han-nah and Smith were at the heart of their respective towns, bearing the hardships of the wilderness Grand Traverse Country while shaping its destiny. Over the years their bond grew and the two men now shared a common view of the future of both Grand Traverse and the country at large.

Grand Traverse County had held its first election on August 4, 1851 - an historical event in which 28 citizens cast their votes at the Horace Boardman house.[252] The ubiquitous George Smith of Northport was elected the new county's Probate Judge. Not long after, Perry Hannah purchased the Boardman sawmill, and in the process of developing his lumber and shipping interests, provided the jobs and boats that brought many of the first Euro-American settlers to Grand Traverse. Now Smith sat at Hannah's dinner table and the two men discussed the anticipated emergence of an independent Leelanau County. In the last Grand Traverse election, more than 600 voters went to the polls – 20 times the number since the first county election only a dozen years before. By 1863, the Leelanau Peninsula hosted a population double the size of incorporated Grand Traverse County, and Northport stood as the largest and most prosperous town in Northern Michigan. Both men understood that the time to recognize an independent Leelanau County had come to pass.

The day of the Smith-Hannah dinner – February 27, 1863 - the lead article in *Grand Traverse Herald* reported on the progress of the Leelanau County legislation in Lansing. Hannah, given his Republican politics and the large ads he placed in the *Herald*, was among the first in Traverse City to receive a copy of the paper. The article of foremost attention read: "The bill for the organization of Leelanaw[253] County passed the House on the 11th by a vote of 66 yeas to 6 nays. It was sent to the Senate on the 12th, read twice and referred to Committee on Towns and Counties. It has doubtless passed that body ere this, and become a law. The County Seat question is left to a vote of the people, and the places to be voted for are Northport, Leeland and Glen Arbor."[254]

The *Herald's* guess that the bill "doubtless passed" showed prescient in this edition, for at about the same moment the weekly paper hit the streets, the Michigan Senate voted in favor of Leelanau's organization. By the time the Smith family took their places at Hannah's table, the bill had been signed into law. In a nation ravaged by Civil War, the government of Michigan had conducted its business with commendable efficiency - only six weeks passed from the time Reverend Smith mailed the petitions from Northport until the bill became law. Although Hannah and Smith could not know it when they sat down, the two patriarchs had dined together on another momentous occasion – the birth of an independent Leelanau County.

The boundaries of Leelanau as originally platted, which made it twice the size as its neighbors, were cut in half during the county's bid for organization. The land to the south of the physical peninsula of Leelanau, where the high ridge country flattens out into a glacial flood plain, was carved off to create unorganized Benzie County. The Fox and Manitou Islands remained as townships within the 1855 boundaries of Manitou County – King Strang's failed kingdom – where they would languish for another 40 years. Even with the reduction in size, organized Leelanau County was home to far more people, and possessed many more miles of lakeshore, than any of its Grand Traverse neighbors.

On March 13, 1863, the *Herald* confirmed: "The House bill to organize Leelanau and define the County of Benzie has passed the Senate without amendment, and is now law." The work of assembling a new county government was set in motion, beginning with elections. In its next issue, the *Herald* reported: "The Republicans of Leelanaw have issued a call for a mass convention...to nominate candidates for County Officers...They cordially invite all persons in favor of supporting the Administration in all its measures for the suppression of the Rebellion, to unite with them." Days later, Reverend Smith wrote: "Went to Carp river in cutter. Mr Dame rode with me to attend County Convention to nominate County Officers. Some 4 or 5 sleighs went. Took dinner at Mr Millers."[255] During this Northern Michigan winter, the business of Leelanau politics was conducted in an open sleigh. Two weeks after Leelanau became a full-fledged county, the state legislature approved Antrim County's petition for independent status. The *Herald* wrote, "The bill for the organization of Antrim County, with Otsego, Crawford and Kalkaska attached, has passed the House... We learn from private sources that it does not detach any portion of Grand Traverse County, and that it will doubtless pass the Senate."[256] In a matter of weeks, the far-reaching hand of Grand Traverse County government lost its grip on two counties that had been attached to it for over a decade.

As winter gave way to spring, news of the international effect of the Emancipation Proclamation began to arrive from Europe. The *Herald* reprinted a "Special Dispatch" from the *Washington Evening Post*, dated April 9, which read: "It is now known, on the very best authority, that John Slidell, the Confederate emissary at Paris, has written to his government that the cause of the Confederacy is utterly without prospect of success.

"He says that neither in France nor England will the new nation be recognized, nor will any measures of intervention be adopted. Both governments may for a time play with the subject, to please the taste of the aristocratic classes, but

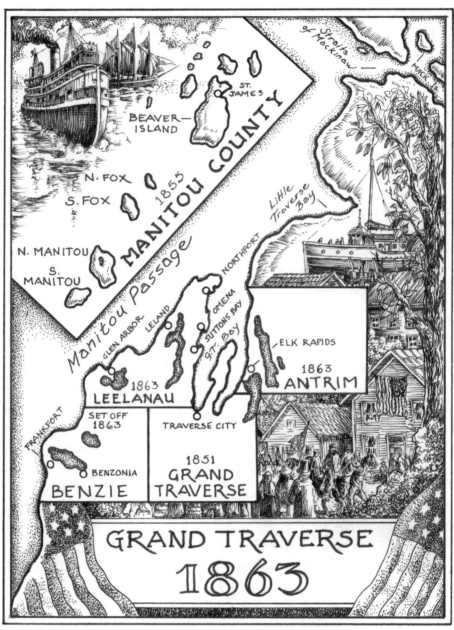

Tom Woodruff

neither of them is strong enough to take a decided step in the face of public opinion. It is understood that he has consequently advised his government to make the best terms it can for a return to the Union. Without foreign aid, the struggle is only a prolongation of misery and ruin. Slidell does not say, but it is well known from other sources, that the strong feeling in favor of the North created by the Emancipation decree, has compelled the ministers to refrain from all acts of hostility toward the Free States."[257]

There was a political genius behind the Emancipation Proclamation, a gift Lincoln's country ways often disguised. The President knew the ruling classes of England and France, who sympathized with the Southern aristocracy and whose fortunes were entangled with King Cotton, leaned in favor of recognition of the Confederacy. This was especially true in light of the unexpected successes the Rebel armies enjoyed in 1862. Lincoln saw that by elevating the conflict to a higher moral ground, European governments could not go against the overwhelming anti-slavery sentiment of their people. Slavery had been abolished in both France and England for more than 15 years, and most of their citizens considered it an archaic and barbaric practice. The Emancipation Proclamation made the choice of sides in the American Civil War clear – the North fought to end slavery, the South to preserve it. Without recognition as an independent nation by the European powers, the Confederates would remain in the eyes of the world a troublesome gang of slavers.

By 1863, the misery caused by the American Civil War had spread to English industrial workers as stockpiles of raw Southern cotton dwindled and mills closed. A clergyman from the city of Manchester – known by the nickname "Cottonopolis" - gave the following instances of the suffering of the working people in his flock. He wrote: "In one house nine persons had been without fire for seven days: in another were ten persons who had lived a week on eighty cents; in the next house were eight grown persons, the wife having just produced twins; there was no food in the house – one of the twins had died, and there was no means of burying it. In a fourth dwelling, the children were trying to keep themselves alive on potato skins."[258] Yet despite their pain, the people of England rallied behind the North. A March *Detroit Advertiser and Tribune* article praised "the grand uprising of the industrial classes of England, in favor of the American Union, and their approval of the Loyal States to put down the rebellion, no matter what the cost."[259]

In his postwar memoirs, President Ulysses S. Grant gave his opinion of the effect of the Emancipation Proclamation abroad. He wrote: "I am told that there was no time during the civil war when they were able to get up in England a demonstration in favor of secession, while these were constantly being gotten up in favor of the Union, or, as they called it, in favor of the North. Even in the mills of Manchester, which suffered so fearfully by having the cotton cut off from her mills, they had a monster demonstration in favor of the North at the very time when their workmen were almost famishing."[260] The *London Times*, which to date had been sympathetic to the Confederacy, began to change its editorial tune. The paper said: "Between North and South there is at this moment raging a controversy which goes deep…into the elementary principles of human nature. The North is for freedom, the South is for Slavery…Free labor is denounced as degrading and disgraceful; the honest triumphs of the poor man who works his way to independence are treated with scorn and contempt."[261]

In a letter written to friends in Chicago, Glen Arbor's Harriet Fisher enunciated her views of how the Union's first step toward abolishing slavery affected relations with the European powers. She wrote: "What is your opinion of England and France taking sides against us? I think they would be glad to see us divided, but I hardly think they will come out openly in favor of the South unless she frees her slaves, as both those foreign forces boast of being enemies to Slavery, but if they come we will be enough for them, crippled as we are, for if necessary, a woman can carry a gun and use it to."[262] Fisher's letter showed that at this point in the war many believed it could devolve into an international conflict.

A Grand Traverse volunteer serving in the 9th Michigan Infantry near Nashville sent a letter to the *Herald* relating his regiment's experiences in Tennessee and his view of the Emancipation Proclamation. Private James Smith wrote: "I was a resident of your beautiful section of the country for two years, and became intimately acquainted with a large number of your generous and enterprising inhabitants, with whom I parted with reluctance to take a part in the defense of the liberty and integrity of my country when this infernal and gigantic rebellion broke out…

"I have now soldiered with the army of the West for nearly two years, and when I say that the present army is a better equipped, drilled, paid, clothed and fed army in the world, I speak but the truth. We were never in such a healthy condition and so eager for a fight as now. There seems to be a great dearth of news everywhere just at present, and in this vicinity there is hardly a man stirring. The calm will soon be broken by the roar of cannon, the rattling of musketry and the dread clashing of steel, announcing that the fearful contest has begun.

"Yesterday the city was thrown into quite an excitement by the announcement that [Confederate General] Van Dorn was marching on the town with fifteen thousand men, and the excitement seemed to be strengthened from the fact that the rebel mail had been captured which disclosed the fact that such a raid on the city was mediated, and I am glad to say that the most vigilant preparations were made to receive them. To-day, however, it is quiet again, but indications are that a battle is close at hand...

"The forbearance hitherto observed towards the rebels and rebel sympathizers in this city has been far too great – it encourages and even invites disloyalty... Men and women have been permitted to boast that they were rebels, and to daily insult our soldiers and officers of the Union army; and while they made bold to assert their disloyalty, a guard of soldiers was given to them to protect their property from molestation by Union soldiers.

"Such things have tended much to dishearten soldiers and tend them to loose confidence in their commanders. But now Gen. Rosecrans set this matter alright by issuing an order to arrest all rebel sympathizers, and has commenced in earnest at the work by arresting a large number of residents of this town and placing them in prison...It is not yet known what disposition will be made of them, but it is altogether likely they will be exchanged for East Tennessee Union men, now held in the loathsome dungeons of the South by these incarnate demons, for no other cause than loyalty to the government of their fathers...

"A great deal has been said and written in regard to the President's Emancipation Proclamation, and the Conservatives would have us believe that it has... united the whole South in hostility to the North. By observation and experience I deny this, and assert on the contrary, it has not made one Southern Union man turn rebel, but they endorse it..."

"Freedom and slavery can never exist together again in this nation, one or the other must be annihilated; and now let the American people endorse emancipation as the only means of saving the country, and meet the issue as becomes a great people. The people are aroused, and all inquire what brought about the rebellion against a mild government that oppressed no man. In other revolutions it has been the oppressed who rebelled, but in this strange rebellion of ours it is the oppressor, the pro-slave faction, the most prosperous men of the nation, a little oligarchy of three hundred thousand people among 30,000,000, who ruled the whole land with a rod of iron.

"We are told by timid men that although slavery be a great evil, yet it would be difficult to remove, and therefore must be let alone. But if slavery be a great evil now, what will it be when the number of the slaves shall be doubled or quadrupled. If it is hard now how much harder will it be for our children? Shall we force upon our posterity the work of removing 8,000,000 of slaves when we are troubled with the presence of 4,000,000? Policy, justice and humanity forbid us to act so dishonorable."[263]

In another part of the letter, Private Smith addressed the issue of how dissention in the North was affecting the troops, writing: "We, the Army of the Cumberland, have read with pain and indignation the course of these disloyal citizens of the North, who by their disloyal speeches and otherwise have imparted confidence to rebels in arms against us…while breathing the free air of the North…We have pledged ourselves to follow the battle flag of our fathers wherever it may go – whether in the sunny fields of the South, against the armed traitors, or against the miscreants, vile and perjured traitors of treason in the North, and for the honor we pledge our lives, our property and sacred honor."

William Sykes, the former Grand Traverse Sheriff and current 1st New York artillerist, expressed similar sentiments in another letter to his friend Powers in Northport. He said: "I am more afraid of the rebels at home, than I am of these here, for *they* are creating divisions in the army in the field. I can tell you…I wish the war was over, but as long as there is fighting to be done I am bound to have a hand in it…When I think of the widows and orphans, and the amount of blood that has been spilled in this cursed rebellion, I am willing to stay three years more, rather than submit to a compromise, for I am confident we can put it down; if we can't do it any other way we will turn around and clean out the North first." After being shown the letter, Reverend Smith commented that it would be something "for Northern sympathizers with the rebellion to contemplate before they proceed much further in giving aid and comfort to treason."[264]

Winter's isolation ended abruptly in Grand Traverse when ice moved out of the Straits of Mackinac. On April 19, 1863, Reverend Smith noted: "Straits broke yesterday *Adriatic…Buffalo…Free State…*came though this morning… Mr D[ame] thinks there may have been 200 vessels in all for both ways."[265] The navigation season of 1863 would prove to be the busiest on the Great Lakes to date, with metals mined in Michigan one of the principal cargoes.

Iron, copper, and lead were the base elements of the Civil War. In the simplest of terms, armies won Civil War battles by effectively projecting these metals into the bodies of their enemies. Now the brutal leading edge of metal would decide the great issues of the day. Mines in the Upper Peninsula of Michigan produced the majority of the nation's supply of iron and copper along with a great quantity of lead. When the Soo Locks opened in 1855, boats carried cargoes of the heavy metals unimpeded from Lake Superior to the growing port

Civil War ordnance depot. *Library of Congress*

cities along the southern Great Lakes, sparking the region's industrial revolution. Again, the advantage in resources, and the ability to shape and distribute them, lay heavily on the Union's side.

A clear indicator of the North's increasing manufacturing output during the Civil War can be found in the annual tonnage statistics for iron ore shipped through the Soo Locks. When the conflict began, Confederates defaulted on loans from northern banks and stopped buying Yankee products. In 1861, less than 50,000 tons of iron ore were shipped from Lake Superior - half the amount of the previous year. By 1862, however, the North had resolved itself to the long war ahead. The nation mobilized, and the natural resources of the Great Lakes were amassed to fuel the Union war effort. Iron was the building block of the war machine, with plentiful capital, coal, limestone, and laborers ready to shape it as needed. The key to it all was shipment by water. Boats on the water highway were the fastest and cheapest way to shuttle bulk materials around the

Workers keep ambulances ready for service. *Library of Congress*

Great Lakes. Advances in docks, locks, and loading procedures streamlined the process. In 1862, over 100,000 tons of iron ore again came through the Soo Locks, and in 1863, the figure doubled to a new high of over 200,000 tons. The rise in volume of the ore shipped from Lake Superior would continue well into the next century. About half the metal passing through the Soo Locks traveled down Lake Huron to Detroit and the manufacturing centers along Lake Erie. The other half went to Chicago, the fastest growing city on the Great Lakes. In these places, factories produced terrible new weapons that propelled Lake Superior ore onto the battlefield in increasingly lethal ways. Untold thousands of Confederate soldiers fell to the hail of Michigan metal during the Civil War.

However, battlefield injuries were never the main cause of death in either army. The worst enemy of all soldiers continued to be disease, which caused two-thirds of all wartime fatalities. Silent battles raged in the tight quarters of winter camps, where sickness spread with ease. That sad fact was again brought home to Grand Traverse when the *Herald's* Morgan Bates received news from a Tennessee river town that shook him to the core. Bates wrote: "We are deeply pained to learn that John Lewis Patrick died in the hospital, at Memphis, on the first of February. He was in our employ as an apprentice to the Printing business for more than two years, and left us last August to join the Mercantile Battery that was raised in Chicago. He was one of the noblest and purest young men we ever knew, and it caused us a heart-pang when he left us to volunteer for the defense of his country. All who knew him loved him, and his early death will cast a gloom over many hearts."

The bad news was made worse by the details of Patrick's death, which were provided by J.H. Hollingsworth, a fellow volunteer in the Chicago artillery battery. In a letter to Bates, he wrote: "It is my sad and painful duty to inform you of the death of Lewis Patrick. When the expedition left [Memphis] on the 20th December, for Vicksburg, Lewis had to be left behind, being quite sick from the measles. He was left in the best hospital in the city, and promised well for his recovery. Since leaving there I have written to him but have received no reply. The first news we received of him was the announcement of his death...We received no particulars with regard to its cause. His death is mourned by many in the Battery, for he was beloved by all. To me it feels as though I had lost a brother, for I loved him as one.

"We have been away from Chicago a little over three months, but we have seen more of the hardships of a soldier's life, and done more marching through the most of the enemy's country than any other Company has done in double the time. We have suffered greatly, and have been treated very roughly by the neglect and meanness of our Captain. He has almost ruined the Battery and we have but 40 men fit for duty to-day. Some are in the hospital, and many here in camp - located in a swamp – so sick they cannot leave their beds. They have little care, and no doctor. Two of our officers have resigned, and the third one has offered his resignation on account of the bad reputation our Captain has gained for us all. While writing, I am in my bed, so feeble I cannot move without assistance. I was taken sick just after the battle of Arkansas Post, and a few days after was taken from my bed, and, with other sick, was left lying on the bank five hours in a drenching rain, and without the least shelter. This was our Captain's fault. He was drunk. Since that time I have been sinking fast.

"Through the influence of one of our men I had a doctor come and see me. He told our Captain I would never be able for duty again and he ought to have me discharged and sent home at once. He would listen to no such talk, and will do nothing for me. I have written to my father to come after me and take me home, but I am afraid he will not arrive in time.

"I am willing to suffer for my country's sake, but it is hard when a man is left to die, far from home, when it can be prevented as well as not. I shall keep up my spirits and courage and perhaps they won't kill me so easy as they do others. It has fatigued me much to write this letter, and I shall have to stop. I can learn nothing of what is going on around me. With much sorrow and regrets for the sad occurrence, I close my letter. J.H. Hollingsworth."[266]

Three weeks after the death of John Lewis Patrick, the drunken captain of the Chicago Mercantile Battery was forced to resign. Fortunately, Private Hollingsworth's determination to keep up his "spirits and courage," mixed with good fortune, helped him hang on to life. Perhaps during his six month struggle to recover, Hollingsworth's father found him and nursed him back from the edge, for all through the Civil War anxious parents traveled to distant battlefields hoping to find, aid, or bury their fallen sons. Although he survived, the artillerist Hollingsworth never fully recovered from his illness, and when he was finally released from the hospital in the fall of 1863, he was transferred to the Veterans Relief Corps, a unit reserved for soldiers judged fit only for limited duty.

Winter's grim reaper was also at work in Virginia, where the 26th Michigan Infantry encamped. In March 1863, Smith wrote: "Mail came…1 from Mr Holden – there have been a good many deaths in the regiment by black measles."[267] Holden had already witnessed William Voice and William Remar die of disease the previous fall at Camp Jackson, and now more of his recruits were succumbing to a deadly mix of typhoid fever, diarrhea, malaria and other maladies.

In consecutive letters to the *Herald*, Oscar Eaton, a Grand Traverse volunteer serving in the 26th Michigan, gave details of the regiment's activities, accounts heavily weighed with scenes of death and dark visions of war. He wrote: "Our regiment is encamped on a large tract of land…about a half mile from town [Alexandria]; on these commons are numerous other bodies of troops encamped, they are also interspersed with half buried horses and some not buried at all – places where the nuisances and filth of the city are left in heaps above the ground to send forth their poisonous and pestilential vapors, aiding in peopling the hospitals, and fast filling cemeteries prepared for all that remains of him who left "the loved ones back home" to go forth "to do battle" with enemies of his country.

"Our company remained in the Regimental camp until January 23rd, when we were detached by Gen. Heintzelman from the regiment…some six or seven miles from town, to the westward, on a U.S. military railroad. There is but one house here, and that is occupied by the switch tender. The railroad here winds its way along the valley of a small stream, bounded on either side by a rough hilly country timbered with a light growth of oak, hickory, chestnut, pine, cedar, &c… The timber is now being stripped by the hundred acres for the use of the army in and around Alexandria and Washington. Our company found a delightful and healthful camping ground, near a splendid spring of soft water a few rods from the railroad track, where we have remained up to the present date. As to our duty here, we were divided into two squads, one on duty one day and the other the next; that duty consisted in aiding the teamsters in loading and unloading that were drawing out wood from the neighboring hills around the railroad...

"Now in regards to the health of Grand Traverse boys, I believe they are in tolerable health, if I except George N. Bigelow of Northport, who is very low with fever in one of the city hospitals, and P.D. Greenman of Whitewater, a nurse in the regimental hospital, who is also very low with bleeding at the nose, which has continued with occasional intermission for two or three weeks, but we hope they will soon be both restored to health, and one day to their families, for they are both heads of families. But alas, we are called to mourn the loss of another of our number by death - Gilbert Lachor, of the Peninsula, died last Wednesday. He had taken the measles and a cold afterward, which caused his death. That makes three from Grand Traverse County that we have lost by death."

Two weeks later, Lakeshore Tiger Oscar Eaton described the last days of a good friend as he clung to life in a Union military hospital, writing: "I came down here...to see a sick comrade and remain with him overnight, that Comrade is P.D. Greenman of Whitewater. In a former letter I think I mentioned his illness, with the hope he will soon be well again; but alas, that hope so far has not been realized. He grew worse until the regimental hospital, which is kept in tents, was not considered a suitable place for him...he was carefully removed in an ambulance to this hospital, which is two or three miles from the city of Alexandria...

"From the window of the room in which I am now writing the prospect is delightful, when the rough edges are taken off of a near view of the desolation of war and mellowed down by distance. A view is here had of the Potomac for a distance of 12 or 15 miles, bearing upon its bosom multitudes of sail and steam crafts of all sizes and descriptions, each intent on accomplishing its own destination. The cities of Washington, Georgetown and Alexandria occupying prominent place in the landscape; the Capitol, which, standing as it does on an eminence...with its lofty dome near three hundred feet in height, stands out in bold relief...

"The room in which Mr. Greenman was placed, and in which he now lies, is on the second floor of what was once the north wing of the Fairfax Female Seminary. He is very low and converses with difficulty. His disease is pronounced by the doctor of the hospital to be Epistoxis; they say that they hope to raise him, but I can see no hope; it seems to me that Death has already claimed him as his own. He has the best of medical attention, the very best of nursing – one man at least is with him to wait upon him night and day – ladies visit him every hour or two through the day rendering him their sympathy and bringing him every species of nourishment and delicacy that their ingenuity can devise…His room is fourteen feet square and twelve feet high, well ventilated and warmed, and he is the only person who occupies it. In short, if I except the absence of the dearest of earthly friends, I can scarcely conceive of a sick man under more favorable circumstances."

Days later, Eaton returned to the letter, writing: "Last week our weather seemed to alternate between winter and spring. On Friday, it snowed and seemed as cold as winter, and on Saturday it rained and seemed more like spring. So it has been nearly all winter." Used to the presence of death in many forms, the Lakeshore Tiger continued: "One day last week as a train was backing up to take on wood, a mule on the track threw off two cars, killing five men and injuring six more, they belonged to the N.Y. 143ʳᵈ." However, Eaton's casual air escaped him when he again turned to the subject of his sick comrade. He wrote: "And now I have to record what to me seems the most melancholy event that has occurred since coming into the service; my friend and former neighbor from Whitewater, P.D. Greenman, is no more. He died yesterday morning, March 22d, at fifteen minutes past twelve o'clock. He left Whitewater last August a robust and healthy man. After returning from the visit which he made his family in November last, he entered the regimental hospital, as nurse, where he remained until he was taken sick, which was about the 12th of February." The previous fall, Reverend Smith had watched the *Galena* steam into Northport harbor carrying "between 30 & 40 volunteers" on leave from Camp Jackson. One of the soldiers was Greenman, making his last trip home alive.

Private Oscar Eaton concluded with the details of his friend's death, writing: "He leaves a wife and three small children to mourn his loss. He died a calm and peaceful death, committing his family to the care of Him who doeth all things well and without whose knowledge not a sparrow falls to the ground. A brother reached him before he died. His body is sent to Sturgis, Mich."[268] This is how another Grand Traverse soldier's life ceased to be in the winter of 1863, one of hundreds of thousands of tragic scenes played out in war-torn Virginia during the Civil War.

Greenman's family could find solace in the fact that he had avoided an anonymous end, achieving the basic requirement of the concept of a "good death" that evolved during the Civil War. To die alone and unknown was for many soldiers the worst of fates, and one all too often realized. A uniform means of identifying the dead, such as the modern "dog tag," had yet to be adopted by either army. The unidentified were frequently wrapped in blankets and buried by the dozens, but the mystery of their vanished lives lingered on to haunt those the lost soldier left behind.

For the Civil War soldier, the horror of losing one's identity came in many forms. The war's chief killer – disease – arrived in epidemics and often overwhelmed a hospital's ability to treat the sick, much less keep track of the dead. When lethal diseases took hold, soldiers were separated from their regiments and carried away to distant hospitals, and in the chaos of war, their records could be lost or left behind, along with friends able to identify them. On the battlefield, a new type of mechanized war introduced weapons that could obliterate any trace of a human being in an explosive instant. Those wounded in combat were often stripped of their clothing prior to surgery or had their pockets emptied by thieves who roamed the battlefield after each bloody engagement. When death finally came, little remained to tell others their names.

The bodies of the dead are collected for burial. *Library of Congress*

In addition to being identified, Lakeshore Tiger Oscar Eaton wrote that his friend Greenman had "died a calm and peaceful death." The fact that his brother was at his bedside to hear his last words and bear witness to his faith in divine providence also brought a measure of comfort to the soldier and those he left behind. Furthermore, the Greenmans had the means to ship their son's body back home. These were the best terms a dying soldier and his family could hope for during the chaotic Civil War. Though fellow Grand Traverse soldier John Lewis Patrick had no loved ones near him when he died, at least his passing was a certainty. Untold thousands of other Americans who sent a loved one off to fight in the Civil War would spend their lives tortured by not knowing what had become of their sons, husbands, and fathers.

April 1863 election results showed that in Grand Traverse and newly independent Antrim County, the vast majority of voters backed Republicans. However, even as local men fought and died for the Union, there was no consensus on the Leelanau Peninsula. In an article titled "Leelanaw County," the *Herald* wrote: "This new County has not done quite so well as we hoped she would do, owing to local divisions on the County Seat question; but Glen Arbor came to the work nobly and has done her whole duty. She saved the Republican County ticket, and must take the front rank as the banner town. No local jealousies or petty quarrels can swerve the sterling Republicans from that town from a straight line. All honor to Glen Arbor!

"We received no figures from Centerville, but understand the Republican majority on the State ticket was 30, and that a Republican Supervisor was elected. There was a terrible splitting of the County ticket. The township of Leelanau (Northport) has fallen from grace and gone back to the beggarly elements of the world, the flesh, and the Devil. The Copperhead State ticket received 14 majority, the County ticket 22, and the Township ticket about the same. George N. Smith was defeated for Supervisor by 22 votes."[269] However, Smith did not leave the election empty handed, having won the race for Leelanau County Coroner.

Republicans like Morgan Bates used the term "Copperhead" to refer to northern Democrats who were opposed to Lincoln and the war. The word derived from an incident in 1861 when a package from Virginia arrived in a northern post office with two copperhead snakes inside. The poisonous vipers, unlike rattlesnakes, gave no warning of their presence or their impending strike. For Republicans, Copperheads seemed like the perfect name for what they perceived were clandestine traitors in their midst. Though the snakes were dispatched without injury, the northern press described the incident as a sneak attack against innocent people. As the war progressed, anti-war Democrats embraced the label, wearing copper pennies on their lapels to identify their stance on the war. The name stuck and was perceived as either an insult or a compliment depending on which side you were on. Copperheads openly criticized the Lincoln Administration throughout the Civil War, revealing not only the deep divisions about the terrible conflict in the North, but also the determination of its people to tolerate free speech even under extreme circumstances.

Later that spring, the question of where to locate the seat of Leelanau County government was settled at the polls. The distances that separated the rival harbor towns of Glen Arbor, Leland, and Northport, and the difficulty of commuting between the places, made the choice of any one of the Leelanau settlements inconvenient for the others. Moreover, the concurrent emergence of the three ports, all striving to attract the prosperous trans-lake ship traffic to their docks, fostered a competitive, rather than cooperative, spirit between them. After the votes were counted, the distinction and power of hosting the county seat had gone to Northport. Reverend Smith wrote: "Today has been held the election...It has been an exciting time. Every poll tolled was for Northport."

As Northport reveled in its new position in Leelanau, its place as the lead town in Grand Traverse Country was being seriously challenged. The long-awaited road connecting Grand Traverse to the outside world neared completion, beginning a new era in transportation to the region. In an article titled "The First Train," the *Herald* reported: "Benjamin Howell, of Delta, Eaton Co., is the Pioneer on the Newaygo and Northport State Road. He came through with his family, his teams, his cattle, his herds and his poultry, cutting his way through the wilderness on that portion of the line which has not been opened, and crossing the Manistee on a raft. He was five weeks on the route, and arrived in good health and spirits."[270]

A week later, wagon trains were rolling North. The *Herald* wrote: "This road is now open and made passable for wagons between Traverse City and Newaygo, a distance of one hundred and ten miles. Emigrant teams have already passed over it. The Little Manistee has been bridged and there is a raft at the crossing of the Great Manistee, suitable for ferriage of teams and cattle, with strong ropes stretched across the river, by which the raft may be drawn from shore to shore.

A permanent bridge will be built at this point in September. Contactors are now busily at work...fourteen miles of the road is also under contract between Traverse City and Northport, and there will be a passable road to that place in October.[271] It was a testament to Northport's prominence that West Michigan's first major road north ended at the tip of Leelanau, but at the same time the new road began to change the dynamics of the region.

Until the Northport-Newaygo road opened, almost everyone arrived in Grand Traverse on boats. The common experience created a shared outlook and a sense of a larger community united by the water highway. The new land road invigorated the area, bringing more homesteaders to settle and relieving to a degree the isolation of winter. The state road also marked a shift away from dependence on water, a move that would redefine the potential and standing of every northern Michigan town. Traverse City was an immediate benefactor of the project, and here a network of rough two tracks began to radiate into the countryside. Just as Northport had evolved as the Grand Traverse center of travel by water, so Traverse City now grew as the hub of road traffic.

Improvements in ship technology also worked in Traverse City's favor. A decade before, schooners and side-wheel steamers were the two main types of vessels working on the Great Lakes. Traverse City, at the head of the bay, was a 60-mile voyage down and back from the main shipping lanes. Schooners risked getting bogged down by gentle bay breezes, and sidewheel steamers, with their voracious appetite for wood, rarely strayed from routes between large ports. Now the growing fleet of fast, propeller-driven ships made easy work of a round trip on the Bay. In June 1863, Hannah, Lay & Co. began building a new 125 foot-wide dock at Traverse City, designed "for the accommodation of vessels loading with wood for the Chicago market."[272]

A subsequent *Herald* article titled "Going Ahead" elaborated on Traverse City's progress. It said: "More buildings will be erected, and more substantial improvements made in Traverse City this season, than in any other previous three years of its history...Traverse City is destined to become, in a few years, one of the most important points in Northern Michigan. This is no vain or idle boast. Its position and natural advantages are such that nothing but the over-throw of the government by the Rebels and Copperheads, and the consequent destruction of the country, can check its future progress."[273]

Despite the North's overwhelming advantage in men and materials, in the spring of 1863 the eventual outcome of the Civil War was very much in doubt. Warm weather brought a new season of military engagement to Virginia and things were not going well for the Union. Although the names of the top Union generals changed, the latest offensive by the Army of the Potomac looked like a replay of previous battles. It was General Joseph Hooker's turn to lead a swollen Union force across Virginia, while the innovative General Robert E. Lee again proved his genius on his home turf. In a series of engagements around Chancellorsville during the first week of May, the Rebel army repeatedly outmaneuvered the larger and better-equipped Union force. Once again, the humiliated Federals straggled back in disarray toward Washington. The two armies suffered more than 30,000 casualties, but the war raged on. Lee knew that for the Confederacy, time was of the essence. For the second year in a row, he began to make plans to carry the fight into the Yankee heartland in hopes of bringing the Civil War to a quick end.

The *Herald's* Bates ruminated on Lee's options for the upcoming military campaign in a May editorial, writing: "It is a cheerful part of the rebel programme that they intend to assume the aggressive. This had not been their policy heretofore. Their rule had been to await attack, not to make it. When they have varied from this rule, they have very oftener failed than succeeded. If they adopt a different policy, it will be from necessity and not from choice. Every week's delay is, to them, equivalent to a loss in battle. They cannot afford to wait. The recent message of Jeff. Davis is conclusive upon this point. To them, inaction is as disastrous as defeat. A long war will be ruin. An unsuccessful campaign can be no worse. They may be whipped if they fight. They will starve if they do not. The Commander-in-Chief says they chose to fight. And they will fight hard. We have official proclamation of their purpose to do so. It is frank and manly of them to give us this warning…and unwise if we do not prepare ourselves to give them a proper reception.

"What will come of this new programme remains to be seen. We expect beneficent results to flow from it, in spite of the terrible slaughter that must ensue. It will be the death throb of the rebellion. Even partial success will be the exhaustion to the enemy, while defeat will be prostration and death."[274] Events transpiring within the next 60 days would once again show the editor's remarkable foresight.

On the western front, General Grant's spring offensive stalled outside of Vicksburg, a city whose near perfect defensive position earned it the name, "Gibraltar of the Confederacy." Vicksburg sat on a bluff high above the Mississippi River, where ships navigating an abrupt u-turn in the river's course ran the gauntlet of well-armed Rebel fortifications. Spring rains had swollen the

Benjamin H. Grierson. *Library of Congress*

swamps of the surrounding countryside, making approach by land futile, as several failed Union attacks in March had shown. The last Confederate stronghold on the great river held on.

A bright spot in Grant's spring campaign was a cavalry raid through Mississippi led by Union Colonel Benjamin H. Grierson. In April, Grierson rode south with 1700 horse soldiers on a diversionary attack, following Grant's orders to wreak havoc in Mississippi for as long as possible and escape as best they could. New York City based *Harper's Weekly* – one of the North's most widely read newspapers - described the action: "The brigade commanded by Colonel Grierson started from La Grange, Tennessee, and rode to Baton Rouge, a distance of 800 miles, through the heart of rebel country. They were seventeen days on the march. They captured over 1000 prisoners and 1200 horses; destroyed for many miles two important railroads, and stores, and property valued at over four millions of dollars; and finally, on May 1, were received at Baton Rouge with great enthusiasm."[275]

Reflecting on Grierson's raid in his memoirs, General Grant wrote: "I first heard through a Southern paper of the complete success of Colonel Grierson… This raid was of great importance, for Grierson had attracted the attention of the enemy from the main movement against Vicksburg."[276] While Grierson's advance distracted the Confederate command, Grant was able to maneuver his forces into position around the Mississippi River city, and by mid-May, Vicksburg was cut off. However, two more frontal assaults on the Confederate fortress failed, and the Union advance settled into a siege.

Though his cavalry inflicted substantial damage on Mississippi railroads and supply depots, Grierson's most important victory was psychological. Until his successes in Mississippi, the more experienced Confederate cavalry regularly humiliated their Union opponents. Horsemanship was a tradition in the South, while most Union recruits, before their stint as soldiers, used their animals mainly to pull plows and wagons on their farms. However, by the spring of 1863, Grierson's cavalrymen had learned their trade and were now riding through the Deep South virtually unscathed. In the process, they demonstrated the advantages of a new way of fighting through enemy territory. Rather than be burdened by supply trains, Grierson's cavalry moved quickly and lightly, foraging for food and other supplies as they advanced.

The Union raiders found that beyond its hard line of soldiers on the front, the Confederate nation was unraveling. The economy of Mississippi, deprived by Union blockades of its cotton economy, had ground to a halt. There were no immigrants, little industry, and few prospects - only uncertainty. *Harper's Weekly* reported Colonel Grierson as saying "that nothing had surprised him more than the utter hollowness of the rebellion. It was, as he expressed it, a mere crust, an empty shell." After the war, Grant asserted: "It was Grierson who first set the example of what might be done in the interior of the enemy's country from which to draw supplies." The success of the tactic attracted the attention of General William Tecumseh Sherman, Grant's trusted corps commander then engaged around Vicksburg. The previous fall, Sherman wrote that Grierson's cavalry, "made some bold and successful dashes" Now he called Grierson's foray into Mississippi "the most brilliant expedition of the war."[277] When later chosen by Grant to lead the Union Army in the western theatre, General Sherman applied Grierson's foraging lesson on a grand scale from Georgia to the Carolinas during his 1864 March to the Sea.

The advance through Mississippi made Grierson an instant hero in the North. In June, a portrait of the Colonel mounted on his horse graced the cover of *Harper's Weekly*. The Union Army promoted him to the rank of brigadier general. It was an unlikely rise for a boy who, at eight years old, had almost died from a kick in the head by a horse, and a man who made his living as a music teacher and band conductor.

Following the Civil War, Grierson distinguished himself on the western plains as a commander of the famous Black cavalry regiment known as the Buffalo Soldiers. In 1896, he retired to Omena on the Leelanau Peninsula, where he built a sprawling cottage he named "The Garrison." His favorite pastime was watching boats steam in and out of Omena - then a booming resort town - from his fourth story watchtower. By chance, General Grierson's next door neighbor

General Grierson built his retirement cottage, named The Garrison, on Omena Bay. *Courtesy Donna Allington*

in Omena was another unlikely Civil War hero, fellow general and Medal of Honor winner Byron M. Cutcheon.

Cutcheon was a University of Michigan graduate and a professor of ancient languages when the Confederates shelled Fort Sumter in 1861. During the Civil War, a university degree was often enough to land the volunteer an officer's rank, and in 1862, Cutcheon joined the 20th Michigan Infantry as a captain. Within 90 days, he was promoted to major. In another coincidence, only a week after Grierson emerged from the Mississippi backcountry a hero, Cutcheon led the charge against a Confederate position that would win him the Medal of Honor. Cutcheon described the action, writing: "After some skirmishing at Monticello, Ky., we had fallen back to the Cumberland River on May 9, 1863…when Morgan's advance attacked our outpost at Horse Shoe Bend that evening. I hastened back to the Bend to take command of the companies stationed there, while Colonel Smith remained behind to hurry up the rest of the regiment. That night the regiment came up, and on the morning of the 10th we were re-enforced by a small body…of the Twelfth Kentucky Cavalry, dismounted, and armed with Henry repeating rifles.

"Before their arrival, Morgan's men made a dash and succeeded in seizing the 'Coffey' house, a large log house east of the road, so called after its owner. We had occupied it as a picket post throughout the night. The house, outbuildings, and garden were filled with rebel sharpshooters, who, though they harassed us throughout the day, did not attempt to advance.

"About 4 o'clock PM – It was Sunday – Colonel Jacob…resolved to take the aggressive, and to drive the rebels out of the house and grounds. To me was assigned the command of four companies…At the signal we went forward at our very best pace. I was then just six feet two inches tall, one-half the length in legs, and an expert runner from practice in college. I took a course directly down the road to the south in front of the companies – one could hardly say 'line', for there was no line; it was a 'go as you please' foot race…The distance was about a hundred and fifty yards, and we made it on the jump. There were three steps up to the porch, but I made only one of them. With my sword in my right hand, and a big Colt's navy revolver in my left, I threw myself against the weather beaten door. A moment later Captain Barnes came to my side, and the door yielded.

"Why we were not both shot down then and there, I have never been able to understand. The rebels certainly missed their opportunity. Instead, we saw Johnnies going out of the back doors and windows, and making for the woods, while the companies coming up right and left of the house, poured volleys into the retreating foe."[278]

The following year, Colonel Cutcheon's 20th Michigan Infantry fought alongside regiments filled with Grand Traverse soldiers in a bloody series of battles in Virginia. In 1891, General Cutcheon received the Congressional Medal of Honor for his sprint at Horseshoe Bend. Not long after, he built a home on Omena's Cottage Row in Leelanau County, where he spent summer days writing about the Civil War.

During the spring of 1863, the blue uniforms of soldiers in transit were a frequent sight on the docks of Grand Traverse harbor towns. Soldiers on leave took advantage of their last chance to visit home before the summer of fighting began. Henry Budd, one of the four Honor Guards who brought the remains of Sgt. William Voice back to Northport the previous fall, spent time in the company of his wife and nine children. Fellow 26th Michigan Infantry volunteer

Charles Clark passed a few days with friends and family near Lake Leelanau. Soon after the ice cleared from Northport harbor, the two soldiers ended their furlough and "left on the *Free State* for the Army."[279] Their families resumed their lives without husbands and fathers, while wives and children carried on the work of the farm. For many, the situation became permanent as news of disease and battlefield deaths reached the northern lakes, as was eventually the case with both Budd and Clark. Every corner of the nation paid the cold, hard cost of a nation divided by war, and Grand Traverse Country was no exception.

In response to growing hardships on the home front, Leelanau County officials set aside "the sum of $5000…to be raised by tax in the year 1863…for a Volunteer Family Relief Fund."[280] Establishing a fund to support the families of Union soldiers was the first fiscal act of the new Leelanau County government and stands as a high point in its legislative history.

Even with the drain of rising enlistments and battlefield losses, Grand Traverse Country continued to grow. The lure of free Homestead Act land drew many more immigrants than left to fight. In May, Smith notes: "*City of Boston* came…some 40 families aboard – 7 stayed here." Northport's story was repeated at ports all along the Great Lakes, the nation's newest coast of opportunity. Harriet Fisher of Glen Arbor wrote to her friends the Boizards in Chicago: "You would really be surprised to see how our country has improved since you left. There is no Government land in our Town. All has been taken and most by actual settlers…There are so many families and land lookers moving in." Several months later, Harriet's husband John seconded her observations, writing to the Boizards: "The country has filled up very fast the past season. It is very different from what it was when you were here."[281] There was no such draw in the South, where laboring whites were considered low class. As a result, every Southern soldier killed was an irreplaceable loss to the Confederacy, while the Union and its army grew in strength in spite of mounting casualties.

It was the job of Michigan recruiters to fill new regiments and in 1863 they worked Grand Traverse Country hard. The thousand plus people in and around the lead town of Northport made it fertile ground for enlistments. Smith recorded the arrival of the first wave of recruiters in May. He wrote: "*Pittsburg* came…2 recruiting officers for the Indians on & 1 Indian recruit came on."[282] The Indian recruiters arriving in Northport on the *Pittsburg* worked on behalf of the 1st Michigan Sharp Shooters, a new regiment of volunteers initially drawn from the Grand River and Kalamazoo River valleys. The very name Sharp Shooters distinguished the regiment from everyday infantry, adding a dash of glamour to the thought of signing up. However, by the spring of 1863, recruiters had already tapped a good many of the men available from the more populous areas of the state. Enlistment in the ranks of the 1ˢᵗ Michigan Sharp Shooters stalled, and recruiters began to search more remote regions. Now they had arrived in Northport.

In 1863, the majority of the Native people of the northwestern Great Lakes continued to live in traditional ways. The rifle had replaced the bow and arrow, but hunting and gathering food still occupied much of the day. The 1st Michigan was a sharp shooting outfit, and recruiters traveled to Grand Traverse where skill with the weapon came at an early age. In order to attract Native American marksmen into the regiment, Michigan's Governor Blair designated Company K of the 1ˢᵗ Michigan Sharp Shooters an all-Native unit, then a one-of-a-kind in the Union Army. In the next two years, the Indians of Company K - many with strong ties to Grand Traverse - would fight and die in some of the deadliest battles of the Civil War.

Indian recruiters were a sign of the changing times. For the first two years of the war, both Natives and African-Americans were not permitted to join the Union Army. Several contingents of Michigan Indians had tried to sign up, only to be rejected. Then in February 1863, Congress passed the Negro Regimen Law, which allowed blacks to serve. The following month the legislature

Black soldier guards artillery pieces at a Union supply depot. *Library of Congress*

approved "an act for enrolling and calling out the national forces," which established the national draft. An across-the-board loosening of race restrictions followed. Soldiers in the field set aside their prejudices when they saw that Confederate minie balls were color blind. Even the most bigoted recruit understood that every soldier of color with a rifle, whether African-American or Indian, meant one less white life on the line. The *Herald* stated succinctly, "The enlisting of negroes goes on briskly. This will save so much drafting of white men."[283]

Soon articles in the *Herald* began to speak of the contributions of black soldiers in the Union Army. One said: "Eighteen regiments of nine months and two year men, chiefly from New England, are now on their way home…What then? Is everything to fall to pieces…and we to lose all we have gained? Not at all, for happily our negro troops are ready to step in and hold the captured points against all comers…Greatly to the disgust of the rebels, and their Northern friends, the new era is fully opened by making the blacks useful in this war against their old oppressors. Loyal men have come to recognize a poetic justice in thus ending the slaveholders rebellion by arming and enrolling the blacks in the armies of the Union."[284]

Another story in the paper read: "It is not alone over rebels in arms that the colored Union troops have won victories. They have "conquered the prejudice" which two centuries of slavery have wrought into the fibre of our American thought. They have stricken down the fallacy that the black man is fit only for menial service, and has not the capacity for progress and improvement. They have shown that the ages of degradation and enforced inferiority have not quenched the vital spark of manliness. They have accepted the severest and highest test to which men are accustomed to subject themselves, and they have not been found wanting. Last, but not least, they have baffled the insidious thought that their presence would demoralize the white troops with whom they fought as comrades. By these their courage is acknowledged, and little will be heard now of the "nigger" question as connected with the army. A few hundred black men filling soldiers' graves in behalf of a flag which had its stars for the white man and too often its stripes for the negro, are an unanswerable argument."[285]

For African-Americans, the desire of the oppressed to join in combat against their immediate oppressor was easily understood. Their stake in the outcome of the war, and their desire to avenge generations of cruelty against their race, compelled many to enthusiastically take up arms. However, the motivation of Native American recruits was more obscure. Company K soldiers were for the most part the sons of Indians who, a quarter century before, had lost their

Michigan lands through the 1836 Treaty of Washington. Since the treaty, Native people experienced little peace, driven at every turn from their ancestral territory and traditions. The Treaty of 1855 was turning out to be another disaster for the Indians of Michigan, with their holdings further diminished by the pact. Yet now the Indians lined up to fight for the government under which they regularly suffered.

The Native soldiers must have entered the Union Army with mixed feelings, with the loss of their homeland still fresh, and the insults to their culture ongoing. However, for a people who for generations traveled freely through the open spaces of Great Lakes region, the brutal confinement of slavery was far more chilling. The intrusion of farmer's fences was one thing, chains and shackles another. Many Native people saw no hope in the Southern slave empire, and felt their turn on the auction block would come if the Rebels succeeded. In a speech printed by the *Detroit Advertiser and Tribune,* an Ojibwa leader warned his people: "If the South conquers you will be slaves, dogs. There will be no protection for us; we shall be driven from our homes, our lands and the graves of our friends."[286]

Moreover, though the nation was still mired in racism, Lincoln's Emancipation Proclamation and the Negro Regimen Law were significant steps toward a more inclusive society. Freedom and equality were still far from reality, but the United States was quickly evolving, and promises made in the nation's founding documents were now backed by law. By fighting for the Union, Native recruits hoped to establish their place in the reforming United States, or at least secure a better chance to hold on to what little land and political power they still possessed. In the end, however, many Indians joined the Union Army simply out of economic necessity, for the enlistment bounties and a soldier's monthly pay were often their only opportunity to provide for their families.

Pvt. Oscar Eaton, who earlier in 1863 described the death by disease of a fellow Grand Traverse soldier to the *Herald,* now sent a spring update of his regiment's actions to the paper. Writing from a "deserted farm" in Virginia on May 20, he said: "I have about made up my mind to bore the readers of the *Herald* for a short time this excessively warm afternoon in regard to the where-abouts and what-abouts of the 26th Mich., Co. A, of which regiment contains most of the Traverse boys, who volunteered in our County, some over nine months ago.

"On the morning of the 20th of April we were aroused at daybreak by the hideous screeching of a railroad locomotive in front of our camp and the announcement…to report…at Alexandria forthwith. We soldiers…in a very short

Hospital wagons awaiting the call. *Library of Congress*

time…had prepared a cup of coffee, and swallowed the same, packed our knap-sacks, transferred our Company moveables – tents included – to the cars, and went whirling long toward Alexandria…At 10 o'clock, A.M., the regiment em-barked on board a transport and were steaming down the Potomac. In leaving Alexandria were obliged to bid adieu to our good old Sibley tents, which for the last eight months had sheltered us from many a heavy storm both of rain and snow, and in which we enjoyed so many soldierly comforts, and betake ourselves to "shelter tents." This, of course, we understand to mean active service in the field, in lieu of guarding cities and handling cordwood. Our regiment reached Suffolk, Va.…and were soon assisting in the construction of rifle-pits, with "rebel bullets" flying over and around their heads…

"On arriving at Suffolk we found the scene that presented itself quite excit-ing. Longstreet was laying siege to the place with over sixty thousand men; our men were actively engaged in strengthening their works, sometimes working night and day…already we have over 16 miles of breast-works and rifle-pits, with a dozen or fifteen forts, with a large number of guns already mounted… throwing shot and shell in the direction of the enemy camp; a continuous fir-ing being kept up by the sharp-shooters on both sides from their rifle pits, by day; a strong force of infantry being thrown out as reserve pickets in the entrenchments by night; regiments were almost constantly arriving both night and day; from the beating of the reveille at early dawn until late in the evening, the atmosphere seemed loaded down with martial music, from brass and other regimental bands; in short we here came in contact with all the paraphernalia of active and vigorous warfare.

"On the 1ˢᵗ of May we were eye-witnesses of a bit of a fight...the 99ᵗʰ N.Y. advanced, only 250 strong, received the fire of more than six times their number of the concealed enemy, which mowed them down fearfully, but the brave fellows advanced steadily up to the enemy's pits without the least signs of wavering or flinching...when we heard the bugle signal to recall skirmishers, when they retired as orderly as they advanced, having lost in killed and wounded 56, in the space of about 15 minutes. As soon as our men had retired a little, our shells made it rather warm for the enemy in their pits, when they broke for the woods in their rear, whereupon all our artillery that could be brought to bear upon them, opened with terrific effect; shells exploded within large groups of men, doing much execution, while the solid shot mowed their paths from different points, cutting them up terribly. Our men skirmished with them two or three days, when they slipped away one dark night and let us have it our own way."

Eaton continued his letter from Suffolk on June 1, writing: "For the dirt and dust that covers this paper and almost neutralizes my ink marks, my apology is, that during my 11 days absence from here, in marching and counter-marching over the most dusty roads imaginable, my only portfolio was my cartridge-box, and my duties will not admit to transcribing.

"On the evening of the 20ᵗʰ we took up our lines of march from the "Deserted Farm" to Winsor, which is a distance from here about 16 miles on the Petersburg railroad, where we lay one day, then advanced some 4 miles further on the Black Water road...where we took up a position in an opening ...surrounded by a thick growth of pine, with the enemy in another opening...in front of the one we occupied. Our business was to hold them in check while our men confiscated about 20 miles of their railroad iron, which they were doing as fast as possible, working night and day with a large force of contrabands, taking up the rails and running them to Norfolk. Our force at this point consisted of four regiments of infantry, a small force of cavalry and six pieces of artillery, which were soon posted...when skirmishing commenced about noon and lasted the balance of the day, the enemy losing quite a number in killed and wounded, and our men none.

"The following day Co. A took up the skirmishing in conjunction with a company of Rhode Island boys, which we kept up through the day with occasional firing until 3 P.M., when some 250 rebels charged on less than 100 Rhode Island boys with one of their hideous yells, and after a sharp struggle succeeded in driving them a short distance, but they were soon reinforced and regained their position; in the meantime our artillery opened up on the enemy with shell, which soon dispersed them, when our men charged through the woods in sight of their forces. Our company was reinforced by Co. E, Capt. Culver, who was in advance of his company reconnoitering, and on returning was mistaken for the enemy by one of our company and received a shot in the arm, which has since proved fatal; this unfortunate affair was the only casualty on our side." It was a bad start for the 26th Michigan Infantry, whose first kill was a captain in their own regiment.

In late June, Lee began to move the Confederate Army north. His offensive into Maryland the previous fall had been checked in the bloody stalemate at Antietam, but recent victories in Virginia again left Union forces in disarray and Southern forces confident. Lee understood that every day the war continued the prospects for the Confederacy grew slimmer. The great defensive general decided his only option was to leave Virginia and attack. The *Grand Traverse Herald* echoed eastern headlines warning "Lee's Whole Army Moving Northward."[287]

Lincoln kept Hooker on as head of the Army of the Potomac even after his disastrous rout at Chancellorsville, though the General's shine had faded considerably. As Lee made his way into Union territory and marched through Maryland, Hooker maneuvered his army between the Confederates and Washington. After a quarrel over strategy and the deployment of troops, Hooker resigned. With the Civil War in the balance, a weary Lincoln replaced Hooker with General George Meade, who pursued the Confederates into Pennsylvania.

Harriet Fisher addressed the apprehension many loyal citizens felt about the Army of the Potomac's revolving leadership and the stuttering way the war was being prosecuted. She wrote: "Quite a number have enlisted here, 13, I think. So you see Glen Arbor has contributed her share towards putting down this Rebellion, and what a terrible war it is. So many lives lost. I wish it would end, but not until the South are whipped. I have no patience with them or those who sympathize with them. It really seems to me as though our Generals are afraid of hurting somebody while the South were fighting to kill. We have been afraid of hurting our Brethren but I think they ought to be dealt with like Enemies they are, and of the worst kind. I always considered family fights the very worst, and what is this but a family fight. If I was a man I would see what I could do. I see by the papers Gen. Mead has taken Gen. Hooker's place. What is the trouble with the Gen's. that they are so often changed. Are they not competent. Are they considered not trusty, or is it politics? I hope the right man will be found, and soon."[288] In light of the week-long lag in communications from the frontlines to Grand Traverse, Fisher could not have known that many of her concerns had already been addressed in the foothills of southern Pennsylvania.

In a story titled "Smelling a Minie Ball," readers of the *Grand Traverse Herald* got a whiff of the odor that would soon become familiar to the tens of thousands of soldiers converging on the Pennsylvania town of Gettysburg. The paper wrote: "A correspondent from the battle field, speaking of the effects of a passing rifle ball, says: the most singular thing…is the effect of those balls upon the atmosphere through which they pass. The passage of one immediately across your face is followed by a momentary sensation of deadly sickness. The air seems thick, stifling and putrid, like that of a newly opened vault, accompanied by an odor of certain kinds of fungi found in the woods, and never willingly disturbed by either man or beast." Another piece in the *Herald* compared the scale of American wars to date, writing: "During the Revolutionary War there were fought thirty-six battles; during the war of 1812, eighteen; during the Mexican war, twelve; and in the present war thus far forty-seven."[289] Battle number 48 was about to change the course of the Civil War.

The opposing armies collided at Gettysburg during the first three days of July in the greatest single battle in American history. By July 10, boats carried the news of the Union's momentous victory to Grand Traverse Country. In an article titled "The Decisive Battle of the War," and below the banner "Lee's Army Demoralized and Flying to the Mountains," the *Herald* reported: "The Propellor *Alleghany*…brings a *Free Press Extra* with news of the Great Battle of the Fourth of July and a glorious Federal Victory over the Rebel army."[290]

The people of Grand Traverse learned of Gettysburg through the eyes of a reporter from the *Cincinnati Gazette,* who described the culminating battle on July 3 – a bloody affair known as Pickett's charge - to readers of the *Herald.* He wrote: "The rebels seemed to have gathered up all their strength and desperation for one fierce, convulsive effort that would sweep over and wash out our obstinate resistance…We had some shallow rifle pits, with a barricade of rails from the fences. The rebel line, stretching away miles to the left…Pickett's splendid division in front…came steadily, and, as it seemed, resistlessly sweeping up. Our skirmishers retired slowly from the Emmettsburg road, holding their ground tenaciously to the last. The rebels reserved their fire till they reached this same road, then opened with a terrific crash. From a hundred iron throats, meantime, their artillery had been thundering on our barricades.

"As the tempest of fire approached its height, he [Union General Gibbons] walked along the line and renewed his orders to the men to reserve their fire.

The rebels – three lines deep – came steadily up. They were in point blank range. At last the order came! From thrice six thousand guns there came a sheet of smoky flame, a crash, a rush of leaden Death. The line melted away; but there came a second resistless still. It had been our supreme effort – on the instant we were not equal to another.

"Up to the rifle pits, across them, over the barricade – the momentum of the charge, the mere machine strength of their combined action swept them on. Our thin line could fight, but it could not oppose weight to momentum. It was pushed behind the guns. Right on came the rebels. They were upon the guns, were bayoneting the gunners, were waving their flags over our pieces. But they had penetrated to the fatal point. A storm of grape and cannister tore its way from man to man, and marked its track with corpses straight down the line. They had exposed themselves to the enfilading fire of the guns on the western slope of Cemetery Hill; that exposure sealed their fate.

"The line reeled back – disjointed already – in an instant in fragments. Our men were just behind the guns. They leaped forward upon the disordered mass: but there was little need for fighting now. A regiment threw down its arms, and with colors at its head rushed over and surrendered. All along the field smaller detachments did the same...the escaped fragments of the charging line fell back – the battle was over."[291]

The fear and confusion that enveloped soldiers from both armies during the furious fighting, and the reluctance of some soldiers to fire on their fellow Americans, was reflected in an unusual report by the Union's Bureau of Ordnance, which said: "On the field of Gettysburg there were 27,574 guns picked up, and of these 24,000 were found to be loaded, and half of them were double loaded. One fourth had three to ten loads in, and many had five to six balls to one charge of powder. In some cases the powder was above the ball, in others the cartridges were not broken at the end, while in one musket 23 balls, 62 buckshot, and a quantity of powder were all mixed up together."[292]

Three miles to the east of the infantry battle, the cavalries of the two great armies collided. In the initial engagement, General George Armstrong Custer rode at the head of the Union charge. Only days before, the 23 year-old Michigander became the youngest man in the Union Army to receive a general's star. Now, as the charging horsemen from the two armies quickly closed the distance between them, General Custer turned in his saddle and called out to his Michigan brigade, "Come on, you Wolverines."

Custer was the third general with ties to Omena to become a Union Army hero during the summer of 1863. Like Generals Cutcheon and Grierson, Custer's rise to the top of the ranks was against the odds. He finished last in the West Point Class of 1861, and his courtship of his future wife, Libby Bacon, was complicated by the fact that her father, Judge Daniel Bacon of Monroe, believed Custer had no future. Despite few positive signs in his early service, Custer's distinct brand of bravado proved well-suited to a cavalry command, and his courage under fire was desperately needed in the Union Cavalry. The expanding war was the land of opportunity for a West Point trained soldier with ambition, and Custer's leadership in a series of minor engagements earlier that spring fueled his meteoric rise. General Custer now commanded a brigade of four Michigan Cavalry regiments. On July 3, 1863, the "Boy General" would dispel doubts as to whether he could handle his new rank.

The cavalry battle began to take shape early in the day. Confederate General Jeb Stuart, acting on Lee's orders, led his men on a wide swing around Union lines in an attempt to split the army in two. Stuart's objective was to link up with Pickett's men when they broke through the center of the Union position. Custer was part of a force detailed to stop any such movement against the Union rear.

With the exception of Grierson's successful raid through Mississippi in April, cavalry clashes between Yankees and Rebels almost always led to Confederate victories. However, in two years of war, Union men had steadily gained martial experience in the saddle, and the ability of the opposing fighters was leveling. What the northern horsemen needed now was a bold leader, and Custer rose to the occasion. A Union captain described his cavalry's charge, writing: "As the two columns approached each other, the pace of each increased, when suddenly a crash, like the falling of timber, betokened the crisis. So sudden and violent was the collision that many of the horses were turned end over end and crushed their riders beneath them. The clashing of sabers, the firing of pistols, the demands for surrender and the cries of the combatants now filled the air."[293]

Battle lines dissolved into the chaos of the close quarter cavalry fight as Stuart scrambled to break through. The horse soldiers alternatively fought sword-to-sword in the saddle and hand-to-hand on the ground. Cavalry units charged through and beyond their opponents, only to reverse direction and charge again. Albert Norris, whose family owned a tannery, brickyard, and mill near the foot of Grand Traverse Bay, fought in the Michigan Cavalry Brigade that day and was wounded in the battle. In the end, Stuart's advance was checked. While the remnants of Pickett's infantry straggled back from their failed charge, General Stuart abandoned his initiative and withdrew. It was the worst day of the war for the South.

Gettysburg had been a devastating confrontation with over 50,000 combined casualties – the bloodiest three days in American history. A total of 7,000 American soldiers and 3,000 horses lay dead on the battlefield. The Confederate drive into Pennsylvania had been repelled, and for a second time in as many years, Confederate General Lee had failed in his attempt to bring the war to a quick end by invading the North. Supporters of the Union took solace as it appeared the momentum of the war was shifting in their favor.

In the weekly edition following the announcement of "Victory at Gettysburg," the *Herald's* headlines cheered a second Union triumph on the Fourth of July, this time on the western front. The paper said: "Vicksburg has fallen, and the back-bone of the rebellion is broken...conjointly with the Gettysburg successes, is regarded as the turning point of the war."[294] The end of Vicksburg was a relatively bloodless affair, as Confederate General John Pemberton – who had served as commander of United States forts at Detroit and Mackinac Island before the war - unconditionally surrendered the wrecked and starving Mississippi River city. The 35,000 troops under his command laid down their arms. Upon receiving the news, President Lincoln proclaimed that "the Father of Waters again goes unvexed to the sea."[295]

Many in the South began to lose hope after the momentous dual defeats on the Fourth of July. The *Herald* printed a letter from "a distinguished Rebel officer captured by General Grant at Vicksburg, wherein the officer says: "The capture of Vicksburg and our army is fatal to our cause. We can never reorganize another army in the West...We have played a big game and lost. As soon as I am exchanged, I shall leave the Confederacy and the cause for Europe."[296]

Exalting over the twin victories at Gettysburg and Vicksburg, President Lincoln made an impromptu speech in Washington on July 7, 1863, the day news of the fall of Vicksburg reached the capital. The *Herald* compiled its report from special editions of New York papers, writing: "At 8 P.M., a crowd assembled in front of the national hotel, and marched up Pennsylvania avenue, headed by the Marine Band, to the Executive mansion, and serenaded, and enthusiastically cheered the President, with repeated cheers for Generals Grant, Meade, Rosecrans, the Armies of the Union, etc. The President appeared at the window, amid loud cheers, and said:

"Fellow Citizens: I am very glad indeed to see you to-night, and yet I will not say I thank you for this call, but I do most sincerely thank Almighty God for the occasion on which you have called. [Cheers.] How long ago is it? Eighty odd years since, on the Fourth day of July, for the first time in the history of the world, a nation, by its representatives, assembled and declared as a self evident truth 'that all men are created equal.' That was the birthday of the United States of America. Since then the Fourth of July has had several very peculiar recognitions. The two most distinguished men in the framing and support of the Declaration were Thomas Jefferson and John Adams – the one having penned it, and the other sustained it the most forcibly in debate – the only two of fifty-five who sustained it being elected President of the United States. Precisely fifty years after they put their hands to the paper, it pleased Almighty God to take both from this stage of action.[297] This was indeed an extraordinary and remarkable event in our history…and now in this last Fourth of July, just passed, when we have a gigantic rebellion at the bottom of which is an effort to overthrow the principle that all men were created equal, we have the surrender of a most powerful position and army on that very day (cheers.) and not only so, but in a succession of battles in Pennsylvania, near to us, through three days, on the first second and third of the month of July: and on the Fourth the cohorts of those who opposed the Declaration that all men were created equal "turned tail" and ran.(Long continued cheers.)"[298]

While the momentous battle raged in far-away Gettysburg, the Native people of Grand Traverse again struggled with one of their worst enemies – small-pox. Smith noted signs of trouble on July 1, writing in his diary: "It is reported there is a case of Small Pox in Pashabe Ville." A day later, he "received a letter and some vaccine." On the 3rd Smith "went to Onumunese Ville & vaccinated perhaps as many as 40," administering one of the few medical treatments of the era that proved effective. On the nation's birthday, Reverend Smith "went to the Bight to celebrate. I spoke by request at considerable length. Topic – The history of Liberty as Connected especially with the history of our Country." [299]

One hundred miles to the south, on the 4th of July 1863, Indians from all along the coast of Lake Michigan converged on a reservation in Oceana County to discuss the Civil War. Numerous Native leaders joined Capt. Edwin Andress of the 1st Michigan Sharp Shooters in addressing the assembly, urging those gathered to volunteer in the Union Army. Indians were not subject to the draft, so the appeal had to stand on its own merits. Though it was clear that the United

States government had been no friend to the Indians to date, Native leaders argued that now was the time to secure their equal status in the changing nation by fighting for the Union. Other orators claimed that the South's enslavement of blacks would soon extend to all people of color if the Confederacy was allowed to secede. In another, more subtle Union victory on that famous 4th of July, 25 Indian volunteers signed up in Company K of the 1st Michigan Sharp Shooters - the largest single enlistment of Native Americans during the Civil War.

A week later, Reverend Smith described a walk he took on the Northport docks, where he "visited some…with Graveroet, a recruiting officer."[300] Though he misspelled the soldier's name, Smith's meeting with Lt. Garrett Graveraet had again brought the Northport minister face-to-face with another dramatic story from the Civil War.

Lt. Graveraet was widely recognized as a model of success for the new generation of Indians living in Northern Michigan. He was born and raised along the Straits of Mackinac, and his mixed French, Indian, and American ancestry reflected his family's deep roots in the Great Lakes fur trading era. Graveraet's knowledge and respect for Native traditions, finished with a broad-based Euro-American education, allowed him to move easily in both cultures. Odawa author John Wright described Graveraet as "a talented young man, an accomplished artist and splendid musician. He was one of the first government teachers of Indians at L'Arbre Croche, and had great influence among the Natives."[301] Graveraet was the perfect choice to bring young men of all races out of the woods of Grand Traverse Country and into the ranks of the 1st Michigan Sharp Shooters.

The history of the Graveraet family provides a look at life in Northern Michigan during the early 19th century. In 1814, at age 7, Garrett's mother Sophie Bailey left her home in the Grand River Valley and moved to Mackinac Island. Her journey north followed the traditional annual migration route of the Odawa and Ojibwa people, who considered the entire east coast of Lake Michigan their home. Sophie's mother was an Odawa and her father a fur trader with the last name of McGuilpin – a respected Mackinac Island family. In 1918, *Michigan History Magazine* wrote of her trip: "Her father hired two trusty Indians to take her from Grand River to Mackinac Island, whither he had preceded her. Drifting down the beautiful river one bright summer's day, they emerged in Lake Michigan, and turning the prow of their little boat northward, started on their long journey through this remote region. They put up a blanket for a sail when the wind was favorable, and paddled along easy stages when it was calm. At night they slept by huge campfires..."

On their way north, the travelers drifted past the landmark Sleeping Bear Dunes and into the Manitou Passage, taking advantage of the lee of the Manitou Islands. When they completed their sail along the west coast of the Leelanau Peninsula, they faced the open waters of Le Grande Traverse – the great crossing – that marked the entrance to the mouth of the Bay. Perhaps here they lit one of the huge campfires the story described and rested for the night, waiting for the morning calm to make the sprint across the big water. If they worked the paddles hard, and the weather was right, they could complete the 75 mile trip from the tip of Leelanau to Mackinac Island before sunset. As an alternative, Sophie and her guides could stop at the Indian settlement of L'Arbre Croche and spend the evening by the fires of relatives and friends.

The *Michigan History* article continued: "When they arrived on Mackinac Island, the battle between the British and Americans was taking place, and the booming of cannons and the strains of martial music could clearly be heard. All was excitement. The little girl along with the women and children of the Island were placed in an abandoned distillery on the west side for safety."[302] Sophie had landed on Mackinac in the midst of the last deadly battle between United States and British armies in the Great Lakes region as the War of 1812 inched towards its conclusion. As Sophie huddled in the shelter of the abandoned building, the American invasion of Mackinac Island went sour, repelled at the cost of United States officer and a dozen of his men. Four months later, the War of 1812 ended in a stalemate. In the treaty that followed, the combatants agreed to recognize the pre-war borders between the United States and Canada, and the British gave up all the territory they had captured in the Great Lakes region during the war. For the fifth time in 60 years, the national flag flying over Northern Michigan changed. The British garrison sailed away from Mackinac Island without firing a shot, just as American forces had just two years before. Sophie Bailey settled into life on the Island as an American citizen.

In 1817, John Jacob Astor built the headquarters of his American Fur Company on Mackinac Island and began to amass one of the nation's great fortunes. For the next 20 years, fur trading on Market Street kept the Island in its historical position as the economic, cultural, and population center of the northern Great Lakes. During this period, Sophie met and married Henry G. Graveraet, Jr. - known as "Grand Chief Crain" in Native circles – a trapper and trader who resided on Mackinac Island in between frequent trips to the woods. In 1839, his brother Robert guided Reverend Peter Dougherty through Grand Traverse Country and helped the Presbyterian preacher choose the site for his settlement on the "Old Mission" peninsula. The well-traveled Henry also spent a good deal of time in Grand Traverse, for the area's vast watershed was a primary source of his furs.

By mid-century, however, fur-bearing animals had been all but wiped out in Michigan, a sign that the region had begun its transition from western wilderness to the nation's heartland. The centuries-old economy of the Great Lakes was dissolving and moving west toward new sources of furs. The Graveraet family stayed in the Straits just long enough to witness a new era on Mackinac Island, as embodied by the opening of the Island House Hotel in 1852 – the first hotel built specifically to accommodate tourists on the upper Great Lakes. The Graveraets then moved to Little Traverse, the site of present day Harbor Springs and the seat of the recently reorganized Emmet County. Here Indians commanded a large voting majority and they elected Henry Graveraet as Emmet County's Probate Judge. Judge Graveraet's announcements of pending probate court proceedings appeared regularly in the *Grand Traverse Herald* through December 1861. It was Henry and Sophie's son, Lt. Garrett A. Graveraet, who arrived in Northport July 10, 1863 as a recruiter for the 1st Michigan Sharp Shooters.

First Michigan Sharp Shooter Payson Wolfe in uniform. *Courtesy Avis Wolfe*

Three weeks after his visit to Northport, the persuasive powers of Lt. Graveraet became apparent when four of the town's men left to join the Sharp Shooters. The Reverend Smith wrote: "It is said that Wallace Woolsey and Douglas Hazle left night before last in Mr Woolsey's boat – leaving notes they need not be followed – that they are going to salt water - it is sad for the parents."[303] Smith's comments on the sadness of parents reflected his own state of mind, for in his next lines he revealed that his son-in-law Payson Wolfe had also enlisted. The Reverend wrote: "*Tonawanda* came AM to UD [Union Dock] and left down. Payson and Charles Allen went on her. They are going to the Mich 1st Sharp Shooters – Dearborn."[304]

As it turned out, the notes Woolsey and Hazle left their parents were lies. Their destination was not the salt-water oceans but rather the ranks of the 1st Michigan Sharp Shooters. The two young men had misled their parents to save them the worry over their fate as soldiers. The truth came out in a letter Reverend Smith received from Payson Wolfe in August, 1863. The preacher wrote: "I went back on horse to Mr Hazle's and Mr Woolsey's to inform them their sons had enlisted in the Mich 1st Sharp Shooters as by Payson's letter yesterday."[305] Hazle and Woolsey had joined Company I of the Sharp Shooters, composed primarily of soldiers of Euro-American ancestry, while Allen and Wolfe enlisted in the all-Indian Company K.

In July 1863, while Lt. Garrett Graveraet scoured Northport and other nearby harbor towns for recruits, his 56-year-old father, Judge Henry Graveraet, traveled to the Dearborn Arsenal near Detroit. The 1st Michigan Sharp Shooters were stationed there to guard the arsenal's coveted store of rifles. The Judge greeted old friends and swapped stories, but he had come with another intention. While at the arsenal, Henry Graveraet misrepresented his age by a decade and signed up in Company K, making him the oldest man in the Sharp Shooters. Days after Judge Graveraet enlisted in the regiment, the 1st Michigan Sharpshooters were abruptly ordered south to Indiana, where Confederate General John Morgan was leading a cavalry raid across the state. A hastily gathered Union force that included the Sharp Shooters caught up with Morgan's rear guard on July 13. They pursued the Rebels for two days, taking a number of prisoners. The Confederate raiders who were unable to escape surrendered, and the 1st Michigan Sharp Shooters returned to guard duty at the Dearborn Arsenal.

As summer progressed, Company K volunteers chose Henry Graveraet as their sergeant. The former judge now reported directly to his son, Lt. Garrett Graveraet. The wheels of fate had been set in motion. Within a year, the Graveraet father-son team faced a hardened Confederate Army on the front lines of the deadliest military campaign in American history, as Grant squared off with Lee in the 1864 Overland Campaign in Virginia. The coincidence that wife and mother Sophie Bailey arrived at Mackinac Island in 1814, during the last mortal engagement between American and British troops in the Great Lakes region, foreshadowed the tempest that would shatter the Graveraet family exactly one-half century later.

Draft riots in New York City soon dulled the shine of the two great Union victories at Gettysburg and Vicksburg, proving there could be no lasting joy in a nation consumed by civil war. The July 13 release of the names of New York City men subject to the draft brought chaos to America's largest city. Angry, anti-war crowds gathered on corners where the lists were posted and soon spilled out onto the streets. There the violence began. The rioters focused their anger on blacks as the cause of the "abolitionist war," killing in random encounters and torching buildings they associated with the draft and the abolition movement. Guards at Horace Greeley's *New York Tribune*, whose headquarters had been besieged, held the rioters at bay with twin Gatlin guns. Pockets of New York City were on fire. It seemed a requirement of 1863 that turmoil accompany every moment. The riots made it clear not everyone in the North embraced Lincoln's Emancipation Proclamation

The uncompromising Bates of the *Grand Traverse Herald*, in a heated blend of editorial and news, blasted the marauding mob in an article titled "Copperhead Riots in New York." He wrote: "The city of New York is under the dominion and control of the Devil and his angels. Carnage, destruction and desolation mark the hour. Fernando Wood[306] and his minions, maddened by the recent rebel reverses and the brilliant success of the Federal arms, have instituted the reign of lawlessness and mob violence; and as of our last advices the streets of New York are filled with blood.

"Resistance to the Draft was the pretext for the mob…The riot commenced on Monday, the 13th and was raging with awful fury as late as the 16th. The military had arrived in large force and was pouring in grape and canisters upon the rioters – mowing them down like grass. The end will come. Law and order and good Government will prevail over Anarchy and Diabolism. But woe to the instigators of this infernal riot."[307]

At the height of the riots, soldiers serving in the Lakeshore Tigers, who had been cutting cordwood and skirmishing in Virginia for months, were ordered north. Grand Traverse men suddenly found themselves in the unenviable situation of fighting their fellow Northerners on the streets of New York City. The *New York Times* wrote: "The 26th Michigan arrived here last night from the Potomac, and will be assigned to duty in this city, until the great riot is quelled. The regiment bore evidences of the hard services it has undergone in the field; but it is composed of as fine a body of brave, intelligent young men as ever shouldered a musket in the cause of civil liberty and civil order...At the present moment the Peninsular State is represented in the three great armies...and Michigan soldiers have won renown for their bravery and discipline throughout the war on almost every battle-field."[308]

Eventually the fires burned out in New York, and the city settled into an uneasy peace. A thousand more caskets were filled through violent deaths, and the Confederates had something to celebrate without firing a shot. Mortimer Boyes, a 19 year-old Northport volunteer in the 26th Michigan, never left the city. He died of disease in a New York hospital six weeks after helping quell the riots, and lies buried in a Brooklyn cemetery. Perhaps shaken by the death of his friend, Lakeshore Tiger George Bigelow, who had shipped out with Boyes from Northport and had himself nearly died of disease earlier in the year, disappeared from the ranks of the 26th Michigan while in New York, his fate unknown.

With Union armies embattled on all front, recruiters continued to fan out across the state looking for new volunteers. Many focused their efforts on Northern Michigan, where the population was young and the sentiment overwhelmingly pro-Union. The Homestead Act attracted an ever-increasing number of families to Grand Traverse in search of free farmland, and the recipients of the acreage understood that it was Union laws and values that created this remarkable opportunity. In addition, the settlers streaming into the region to stake their claims were for the most part New Englander who believed the time for universal freedom was at hand. On their recent journey from the Atlantic States, they traveled across a thousand miles of countryside where there were no slaves, and witnessed for themselves the vitality of the North even in the midst of war. Few considered heading to the South where African Americans – the nation's involuntary immigrants - were forced into labor, and whites who worked with their hands were scorned. The recipients of free Homestead Act land felt indebted to their government – a government that was fighting for its life. It was hard for these potential volunteers to say no when recruiters came calling at their homestead doors.

When trying to persuade young men to enlist, the glamour of the cavalry always helped in the recruitment process. Now the well-publicized forays of Michigan's "Boy General," George Armstrong Custer, were attracting scores of Grand Traverse men to Union cavalry regiments. Lt. E.J. Brooks of Northport, who had seen his share of hard fighting during the first two years of Civil War while serving in the 1st New York Light Artillery, had switched hats and now worked as a recruiter for the 10th Michigan Cavalry. The call for volunteers rang out in every town along the coast of Grand Traverse Country. Harriet Fisher of Glen Arbor noted: "They are trying to raise two more Regiments in the Northern part of Michigan. A Mr. Brooks speaks in town Saturday evening. War, of course, is the subject and to raise volunteers the object of the meeting. If ladies are allowed to, I shall attend." A subsequent *Herald* article detailed the recruiter's work, writing: "Edwin J. Brooks of Northport, has received authority to enlist recruits for Kellogg's 10th Cavalry Regiment. As a draft will soon be made under the Conscription Act, we hope all of those who prefer volunteering to the draft will avail themselves of this opportunity to join what will be a "crack" Regiment. Each recruit will receive one month's pay in advance, and a bounty of $100 from the U.S. Government and $50 from the State. The State bounty and $25 of the Government bounty will be paid in advance. Now is the time."[309]

Though Lt. Brooks had recently failed in his bid as the Democrat candidate for Leelanau County's Prosecutor, there was no arguing his success as a recruiter. Lt. Brooks' presentation to potential enlistees, as noted by Harriet Fisher, must have been stirring, for over a dozen Glen Arbor recruits signed up in the 10th Michigan Cavalry after his speech. In a 90-day stretch following the Battle of Gettysburg, the former Northport school teacher brought more than 20 Grand Traverse volunteers into the forming regiment. Even Republican Bates had to admit that "Lieut. Brooks deserves great credit for his energy and perseverance in raising recruits for the 10th Cavalry."[310]

Harriet Fisher may have joined the cavalry with her fellow Glen Arbor citizens if army rules had permitted her to enlist. After contemplating the idea of European powers entering the war on the Confederate side, she had defiantly written friends: "If I was a man I would see what I could do...for if necessary, a woman can carry a gun and use it, too." She possessed the frontier skill of handling a horse, and a *Herald* article noted: "Mrs. John E. Fisher...rode on horseback from Glen Arbor to Traverse City, 30 miles, on Wednesday last, transacted business...at the Land Office, and returned the next day." Fisher confirmed her pledge to fight if necessary, adding, "Now don't laugh at the idea, for I am seriously in earnest," making it clear the gender restrictions of the day were the Union's loss. Before leaving Grand Traverse for the front, Lt. Brooks stopped in his hometown of Northport to pitch the 10th Michigan Cavalry, and had some success. On September 22 Reverend Smith wrote, "On E.J. Brooks' order I paid $3.00 being one dollar each for 3 volunteers for which the people of the village agree to make a home bounty of $25.00."[311]

The *Herald* article featuring Lt. Brooks and the diary notations of Reverend Smith both mention the bounty system – a key incentive that persuaded men to enlist in the Union Army. The Federal government preferred to lure willing recruits through a bounty rather than force them into service by the draft, hoping to avoid such humiliating national events as the recent draft riots in New York City. When signing up from Northport in the summer of 1863, the volunteer received a total of $200 from federal, state, and village governments, more than an average year's pay at the time. With it, the recruit could build a solid house on free Homestead Act property and secure his claim. Any left over money, in addition to a soldiers monthly pay, helped his family get by when he was ordered off to the front.

Lt. Charles W. Holden returned to Grand Traverse in 1863 to again recruit for the 26th Michigan Infantry. The previous summer, Holden had signed up Sgt. William Voice and over 60 other area men in Company A of the Lakeshore Tigers, creating a contingent of Grand Traverse soldiers within the forming Michigan regiment. Holden had developed a close friendship with fellow Republican George Smith and throughout the war, the two men corresponded regularly. Soon after the battle of Gettysburg, Holden was promoted to Quartermaster of the 26th Michigan Infantry, assuming the difficult duty of keeping the regiment supplied in Confederate territory during the worst fighting of the Civil War.

In the fall of 1863, Reverend Smith's diary spoke of the continuing cruelty of the year, which extended its grip into Grand Traverse. In September, he wrote: "*Ogdensburg* came AM...She lost her 2nd mate overboard out of the Mouth of the Bay & could not save him." A few days later he witnessed a frontier family's agony in the extreme, writing: "I was called on to attend the funeral of a daughter of Mr Kenedy's between 3 & 4 years who died yesterday morn. I went in wagon, Mrs Smith with me. We arrived ½ past 10, another daughter over six years died about ten minutes before we got there. We found the family in great distress. They are said to have been lovely little girls, much attached to each other - they died alike." On September 10, Smith "got a letter tonight from Joseph Wakazoo...saying he was arrested as a deserter and requesting me to come at once." Then nature itself turned against the diarist, and Smith awoke to find a "hard frost this morning, the first to injure my things we have had. All vines appeared to be killed, much damage done."[312] All the while, the preacher worked to save the deserter Joseph Wakazoo from a charge that in 1863 often led to death by a military firing squad. By the end of the month he succeeded, writing that his friend Lt. E.J. Brooks had agreed to make a horse soldier out of Wakazoo, and the charges were dropped.

Throughout the war, Smith looked after Indian interests, especially Native soldiers, and in particular his son-in-law Payson. He wrote: "I went and presented Payson's certificate of enlistment to Supervisor Mr Wood – he said nothing could be done until the annual meeting of the Board – none of the families of volunteers have received anything for some 6 weeks." The Democrat Wood appeared hesitant to support the war effort on any front, including his neighbors in need. Cold weather set in and the Indians again battled their centuries-old enemy. Smith wrote: "Meeksemaig & wife died last Friday night of Small Pox; their child was not expected to live."[313]

Despite the perilous times, ports along the coast of Lake Michigan – anchored by Chicago – continued to enjoy prosperity and unparalleled growth. Chicago celebrated the opening of the world's largest grain elevator, reflecting the success of free labor farms throughout the region. The *Grand Traverse Herald* commented: "The increased production of grain in the Northwest is perhaps shown in no way more clearly than the rapid increase in Chicago of the facilities for receiving and shipping it." Local homesteaders were doing their part to keep Great Lakes grain elevators full. The *Herald* wrote: "Our farmers are engaged in busily harvesting their wheat…the crop is fully up to average." The paper also sang the praises of fruit received from Omena's Reverend Peter Dougherty, calling them as "fine a sample of apples that ever grew in any part of this state. They are large, handsomely formed, of rich flavor and perfectly free from blemish." Many more acres would be planted in Grand Traverse next season, for throughout the region, large swaths of forest fell as new farmers rushed to improve their Homestead Act claims before winter set in. A late October story in the *Herald* titled "Rapid Settlement" said: "One hundred and twenty persons arrived here and settled in this County within the last two weeks,"[314] about the same number of all Euro-Americans living in the Grand Traverse region only a decade before.

The *Herald* noted more good news from Michigan's Upper Peninsula mining district, which supplied much of the metal used by the Union war machine. It said: "There is considerable excitement just now in business circles connected with the Lake Superior trade, in consequence of the discovery of an immense deposit of silver bearing lead in that famous region. Marquette Co. is the fortunate locality of this new discovery. It is stated that the ore yields twenty per cent of pure lead, and that every ton of lead yields twenty five pounds of silver…"[315] Not only was there a new source of silver for the treasury, there was also a fresh supply of lead available to mold into minie balls for Union rifles.

The reports of plenty in the North sharply contrasted with the news printed in the Charleston, South Carolina *Bulletin*. The paper said: "We again appeal to the people of North Carolina to give what aid they can to the starving population of Charleston. We dislike exposing the necessities of our people, but our friends can avert starvation, and we believe that they will do it when they know it is absolutely necessary."[316] Northern papers loved to write of the agony of anything Charleston, the cradle of the rebellion. It was their editorial way to shoot back at those who opened fire on Fort Sumter and started the devastating war. Charleston would pay again and again for its initiative, and by the end of the war, the city lay in ruins. In the meantime, good news emanating from the northern Great Lakes continued to bear bad tidings for the Confederacy.

Throughout the South, signs of desperation mounted. A Confederacy formed under the banners of decentralization and states' rights began to tilt toward totalitarian government. The *Herald* wrote of "a proclamation by Jeff Davis, calling out under the Confederate Conscription Act, all white men between the ages of 18 and 45 to serve for three years, under penalty of being punished for desertion in case of disobeying the call." Other measures considered by the Rebel government included the "application of martial law to the whole country as if in a state of siege…taking absolute control of all trading…and the material enlargement of the President's power to…make appointments and get rid of incompetent officers."[317] The "decentralized" South began to function like an old-fashioned European monarchy as their position in the war deteriorated.

On November 18, 1863, President Lincoln traveled by train from Washington to Gettysburg to speak at the dedication of the town's new Federal cemetery. The next day, Lincoln delivered what is widely recognized as the greatest speech in American history. In his Gettysburg Address, the President said: "Four score and seven years ago our fathers brought forth upon this continent a new nation, conceived in Liberty, and dedicated to the proposition that all men are created equal.

"Now we are engaged in a great civil war, testing whether that nation, or any nation, so conceived, and so dedicated, can long endure. We are met here on a great battle-field of that war. We have come to dedicate a portion of it as a final resting place for those who here gave their lives that that nation may live. It is altogether fitting and proper that we should do this.

"But in a larger sense we can not dedicate – we can not consecrate – we can not hallow this ground. The brave men, living and dead, who struggled here, have consecrated it far above our poor power to add or detract. The world will little note, nor long remember, what we say here, but can never forget what they did here. It is for us, the living, rather to be dedicated here to the unfinished work which they have, thus far, so nobly carried on. It is for us, the living, rather to be here dedicated to the great task remaining before us – that from these honored dead we take increased devotion to that cause for which they here gave the last full measure of devotion – that we here highly resolve that these dead shall not have died in vain, that this nation shall have a new birth of freedom, and that this government of the people, by the people, for the people, shall not perish from this earth."

Confederate prisoners wait at the railroad station in Chattanooga, Tennessee. *Library of Congress*

The final great battle of 1863, fought in two states over two months, began in the hill country of northern Georgia, just south of the city of Chattanooga, Tennessee. In September, near a small creek named Chickamauga, Union General William Rosecrans led his forces into battle in a rare instance when the

Confederates commanded superior numbers. During the two most costly days in the western theatre of the war, the opposing American forces suffered a combined 35,000 casualties. Federal armies were driven back to Chattanooga, with the Rebels in close pursuit. Though still in possession of the important city, the Union Army found itself surrounded, cut off from supplies, and under siege. Gettysburg had turned the tide of the war in favor of the Union in the east, but in spite of the fall of Vicksburg, Confederates were now having their way in the west. A broken General Rosecrans was relieved of his command, and once again General Grant was called upon to save the day.

Six weeks later, with the Federal forces in Chattanooga facing starvation, Grant succeeded in punching through a line of supply to the besieged city. The General described the scene in his memoirs, writing: "With the aid of steamers and…teams, in a week the troops were receiving full rations. It was hard for anyone not an eye-witness to realize the relief this brought. The men were soon reclothed and also well fed; an abundance of ammunition was brought up, and cheerfulness prevailed not before enjoyed in many weeks. Neither the officers or men looked upon themselves any longer as doomed." Not long after, the revived Union Army turned on their captors at Lookout Mountain, charging up hill against an entrenched enemy and sending them running.

Knowing that the rescue of Chattanooga helped seal the Confederacy's fate, Grant digressed, exposing the contemplative mind of the warrior Lincoln would soon raise to commander of all Union forces. He continued: "There was no time during the rebellion that I did not think, and often say, that the South was more to be benefited by its defeat than the North. The latter had the people, the institutions, and the territory to make a great and prosperous nation. The former was burdened with an institution abhorrent to all civilized people not brought up under it, and one which degraded labor, kept it in ignorance, and enervated the governing class. With the outside world at war with this institution, they could not have extended their territory. The labor of the country was not skilled, nor allowed to become so. The whites could not toil without becoming degraded, and those who did were denominated "poor white trash." The system of labor would have soon exhausted the soil and left the people poor. The non-slave holder would have left the country, and the small slave holder must have sold out to his more fortunate neighbor. Soon the slave would have outnumbered the masters, and, not being in sympathy with them, would have risen in their might and exterminated them. The war was expensive to the South as well as the North, both in blood and treasure, but it was worth all it cost."

Grant had 30 years between the end of the war and the writing of his memoirs to evaluate the conflict and praise its gains in spite of the bloodshed. But
for the moment, the escalating cost of the war stunned the nation as it brutally
struck one household at a time. Word filtered back to Grand Traverse that Albert Norris, the son of the East Bay tanner who had been wounded while fighting beside General Custer at Gettysburg, had died of disease on December 7.
No one could imagine that the terrible number of casualties suffered thus far in
the Civil War was only half the grand total.

In order to replace casualties and expiring enlistments, Lincoln issued another call for 300,000 troops and raised the bounty paid to new recruits and
returning veterans. The *Herald* commented: "Every incentive is now offered to
induce volunteering. Not only are the very liberal provisions made in the way of
bounties a great inducement, but there are other considerations. The rebellion is
daily growing weaker, and our arms are now universally successful whenever an
engagement takes place. Our forces are commanded by experienced Generals,
men noted for gallantry and heroic conduct on the battlefield…recklessness and
incompetency which was once so plainly observable on almost every battlefield,
is now seldom if ever seen. Victory everywhere crowns the onward march of our
brave and noble army."[318]

As the winter's hard freeze began to grip Grand Traverse, a delighted editor
Bates wrote: "The Bridge across the Manistee River…is completed, and Mr.
Hannah, the Commissioner, assures us it is built in the most substantial manner…We now have a winter road." Bates would no longer have to suffer excuses
about the mail stuck "outside" on drifted footpaths, or rail against the negligence
of sloppy mail contractors. Never again would he have to dig dated papers from
the trash to fill his columns on the weeks the mail failed to come through. It was,
he concluded, "A new era in our history."[319]

In the paper's next edition, Bates had the last word on 1863 as he summed
up his half-decade of publishing in the region. He wrote: "This number closes
the Fifth Year of the *Grand Traverse Herald*. The experiment of establishing a
newspaper in the wilderness has proved successful; and we look back upon five
years of humble effort to develop the resources and encourage the settlement,
growth and prosperity of a beautiful and fertile region of the country…

"The greatest difficulty that we have had to encounter and overcome, was
the ill-founded prejudice against Northern Michigan, and especially the northern portion of the Lower Peninsula, which was fostered and encouraged for
years by the old Steamboat Combination on the Lakes, and by large speculators

in western lands. This, in a great measure, has been eradicated, and the tide of emigration has turned in our favor. The country will bear inspection, and almost every man who has visited the region around Grand Traverse Bay has been pleased with the country…As evidence of this the Books of the Land Office at Traverse City show that since the establishment of the *Herald,* 530 purchases have been made for cash, of land in…Grand Traverse, Antrim and Leelanaw – the three Bay Counties; and 678 entries under the Homestead Law…

"We have every reason to anticipate a large influx of population next spring. Hannah, Lay & Co. will place a new Propellor on the Bay, which in connection with propellors at Northport, will give us a daily line of communication with Detroit and Chicago…

"We mark out no new course in the conduct of *Herald.* I will pursue the even tenor of its way, and give cordial and hearty support to the Administration in all its efforts to crush the Rebellion. While the war continues, we will wash our hands of all *Conservatism.* Desperate diseases require desperate remedies… The cause must be removed before any diseases can be cured. Slavery is the cause of this Rebellion, and Slavery must die. On this point we are *Radical.*"[320]

Former Northport merchant and recently promoted Captain Sam McClelland of the 1st New York Light Artillery, 1864. *Library of Congress*

CHAPTER SEVEN

1864
A Fearful Time

On New Years Day 1864, the people of the North worried less about a Confederate victory and more about the cost of meeting and defeating a determined enemy on their home territory. Since the battle of Gettysburg and the fall of Vicksburg on the Mississippi, and in light of the widening gap in manpower and materials between the two sections of the country, northern citizens felt a growing confidence that the Union would prevail. However, the feeling was mixed with a dreadful anxiety about the year ahead and the toll it could exact.

In 1864, Union troops would again invade the South and pay dearly for the venture. Lee's army had been whipped at Gettysburg and driven back to Virginia, but the Rebels had yet to lose a major battle on their own turf. Larger Federal armies routinely suffered at the hands of the Rebels whenever they marched south of the Potomac River. There was no doubt that the Confederate Army, the masters of defense, would fight with fearful resolve to hold on to their homeland. The North, in turn, led by the fighting General Ulysses S. Grant, would attack relentlessly with superior force, spelling disaster for families of soldiers on both sides of the line.

In Grand Traverse, the unusually severe weather of the New Year reflected the state of a nation held hostage by the raging Civil War. On January 1, Reverend Smith reported from Northport: "A most furious gale – Snow drifting so that we can scarcely see & piled up in great banks every where, so it is almost impossible to get out the door anywhere. It is probably 4 feet all around our west door, the window near by banked up! It is a fearful time. I think I never knew so severe a day. Thus begins the New Year – Oh that we are able to live more for God & heaven than any past year of our lives."

The blizzard showed no sign of letting up, and on January 3, Smith wrote: "Cloudy, furiously tempestuous, snow drifting fearfully. No possibility of getting away any where…I can't get a horse from the barn to the house – have to carry water to them over the drifts. I had to shovel a long time to get my pigs out so I could give them drink. This is the 3d day since they had any, they were literally buried. One of our roosters froze to death today. It is altogether the worst storm and of the longest continuance I remember ever to have known."

Ten days into 1864, there was still no break in the Grand Traverse storm. Smith wrote: "We walked over the top of our picket fence on Snow drifts…I shoveled out the N gate so I could get out with my horse and cutter. I started… but met Mr Rose. He said it was impossible to get through - the road was completely blocked up. Mr Woolsey tried to get through with oxen and sled last night with Mrs Woolsey – got into a snow bank & had to leave his sled & go home on foot I never have seen such a time since I have been in this country."[321]

The *Grand Traverse Herald* described the reach and gravity of the blizzard, writing: "At Kalamazoo the mercury sunk to 20 degrees below zero…and at Milwaukee to 40! A large number of cattle and hogs were frozen to death on weather bound trains…A severe storm raged at Buffalo…All the railroad tracks were washed away and canal boats were left high and dry in the streets… several persons were frozen to death at Milwaukee; and the soldiers in camp… suffered terribly. A German family, consisting of the parents and five children, were frozen to death about 30 miles from the boundary line between Indiana and this State."[322]

The bitter winter weather that enveloped the Great Lakes in January 1864 was nature's introduction to what would be the worst year in the history of the United States. The violent home stretch of the American Civil War was at hand. The intellectual wordsmith George Smith must have seen the similarities between the storm and the state of the war during the long days of being frozen within the confines of his Northport home. He wrote it was "impossible to get out the door" until the storm – and the bloody Civil War - were borne to their conclusions. The year 1864 would bring "the worst storm of the longest continuance" in terms of death and destruction the people of the United States would ever suffer, the horror magnified by the fact that the carnage was created by neighbors and fellow citizens fighting and killing each other. It would take

"God and heaven" to bear the intense pain hundreds of thousands of Americans would feel as news of the death or maiming of a loved one reached their doors. Reverend Smith summed up the national mood on New Years Day 1864 when he wrote, "It is a fearful time."

At the height of the New Year's blizzard, half a dozen Leelanau men decided to volunteer in the Union Army en masse. On January 4, Reverend Smith wrote: "Mr Woolsey spent PM here, took supper with us. He has enlisted & expects to leave soon." Ten days later, Smith revealed the extent of the North-port contingent by name when he wrote in his diary, "Mr Woolsey & Mr Middleton came. I gave them & Mr Kehl each a Bible $0.75 as volunteers – gave Charles Waltz, [Jacob Haines], and Thomas McCormick each a Testament. The above 6 Volunteers started PM for Grand Rapids in Company with Fox who is going to Traverse City with horses and bobs."[323] In his first job as a minister in Michigan, Reverend Smith distributed Bibles to struggling pioneer and Indian families in the Kalamazoo River Valley. For Smith, the current president of the Grand Traverse Bible Society, the handing out of Bibles was a 30-year tradition, and he did his best to put one in the knapsack of every soldier that departed from Northport to fight for the Union.

Chauncey Woolsey, Joshua Middleton, and John Kehl landed at Northport harbor only a few years before the outbreak of the Civil War, part of the wave of settlers that built the mission village into Northern Michigan's leading port town. Though from diverse backgrounds, all three men were well-educated and well-traveled before they arrived. Woolsey, 45, was a ship captain from Buffalo who witnessed from the deck of his schooner the rapid growth along the coast of Lake Michigan, and in particular Northport harbor. The previous summer, his son had joined the 1st Michigan Sharp Shooters with Smith's son-in-law Payson Wolfe, and the senior Woolsey believed it was his turn to serve. Joshua Middleton, 39, was a pacifist Quaker farmer who moved his family north from Ohio by way of the Manitou Islands seeking new opportunities. His letters and diary notes recorded the violence in Virginia in 1864 from the perspective of a soldier trained from birth to avoid fighting. The 40 year-old John Kehl sailed the world as a Nantucket whaler and worked in Buffalo as a master shipbuilder before landing in the region. In their ongoing struggle to put down roots on the Leelanau Peninsula, the men formed a bond that was common on the frontier, pooling their diverse talents and resources when needed. Together they cut forests, planted fields, rigged sails, built barns, unloaded schooners, and cooperated in a variety of other ways, knowing that success at the edge of wilderness was a group effort. These deliberate, middle-aged men had contemplated the meaning of the war and committed to face its horrors due to the high-stakes principles involved.

Most of the 100 or so volunteers in Company A of the 26th Michigan Infantry were from Grand Traverse, including the regiment's leader, Captain L. Edwin Knapp, and Grand Traverse County Prosecutor turned Union recruiter, Lt. Charles Holden. Since the death of Sgt. William Voice shook Northport in the fall of 1862, most of the town's men joined Voice's Company A of the Lakeshore Tigers in honor of their fallen friend. This new batch of Northport men was no exception.

Joshua Middleton began the description of the volunteers' nine day, snow-covered journey to the regiment's headquarters in Grand Rapids, writing: "I left home Thursday 4 A.M. At noon left Northport for Suttons Bay…We arrived in Traverse City Friday night, tired, cold, and hungry. Snow had been three feet deep with much of the road not broken through most of the way." Reverend Smith had also braved the weather that day but the blizzard turned him back. He wrote: "9 AM…started for Traverse City…near Manseau's Mill met Fox & McAuly coming home. They said it is utterly impossible to get along. They liked to have ruined their horses in the attempt. The volunteers went on. I took my grain to the mill. It was ground around 4 PM & we started for home. As we started a man hailed us from a distance to know if we would [give] one old soldier a ride. He came up and it was Albert Powers on furlow."

Reverend Smith's chance encounter with Albert Powers again demonstrated that news from the front lines in the Civil War was not always reliable. Smith last mentioned Powers in his diary in January 1863 when he wrote: "Albert Powers lost one of his legs in the Battle of Fredericksburg & is in the hospital in Baltimore…I carried the word to his parents." The report of Albert's lost leg was obviously incorrect, and before this meeting with Powers, Smith must have made a more pleasant second trip to inform his parents of the truth – in fact their son was whole. Now the veteran Powers climbed into Smith's sleigh on his own two legs and together they forged on through the snowstorm toward Northport.

Middleton continued with his account of the six friends' trip to Grand Rapids, writing: "From Traverse we hired a team of horses, but through our haste proved only worthy of carrying our baggage. The teamster turned back within five miles of Benzonia, and it was snowing, cold and disagreeable. We managed to find a place to stay over night in a new settlers home. They were very nice folks, with the women taking a great fancy to some cheese we had, in our mea-ger supplies. But we dare not refuse for fear of consequences. It turned out they charged us a very reasonable price for our stay, they wished us well on our way."

After a day spent trudging through waist deep snow on little more than a footpath, Middleton wrote: "We ate dinner in the woods on the way, a cloudy day. We kept going until nightfall when we realized we had taken the wrong road. Having to turn back, we were so very tired and lame, our minds were made up to turn back and go home. We instead kept on and when almost discouraged, managed to find the right guide marker of our route. We slept over night…in [a] small log house, with no bed. We had very little extra clothing with which to cover us, and we were so cold we could not sleep at all. We did have plenty to eat, though we paid high for it. John [Kehl] told the women I had fourteen children, only one inch difference in their sizes - from the oldest to the youngest - stand them in a row and it was like looking at a line of steps." If the volunteers had known the fate that awaited them in Virginia, they may have wished they had stuck to their decision to "turn back and go home." However, the road home was most likely now impassable, for on January 17, Smith observed: "In the open country it has drifted immensely…there are banks 10 to 12 feet high." Five days later, after what Middleton described as "a very hard tramp," the recruits arrived in Grand Rapids, having had "no sleep or anything to eat" during the last 48 hours. The six men had walked most of the 150-mile journey through an especially hard winter storm, a tough first step on their march to war.

For the balance of the Civil War, the diary and letters of Northport's Joshua Middleton preserved one Grand Traverse soldier's experience in the midst of the deadliest fighting in American history – first as a Lakeshore Tiger wound-ed at the Battle of the Wilderness, then from a Union hospital ward where he recovered from battlefield wounds. More Grand Traverse soldiers would fight and die in Virginia during 1864 than in all other places and years of the war combined, with the Lakeshore Tigers in the thick of the worst fighting. The Quaker Middleton's observations recorded the pacifist's logic for joining the Union Army, where many volunteers risked their lives for high ideals. Middleton wrote: "As for liking the service…a majority of soldiers see nothing lovely in it, but it is the glorious principles which we are fighting for which fill every soldiers breast, there is the Secret, which animates our troops and carries through triumphantly in all their arduous duties."[324]

On February 10, Reverend George Smith received "a letter from Messrs Woolsey Middleton & Kehl and W & M's photographs." Before leaving Grand

Northport volunteers Chauncey Woolsey, Joshua Middleton, and John Kehl posed for photographs in Grand Rapids after joining the 26th Michigan Infantry, the regiment known as the Lakeshore Tigers. *Leelanau Historical Society*

Rapids for the winter camps, the Northport volunteers had donned the uniforms of the 26th Michigan Infantry and posed for posterity. The same day Smith received the letter and photographs, his three friends arrived in Washington by way of a two-day train ride through the heart of the Free States. Middleton wrote that they traveled from "Detroit to Toledo, by Pittsburg, through Little York, then to Harrisburg about sundown. In Baltimore we got breakfast, arrived in Washington about 3 O clock." On their way to the front, the Grand Traverse volunteers and hundreds of thousands of soldiers like them saw the expansive America they were going to war to help preserve. After a day in the nation's capital, Middleton and his fellow recruits joined the 26th Michigan in Alexandria, "9 miles from Washington and received our equipment and here we are near Dixie. Stayed two days and off to the front. Went to Brandy Station and from there to our camp. Built us a cabin and began to soldier. Done duty through the winter Pickiting on the Rappahannock."[325]

The winter camps soldier Middleton described in 1864 had come a long way since the first years of the war. The Lakeshore Tiger wrote: "We have everything as comfortable as a soldier can expect. We live in log huts. Our shelter tents make roofs. We have a fireplace in each hut, four persons in one. We have plenty of rations and mostly good. Our Regiment has been doing picket duty all winter. Our lines are about three or four miles from the rebs lines.

"We have to stand about 3 days out of every nine on picket. We leave camp, take our rations for 3 days and camp out in the field or woods just where our post happens to be and keep a sharp look out for Bushwackers. Our cavalry boys are picking them up pretty fast this spring. I don't know how I shall stand when we march, I shall try and do the best I can."[326]

One hundred miles to the southeast, a Union naval officer from Grand Traverse, Capt. Robert McLaughlin, described an action his ship engaged in along the Atlantic coast in a letter dated March 7, 1864. His missive, sent from the U.S. Steamer *General Foster* to the *Grand Traverse Herald*, began: "Nearly three years of war have by no means erased from my memory Grand Traverse and its past associations; and I judge from my desire to hear from "friends at home" that a letter from a "Traverse Boy," now at the seat of war, will be perused with interest by many of my former acquaintances…I will give you an account of a late expedition up the Alligator River, N.C., the result of which the conclusion of this letter will show."

A dozen years before the Civil War began, Reverend Smith arrived at the site of the future town of Northport aboard the schooner *Hiram Merrill*, owned by his friend James McLaughlin. The ship master had come to instruct the mission Indians in farming techniques, a job paid for by the U.S. government under terms of the Treaty of 1836. McLaughlin brought with him two boys named James and Robert, whose mother had drowned a decade earlier when their boat capsized in the Kalamazoo River. The McLaughlins learned to sail and work a schooner on the waters of Grand Traverse Bay and now Robert was a captain of a Union Army gunboat.

A Union Army gunboat patrols a river along the Confederate coast, 1864. *Library of Congress*

Soon after the Rebels opened fire on Fort Sumter to begin the Civil War, President Lincoln proclaimed that "a competent force will be posted so as to prevent entrance and exit of vessels" from Southern ports. The Union naval blockade of the Atlantic coast had begun. With only 90 ships to its name, the U.S. Navy at first struggled to enforce Lincoln's edict, intercepting only 10% of the ships destined for Rebel ports in 1861 and 1862. However, by the time Capt. McLaughlin wrote to the *Herald* from the helm of the *Foster*, over 400 Union vessels patrolled the Confederate coasts, and the blockade stopped one of every two ships that attempted to run it. During 1864, the Carolinas hosted the last remaining southern harbors open along the Atlantic seaboard, and in addition to blockade duty and provisioning troops, Union gunboats like the *Foster* launched raids aimed at closing the South's salt-water trade for good.

Back in the spring of 1862, George Smith returned by ship from Chicago and noticed that "Robert McLaughlin was on board. He belongs to the Navy, is recruiting." The following summer, brothers James and Robert visited Northport, and Smith wrote that "Robert is a captain in the NY artillery." Both statements were true, for the new style Army gunboats McLaughlin commanded had the capacity to deploy land-based artillery and troops. While in Northport, Capt. Robert McLaughlin had the occasion to meet Smith's 16 year-old daughter Annie, and the two began to correspond after he returned to the war. The day before Thanksgiving 1863, Smith mailed a letter from his daughter to McLaughlin, which the captain answered in the first week of the New Year 1864, complete "with a photograph to Annie." Two months later, Capt. McLaughlin was in command of the steamer *Foster* off the coast of North Carolina, where he described to readers of the *Grand Traverse Herald* the famous expedition he made up the Alligator River. He wrote: "Leaving Plymouth, N.C., on the evening of the 16th February…I sailed for the Alligator River with instructions to stop at a point on the river twenty-seven miles from its mouth, for the purpose of picking up refugees fleeing from the rebel conscription. Owing to bad weather I did not reach the point indicated – Gum Neck Landing - until the evening of the 17th, that being as far up the river as any steamer had ventured since the commencement of the war. I here landed a party of thirty men under command of Lieut. Kingsbury, but did not find any of the parties I expected to meet, but the Lieutenant picked up three rebel prisoners home on furlough.

"At ten o'clock in the evening a boat came down the river from Fairfield and from one of the boatmen I learned that Capt. Spenser and a portion of his company were at that place. I determined to make an effort to capture them and rid the country of one band of "Independent Rangers." Getting my detachment on board, I started up river, which, being very crooked and narrow, found us but ten miles above Gum Neck Landing at daylight. Wishing to surprise them in the night, I made the vessel fast to the bank, posted pickets on the only road leading to Fairfield, and waited until the evening of the 18th, when we again started up the river. Four miles further and we were blocked, the river becoming so narrow that the sides of the vessel touched the bank on either side. Leaving the *Foster* under command of Lieut. O'Malley, I embarked sixty men in two launches and one cutter and pulled five miles through a driving snowstorm to the mouth of a canal leading to Fairfield, still four miles distant. Here we landed, many of the men being so numb with cold they could scarcely stand.

"The night was intensely dark and well fitted for a surprise – objects being visible only by the reflection of the snow on the ground. Forming my men into two companies…we commenced our march for the enemy's camp. It was now 2 o'clock A.M., the snow driving furiously, and the wind howling through the leafless and frozen branches of the trees. After a march of one and a half miles a light gleams through the driving snow, which on closer observation proved to be the fire of the enemy's picket station. Thinking the inclemency of the weather would prevent the "Yankees" from disturbing them, they built a fire among the bushes to keep the cold away, near which two of the enemy lay, while the third one walked his post and kept a lookout for the "Yankees" in the direction we were coming. But now we had "the best of them," having discovered their exact position, while they were ignorant of our presence and supposed that a space of eighty miles or more intervened between them and any "Yankees."

"Eight men sent to surround the picket post soon had them all secured, without them being able to give any alarm. We then had a clear coast to Fairfield, whose single street we entered at precisely three o'clock on the morning of the 19th. I learned from a Union man that Capt. Spenser, one of his officers, and a few enlisted men occupied one building, while the balance of his men were asleep in an adjacent store. Posting a guard of ten men around Capt. S.'s quarters and a picket of ten more to the rear of the building occupied by the soldiers, we made an assault with the remainder of the party – forty in number – upon the front door, which soon gave way and we "went in."

"A light from a dark lantern in the hands of one of my men gave us enough light to do our work handsomely, and before any resistance can be made, a bright bayonet with a blue jacket to push the matter, if further argument was necessary, was at the breast of every reposing rebel, all who were comfortably nestled among an abundance of straw. Securing their arms and putting the rebel under a strong guard, we immediately gave Capt. S. and companions our special attention. So well had the first part of our job been performed that the officers knew nothing of our intended visit to their abode until his door went in with a crash, and he was summoned to surrender to a Yankee Captain he had boasted he would like to meet. He took it like a sage, and while he yielded to the fortunes of war, he delivered his sword to his unwelcome visitors. Lieut. Sparrow of his company, seeing resistance useless, did likewise; and we found ourselves in possession of one Captain, one Second Lieutenant, and twenty-six enlisted men, together with sixty stands of small arms, a small amount of ammunition, cavalry saddles and a stand of rebel colors.

At daylight, we returned to our boats at the mouth of the Canal, where we embarked our prisoners and arms, and pulled back to our steamer, arriving on board at 10 o'clock A.M., well fatigued and very cold, amid the cheers of the part of the crew that remained on board the ship."[327] The cheers continued when General John Peck, commander of Union forces in North Carolina, wrote: "I have the honor to report that General Wessels…dispatched the Army gunboat *Foster* on the 16th to the Alligator River upon a reconnaissance. Her crew was re-enforced by Lieutenant Helms and 30 men of the One Hundred and First Pennsylvania Volunteers. Hearing that Spencer's Rangers were quartered at Fairfield, Captain McLaughlin proceeded in two launches, surprised the outpost, and captured the whole company, consisting of Captain Spencer, 1 lieuten-

The crew of the U.S. Army gunboat *General Foster* drills on shore with howitzers. *Library of Congress*

ant, and 26 privates. Much property was taken. The enterprise was conducted in a heavy snow storm, and entitles all concerned to highest praise. Another proof is added to the value of our gun-boats.[328] Robert McLaughlin, who as a young man learned to sail aboard the schooner *Hiram Merrill* on Grand Traverse Bay, had just become a Civil War hero.

The opposing American armies had refined their fighting skills in the three years since the Confederate attack on Fort Sumter. By 1864, the heat of battle had molded green recruits into hardened veterans efficient at killing. In 1858, the entire United States Army consisted of 16,000 men; by 1864 the two armies of the divided nation held well over a million soldiers. Many of these veterans had stood close to booming cannons, smelled the sharp scent of lead minie-balls, and saw friends who fought beside them fall and die in the fury of battle. Together the two fearsome armies could have conquered any nation or repelled any foe. As it was, they would continue to wreak havoc on each other until one or the other ceased to exist.

Throughout the winter of 1864, Grand Traverse men signed up and left for the front in increasing numbers. There was a feeling of urgency in the air and the hope that the spring's campaigns would bring the disastrous war to an end. By now, Grand Traverse men had been dispatched to every front of the war. Families left behind did their best to survive after their men left for the war. Mothers raised children and tended crops while the price of everything rose. To add to the bitter times, all too many saw their lonely situation become permanent as bad news poured in from far-away battlefields.

Reverend Smith advocated for the families of both white and Indian soldiers, writing in February, "Shak ko's wife & son came & I wrote her a letter to the Supervisor to get her help from the relief fund."[329] The Democratic Supervisor of Leelanau Township - whose opposition to the war was well-known – was uncooperative when it came to helping out the families of those who served. In a letter to his family, Joshua Middleton also expressed his dismay with Northport politicians and their disregard for the needs of those left back home. In April 1864, he said: "Anna writes the copperheads have elected their Supervisor and they have small hopes of getting any relief from the county. They claim the soldiers wives must work out and make their own living."[330]

As scarce as things were becoming in the North due to the demands of war, conditions were considerably more desperate for Southern soldiers and their families. Their movement as a united nation was collapsing and there was little of substance left in the South except for a hard-fighting army. A Union naval blockade all but stopped the export of cotton, which rotted in plantation fields throughout the Deep South. The labor force of black slaves escaped North, many ending up dressed in Union blue. There were few farmers left to plant food crops, due in part to the traditional Southern attitude that field labor was the work of slaves and low-class whites. In the Confederate Army, rations were cut and powder, shot, and medicine became increasingly hard to find. The *Grand Traverse Herald* wrote: "The dissatisfaction of Lee's army, in consequence of the reported reduction in their rations, has reached such a point as to require that commander to issue a general order, appealing to their patriotism and their religion to prevent mutiny."[331] As the dreaded spring campaign approached, Rebel soldiers held out little hope that the cause they were likely to die for had much chance to succeed.

Another *Herald* story titled "The Last Efforts of the Rebellion" gave the paper's take on the state of the Confederacy. It said: "The traitors of the South acknowledge that unless they can accomplish a loan and conscription by April, their cause is lost. The loan must be for one thousand millions of dollars, and the draft of all males between the ages of fifteen and forty five, and not less than half a million will meet the emergency. With a currency worth only seven or eight cents on the dollar, and an exhausted population, how can the rebels hope to escape the ruin impending over them? The hand writing is on the wall."[332]

In March 1864, the *Herald* compiled its latest survey of the Grand Traverse Country, the first comprehensive description of the region since the Civil War began. The most notable change, other than a general increase in settlers throughout Grand Traverse, was the shift in population to Traverse City, which had sprinted to a tie for the lead with Northport as the area's largest town. When first examined by the *Herald* in 1858, Traverse City held only 100 people, most of them working for Hannah, Lay & Co., while the booming harbor town of Northport boasted a population of over 300. Now the two Grand Traverse towns were even in population, each with over 400 residents, and many hundreds more working their Homestead Act claims.

Potatoes and wheat ranked as the most important crops grown on Grand Traverse farms. The soil beneath the cleared hardwood forest proved especially fertile for these staples. Surplus produce could be shipped inexpensively to Chicago, the largest farm market on the Great Lakes. Due to the moderating effects of the waters of Lake Michigan on the weather, fruit trees also thrived in Grand Traverse, and with this in mind, many homesteaders prepared ground for an orchard on their acreage. The *Herald* credited Northport's George Smith as the person who "probably paid more attention to the cultivation of fruit than any other man in this region. He settled there fifteen years ago as a missionary to the Indians, and commenced testing fruit the first year." In an interview with the paper, Smith said: "My cherries succeeded equally well as my Plums; I have several excellent varieties, all flourishing, but the birds regard them as legitimately their inheritance." Time proved that cherry trees benefited most from the region's distinct climate and soils, earning Traverse City the modern day title, "Cherry Capital of the World."

By 1864, almost all Grand Traverse ports had a wooding dock to take advantage of the demand for cordwood fuel for ships. The *Herald* noted: "The wood is of superior quality, bringing twenty-five to fifty cents more per cord in market than wood from any other quarter. Many farmers in the immediate vicinity of the Bay find it to their profit to cut their timber into wood and sell it rather than to burn it." It speaks to the omnipresence of the forest covering Grand Traverse at the time that the *Herald* made news of the potential value of its wood. The paper concluded that "lumber, like every thing else, has greatly advanced in value since the breaking out of the war."

Within the survey, the *Herald* examined the population and demographics of Grand Traverse and found: "The number of inhabitants in the Grand Traverse region, according to the census of June, 1860, was 3,627. There has been a constant influx ever since. The population has probably more than doubled." Though a catastrophic Civil War split the nation and called hundreds of area men off to fight, the region was in the midst of a full-fledged population boom. The paper continued: "Settlers that have come here are from nearly all the Northern States – some few are of foreign birth. New York has probably a larger representation than any other State."

A section of the survey titled "Why this Region was not Earlier Settled" revealed more about Grand Traverse and the economics of westward expansion. It said: "It may seem strange to some that this region should be so long left a wilderness while other portions of the west were so rapidly settling. For this there are doubtless various causes…

"First, in an earlier day, before the time of railroads, when the tide of emigration was settling westward, the proprietors of boats found it for their interests to persuade emigrants to go as far west as water would float them. At a later day railroad companies did the same thing, that is, they induced them to go as far as the railroad could carry them. Hence, Illinois, Wisconsin and Iowa have been filled up while this region had been run around and entirely overlooked.

"Another reason doubtless is that the impression has quite extensively prevailed that all this north part of Michigan was one vast Pinery, and therefore not adapted to agriculture. It was not until recently that the public have learned to the contrary…The greater portion of all this country is of the best quality of hard timbered land. Then again this region has been looked upon as cold, and therefore barren. The prevalence of this idea has doubtless deterred many from coming here…The truth is we do not have as cold weather here as they do in most regions much further south. Our winters are milder by several degrees than in the southern part of the State." The waters of Lake Michigan created the moderating effect on the weather the paper described, an anomaly that accounts for the historic success and modern importance of cherry trees and grape vines in Grand Traverse.

In advising travelers how to get to Northern Michigan, boats were the sole means of transport the *Herald* recommended. The road north from Grand Rapids was open in sections all the way to Northport, but the land route was still a comparatively rough trip. The paper suggested boarding the Traverse City based *Alleghany* on any of her stops between Detroit and Chicago as "the most direct route" to Grand Traverse. As an alternative, it said: "Find a Propeller at Cleveland, Buffalo, or Detroit, that will land you at Northport. At this point you can take passage any day on the Bay Propeller for Traverse City…a large number of Propellers stop at Carp River for wood – a little village on Lake Michigan, fifteen miles south of the entrance to the Bay – so also at Glen Arbor, 20 miles south of Carp River and 30 miles west of Traverse City. But neither of these points is a convenient place for those wishing to reach the Bay." The Manitou Islands had a bad reputation with travelers and the *Herald* warned its readers to stay away. The paper said: "Visitors will not allow boat Captains to persuade them to land at the Manitou Islands, as it will cost them more to get from there than their whole expense from home."[333]

The late winter weather in Grand Traverse carried with it a dose of sickness and disease. On Sunday, March 20, Smith wrote: "Had no meeting here today. The fear of Small Pox is the reason – people are afraid."[334] Instead of preaching, he mentioned writing letters to Northport friends, including 1st Michigan Sharp Shooters Payson Wolfe and Charles Allen. Later, Smith's daughter Mary received a letter from her husband Payson Wolfe, containing ten dollars and "a picture of Camp Douglas," where the 1st Michigan Sharp Shooters were stationed as guards. Much has been made of the horrors of the infamous Andersonville Prison in Georgia where so many Union prisoners died, but little has been said

Confederate prisoners of war in Camp Douglas, Chicago, circa 1863, the last place the 1st Michigan Sharp Shooters were stationed before heading off to fight in Virginia. *Library of Congress*

about Camp Douglas, its Northern equivalent. The truth lays in Oakwood Cemetery in Chicago, where 6,000 Confederate soldiers who died at Camp Douglas are buried in a one acre plot – the largest mass grave in the North. Both prisons came to epitomize the brutality of the American Civil War.

In the same letter that held the photograph of Camp Douglas, Payson wrote that the 1st Michigan Sharp Shooters would soon be deployed to Annapolis, Maryland to take part in Grant's Overland Campaign. It would prove to be a disastrous assignment for the regiment. In one of the many ironic and often catastrophic turn of events common in the Civil War, by the end of the summer of 1864, several dozen of the Camp Douglas guards from the 1st Michigan Sharp Shooters would themselves be prisoners of war, confined at Andersonville. Only a few made it out alive.

Inside the pages of the *Herald*, Hannah, Lay & Co. – which had diversified beyond the lumber business and now owned and operated the largest mercantile store in the north – expanded the size and subject matter of its advertisements. The new, half page ads came complete with an introduction titled "State of the Markets," which charted the effects the Civil War was having on the commodities the store stocked. In April, their ad said: "The tendency of markets is strongly upward…Brown and bleached cottons are scarce and higher…Groceries are very firm with a constant increase in price of most goods; in tea and sugar particularly…furs are falling off…owing to immense stocks in Europe, the war in Poland, the mild winter on the continent." The advertisement included the company's take on the most recent increase in the draft, writing:

"The unavoidable effect of the present call, on all manufactured articles in which labor is the prominent element, will be to materially advance the cost of production and consequently the price of sale."[335] Following this introduction, Hannah, Lay & Co. listed over 200 categories of goods available – from apples to "nice, fresh" Baltimore oysters – confirming that although prices were rising, goods were available in plenty. In contrast, at this point in the war, most of the items in the advertisement could not be found in the South at any price.

April started on a bad note for Reverend Smith, setting the tone for the upcoming summer. He wrote: "I buried my old Dog Major…in my Garden. He was worth more to me than a cow as he saved my fruit from being stolen." Throughout Grand Traverse, the cold winter of 1864 lingered way past its welcome, freezing out lake travel and commerce. In spite of the weather, the *Herald* reported: "A good many land-hunters have come in already, overland, and have selected and entered the Homesteads at the Traverse City Land Office. There will be a great rush as soon as navigation is fairly opened and Propellers are enabled to get through the Straits of Mackinac." On April 29, the *Herald* wrote: "The *Alleghany* arrived from Sarnia, having made the round trip in five days. She is the first propeller of the season to make the passage through the Straits to the Lower Lakes, and return." However, due to the renewed presence of ice on the bay, "she was not able to get to the dock when our paper went to press, and we have received no news by her." Without the usual bundle of national papers as sources, the *Herald* turned to local news, writing that "seventy-three Homestead entries were made at the Traverse City Land Office during the month of April." Commenting on the effects of the Homestead Act to the west of the town, the paper said: "Three year ago the region…was an unbroken wilderness. The land is now taken up by actual settlers, and Glen Arbor and Traverse City are becoming near neighbors."[336]

When the ice finally broke up, the worker-bee schooners of Great Lakes commerce swarmed to the area's docks. The *Herald* noted: "There are four schooners at the Wharfs on Hannah, Lay & Co. loading with lumber for Chicago." With the water highway open for the navigation season, Hannah, Lay & Co. updated their commodities forecast, writing: "Navigation may be said to be open and as a consequence we are compelled to notify our friends that what we have predicted is upon us, viz: a general advance has taken place, and that not on a few isolated items, but on nearly everything.

"With gold at 180; an entire lull in our military affairs; a necessary increased demand and price for all kinds of labor; a scarcity of many kinds of artisans, on account of the Draft and enlistments; a want of faith in our country Banks; the sure increase of taxation to meet the demands of government; these and various other causes combine to insure the advance now beginning to be seriously felt.

"Provisions are much higher, especially meats of all kinds. Sugars are pretty much out of sight, and Teas keep close behind. Coffees are out of reach. Seeds are enormously high, and cottons firmer. Hardware has advanced about 30 and boots and shoes fully 25 per cent. Tobacco is about as high as it should be. Furs are quiet. Tin steadily advancing. Leather very firm, with an upward tendency. Windows and doors have been advanced again largely." Then, as if contemplating the whole sad state of a country at war with itself, the Hannah, Lay & Co. ad concluded, "The end is not yet."[337]

A rush of new settlers came to stake their claim in Grand Traverse. The men of the family often enlisted soon after and left to fight in the Civil War. Paul Gravel was one of a dozen Traverse City men to join the 14th Michigan Infantry that spring and described the regiment's journey south to Tennessee in an April, 1864 letter. He wrote: "On arriving at Grand Rapids, we were placed in camp Lee for drill and instruction and to wait till we were paid. This camp Lee, I am happy to hear, is now broken up and soldiers transferred to Jackson. It consisted of several board shanties with no ventilation except that afforded by the cracks and crevices. The dirt and discomfort was far advanced of any prison I have ever seen, while sickness and vermin were common complaints. But it is removed, and one disgrace to the State abolished, so let it pass. From here we were transferred by stage to Kalamazoo, where the rigid rules of Camp Lee succeed a freedom that was appreciated to the full. Our officers showed us confidence, and the men did not violate it…This pleasant state of things continued till all the absentees arrived, when…we started on the M.C.R.R.[338] for the South. We traveled all night, and in the morning it was discovered by the blood on the brakes and wheels that someone had fallen off in the darkness. It proved to be a member of Co. G. and his mangled remains were found by the night express train and forwarded home.

"All the next day we rode through a flat prairie country nearly submerged in water and with hardly a settlement worthy the name, till evening, when we neared Indianapolis. Here the country changed, becoming hilly and more populated. Arriving in Indianapolis just at dusk, and not having time to stroll about, our view of the city was confined…to a huge, heavy, dirty looking building called the State House, and a nearer sight of a host of smoky machine shops, saloons and shanties which invariably surround a depot. We arrived at Jeffersonville, Ind., about three o'clock in the afternoon, and immediately took a ferry for Louisville, Ky., and on landing we were marched to a spot which was denominated the Soldier's Home. This was a long building about 50 by 150 feet, devoid of furniture except four or five sinks for washing purposes. It was occupied on one side, on our arrival, by an Illinois veteran regiment on their way home on a furlough. They were about as dirty a set as you often meet, but the place itself almost surpassed description. The floor was covered with a thick stratum of filth, and over this was strewn old shoes, pipes, pork fat, bones, cast off accoutrements, bread and everything in the shape of refuse which a regiment just from the front would be likely to throw aside on reaching a place where a new outfit could be bought.

"After staying here three days we took the cars and arrived safely the next morning. We were first marched to Barrack No. 1, which is an immense building said to contain 365 rooms. It belongs to the confiscated estate of the late rebel Gen. Zollicoffer, who intended it for a hotel; but the war was coming on, it was left unfinished, and is now used by the Government. After knocking about two or three weeks and changing quarters about the same number of times, we are at last posted as guards around what was once the Nashville Female Institute, now occupied by the Government as a barracks, where regiments which only stay a short time in the city are stationed. Our duties as guards occupy us eight hours every other day, so you can see we are not likely to break down from fatigue just yet."[339] However, for Gravel and the rest of the 14th Michigan Cavalry, fatigue was on its way. The regiment would soon have the misfortune of being designated 'dismounted cavalry,' and spent the rest of the war marching with Sherman to the sea.

The monotonous routine the soldiers of 14th Michigan endured since their arrival in Tennessee contrasted with the experience of the 10th Michigan Cavalry, who had just fought their first engagement in the border state. Lt. E.J. Brooks and the Grand Traverse men he recruited were in the midst of the battle, with Brooks demonstrating the skills he acquired during his two years of service with the 1st New York Light Artillery. The 10th Michigan Cavalry's regimental history records the scene as they faced the Confederate in mountainous country. It said: "The bridge was defended by the rebels…with a strong force, occupying a strong redoubt, with extensive and well-constructed rifle pits. The Union force had one mountain howitzer, commanded by Lt. E. J. Brooks, but allowing to a very limited amount of ammunition, he was unable to accomplish much, yet made some remarkably telling shots.

"It was soon ascertained that there was no possible way of reaching the bridge without first dislodging the enemy from their strong position, and this had to be accomplished at much risk by passing over perfectly open ground for a distance of two hundred yards, swept by a very sharp and hot cross-fire from the opposite side of the river. Yet, being the first heavy undertaking of the regiment, Col. Trowbridge felt unwilling to retire without accomplishing something, as it would produce an unfavorable effect upon his command. He therefore decided to make an attempt, dismounting about one-third of his men. With this small force he ordered an advance upon the enemy's position at double-quick, when they gave way in great disorder, leaving their works, and taking shelter in a large mill near at hand…As soon as the redoubt was taken, an attempt was made to drive the enemy out of the mill, but the charging force was met with such a terrible and destructive volley that it was abandoned. In this daring and gallant attempt Captain Weatherwax lost his life, being shot in the heart.

"The fight was a brilliant success, though obtained at the loss of seventeen killed and wounded, and must be recognized as an uncommon victory, considering it was gained by dismounted cavalry, new and undisciplined, over a much superior force of well-trained infantry, holding strong defensive works, and…should be classed among the most gallant minor victories of the war."[340] The Grand Traverse men in the 10th Michigan Cavalry had now done some real fighting and Lt. Brooks was soon promoted to the rank of captain. However, there would be no toasting the minor victories in 1864; they simply blended into the space between the great battles, as did this forgotten engagement in Tennessee. The scale and frequency of the fighting had surpassed the worst of expectations and dulled the nation's nerves. Yet nothing to date had prepared the forlorn American people for the slaughter that was about to take place in Virginia, in what would become the most lethal 90 days in American military history.

During the last two weeks of April, Reverend Smith corresponded with Payson Wolfe and Charles Allen of the 1st Michigan Sharp Shooters, and Lakeshore Tigers Chauncey Woolsey, Joshua Middleton, John Kehl, and Thomas McCraney - all Grand Traverse volunteers serving in the Army of the Potomac. They were six of more than 100,000 Union soldiers who saw the cherry trees blossom as they assembled around Washington and awaited the start of the 1864 Overland Campaign. The President had just placed the Army's command in the hands of the Union's most aggressive leader, General Ulysses S. Grant, the hero of the western front. With Congressional approval, President Lincoln went so far as to resurrect the rank of Lieutenant General of the Army for Grant, a title previously held by George Washington. The majority of soldiers from Grand Traverse now marched to the Lieutenant General's orders and would start paying the cost of Union victory as the army advanced on the Confederate capital of Richmond. Two of the six abovementioned Grand Traverse soldiers would be killed in action within a month, another two seriously wounded during the upcoming summer's battles.

While drilling for the fight near the banks of the Potomac River, Northport's Joshua Middleton wrote: "There is nothing new going on at present. But there is getting up a big ready for the spring work. Grant is a going to Boss the job. We expect to have some hard fighting." In the same April 1864 letter, soldier Middleton tried to explain to his sister why he left his Quaker-based pacifist principles behind to join the Union Army. He said: "You may think it was wrong of me to leave home, situated as I am, but why not I as well as others. I thought long and seriously about it. Sometimes it would seem as if I could not go but must stay at home and take care of my family, but that did not satisfy me. I could not get rid of the thought that I would be into it sooner or later, and I felt my duty and I could not resist. And now I am here, I feel as if I am doing my duty to God and my Country. And if I should fall I shall leave a name that they need never blush to own."

In the late 17th century, the Society of Friends, more commonly known as the Quakers, was the first religious group in America to formally protest against the institution of slavery. One hundred years later, George Washington complained that "a society of Quakers, formed for such purposes"[341] had attempted to liberate a neighbor's slave. The organization Washington referred to would eventually become known as the Underground Railroad, which helped thousands in bondage escape to the North before the Civil War. As the 19th century unfolded, Quakers took on an increasingly active role in non-violent resistance to slavery, and through their political activism, helped convert many to the cause of abolition. In the process, they helped foster the national divisions that led to the war. Now, for Grand Traverse soldier Joshua Middleton, the time for talk had passed, and he struggled to reconcile his Quaker belief that God dwelled in all people with his decision to volunteer in the Union Army – a course that may well lead him to kill a fellow human being.

Middleton drafted his next letter from a make-shift desk in a log and canvas barracks somewhere in Virginia, writing: "You must excuse the smut on the paper, for it impossible to keep clean in our smoky cabins…We had a grand review yesterday, the entire Corps about 70 regiments. It was a splendid sight.

We all passed before Gen Grant & Gen Mead. Who can tell how many will be left to pass in review next spring? God only knows. Both armies are making tremendous efforts for the spring campaign. Unless G`en Grant does some smart engineering, we have a big job before us, before we get Lee out. Our regiment is always in front, acting mostly as skirmishers and flankers."[342] It was an honor for the regiment to be chosen as skirmishers, for it spoke to the stealth and marksmanship of the unit. However, the honor would soon put the Lakeshore Tigers on the leading edge of the greatest clash of armies ever staged on the North American continent.

The drawing of a crossroads at Kelley's Ford, Virginia, made by Joshua Middleton before the Battle of the Wilderness, portrays battle-scarred buildings and bears a crease that corresponds to the size of Middleton's Bible. *Courtesy Donna Allington*

In his letter, Middleton gave further insight into his own internal conflict as a fighting Quaker. He wrote: "Why does it seem so strange that I am here? Have I no interest at stake? Am I not an American, and I wish to see transmitted to my children the glorious privileges that I have enjoyed? For this I have left all I hold dear on Earth, for to battle in the cause of God and Humanity." Middleton concluded: "We are packed up and ready for a start at any moment, it may be tomorrow, it may not come for a month. No one knows anything of Gen Grant's plans until he is ready to move. One thing is certain, he would like nothing better than to have Lee attack us here and we could give him a worse cleaning out than he got when he went into Pennsylvania." However, Grant had been chosen as a general who attacked the Rebels, not one who waited for others to start a fight.

Ten days later, the 26th Michigan was ordered out of their entrenchments and deep into the Virginia heartland, where Lee's fabled army waited. Middleton

Tom Woodruff

described the fateful move, writing: "Was on picket when ordered to break camp. Left on the 3rd of May about 11 o clock marched all night, crossed Eli ford about 8 o clock in the morning. Reached Chancellorsville about noon, we stole a march on Lee and got possession of our field ahead of him, in the Wilderness."

On May 6, Grant's Army of the Potomac collided with Lee's Army of Northern Virginia in the desolate area named the Wilderness – the first battle of the Overland Campaign. The 1st Michigan Sharp Shooters and the 26th Michigan Infantry were among the many regiments that advanced as skirmishers, testing the Confederate strength ahead of the main body of troops. The Wilderness was choked with a dense, second-growth forest where vision was limited to a few feet ahead and close in fighting would be the rule.

As the opposing armies approached each other, Indian soldiers in Company K saw the problem of their bright blue uniforms standing out against the green foliage. An officer in the 1st Michigan Sharp Shooters wrote: "They, on the very first day on the front, caught on to the great advantage our enemy employed over us in the color of uniform. Ours was blue, and could be seen at a long distance; while the "Johnny" (as we called them) could not be spotted at a comparatively short distance, even while lying in an open field.

"This disadvantage to us was appreciated almost immediately that these Indians got in the field, and they would go out and find a dry spot of earth and roll in it until their uniform was the complete color of the ground before going out on the skirmish line; and if the day was wet they would not hesitate to take mud and rub it over their clothes, for as soon as this dried a little they would have what they were after – the color of the earth. This custom was adopted by my whole Regiment; and it was often remarked that our Regiment could do the closest skirmishing at the least cost of any Regiment in the Division."[343]

In his memoirs on the Battle of the Wilderness, General Ulysses S. Grant wrote: "More desperate fighting has not been witnessed on this continent than that of the 5th and 6th of May."[344] The Army of the Potomac's Second Corps, which included the 26th Michigan Infantry, spent the two days battling Lee's troops in the tangled Virginia countryside. Northern Michigan soldiers, whose rifles had never aimed at anything more than animals in the wild, now sighted in on their southern countrymen and pulled the trigger. Others struggled hand to hand, fighting through the smoke and underbrush with rifle butts and bayonets. On the 5th the Union gained the field, only to be driven back the next morning by Rebel forces under the command of General James Longstreet. In this war that divided so many houses and exposed so many bitter ironies, it was only a footnote that Generals Grant and Longstreet had been best friends while attending West Point in the early 1840's, or that Longstreet was an honored guest at Grant's wedding in 1846, for today in the Wilderness the past was forgotten.

Northport's Joshua Middleton described the scenes the Lakeshore Tigers were part of over the next two days, writing: "We was put right out on the line. We was kept there till 3 o clock in the morning. We was in a swamp. You could hear the balls - whiz spat chug - but could see no one. Two struck near me one in the tree beside me, another over my head, but thank God none touched me. We took 3 prisoners that night.

"We was moved to the left of the line the next morning and we went to work to build the breast works, the rebs shelling our line. Hurt no one though. Started out to drive them out of the woods in front of us. On the 6th of May Friday drove them two miles and was wounded just as we got through the fight. Was sent to Division Hospital along with Henry Holcomb who was mortally wounded. Left there that night, was ordered back by way of Chancellorsville, was knocked over an embankment - hurt me bad." May 6 had been a terrible day for Grand Traverse soldier Joshua Middleton, having been hit in the hand by a Confederate minie ball and then knocked off a narrow Virginia two-track by a fast moving supply wagon. Although that evening he lay wounded and battered at the base of an embankment, in light of the battle's great losses, he could consider himself lucky to be alive.

Throughout the first day in the Wilderness, Federal reinforcements, including the 1st Michigan Sharp Shooters, pushed forward to help stabilize Union positions. While maneuvering through the thick woods, Sgt. Charles Allen of Northport, who over the years helped preachers Smith and Dougherty translate their Sunday services, was shot in the chest, the first Indian soldier from Company K cut down by enemy fire. The night of May 6 was a scene from hell as fire swept the day's battlefields, burning many of the wounded alive as they cried for help. Veterans of the worst battles of the war later cited the scenes of smoke and fire, and the screams of desperate soldiers, as the most dreadful experience of their Civil War service. By dawn of May 7, Charles Allen lay seriously wounded in a field hospital, and Northport neighbor Henry Holcomb was dead.

Sgt. Charles Allen had left Grand Traverse the previous summer aboard the propeller *Tonawanda* with Reverend Smith's son-in-law Payson Wolfe. The two men steamed away to enlist in the all-Indian Company K of the 1st Michigan Sharp Shooters, who were then stationed in Dearborn to guard the Detroit area arsenal. Almost immediately, Allen and Reverend Smith began to correspond by mail. For a number of Northport soldiers like Allen, letters to and from Reverend Smith were their main contact with home. The preacher's diary is filled with notations citing the receipt and posting of mail, often carried by captains of passing vessels who had become friends with Smith during their time in Northport harbor.

On May 18, 1864 - 11 months after Charles Allen and Payson Wolfe left on the *Tonawanda* for the Union Army - George and Arvilla Smith and daughter Annie were aboard the same ship, traveling the same route to Detroit. Reverend Smith planned to attend the state convention for Congregational ministers, while the rest of his family enjoyed a change of pace and the culture of Michigan's largest city. George Smith wrote: "We started from Northport a little before midnight…AM passed Mackinaw had a fine prospect with the glass. Arrived at…Saginaw Bay about sunset – a splendid day's sail…wrote on board letter to Payson, 1 to Charles Allen."[345]

The delivery of mail to and from the front lines was a difficult task for the postal service. With armies on the move, and pitched battles in progress, it was hard to get ammunition, food, and medicine to soldiers - much more so the mail. The trail of correspondence Smith shared with the 19 year-old Allen showed that the lag time between posting mail and having it safely delivered was considerable. Two weeks after the Battle of the Wilderness, Smith did not yet know that Allen had been mortally wounded, much less that he had died in a Fredericksburg hospital at about the same time his family steamed out of Northport aboard the *Tonawanda*.

Though the worst of the Battle of the Wilderness was over, fighting continued as the two armies maneuvered south. On May 7, General Grant noted, "General Custer drove the enemy's cavalry from Catharpin Furnace to Todd's Tavern."[346] The skirmish renewed the rivalry between Custer and Confederate General Jeb Stuart and set the stage for their final meeting in the week ahead. During the Battle of the Wilderness, another 29,000 American casualties - the majority Union – were added to the toll of the Civil War. The columns of wounded soldiers straggling back to Washington shocked even the war-hardened citizens of that city. In the past, northern armies had retreated in defeat after such heavy losses, but for Grant, the Overland Campaign of 1864 had just begun.

For days following the battle of the Wilderness, the wounded Joshua Middleton tramped in a daze through northeast Virginia, then the most dangerous place on the continent. Thousands of men like Middleton, whose wounds were not life threatening, were left to fend for themselves, for the overwhelmed hospitals at the front could attend only to the critical. Middleton wrote: "May 10 1864. Arrived at Fredericksburg. I am almost crazy with pain, and have had no provisions since leaving the field Hospital. It has been awful hot and dirty, and we have been forced to drink muddy water. Even this we are happy to get."

The conflict in Virginia was now a war of attrition, and Grant knew the odds were heavily in his favor. On May 11, the General telegraphed the War Department in Washington from his headquarters in Virginia, writing: "We have now ended the 6th day of very hard fighting. The result up to this time is much in our favor. But our losses have been heavy as well as those of our enemy. We have lost to this time eleven general officers killed, and probably twenty thousand men. I think the enemy loss must be greater…I am now sending back…all my wagons for a fresh supply of provisions and ammunition, and purpose to fight it out on this line if it takes all summer."[347] Grant understood he had been chosen to bring the conflict to an end at whatever the cost and the Overland Campaign was shaping up to be a large part of the payment. The mission of the Army of the Potomac was clear. After pledging to "fight it out," Grant ordered his force south toward Richmond, and the bloodiest campaign of the Civil War continued.

The Confederate strategy to hold on to Richmond was to maneuver between the Union Army and the South's capital city, using the terrain and their familiarity with home territory to compensate for inferiority in numbers. Contrary to Grant's optimistic assessment, in the Wilderness the Rebels had inflicted nearly two casualties for every one they absorbed. The problem for the Confederates was that every soldier lost was irreplaceable – by the spring of 1864 the South already enlisted almost every available man. The North, however, had started the war with twice the base population of the secession states, and three times the number of free white men. In addition, the flood of immigrants into the North, and the acceptance of men of color in the ranks, more than replaced the casualties suffered by the Union Army. Northern commanders continued to add to their ranks with the help of cash bounties and the draft. New Confederate enlistments dwindled to such a desperate state that the part of the country that viewed slavery as a God-given right now considered freeing any slave who would fight in the Confederate Army.

The next battle in Virginia bore the name of a clapboard building known as Spotsylvania Courthouse, one of the few signs of civilization in the densely wooded corner of Virginia. Skirmishing commenced on May 10th as troops from both armies concentrated in the vicinity of the courthouse. In the midst of prolonged showers, soldiers from the two huge armies exchanged heated fire while behind them the main forces struggled through mud to find the best ground for the battle ahead. While most of the Army of the Potomac moved on Spotsylvania, Grant ordered a detachment of 10,000 cavalrymen to ride toward Richmond in a move designed to draw Confederate Jeb Stuart's forces into open battle. General Custer and his Michigan Cavalry Brigade had stopped Stuart at Gettysburg the year before and now prepared to face their rival for the second time in a week. Glen Arbor's Thomas Daly and Casten Miller and Leelanau's Thomas Harmer - who had all joined the 7th Michigan Cavalry only months before – rode with Custer into the fray. Possession of the field shifted as the day wore on. In the confusion of battle, General Stuart halted to scan the road ahead with his field glass, unaware of a company of Michigan cavalry riding nearby. A Union soldier drew his pistol and shot Stuart from his saddle. The renowned Confederate commander died in a field hospital, and the divided nation lost another of its great leaders. As the sun set on Spotsylvania, the rain-soaked soldiers in both armies pitched their overnight camps, built fires, and slept as best they could. They knew the battle would begin again in the morning.

May 12, 1864 quickly evolved into one of the worst days of the war for Grand Traverse soldiers. In battles to date, Northern Michigan men had fallen by ones and twos – today at Spotsylvania their casualties would be measured by the dozens. Morning rain continued to soak the Virginia countryside and confound the movement of the heavily-equipped Union Army. As was the case at the Wilderness, thick woods and thin roads neutralized the North's superiority in artillery and made it difficult to concentrate on any one point along Rebel lines. However, Grant pledged to take on the Confederates wherever he found them. By noon, the leading edge of the Union Army had closed to within striking distance of Confederate positions, and the General ordered a charge.

The 26th Michigan Infantry led the Union assault on the Rebel works and suffered dearly during the long hours of combat that followed. The ferocity of the Battle of the Wilderness the week before had hardened the Lakeshore Tigers into fighting soldiers, and the regiment pressed on through the volleys of Confederate rifle fire and exploding shells. Once again, hometown friends fell next to each other and neighbors lay scattered about the field. Through it all, Union soldiers continued their advance until they crashed into Rebel lines. In the desperate, individual struggles that followed, the righteous ideals and grand causes the soldiers fought for dissolved into a pitiless frenzy of kill or be killed. Face to face, the Rebels they attacked were not the whip-toting, slave holding villains that the *Grand Traverse Herald* described as their enemy, but rather American soldiers like themselves trying to avoid premature death. For most of the men, immediate success in battle had nothing to do with union or secession, abolition or slavery, but simply living to see another day.

When the sun set on the Spotsylvania battlefield May 12, Jacob Haines of Company A, 26th Michigan – one of the six volunteers who left Northport during the January blizzard to enlist in the Lakeshore Tigers - lay mortally wounded, with friend Henry Lemmerwell of Leland dead beside him. Neighbors James Adameson and Lewis Gremmulbaker from Leelanau were torn by Confederate shot and shell and soon died from their wounds. As was often the case when a Union regiment recruited from a particular area was heavily engaged, every town in Grand Traverse suffered from the May 12 carnage. Leland's 44 year-old David Hollinger took bullets in both the neck and hand but survived. While fighting side by side, friends Sgt. Levi Bailey of Glen Arbor and John Dechow of Port Oneida fell to Confederate fire. The pair made it home to Grand Traverse, though a Confederate minie ball had cost Dechow the use of his right arm. Another Lakeshore Tiger, John Hopkins of Traverse City, lost a leg to an exploding Confederate shell. The worst fears of many Grand Traverse families had come to fruition in the woods of Virginia.

Writing from his hospital bed outside of Baltimore, Joshua Middleton filled in the casualty list of Grand Traverse soldiers fighting in the 26th Michigan Regiment at Spotsylvania on May 12. He wrote: "Little Tom McCraney was shot dead…Charley Clark and John Eglas were both wounded at the same time."[348] McCraney, the 26 year-old Leelanau school teacher who corresponded regularly with George Smith, never received the letter the preacher had written to him only five days before. John Egeler Jr., a 43 year-old Lake Leelanau farmer who Middleton referred to as Eglas, soon died from his battlefield wounds. Nineteen year-old Charles Clark of Leland survived being shot at Spotsylvania only to be killed in another Virginia battle the following spring.[349] The number of Lakeshore Tigers falling in the 1864 Overland Campaign began to mount.

Nearby, the battle-hardened 1st New York Light Artillery supported the charging Union forces with a steady barrage of artillery shells. The veteran unit was home to a number of Grand Traverse men who volunteered in the early days of the war. The soldiers of the 1st New York had previously fought and died in Virginia, distinguishing themselves at the battles of Fair Oaks and Malvern Hill in 1862 and almost every major battle in the east that followed. After Malvern Hill, former Grand Traverse Sheriff William Sykes wrote the *Herald*, saying: "Why we were not killed God only knows." Now, two years later, at another Virginia address made famous through bloodshed, Sykes ran out of luck. Confederate metal found its mark and the former Grand Traverse Sheriff was carried from the field mortally wounded.

Captain Ames of Battery G, 1st New York Artillery, described the action at Spotsylvania in which Sheriff Sykes was struck down, writing: "May 12, at 3 a.m., we marched to the left about five miles, and at the break of day…charged the enemy's works at the bloody angle of Spotsylvania Court House, and at once became hotly engaged with the enemy at close cannister range. In a few moments, fearing in the smoke and fog we might injure our own men, I asked permission of General Hancock if I might advance the battery to the extreme front, which was granted. Reaching the position, we at once engaged the enemy, much of the time not fifty rods away. Some of the artillery of the corps not having reported, General Hancock sent a staff officer to me, asking if I could work some of the twenty-two guns we had captured from the enemy. I informed him I would if he could give me some of the infantry to take the place of the drivers and aid in bringing up ammunitions. He readily gave us all the men we wanted, and from then on we fought not only with our six guns, but also nine of the enemy's, using the enemy's ammunition. It seemed to madden the enemy to desperation to be thus slaughtered by their own guns and ammunition. Charge after charge was made by the Confederates to retake their position and the guns they had lost, but our men stood firm as a rock, determined to hold the position or die in the attempt. Thus the battle was fought from 4 o'clock a.m., May 12th, to 3 a.m., May 13th, when the enemy relinquished the attempt to retake the position and fell back to a new line in their rear.

"But what a sight to our eyes! The dead lay in piles. Trees sixteen inches in diameter were cut off by musket balls and cannister. Of the infantry that helped work the guns, several were killed or wounded, and I regret I am unable to give their names and regiments."[350] After several more months of fighting in Virginia, the term of Captain Ames' service expired, and Lt. Samuel A. McClelland of Northport was promoted to captain of the battery he and a score of Grand Traverse volunteers served in since the fall of 1861.

At another forlorn point along the battle lines at Spotsylvania, the 1st Michigan Sharp Shooters marched towards the Confederate breastworks. They met the same fierce resistance as the 26th Michigan, facing dug in troops protecting their country and capital state. Like the scrubby woods of the Wilderness, the dense foliage they now marched through often made it difficult to see more than a few yards ahead. Artillery shells tore through the branches above and dropped limbs and trunks on the advancing Sharp Shooters. Every explosion blasted a torrent of water off the rain soaked trees, showering the men below.

The 20th Michigan Infantry, commanded by Lt. Colonel Cutcheon, maneuvered up alongside their fellow Michiganders, their pickets probing the uncharted ground. The whole Union line now moved blindly forward, having had no time for reconnaissance, and not knowing what lay ahead. As the brigade approached newly opened ground in front of the Confederate works, an exploding shell killed four soldiers from the 20th Michigan, right next to the advancing Sharp Shooters. Through the haze they saw the log fortifications and sharpened pike poles which the Rebel Army waited behind. On this day in May, the Confederate command believed this was the battle that would drive a beaten Army of the Potomac back to Washington, and possibly even end the war. The order from the generals of both armies was simply "Attack."

As the 20th Michigan and the Sharp Shooters advanced, five regiments of North Carolina soldiers left their trenches, advanced through the woods, and collided with the Union line. The Carolinians rolled over the first two Union regiments they engaged and into the flank of the 20th Michigan. At the same time, Rebel fire erupted from the trenches, and the Union soldiers were hit from the front and side in addition to artillery fire exploding above. In a half hour of close combat, over 100 soldiers of the 20th Michigan were casualties, and the Confederates continued to surge forward. Next in line were the 1st Michigan Sharp Shooters, who were now attacked from three sides and at risk of being surrounded. The regiment had no choice but to fight it out.[351]

The North Carolinians pressed forward and the battle intensified. The Michigan woodsmen in the Sharp Shooters returned deadly accurate fire. The Indians of Company K followed each volley with a distinctive war cry that rattled the Confederates in the same way the Rebel yell unnerved Yankee troops. The Sharp Shooter's regimental history described the fighting as "slowly, sullenly, disastrously rolling down from the left...everything on the left of the sharp-shooters had been swept away, and the attack on their front and flank, with both infantry and artillery pouring in shot and shell, was terrific, but they gallantly held their ground. On the left of the sharp-shooters were a company of...Indians, in command of the gallant and lamented young Graveraet; they suffered dreadfully, but never faltered or moved, sounding the warwhoop with every volley, and their unerring aim quickly taught the rebels they were standing on dangerous ground."[352]

Soldiers on both sides fell in waves as the distance between the two armies closed. Lt. Garrett Graveraet and his father, Sgt. Henry Graveraet, moved among their men, cheering them on, settling their nerves. In an instant, the 57 year-old Henry Graveraet fell dead, shot in the head in sight of his son. The *Grand Traverse Herald* reported that Lt. Garrett Graveraet: "while fighting by the side of his father…had the misfortune to see his father shot dead by his side. He bore the body of his parent from the trenches to a safe spot, where weeping bitterly, he dug a grave, with an old tin pan, and buried it. This done, the devoted son dried his tears and returned to the battle. His rifle told with terrible precision among the rebel officers." [353]

Native soldiers in the 1st Michigan Sharp Shooters continued to fall. Jonah Debasequam, recruited from Little Traverse by his neighbor Garrett Graveraet, lay dead beside the lieutenant's father. Northern Michigan friends Samuel Going, Thaddeus Lamourandiex, and brothers James and John Mashkaw were four of the 25 Indians who together joined Company K on July 4, 1863. In one hour

Wounded Native Sharp Shooters outside a Fredericksburg hospital, May 1864. *Library of Congress*

of intense fighting, all four were killed in action at Spotsylvania. Another dozen men from Company K were carried from the field seriously wounded. With ammunition running short and their position deteriorating, the regiment was ordered to withdraw. By sunset, the Union assault had failed, as had the Confederate counter-attack, and another Virginia battle had accomplished little more than making work for surgeons and grave diggers.

Lt. Graveraet returned to the battlefield the next day and reburied his father in a deep grave, marking the site carefully. He vowed to return to Spotsylvania and bring his father back to Northern Michigan. However, the Civil War had other plans for the young lieutenant. Later that night, another storm rolled into Virginia and stayed for a week, bogging both armies down in the trenches, and reducing the action to heated skirmishes and sporadic sniper fire.

During the battle of Spotsylvania, the 26th Michigan Infantry lost 167 of its soldiers, including the commander of the regiment who was wounded four times. Seven of the Lakeshore Tigers' nine color guards were killed or wounded. The 1st Michigan Sharp Shooters suffered 162 casualties, among them their two top officers. The 20th Michigan, who fought beside the Sharp Shooters, came out of the battle with 194 fewer men – one was their wounded regimental commander, Colonel Byron Cutcheon.

An article in the *Richmond Examiner* titled "A Tree Hewn Down by Bullets" lent perspective to the ferocity of the fighting on May 12. It said: "Most people had doubted the literal accuracy of the dispatch concerning the battle of Spotsylvania, which alleged that trees were cut down under the concentrated fire of Minie balls. We doubted the literal fact ourselves, and would doubt it still but for the indisputable testimony of Dr. Charles McGill, an eye-witness of the battle. The tree stood near our breastworks at a point upon which at one time the most murderous musketry fire that ever was heard of was directed. The tree fell inside our works, and injured several of our men. After the battle Dr. McGill measured the trunk, and found it twenty-two inches through, and sixty-one inches in circumference, actually hacked through by the awful avalanche of bullets packing against it. The foliage of the tree was trimmed away as effectually as an army of locusts had swarmed on its branches. A grasshopper could not have lived through the pelting of that leaden storm; and but for the fact that our troops were protected by breastworks they would have been swept away to a man."[354]

General Grant commanded a force of 118,000 soldiers when he started toward Richmond in early May 1864. In the first two weeks of fighting along the Wilderness-Spotsylvania front, the Army of the Potomac suffered 38,000 casualties, compared to Lee's losses of 20,000. Grant had succeeded in pushing the battle lines steadily south toward the Confederate capital, but at a daily cost never seen before in the Civil War. However, the General did not waver, and when the weather cleared, he again ordered his troops south toward Richmond, keeping his promise to "fight it out on the line if it takes all summer."

Far from the carnage in Virginia, news had yet to reach Grand Traverse about the tremendous losses suffered by local men. Cherry trees blossomed, the woods filled out with leaves, and smoke trails of steamers and propellers streaked the sunsets over the western islands. Homestead farmers worked their axes and saws from dawn to dusk in the race to clear land and plant crops. Families with husbands and sons serving in Grant's army could still hope that their loved ones had been spared the worst of the fighting.

On May 20, the Smiths arrived in Detroit aboard the *Tonawanda*. The family settled in for the week in Michigan's leading city, where George attended to church business and checked on benefits due Grand Traverse soldiers at Union Army headquarters. The propeller *Nile*, whose weekly trips through the western lakes included scheduled stops in Grand Traverse, arrived later in the day and tied up close to the *Tonawanda*. The propeller remained at the wharf overnight before resuming the trip up the lakes toward Chicago.

The next morning, the *Nile* fired her boilers with cordwood and made steam for the voyage ahead. Awaiting passengers boarded the ship and headed for the salons. Among those traveling back home on the *Nile* was Traverse City's Albert W. Bacon, the brother of Libby Bacon, who had recently become the wife of General George Custer. Albert Bacon arrived in Grand Traverse Country in 1852 at the age of 20 and worked as one of the area's first surveyors. In the ensuing dozen years, he met many of the region's early settlers through his field work, and rose to become one of Traverse City's most respected pioneers. The *Grand Traverse Herald* described him as "more thoroughly acquainted with the country and its resources, from actual exploration and observation, than any other man."[355]

It was inconceivable that another promising young Grand Traverse man was about to perish in the exceptionally cruel month - especially so far from the battlefields. However, in May 1864, the grim reaper was having his way. Reverend Smith wrote: "Propeller *Nile* exploded her boilers at the dock...instantly being blown almost to atoms. A.W. Bacon was just aboard & was thrown far above a warehouse...in all 6 dead have been recovered. A considerable [number] are in the wreck. Much damage was done in the city. One man was killed by a stick of timber thrown over buildings some distance - went through the wall of a brick building – struck him in the side & killed him."[356]

In an article titled "The Late Albert W. Bacon," a shaken Morgan Bates described the disaster in Detroit, where by chance he, Reverend Smith, and Bacon were all visiting at the time. The editor wrote: "On the morning of Saturday, the 21st of May last, while the Propellor *Nile* was lying at the wharf …in Detroit, her boiler exploded and the vessel was torn into fragments. Albert W. Bacon, of Traverse City, had stepped on board an instant before the explosion, and was thrown entirely over and thirty feet above a four story building, falling headforemost on the pavement of the street. He was killed instantly.

"We never received a greater shock than when, on the evening of that day, while in the act of registering our name at the office of the Michigan Exchange in Detroit, the Clerk informed us that Mr. Bacon was a corpse in the house. We had seen him only a few days before, full of health, life, hope and energy. A mangled corpse is all that remained of our noble, generous, warm-hearted friend."[357] Bates had inadvertently written a eulogy to the many Grand Traverse soldiers whose names soon appeared on the casualty roles arriving back North. With the death of Bacon, it seemed as if some tragic force was making sure that May was the month Northern Michigan paid its share of the cost of the Civil War. The sad fact was there were still ten days left in May - time enough for more Grand Traverse men to die. Worse yet, May would proved to be only the first month of a summer of desperate fighting in Virginia. Grant chose as his next target the town of Cold Harbor, which lay a dozen miles north of Richmond. As Grant had promised, the Army of the Potomac would continue to attack.

Three days after the tragic accident that killed Bacon, Smith visited Union Army headquarters in Detroit, "getting Certificates of enlistment & Credits to Northport of 8 soldiers to our town." The credits Smith mentioned represented the number of recent volunteers from Northport, which reduced in like number those subject to the draft. Later Smith toured Detroit in "a fine Span of horses & carriage," but as his party approached the Union Army camp at Fort Wayne, the guards "would not admit us unless we had Special business with the Officers." However, they were allowed to "follow the road around, inside the ramparts. This gave us a fair chance to see. They are very stringent in their regulations. Many hands are at work building a wall around the whole." Fort Wayne had become an important Union supply depot, a holding ground for the many weapons now being manufactured in the vicinity of Detroit. However, the city remained a Copperhead stronghold, and the government was taking no chances in regards to the fort's security.

The next day, the Smiths began their journey home on the Great Lakes water highway. The diarist described a part of the country that was far removed from the agonizing scenes playing out in Virginia. He wrote: "*Badger* came bound up, fare $6.00 each...left Detroit abut 11 AM. Had a beautiful time crossing lake St. Clair & the flats – 5 PM stopped to take wood on the Canada Side of the St Clair River." The following morning the ship "passed Pointe O Barques breakfast time...seas run pretty high. We have a beautiful boat - is very steady and we are treated in fine style. We are all bound for Northport some 12 in number." That same day in Virginia, Henry Budd, the father of nine who served as an honor guard at Sgt. William Voice's 1862 funeral in Northport, was wounded by Rebel fire in the fields of Spotsylvania.

On the last day of May, Reverend Smith made his rounds and took notice of a new boat in Northport harbor. He wrote: "*Sunny Side* came to Union Dock. A large number went on board...She was built by Hannah, Lay & Co in Detroit. She is to run on the Bay. She is a beautiful Propeller for passengers & freight."[358] Perry Hannah knew that the success of Traverse City depended on fast and reliable transport up and down the Bay. The big trans-lake steamers preferred to stay close to the shipping lanes, which gave the advantage to rival Northport in the contest for the title of Grand Traverse Country's lead harbor town. Now the brand new *Sunny Side* made the trip along the Bay easier, faster, and less expensive than it had ever been, minimizing Northport's geographical advantage. The speedy propeller made daily stops at the growing ports along the coast, closing the distance between them and enhancing a sense of the greater Grand Traverse community.

For Hannah, Lay & Co., there was an added advantage in operating the *Sunny Side* – the vessel served as a delivery truck for their store in Traverse City. Farmers could send their shopping lists to the store on the *Sunny Side*, often receiving their goods at the nearest dock the next day. The *Herald* summed up Traverse City's reaction to the *Sunny Side* in an article titled "A New Era." It said: "We welcome with hearty satisfaction the arrival of the new and beautiful little steamer "*Sunny-side.*" We are now in direct daily communication with the "outside" world."[359] It was remarkable that at the height of the Civil War, when the Union was arming and equipping the world's largest military machine, that there was still enough industrial capacity left to build a steamboat for use on Grand Traverse Bay. Steaming along aboard the *Sunny Side,* the war seemed another world away. However, many of the men who volunteered from Grand Traverse and now served in the Army of the Potomac had found the war's red hot center.

About the same time the Smiths arrived back in Northport on the *Badger*, the weather cleared in Virginia. True to his word, Grant pushed his troops steadily toward Richmond, with the 26th Michigan Infantry again acting as skirmishers. On May 31, Northport friends John Kehl, the ship builder, and Chauncey Woolsey, the ship captain, scouted ahead of the main Union force as they approached Cold Harbor. They were probing the woods, trying to find where Rebel forces had concentrated. The Lakeshore Tigers soon encountered stiff resistance, with the exchange of rifle fire reverberating down the advancing blue line. Kehl and Woolsey lay side by side as forward pickets, firing at anything that moved. When the order came to withdraw, Kehl sprang to his feet, surprised Woolsey had not joined him. Then he saw his friend was dead, shot through the head by a Confederate minie ball. Nearby, Charlie Waltz, who left Northport with Kehl and Woolsey during January's fierce blizzard, had also been hit by Rebel fire. Four months after leaving Grand Traverse, four of the six Northport men were casualties – one dead, one dying, and two badly wounded. Only John Kehl and Tom McCormick were still able to fight.

Joshua Middleton, recovering in a Baltimore hospital from his Wilderness wounds, wrote to his sister: "Our friend Chauncy Woolsey is gone; he was shot on the 31st of May and Charley Waltz, a young fellow who went with us, was wounded at the same time, shot through both thighs."[360] That same day, in a nearby hospital, former Grand Traverse Sheriff William Sykes of Northport lost his battle with injuries suffered at the Wilderness and died. Not yet satisfied with the toll it had exacted from Grand Traverse, deadly May in its last day had taken two more of its leading citizens. The gruesome statistics kept adding up. Though the Army of the Potomac suffered the majority of the casualties, Grant understood that the Overland Campaign was working, for the Rebels had lost a higher percentage of their available fighters, and there were few southern civilians left to fill the depleted Confederate ranks. The war of attrition was being won.

Grand Traverse soldiers engaged the Rebels almost every day during June. The first battle of the month erupted around Cold Harbor, then hotter than the steamiest summer day in Grand Traverse. Here, for three days, the Federal Army suffered losses similar to those inflicted on them at Fredericksburg the year before, as they repeated the scenario of attacking fortified Confederate positions over open ground. On June 3, nearly 7,000 Union soldiers fell in less than one hour in an advance that was the northern version of Pickett's Charge at Gettysburg. Charles Mann, the letter-writing Oscar Eaton of Traverse City, and Horace Philips of Yuba - all serving in Company A of the Lakeshore Tigers - were wounded in assault not far from where Chauncey Woolsey was killed three days before. The sergeant of Company A, Northport's Charles Lehman, was also downed by a Confederate minie ball. Once again, the Rebel lines held. Grant ordered a last charge, but his generals defied him, not willing to sacrifice any more of their men to futility. Grant soon withdrew the order and later confessed in his memoirs: "I have always regretted that last assault on Cold Harbor was ever made...At Cold Harbor no advantage whatever was gained to compensate for the heavy losses we sustained."[361] When news of the lopsided casualties reached home, the northern press, which a month before had elevated Grant to the status of a savior, now began to describe him as a butcher. The war of attrition was wearing down the Confederates, but also the patience of northern voters. Without battlefield victories, the reelection of Lincoln in November was becoming very much in doubt.

Though there would be no more grand charges, fighting continued around Cold Harbor, and for miles around the town, every soldier knew he could be killed at any moment of every day that passed. The fact was a great burden to carry, and soldiers on both sides grew increasingly weary. For Grand Traverse soldiers who dreamed of cool breezes off Lake Michigan, the scorching heat and suffocating humidity of a Virginia summer made their lot all the more difficult. After two weeks of exchanging fire from the trenches, the Army of the Potomac slipped away from Cold Harbor. They moved south toward the important railroad junction at Petersburg, only six miles from Richmond. There was a brief period when Union forces could have overrun the exposed Rebels and marched on unopposed to the Confederate capital, but Union generals in the field hesitated, and the time had come and gone. By mid-month, the Rebels had dug in before Petersburg and now maneuvered within an elaborate network of trenches protected by earthen embankments, sharpened logs, and carefully placed artillery. It was a deadly mix, one the troops in blue, at heavy cost, found impenetrable.

The vanguard of Union forces approached the Petersburg area on June 14. In one heated skirmish, Northport Sharp Shooter Jacko Pasauoquot was captured while charging a Rebel position and was eventually sent south to Andersonville Prison in Georgia. Before long, several dozen of his friends in the regiment would also fall into Confederate hands and join him at the prison. For the next two days, the battered Army of the Potomac trudged toward Petersburg, hoping that here Lee would finally fall to their superior force. The men were showing signs of fatigue from six weeks of nearly constant marching and battles. They saw their fighting strength decline by the day through death, wounds, sickness, desertion, and straggling. The soldiers left on the field were increasingly angry at what they perceived as the useless slaughter brought on by bad leadership, but they were also resigned to more tough fighting ahead. Their brief but intense experience in Virginia had hardened them into soldiers who were ready and able to kill to stay alive. They no longer flinched at the roar of gunfire or the wretched sight of dead and wounded friends.

On June 16, the Lakeshore Tigers joined the Petersburg line and prepared for another day of fighting. The 1st Michigan Sharp Shooters were also on the march, traversing 30 miles of rugged country with little rest before arriving at Petersburg the morning of the 17th. The Sharp Shooters were thrown immediately into the fight and found themselves on the far left flank of the Union line. Early in the engagement, the exhausted marksmen took their toll on the Confederates, picking them off as they rose to fire from their trenches. As the sun began to set, the regiment received orders to charge the Rebel works. Summoning what little strength they had, they stormed the Confederate positions and sent the enemy running. However, the hastily drawn battle plans quickly evaporated into chaos. The Sharp Shooters discovered they were alone and under fire from three sides. Confederate artillery soon focused on their position. While urging his men on, a Rebel shell burst above Lt. Garrett Graveraet, the shrapnel shredding his left arm. He was rushed to a field hospital, and the following day he was driven by wagon to a Washington hospital, where his arm was amputated. The lieutenant appeared to be recovering when infection set in, which consumed Graveraet on July 1. Two of Northern Michigan's most beloved Native citizens – father and son Henry and Garrett Graveraet – had met their destiny in Virginia. Exactly one half century after Sophie Bailey arrived on Mackinac Island in the midst of international warfare, her husband and eldest son were taken from her by the brutal American Civil War.

The importance of the Graveraets to the greater Grand Traverse community was reflected by their eulogies in the *Grand Traverse Herald*. During the most deadly summer in American military history, when local soldiers appeared so often on the death rolls that their passing was rarely mentioned in the paper, the loss of the father-son team of Sharp Shooters garnered more ink in the *Herald* than any other Civil War casualties. A *Herald* article of July 29 said: "Lieut. Garrett Graveraet, of Little Traverse, a Sharp Shooter under Colonel Delane, died in hospital recently, of wounds received in one of the late battles. His body has been embalmed, and he will be sent home in October."[362]

An unprecedented second article titled "Death of Another Brave Young Officer" appeared in the *Herald* two weeks later. It said: "In the fight before

Petersburg…Lieut. Garret A. Graveraet, of Little Traverse, gave his life for his country. He was Second Lieutenant of Company K, 1st Michigan Sharp Shooters, Burnside's Corps. He was a young man of extraordinary attainments, and was highly esteemed as an officer and a gentleman. His bravery and accomplishments endeared him to the company, and at their request he was promoted to Lieutenancy. In the fight before Petersburg…he fell, badly wounded in the left arm. Lieut. G. was brought to Washington, where his arm was amputated at the shoulder, which resulted in his death. His body was embalmed by Dr. Thomas, who had it deposited in the Congressional Cemetery, to await the order of his mother and friends, who reside in Little Traverse. Lieut. G. was but twenty-four years of age, was highly educated, being master of several modern languages, beside the Chippewa tongue, a fine portrait and landscape painter and a thorough musician. The tidings of his death will be received with much regret, by his relatives and acquaintances."363

Headstones in St. Anne's Cemetery, Mackinac Island, honor Civil War heroes Henry Graveraet and his son Garrett, who were both killed in Virginia in the summer of 1864. Henry's body remains in Virginia.
John C. Mitchell

Lieut. William Driggs of Company K wrote that Graveraet "never shrank from danger. At the battle of the Wilderness and at Spotsylvania he remained constantly with his men...encouraging them to stand their ground...He was the most popular officer in the regiment, and his loss was deeply felt." Though the exploding Confederate ordnance prevented Garrett from keeping his promise to carry his father's body home, Driggs' father, a U.S. Congressman from the Saginaw area, was instrumental in bringing the lieutenant's body back to Mackinac Island for burial in St Anne's Cemetery.

In the battle before Petersburg, the position of the Sharp Shooters disintegrated within hours of the wounding of Lt. Graveraet. The Rebels, aware that the Sharp Shooters were alone with no reinforcements in sight, resolved to retake the entrenchments they had lost earlier in the day. Shortly after dark, 500 North Carolinians charged the Sharp Shooters, whose numbers had been reduced from 700 to 200 soldiers during the six weeks of fighting in Virginia. After a few violent minutes, the Rebels were repulsed, with over 80 taken prisoner. The captives were marched to the rear of the lines, guarded by a contingent of Sharp Shooters. The strength of the regiment on the line was now down to around 100, who stood alone in their advanced position. Soon Confederate troops regrouped and descended on the isolated Sharp Shooters in waves. This time there was no stopping the onslaught. Seeing nothing but bloodshed around him, with no chance of turning the tide, the commanding officer of the 1st Michigan Sharp Shooters called on his men to surrender. Now it was 80 Michigan soldiers who found themselves prisoners of war, including a number of Grand Traverse men.

Scrounging through the spoils of war, the Rebels took a particular interest in the Indians' rifles, whose wood stocks displayed elaborately carved images of birds, turtles, fish, and other forest animals. Among the Indians surrendering their weapons was Payson Wolfe, George Smith's son-in-law. Wallace Woolsey of Company I - son of the late Chauncey Woolsey - was lucky enough to have escaped the trap. He was one of only 61 Sharp Shooters to answer the morning roll call on June 18. The battered regiment, now less than the size of a company, was pulled back from the front to rest and refit. In his memoirs, General Grant underscored the futility of the battle when he wrote: "During the 17th the fighting was severe and the losses heavy; and at night our troops occupied about the same positions they had occupied in the morning."[364]

Seven weeks of deadly combat had knocked the fight out of both the Union and Confederate armies. Sixty-five thousand Union soldiers had been killed, wounded, or were missing in action - a number equal to 60% of all casualties in the three years of war to date, or half of the soldiers who marched with the Army of the Potomac at the outset of May, 1864. Throughout the Union Army, desertion in the ranks became a nightly occurrence, and blue-coated stragglers lined the roads all the way north to Washington. Lee's men were also abandoning their positions in droves, preferring to risk hanging or the firing squad rather than face another deadly day on the front lines. Those who remained dug deep trenches along the Petersburg line, though their physical and mental ability to fight hard was gone. Grand Traverse soldiers had died by the dozens with many more wounded or captured. But the fighting continued and soon the *Herald* published the names of another two dozen men drafted from the region, as the Union war machine moved on to the next field of battle.

On the morning of June 20, Reverend Smith wrote: *"Bradbury* came…It is said Joseph Wakazoo landed on her." Joseph Wakazoo, who in the summer of 1863 had been arrested for desertion, now returned to Northport to recover from wounds he received in action with the 10th Michigan Cavalry. The Native

Soldiers' graves crowd a cemetery outside General Hospital, City Point, Virginia, 1864. *Library of Congress*

community rejoiced at having one of their sons back home. The celebrating abruptly ended a few hours later when Smith visited the Northport docks. He wrote: "*Sunny side* came PM to Union Dock...report says Mr Woolsey was killed while doing picket duty."[365] Later in the week, the Reverend continued: "I preached the funeral of Br Chauncey Woolsey from Genesis 18:25. It was a very solemn and afflictive season. The entire Congregation were mourners – the widow and 7 children & friends were almost inconsolable."[366]

By now, wounded Lakeshore Tiger Joshua Middleton had recovered sufficiently to act as an assistant in the wards at Jarvis Hospital in Baltimore, a sprawling complex that attended to the mounting numbers of Union war wounded. He wrote his sister on June 30, 1864, providing a look at what happened to soldiers who had healed enough to work but not to fight, as well as news from the front. Middleton said: "I am helping nurse in this ward, our patients are all doing very well...poor fellows how awfully some do suffer...

"They are making preparations for a grand 4th of July. They intend to have a grand dinner for the patients. There is not much news from the front, we are steadily gaining ground, but there must be some very hard fighting yet. Expect another lot of badly wounded soon, they are building 12 new wards, the hospital will hold about 1000 patients then." Despite having seen hundreds of soldiers dead on the battlefield, and thousands more hospitalized, the wounded Middleton was still forced to worry about his family's finances back in Northport. He complained: "It cost so much to live now everything is so dear at home...Anna has had to buy a new stove... she can get nothing from the Supervisors, they are all copper.[367] I sent her all I could rake and that scarce keeps her along. One of the oxen...died this spring, how they can manage to get along without a team I don't see. It will cost me some thirty dollars to go home, but I shall have to deny that pleasure, for their comfort."

The previous summer, Smith had made the same complaint against Leelanau's "copper" Democratic Township Supervisor when he tried to get help for the family of son-in-law Payson Wolfe. The war had divided not only a great nation, but pit neighbor against neighbor in every corner of the once-united country. Middleton could not know that on the same day he penned his letter, help for his family was on the way. Leelanau County representatives had again voted to raise money for soldiers' families, easing the anxiety and daily burden of those left behind. The *Herald* also reported that Grand Traverse County also had "money enough left in the Treasury to pay all orders that will be drawn on the Volunteers Family Relief account."[368] Middleton finished his letter on a poignant note, expressing the feeling of abandonment many soldiers felt far from home. Having received no letters in a while from his son, he wrote: "Sam I guess forgot to write, but no matter, I am most used to being forgotten. God grant they may never have to feel it, is my prayer."[369]

On July 5, Reverend Smith and family visited Presbyterian minister Peter Dougherty in Omena, but rather than enjoy themselves, they came home mad. Smith wrote: "Mr Dougherty talked to us in such a way about the war as to make us almost disposed to leave without tea. He nearly took & in many quite took the copper head position – I had all I could do to endure his talk – I shall not be forward to go there again." Dougherty was older and comparatively "old school" in thinking than the progressive Smith. He had seen not only the nation divided by the new ideas of the time, but also witnessed his Presbyterian Church ripped asunder by issues that had brought on the war. Dougherty was tired of it all, and ready to accept peace on any terms.

Smith and Dougherty represented the divergent points of view common among the people of the Northern states in the summer of 1864. While a core of men like Reverend Smith backed the war unconditionally as a terrible yet unavoidable instrument of social justice, every day more loyal citizens despaired that the end of the conflict was nowhere in sight. If in the next 100 days the Union armies failed to prove through battlefield victories that the war was nearly over, the public may well vote to end it through compromise by electing a peace candidate. As long as the campaign in Virginia remained in a stalemate, and no significant progress was made on other fronts, Lincoln's prospects for reelection declined.

The *Herald's* Morgan Bates urged his readers to stay the course with Lincoln, writing: "The people feel for one thing…to put down the rebellion. Mr. Lincoln's policy is developed; and no new concern or anxiety is needed to settle the matter. We have only to go on as we have begun, and the war ends with the rebels conquered." However, the questions remained - how much blood would need to be shed, and when would the Rebels be conquered? In the meantime, the political battles leading up to the Presidential Election promised to be as bitter as those on the field.

Sensing an opportunity, Confederate politicians pushed their remaining friends in England to help broker a cease fire with the Union and end the war through negotiation. Many Europeans were appalled at the casualty figures coming out of Grant's Overland Campaign. However, the leader of the British House of Commons announced in July that "no advantage would be gained by meddling" in the American conflict, slamming the door in the Rebels' face. The South's only hope now lay with their enemy – the Yankee voter – and their rising discontent with Lincoln and the war. Editor Bates recognized the danger of a divided North and wrote: "When the loyal States stand shoulder to shoulder as earnest for Liberty and Union as the rebels are for slavery, the glorious end of the contest will be near."[370]

Northern disillusionment spiked during July after a corps from the Army of Northern Virginia under command of General Jubal Early rode out of the Shenandoah Valley and invaded Maryland and Pennsylvania. The citizens of Hagerstown and Frederick were forced to pay tribute to the Confederates to prevent their towns from being torched. With the exhausted Army of the Potomac bogged down outside of Petersburg, and General Sherman approaching Atlanta, there were few troops left between Early and Washington. A panic spread through the city as the Rebels continued to march almost unopposed toward the nation's capital. Learning of the gravity of the situation, Grant diverted reinforcements that were heading for Petersburg to Washington, where they arrived in force on July 11. Early ordered the attack on July 12, having previously scouted Federal positions outside the city and found them sparsely manned. However, the situation had changed overnight, and when they advanced, they found the Union fortifications filled with fresh troops. In the ensuing battle, the Confederate invaders were repulsed. Early fled back to the Shenandoah Valley but even in defeat he had won a psychological victory. A superior Union Army had relentlessly attacked the Confederates in Virginia for two bloody months, yet the Rebels were still able to mount an offensive from the state.

The following week, the Smith family and their Indian friends received terrible news from Virginia. On July 19, Smith wrote: "Mail came…letter from Albert [Powers] stating that Payson is a prisoner probably in Richmond. He counted only 14 of the company left."[371] Payson Wolfe had been captured by Confederates, and confinement in their prisons was often the equivalent of a death sentence. Through the battles at the Wilderness, Spotsylvania, and Petersburg, over two dozen of the Indian soldiers had fallen into Confederate hands and now faced the horrors of a rebel prison camp. Company K, which only months before teemed with over 100 of the most promising young Native Americans in Michigan, had been decimated.

July 22 and 23 provided two of the few bright moments in Northport during the summer of 1864, when the hero of the Michigan Cavalry Brigade paid a visit to the Grand Traverse harbor town. Reverend Smith wrote: "*Oneida* came

PM to Rose dock...Gen. Custar and Lady came on her."[372] The lady mentioned was Libby Bacon Custer, the bride of cavalry General George Armstrong Custer, whose name Smith had misspelled. Since departing for the front after their wedding, Custer had fought his nemesis Jeb Stuart to the death and supported the Army of the Potomac in every bloody battle of Grant's Overland Campaign. Libby had lost her brother in the explosion of the propeller *Nile* during the same time. Her family owned extensive tracts of timberland in Omena, and the newlyweds took advantage of the peace afforded in the North Country to recuperate from the harsh events of the summer. The next day,

General George and Libby Custer, seated, with Tom Custer, 1864. *Library of Congress*

Smith wrote: "*Sunny Side* came PM & left for T[raverse]City...Gen Custar left on her...had a short interview with him." The Northport preacher had again made himself part of a significant Grand Traverse Civil War scene.

In Virginia, the armies continued their bitter stalemate outside of Petersburg. As usual, the 1st Michigan Sharp Shooters held one of the most dangerous stretches of the line, where the crack of sniper fire kept men huddled in the trenches and one wrong move could get you killed in an instant. The intense Virginia sun beat down on the tightly-packed and war-weary soldiers, water was scarce, and the men were compelled to live in their filth rather than risk exposure to a hail of minie balls. Regiments of black soldiers fought near the Michigan troops, which further focused the wrath of Confederates fire on their position. Grant searched for a way to breach the Rebel lines and advance on Richmond with the hope of ending the Civil War. However, Cold Harbor had taught him the bloody futility of charging entrenched positions, and the General was ready to consider any and all alternatives to a frontal assault.

The commander of a regiment of Pennsylvania coal miners came up with a plan that he submitted to Grant. At one section where the trenches of the two armies came particularly close together, he proposed that his miners dig a shaft under the Confederate fortifications and pack it with explosives. When detonated, the explosion would blast a hole in the Confederate line that Union soldiers could charge through all the way to Richmond. After initial hesitation, Grant decided to give the idea a try, anxious to find some way to end the stand off without another Federal disaster.

After a month of digging, the Pennsylvania miners placed over 400 kegs of gunpowder at the end of the tunnel and waited for orders. Just before dawn on the morning of July 30, the fuse was lit, and an earth-shattering blast followed. The ground below the Confederate trenches erupted as planned, and their position disappeared in a plume of smoke, earth, and fire. The bodies of Rebel soldiers whirled about in the debris – over 300 men were killed instantly. One-ton Rebel cannons and the artillerists who staffed them were thrown about like sticks. Several Confederate companies evaporated in the inferno. When the dust cleared, a gaping hole 30 feet deep, 170 feet long, and 80 feet wide appeared where the Confederate lines had been. The Battle of the Crater was on.

Properly exploited, the gap in the Rebel front might have allowed Union troops to win the field. Two flanks of the Confederate line lay open and the ground beyond was lightly defended. Once again, Union troops were in the position to bring about an end to the war. However, even before the battle began, the chance for victory had passed. Problems near the mine surfaced days before when African-American regiments, who had trained to lead the attack, were replaced with inexperienced white troops. Pressure from abolitionist politicians had forced the move, for they feared if the assault failed, and black troops were slaughtered, there would be widespread protests in the North. The general in charge of the ground attack, James Ledlie, had received the day's command through the act of drawing straws, and was widely recognized as the worst possible choice for the crucial position. After ordering his troops to advance, the general retired to a bunker, where he proceeded to get drunk. In another sign of disaster ahead, the order to remove obstructions in front of Union lines was never executed. The attacking Federals found themselves stuck behind their own defenses, slowing the assault to a crawl.

Precious time ticked away. Hundreds of Confederate soldiers were shaking off the shock of the concussion and replacing their fallen comrades along the shattered earthworks. The "whiz splat chug" sounds of the minie balls increased

The Union siege cannon "Dictator" aimed at Petersburg, 1864. *Library of Congress*

in crescendo, as did the cries of those falling from their effect. General Ledlie had failed to explain Grant's battle plan and Union troops approaching the crater were unsure of what to do next. Rather than going around its perimeter and securing the Confederate trenches, most charged into the pit. Soon thousands of men crowded into the quagmire and became easy targets for the reforming Rebels. No Union advance was made beyond the gaping hole

Judged in terms of sheer carnage per square foot, the Battle of the Crater degenerated into one of the worst engagements of the Civil War. Union soldiers realized their predicament and tried to claw their way out of the hole, but were gunned down as they crawled over the rim. The dead and wounded tumbled back upon those who followed. Soon the men trapped in the crater stacked the bodies of their fellow soldiers as shields against the minie balls and cannon shot. However, the gruesome piles afforded little help, for Rebel fire now rained down from all sides. Black soldiers, who were spared the point of the charge but followed their white comrades into the melee, became favorite targets for Rebel marksmen. Another Union offensive in Virginia had fallen into chaos.

If there was a bright spot anywhere in the raging battle, it was at its far left side, where the surviving 1st Michigan Sharp Shooters again found themselves in the midst of some of the fiercest fighting of the war. The few soldiers left in the regiment dug in along the edge of the crater, rising occasionally to pick off a Rebel foe. At this point, the individual instinct to survive the battle consumed most soldiers. An everyman-for-himself retreat ensued. However, a handful of Sharp Shooters stood their ground, covering the stampede back to Union lines until the entire crater was surrounded by Rebels. A lucky few successfully ran the gauntlet back to Union lines; those unable to escape were added to the lists of prisoners of war. Antoine Scott of Company K and three other Sharp Shooters were recommended for the Medal of Honor for their bravery in providing cover fire for retreating soldiers. Of the 100 Sharp Shooters who entered the fray that morning, half were listed as casualties. The Battle of the Crater joined the list of Union disasters in Virginia where Grand Traverse men fought and died.

In his memoirs, Grant railed against Union leadership at the Crater, reciting the complaints that the foot soldiers had been repeating for years. He said: "The effort was a stupendous failure. It cost us about four thousand men…all due to the inefficiency on the part of the corps commander and the incompetency of the division commander who was sent to lead the assault."[373] There was plenty of blame to go around, but in the end it was Grant's Overland Campaign that had stalled, and his Army of the Potomac that lay battered and exhausted just outside the Rebel capital. The events of the last ninety days had sapped their will to fight, and citizens throughout the North began to feel that the horrible losses suffered during the summer of 1864 were in vain.

The bad news kept on coming. The same day of the fiasco at the Crater, a Confederate force under General Jubal Early again rode out of the Shenandoah Valley and invaded Pennsylvania. When the citizens of Chambersburg – only a few miles from Gettysburg – did not pay the ransom the Rebels demanded, Early ordered his troops to burn the town to the ground. The Northern press decried the twin humiliations of the Crater and Chambersburg, and Lincoln's chances for reelection continued to plummet. It was another low point of morale in the Union, for only 90 days before the northern public believed that Grant's Virginia campaign would sweep the Confederates from the field. Now Grant's May statement that he would "fight it out on the line if it takes all summer" seemed conservative, for there was still no end to the carnage in sight.

Only days after the debacle at the Battle of the Crater, Reverend Smith wrote: "Got a letter from George Azh klenk July 5 saying Payson & the other prisoners were sent to Georgia."[374] Smith's heart must have sunk when he read the letter, for "sent to Georgia" meant his son-in-law was headed for Andersonville Prison. A Union soldier fighting on the most violent stretches of the front lines had better chance of coming out alive than one walking though the gates of the infamous Southern stockade. Guards herded thousands of Union prisoners into a filthy, open field and let them fry in the heat of the Georgia sun. In August 1864, when Payson Wolfe and other Sharp Shooters arrived at Andersonville, they joined 32,000 other Union prisoners who were packed into the 26- acre stockade.[375] This was as overcrowded as the perpetually packed prison had ever been. There were no barracks of any kind on the grounds, and the stream that ran through the camp served both as the prisoners' water supply and their latrine. Hundreds of men died every day from starvation and disease. In its 14 months of operation, 13,000 of the 45,000 total prisoners who were crammed into Andersonville never made it out alive.

Some of the brutality in the prison camp was calculated; some reflected the condition of the South. The Confederacy's own soldiers lacked every kind of supplies and on many days fought in a state close to starvation. Often there was simply nothing available to feed and clothe the prisoners. But even allowing for the Rebel's increasingly desperate situation, history has judged the treatment of Union prisoners at Andersonville as an American tragedy. It is a testament to the horrors of the place that in a war that caused such widespread death and destruction, the only person executed for war crimes at the end of conflict was the commander of Andersonville prison.

An article in the August *Grand Traverse Herald* presented another view of the carnage caused by the Civil War. It said: "One hundred and seventy-four thousand horses have been purchased by the Government during the last year. Nearly sixty thousand of those have been killed, and rendered useless or sold. Eighty-six thousand mules have been purchased, and over seventeen thousand of these have been captured, condemned, sold or killed." It was estimated that four out of ten farm animals in the South were also killed during the war.

News of the disastrous Battle of the Crater arrived in Grand Traverse a week after its conclusion. The *Herald* wrote: "The failure of the late attack on Petersburgh, which it is feared will have the effect to intermit large military operations in Virginia for some time, once again centers the main interest of the war in the military situation before Atlanta."[376]

Union forces in the western theatre, commanded by General William Tecumseh Sherman, had spent the summer chasing the Confederates through eastern Tennessee and into Georgia without a decisive engagement. The 15th Michigan Infantry, the regimental choice of many Grand Traverse volunteers, were part of Sherman's force. For months, General Joseph E. Johnston maneuvered just out of the grasp of Grant's trusted friend and favorite general. By mid-August, Sherman's army was approaching Atlanta, and the Rebels had to stand and fight in order to save this essential manufacturing and railroad center. Confederate President Jefferson Davis said Atlanta was the "military key of the continent, and must never be given up,"[377] and another desperate encounter was shaping up in Georgia.

In Virginia, the fighting in front of Petersburg settled into a prolonged siege. Snipers exchanged continual fire and skirmishers constantly tested their enemy's strength. A heat wave descended on the region, making life in the trenches all the more unbearable. On August 16, in action before Petersburg, a Confederate minie ball shattered the arm of Lakeshore Tiger Herman Dunkelow, which doctors later amputated above the elbow. Dunkelow, the hospital attendant who had bought the doll for the dying William Voice in November 1862, now lay critically wounded in a field hospital bed of his own. No specific record exists of Dunkelow's surgery, but amputees often faced the saw without anesthetics, and many later died from infections contracted on filthy operating tables. Every day, soldiers like Dunkelow were maimed and killed, with no change in the status of the war.

Death and disease continued their summer rampage through Grand Traverse. The same day Dunkelow was shot down in Virginia, Reverend Smith wrote, "Was called again to see the sick man at the Dame House…he has Symptoms of Smallpox." The following afternoon the "*Free State* came …J. Deerwood's wife came on her with her child dead…died on the boat. That Sunday, Smith cancelled Church services "on account of the Small pox," and was later called to doctor "a girl of 12 – I found her sick of fever." A few days later, "*Galena* came in morning…while She was lying at the dock, a woman died on board, of consumption."[378]

Meanwhile, the constant combat in Virginia took its toll on Grand Traverse soldiers in other ways. A week after the wounding of Dunkelow, Reverend Smith wrote: "Went in wagon… to Mr Kehl's. He reached home Sabbath eve on sick furlough. I talked many things with him about the army. He is excellent in describing marches and battles. His health is poor, he looks bad."[379] The gaunt visage of Kehl was a reflection of the state of Union soldiers serving in Grant's Overland Campaign, his body and mind ground down by three months of continual fighting. Of the six Northport volunteers who in January walked 150 miles through a blizzard to join the Lakeshore Tigers, only one now remained at the front.

The strain of the war lent a gloomy tone to Hannah, Lay & Co.'s "State of the Markets" report in an August 1864 *Herald.* The advertisement said: "Gen. Grant has not yet taken Richmond...Labor is continually becoming scarcer. A new call for half a million men is about to be made. A large increase has been made in our Revenue and Income Tax; as also on all classes of imports, and Raw Materials have advanced beyond all precedent. Supply is falling behind demand in almost everything. Appearances point to a short crop in many staples, resulting of course in an immense advance on any previous known rate. Speculation is rampant.

"There is much difficulty in replacing articles with the amount received for the same when sold. No one seems anxious to sell, but on the contrary, all prefer to hold for a still further advance." The report came to essentially the same conclusion as it had in May, but now reflected the widespread exhaustion felt by a nation. It said: "To form any opinion when and where this state of affairs is to end is simply idle; while it is safe to say, "the end is *not* yet."

Editor Bates tried to spin the events of the terrible summer in the best possible light, writing: "The rebels are losing a regiment a day," says Gen. Grant... and we are adding to our army in Virginia a regiment and a half a day, according to our dispatches...Courage, patience, hope. Let the people cherish these qualities, hold out a little longer, and out of our period of sacrifice and peril we shall win a new life for our ransomed nation, and a fresh birthright for all who come after us."[380]

President Lincoln despaired over the deadlock in Virginia, sickened by the carnage of Grant's Overland Campaign and knowing that without a major victory his chances for re-election were slim. If a peace candidate was elected and hostilities ceased in a draw, all the suffering to date would be in vain. There would be little chance of re-uniting the country, and slavery would likely continue in an independent South. The battle of the ages would be lost. In an August 23 letter titled "Memorandum on the Probable Failure of Re-election," Lincoln wrote: "This morning, as for some days past, it seems exceedingly probable that this Administration will not be re-elected. Then it will be my duty to so co-operate with the President elect, as to save the Union between the election and the inauguration; as he will have secured his election on such ground that he could not possibly save it afterwards." For the moment Lincoln pocketed the letter and returned to the ugly business of war.

Rather than falter in the face of looming electoral defeat, Lincoln stepped up the war effort to new heights, knowing time was of the essence. In 1864,

a sitting President who was not reelected remained in office for four months
before his successor was inaugurated. Should his bid for a second term fail, Lincoln understood he would have only half a year to bring the war to a successful
conclusion. He issued another massive draft call, knowing the war would soon
be over, or lost. He called on northern industry to ratchet up war production and
worked to supply his generals with every item they needed. The patience and resources of the loyal states were pushed to the limit in this final surge of the war.
Fortunately for Lincoln, events in Atlanta and the Shenandoah Valley would
soon change the tone of the desperate state of affairs the President faced.

As Sherman's 50,000 man army began to roll up upon Atlanta, the Confederates changed their strategy. Although military experts considered Johnston
one of the South's finest generals, President Jefferson Davis appointed a more
aggressive leader for the defense of the city. He replaced the evasive tactician
Johnston with the hard fighting General John Hood, who had been wounded at
Gettysburg and later lost a leg leading his troops at the Battle of Chickamauga.
As was most often the case when politicians meddled with soldiers in the field,

General Sherman at the outskirts of Atlanta, September 1864. *Library of Congress*

Davis's choice of generals turned out to be a disaster. Hood immediately lived up to his aggressive reputation, launching a series of costly assaults on Sherman's larger army. The Confederates took losses far greater than they could afford, and in the reverse of the Virginia campaign, suffered casualties at two and three times the number they inflicted on Union soldiers. By the last week of August, the Rebels had been driven back to trenches on the outskirts of Atlanta.

One month after the disastrous Battle of the Crater, Sherman's men succeeded in cutting all supply routes to the embattled Georgia city. The next day, August 31, Federal forces heard the rumbling of explosions within Atlanta as the Confederates demolished everything that could be used by the Union Army. On September 2, Atlanta surrendered to Sherman. The General wired Washington: "Atlanta is ours, and fairly won." Lincoln and the Union Army had the military victory they needed to assure the Northern public the war would soon end in their favor. Upon receiving the news at Jarvis Hospital, the recuperating Joshua Middleton wrote his sister: "100 guns was fired for Atlanta, old Abe is safe."

In the same letter, Middleton spoke about the human cost of the war through the eyes of a hospital orderly, including his personal recovery from injuries suffered at the Battle of the Wilderness. He wrote: "I have received no pay for six months. I am still nursing…we are kept busy now. We have 1200 patients in this Hospital. They are coming and going all of the time…The dressing of the wounds affects my lungs. I am taking Iodine for my neck. It has done no good yet as I can see. It pains me considerable at times." Eight months of separation from home and family also weighed on Middleton. He said: "I do indeed wish you would write often for I form no new friends in this place and it is very lonesome at times."[381]

Later, Middleton gave more insight into life in a Union Hospital in 1864 – details many Grand Traverse soldiers fighting in Grant's Army had become familiar with. He wrote: "Sunday everywhere in the Army is a General day of Inspection. Every one and every thing must be in its proper place, boots blacked and clothes brushed and all in as good order as possible. Why it would be on Sunday is more than I can inform you…but it is Military and like a good many other things there is not a particular reason for it. It is soon over and then if so disposed you can generally find a place to hear Divine Service, for most every regiment has a chaplain. We have Chapel in here and Service every Sunday, there is a funeral sermon preached almost every day…Before Spring I hope the war will come to a close, they talk of arming their slaves, they dare not do it, only in desperation will they do it, it is there last hope." Middleton concluded:

Sunday prayers. *Library of Congress*

"We had a splendid Thanksgiving dinner and then a concert in the evening, a prayer by the chaplain and a speech by Colonel Somebody then we eats and how we made the turkeys fly."[382]

Stuck in a stalemate outside of Petersburg, Grant decided to attack General Jubal Early's base in the Shenandoah Valley and end the embarrassing forays into Union territory for good. Grant knew that the Shenandoah "was very important to the Confederates, because it was the principle storehouse they now had for feeding their armies about Richmond."[383] With Confederate forces stretched to hold the line outside the South's capital city, Grant correctly predicted that Rebels in the valley would receive little help from Lee.

Grant selected cavalry officer Philip Sheridan to solve the problems in the Shenandoah, putting him at the head of a force of 30,000 men. When General Sheridan asked for more soldiers, he told Grant "he was perfectly willing to take the raw troops being raised in the North-west," for Lake Michigan soldiers had proved their ability to apply their frontier skills to the art of war. Sheridan gave Custer command of the Union Cavalry in the Shenandoah – with the Michigan Cavalry Brigade riding the point - knowing the young general was a hero who western men followed without question. Grant ordered Sheridan's assembling army to destroy both Early and the Valley so that neither could again support the Confederate cause. The war had entered its final, brutal phase.

By mid-August, Sheridan's forces were on the move. For a month, the Union Army marched through the Shenandoah's lush countryside, skirmishing whenever they met the Rebels. Up to this point in time, this bountiful region of Virginia had been unscathed by the war, but now every building and ripening field was a target. The Shenandoah and all sense of civility were put to the torch by Sheridan's scorched earth policy, which Custer liberally applied. The Michigan Cavalry Brigade soon became a focus of Confederate hatred. The Rebels fought back, ambushing Union patrols on country roads and taking no prisoners. In turn, Union soldiers hung men in civilian clothes they suspected of being spies. Destruction and death were transforming the verdant valley into a gray and ashen place. A dozen years later, when Custer was killed at Little Big Horn, few in the Shenandoah Valley mourned his death.

On September 19, Sheridan caught up with Early near Winchester and routed the Rebels. Two days later, the Union Army again cornered the retreating Confederates and dealt them a second severe blow. In an article titled "The Great Victory," the *Herald* said: "The news from the seat of war is most cheering. Sheridan has gained two great victories over the rebels in the Shenandoah Valley; and the proud army of Early is shattered, broken, and reduced to a mere mob. The power and strength of the Rebeldom have departed forever. Richmond and Petersburg will soon be ours. Who, in the face of these great victories, will dare to prate about the inability of the Government to sustain itself against Rebellion and to *conquer* a peace. Who asks for an armistice now?"[384]

Even in the midst of the worst year of warfare the nation had ever experienced, and a summer filled with death at home and in Virginia, Grand Traverse Country as a whole prospered as if peace reigned. The region lay directly in the path of a national land rush west, and free Homestead Act land continued to draw people in droves. In September, Reverend Smith wrote: "*Tonawanda* came...

brought good many passengers & good deal of freight. Several French families I am told stop here."[385] Then the "*Mohawk* came...left Pm up – about 30 passengers came on her going to Benzonia." In addition, the perseverance of Grand Traverse Indians was finally paying off, and several times that month Smith mentioned that a government official was "delivering certificates of land" to the Natives as guaranteed by the Treaty of 1855.

Due to the constant influx of Homestead Act settlers, in the fall of 1864 there were still plenty of Grand Traverse men available and ready to fight for the country that had just given them land and a future. While a stream of boats delivered new settlers, they also carried soldiers off to the war. Smith wrote: "*Sunny Side* came...James McLaughlin & some ½ dozen Volunteers with him went on her." McLaughlin was the son of the owner of the *Hiram Merrill* - the schooner that in 1849 brought Reverend Smith and his party to Grand Traverse. In 1863, Lt. E.J. Brooks of Northport talked McLaughlin into joining the 10th Michigan Cavalry. Brother Robert McLaughlin had already spent time recruiting for the Navy in Grand Traverse before becoming a noted Union Army gunboat captain. Now it was James' turn to recruit for the cavalry back home, a task made easier by reports filtering back from the front of Lt. Brooks' courage under fire in Tennessee. Following a battle earlier in the summer, the commander of the 10th Michigan Cavalry wrote:

"I was ordered to go up near the Virginia line to capture a large number of horses that were said to be in pasture. It was not expected that I should meet the enemy before Kingsport, but unfortunately for the success of my enterprise, I met them at Bean's Station. I at once ordered Capt. Roberts, with two companies, to charge them. One of the companies was commanded by Lieut., afterwards Captain Brooks. Brooks was smarting under some ill treatment from a superior officer, and immediately dashed forward with his company. After routing the rebels handsomely and charging them for a couple of miles, Capt. Roberts wisely ordered a halt; but Brooks had gone ahead with a few men, and actually kept up that charge with three men with him for a distance of ten miles and a half. Captain Brooks was afterwards rewarded for his gallantry by the brevets of Major and Lieutenant Colonel."[386] Grand Traverse volunteers, and in particular men from Glen Arbor and Elk Rapids, were swayed by the chance to serve under the local cavalry hero.

Hope was on the rise that recent Union victories in Atlanta and the Shenandoah Valley signaled the closing act of the war. Lincoln's chances for reelection improved, but the approaching Presidential race was still anyone's contest. At their nominating convention in Chicago, the Democrats adopted a peace platform that called for a truce and negotiation with the Rebels. General George McClellan, who had built the Army of the Potomac but failed to unleash its power against the Confederacy, was chosen as the Democratic candidate for President. The Democrats hoped that McClellan's name would bring the soldiers' vote their way, for there were many men in the ranks who looked back with nostalgia on his cautious leadership, especially in light of the Army of the Potomac's recent mauling in Virginia. McClelland as President was the Confederate's last hope for survival, as South Carolina's lead paper, the *Charleston Mercury,* explained: "If we hold our own and prevent further military successes on the part of our foes, there is every prospect that McClellan will be elected, and his election…must lead to peace and our independence."[387] Though McClellan rejected the peace platform, Morgan Bates of the *Herald* went on the attack, determined to sway every possible Grand Traverse vote to Lincoln. The paper made it known that the soldiers' vote did not belong to McClellan, publishing a letter from a well-known Grand Traverse volunteer who was off fighting the Rebels.

Aaron Page was one of Northport's earliest Euro-American settlers. He arrived at the mission settlement in 1854 in response to Joseph Dame's letter of praise of Grand Traverse that ran in the *New York Tribune*. Page shared Dame's assessment of the area, and after marrying the writer's daughter, he took a job as Northport's first postmaster. In 1859, Page moved his family south to Omena, where they built and ran a boarding house for lumbermen. Page was one of the group of 20 Grand Traverse volunteers who joined the 1st New York Artillery in 1861 and fought under General McClellan in Virginia. He stayed with his decorated regiment throughout the war, and his long service gave credence to his perspective of the approaching election. In an article titled "How the Soldiers Feel," the *Herald* wrote: "We have been permitted to make the following extract from a private letter written by Aaron B. Page of Leelanaw to his wife. The writer had formerly been a Democrat, and we ask those of his old friends here who still adhere to that shattered faith to read what Mr. Page says and ponder well his words."

Page's letter to his wife said: "Remember we have a pleasant home of our own, increasing in value every day, in part of the country where the ravages of war will not be likely to come; still what would our house be worth without a Government, or even with a Government if it be one of Tyranny, ruled by men pledged, soul and body, to the maintenance and extension of Slavery, and who would not hesitate to sacrifice the liberties, happiness, and even life itself, of the whole nation to carry out their base desires to that end. It behooves every man, with the spark of genuine patriotism, to rise in their might and swear by all that is pure and just, that they will stand by the good old Government established by our fathers, and fight to maintain so long as there is one patriotic arm to wield the sword in its defense. Let their motto be, Death to Traitors – no compromise, no sheathing the sword as long as the traitor is seen, unless they lay down their weapons and come back to their allegiance. This is how I feel, and had I a thousand lives I would sacrifice them all on the altar of my country rather than see our own happy Union destroyed or severed in twain.

"If "Old Abe" is elected this Fall, as I have no doubt he will be, I think the Rebs will give up all hope of establishing their independence. All that keeps them up now is the faint hope held out to them, by the villainous, traitorous, Copperheads North, that a Peace man will be elected. O, would to God that I had the power, I would not leave a vestige of such men to suck the lifeblood of the Nation. Even the rebels hate and despise them, for they know they are men of no principle, who merely seek position, and would not hesitate to turn against them if they could thereby carry out their base desires and get the reins of Government in their own hands. But this is God's war, and justice will triumph, and the time will come when these "hellhounds" will call on the rocks and mountains to fall on them."[388]

Individual states held their elections a month earlier than the national Presidential ballot, and the October vote reflected recent Union victories on the battlefield. Editor Bates sent his paper this dispatch from Chicago: "I arrived here this morning just in time to miss the morning train for Detroit. We had a very pleasant trip all the way, as I always have on the *Alleghany*. I was greeted on my arrival with the glorious news from Ohio, Pennsylvania, and Indiana, where the State election were held yesterday. Ohio gives 75,000 Republican majority! Pennsylvania 40,000!! And Indiana 25,000!!! In the language of the *Tribune* this morning, the notes of these victories will be welcomed throughout the civilized world, wherever America has a sympathizing heart, or Liberty a friend. Not only is the Presidential question settled, but the greater question of the Rebellion is settled by the emphatic voice of not less than one hundred thousand majority in three states, two of which were confidently counted upon to vote for "an immediate cessation of hostilities." The election in November is now a mere formality. McClellan can not carry a Northern State. The war for Union will go on as long as a traitor remains to handle a weapon against the Government and Constitution of the country."[389]

During October, Reverend Smith attended to the technical details of the approaching election in Leelanau. This would be the first Presidential election since the Peninsula organized as an independent county in February, 1863. As a matter of pride, Smith was determined to make everything go smoothly. Only a dozen years before, the sparsely populated Leelanau Peninsula had been attached as a township to adjoining Grand Traverse County. A total of 28 citizens cast their ballots in the 1851 election held in Grand Traverse – a sprawling geographical area encompassing modern Leelanau, Benzie, Antrim and Grand Traverse Counties. Now, in 1864, Leelanau County boasted five of its own townships,[390] and its lead town of Northport was the largest and busiest port in the northern half of Michigan's Lower Peninsula.

More than any other time in the history of the United States, the immediate fate of the nation depended on the outcome of the election that was only two weeks away. Yet after four years of war, and the suffering and dying of so many local men in Union blue, how Leelanau, and especially the county seat of Northport, would vote in the upcoming election was very much up in the air. Four years before, the harbor town voted heavily for Democratic Stephen Douglas over Republican Abraham Lincoln. Recently, under the Lincoln administration, Leelanau soldiers had been mauled in Virginia, and the just released draft roles called over 100 more of the peninsula's men into the Union ranks. The answer to whether citizens in Northport would again vote against Lincoln and the war, or now support the Union to the bitter end, could well predict the wider Presidential vote. It was one of many small northern towns that would soon decide the fate of the war and the nation.

As summer passed into fall, Reverend Smith paused to reflect on his life as a missionary along the shores of Lake Michigan. He wrote: "I am 57 years old today. Am enjoying good health as I have for many years. Have much cause of gratitude to God for all his mercies."[391] For 15 years, Smith helped shape and record the social and economic emergence of the western Great Lakes from his home in Northport. The years of sustained growth Smith had witnessed owed much to the long, peaceful border between the United States and Canada, including a thousand miles of Great Lakes shoreline. For 50 years, the two countries had enjoyed friendly relations, and both shared in the growth and prosperity the Erie Canal had brought to the western lakes. There had been no standing navies or naval standoffs anywhere on the Great Lakes since the War of 1812, and no shots fired in anger between the two nations. However, the American Civil War had now put the tranquil border in jeopardy.

Canada during the Civil War was ruled by the British and officially neutral. The country was far ahead of the United States on the issue of slavery, having banned the practice in 1838. Prior to the Civil War, the dream of escaped slaves was to reach the free soil of Canada, where many of the country's citizens co-operated with the Underground Railroad. However, the war had changed the demographics of Canadian border towns. Draft dodgers and anti-war activists clustered on the Canadian side and Confederate sympathizers and soldiers walked the country's streets under the protection of the government. By 1864, Confederate raiders plotted actions against the Union from Canadian camps along the northern Great Lakes and on up through New England. Recently, Union General Sheridan's destruction of the Virginia's beloved Shenandoah Valley had enraged the South, and the Rebels considered desperate measures to strike back at the Yankee homeland. Their first target they set their sights on was the Great Lakes region.

Tom Woodruff

In a September article titled "A Copperhead Plot," the *Grand Traverse Herald* reported: "The Rebels in Canada and their Copperhead friends in Detroit concocted a nice little scheme, last week, to release the rebel prisoners on Johnson's Island, near Sandusky. They seized two steamers which ply between Detroit and Sandusky, and intended to capture the armed steamer *Michigan,* and go to the release of the prisoners. The plot was detected in Sandusky, and the whole scheme failed." Confederate soldiers in civilian clothes had hijacked the steamers *Philo Parsons* and *Island Queen* on Lake Erie, not far from where over 3,000 Rebel officers were held on the island prison. When their intentions were discovered, "the rebels sunk the steamers and made their escape to Canada." Bates filled in details of the plot by publishing a story from the *Cleveland Herald,* which read: "The ringleader of the pirates, a man named Charles H. Cole, appeared in Cleveland about six weeks ago, made a large display of gold, entertained into negotiations for the purchase of two schooners, pretended to be very loyal, made the acquaintance of the officers of the United States steamer *Michigan,* gave them suppers; and created sensations generally. Two weeks ago, however, he was recognized by a Southern refugee as a former captain in the rebel service. Information of his real character was given to the police, and he was placed under surveillance...

"A close investigation into his proceedings showed that he was a frequent visitor to the house...of a noted Copperhead, who had living with him the wives of two rebel officers who were confined on Johnson's Island. A sewing woman who worked for the female rebels occasionally, was witness to much talk of a treasonable nature that took place between Cole and the women. Dispatches were repeatedly received by Cole in reference to shares in stocks, transactions in cattle, and other matters which were ascertained to be mere blinds to conceal the reports of the movement of men and the progress of the conspiracy between the Copperheads, having in view the release of the rebel prisoners.

"The evidence of the treason of Cole accumulated rapidly, and it was deemed best to bring matters to a head. The opportunity was soon provided by Cole himself. He invited all the officers of the *Michigan* to a grand supper to be given on shore...most of the officers agreed to come, but word was sent to him...that one of the number could not get away without permission of the Commander, who would only grant leave on the direct application of Cole himself. It was represented that the officer was very anxious to come, and Cole was asked to come on board and intercede for him. Cole did so about seven o'clock in the evening, and was immediately arrested. Finding himself in a bad position, his true character known, he at length confessed a part of the plot in which he was engaged. He said the officers were to be feasted high and their wine drugged… They were then to be put out of the way by the Copperhead conspirators, when the confederates…were to make an attack on the *Michigan* and capture her.

"On these disclosures and other evidence, six Sandusky Copperheads were arrested and sent to Johnson's Island. Subsequently Cole disclosed more of the plot. He said that a number of his confederates were to come down that morning from Detroit on the steamer *Philo Parsons,* capture her, take the *Island Queen,* then, on the proper signals being made from the *Michigan,* steer in and attack the troops on the Island. He said he had no further need of concealment of that part of the plot, as it was undoubtedly effected. Cole was then put ashore under guard on Johnson's Island, and the *Michigan* got ready to give chase to the *Parsons.*

"On the way out a small boat was hailed and taken on board…on their way in with the intelligence of the capture by the rebels of the steamers *Philo Parsons* and *Island Queen,* the sinking of the latter, and the flight of the former towards Canada. The *Michigan* gave chase, but returned yesterday afternoon unsuccessful."[392]

Although the Confederate action on Lake Erie failed in its immediate intentions, it left the Great Lakes region in turmoil. Another story in the same *Herald* said: "A rumor reaches us by way of Northport that a large fire has occurred in Detroit, supposed to be the work of rebel incendiaries."[393] There was no fire in Detroit, only fear that one could be set at any moment by Confederate conspirators.

Further east, a former Confederate prisoner of war named Bennett Young received an officer's commission to lead Rebel cavalrymen across the Canadian border to rob New England banks. The Confederates hoped the raids would force the Union to withdraw troops from the South to defend their northern border, and they would use the captured loot to shore up the Confederate treasury. The first place the raiders chose to attack was St. Albans, Vermont – George and Arvilla Smith's former hometown.

During the first two weeks of October, a score of Confederate soldiers arrived by ones and twos and checked into the hotels and boarding houses scattered about St. Albans. They scouted the town's three banks and noted other assets of the prosperous New England settlement. On the afternoon of October 19, plain-clothes Confederate cavalrymen stormed all three St. Alban's banks and emptied their vaults. While the robberies were taking place, other

Rebels rounded up the townspeople and held them at gunpoint on the village green. One citizen was killed and another shot in the scuffle. After loading over $120,000 in banknotes and mounting the town's best horses, the Rebel raiders began their 15-mile sprint north to the Canadian border.

Word spread through the Vermont countryside of the Rebel incursion and the local militia began their pursuit. The bandits' trail was easy to follow, for the road north was speckled with Yankee greenbacks flying from hastily packed saddlebags. The Vermont militia pursued the bank robbers across the border where they caught up with Young, but they were forced to surrender their prisoner to British Army regulars stationed in Canada, bringing the incident to an international stage. A Canadian court ruled the Rebel raiders acted under orders, and because of Canadian neutrality, they could not be handed over to the United States. Tensions mounted as the two governments failed to agree on how to proceed with prisoners and their trials. Relations between the two countries teetered near collapse.

The *Grand Traverse Herald* followed the disintegrating situation, noting that "Gov. Blair has authorized the raising of the 30th Michigan Regiment…to be exclusively for State service." Blair was responding to a telegram from Union General Joseph Hooker, the army's chief administrator, who wrote: "In consideration of the number of outlaws and sympathizers in Canada, and the exposed condition of the frontier, and the very limited number of troops to guard it, I deemed it prudent to call on the Secretary of War to give you authority to raise a regiment of volunteers…intending to post them along the Detroit River at such points as their services were most needed…I deemed it very important… that the regiment should be raised and equipped ready for service before the river is frozen over." In another correspondence concerning the formation of the 30th Michigan Infantry, Hooker said: "No lesser force can render the frontier of Michigan secure from the incursions of the disaffected from Canada." With the 1864 Presidential vote only a week away, he added: "In view of the election, I have thought proper to order two hundred drafted men here…and shall send a little steamer in the government employ, with a small detachment of men, up river to-morrow as far as Port Huron, the men to go ashore and remain there until the polls are closed. These dispositions, I trust, will prevent any irregularity to the polls at the points at which it is apprehended."[394] The peaceful international border was for the moment a thing of the past.

Late in October, Reverend Smith boarded the "3 masted schooner *Emeline*" and "Reached Chicago about Sun-rise." The schooner anchored off the Great

Lakes fastest growing city and Smith waited for "a Tug to take us into the Creek." Earlier in the summer, Smith was in Detroit when the *Nile* exploded, killing his friend and General Custer's brother-in-law Albert Bacon. Five months later in Chicago, Smith wrote: "I spent the day in visiting…the *Tonawanda*…she was blown up a week ago today. 2 were killed."[395] Two of the Great Lakes finest steam-powered vessels, the *Nile* and the *Tonawanda* – both regular visitors to Grand Traverse harbors – added their names to the long list of victims of the year 1864.

Smith stayed in Chicago into the first week of November, at one point visiting Camp Douglas, where thousands of Confederate prisoners of war were held. His son-in-law Payson and two dozen of his Indian friends from Company K, who only months before served as guards at Camp Douglas, were at the moment captives at Andersonville Prison in Georgia. Smith made no comment about the agonizing turn of events. When Smith finally completed his business in Chicago and boarded the *Alleghany* for the trip back north, the weather had turned sour. November gales made the month the most dangerous time for a voyage on the Lake Michigan. On the 4th he wrote: "We have a fearful North Easter," and his ship was unable to leave the harbor. The next day the *Alleghany* "left Chicago 3 AM…struck the bar several times – heavy squall day." On Sunday, conditions on the lake deteriorated further. Smith continued: "Gale… blew furiously. Cloudy most of the day. We left Milwaukee about midnight. The lake was very rough & continued so all day. Most of the passengers scarcely left their berths, I was quite unwell…I reached home about midnight. Several hours before we arrived it seemed as though the boat could not out live the storm."[396] Once more, when the winds of fate threatened to consume him, Smith escaped unscathed.

A number of local soldiers who had long braved the tempest of war also arrived safely back in Grand Traverse in early November, 1864. The *Herald* wrote: "Matthew Harper and Isaac Winne, who have faithfully served their country three years, been engaged in a hundred battles, and received honorable discharges, returned on Monday last. They look as healthy, fresh and vigorous as they did when they departed three years ago.[397] When the two lumberjacks left the pine forests of Hannah, Lay & Co. in 1861 to join the Union Army, the paper called them "as stalwart and noble hearted young men as ever shouldered a musket," and Hannah "made each a handsome present." Now fate had given them their best gift yet – they were alive, intact, and back home for good.

In the last *Herald* printed before the 1864 Presidential Election, Morgan Bates summed up his view of the contest. In an editorial titled "A Word Before the Battle" he wrote: "The contest of next Tuesday will decide the fate of this Nation for ages. If Abraham Lincoln should be elected President of the United States, the Rebellion will be crushed, and we shall become a great and mighty people whose God is the Lord. If, on the other hand, McClellan should succeed, an armistice will be declared, our victories and conquering armies disbanded, a disgraceful and humiliating Peace proclaimed which will only last until the South can recuperate its exhausted energies..."[398]

Fearing he may not have made his case in the editorial, Bates turned the news section of the paper into pro-Lincoln advertisement. One article said: "The Rebel leaders admit that their last and only hope of success is the election of McClellan to the Presidency. Every man, then, who votes for the so-called democratic ticket gives "aid and comfort to the enemy" – and this is Treason." Another argued: "A vote for McClellan will be a vote for the Rebellion at a time when the Rebellion is nearly crushed." A third read: "Remember! – Next Tuesday is election day. Let every man turn out. Vote early. Vote for Abraham Lincoln. Vote the entire Republican ticket."

Reverend Smith, like Bates, was also doing all he could to sustain Lincoln. The day before the Presidential election, he wrote: "Took my horses & waggon...& went to Onumunese Ville – held a Council with the Indians. I think they have opened their eyes & they will vote right." Smith went so far as to arrange a dinner for Indians who voted Republican. With the ballots cast, Smith commented: "Today has been one of the most important if not the most important in the history of this country, the election of President. Oh that the wicked enemies of our country may not be permitted to destroy it – by our efforts we carried 11 Majority."[399] The swing town of Northport had gone Republican. The next day, Reverend Smith added: "We have a large Majority Republican in our G.T. Country – I hope in our land."

In a letter to his sister, Joshua Middleton, who continued to work the wards while recuperating from wounds at Baltimore's Jarvis Hospital, said: "Hurrah for Old Abe. I acted as clerk of Elections in this City for Michigan Soldiers. They went 20 to one for ole Abe, poor old Mac. Ohio gave him one out of 40 that was cast at our polls."[400] One of those voting at Jarvis Hospital may have been Sgt. Frederick Cook of Company A, 26th Michigan Infantry and Leland, who was wounded in the summer's Overland Campaign and would be discharged from the Union Army on disability later that month.

The *Herald* of Friday, November 11 only printed news of the local vote – the national tally had yet to arrive by water. The paper said: "We do not expect to receive news of the Grand result of the election until the arrival of the *Alleghany* from Chicago next Monday, or Tuesday. There is a probability, however, of getting it sooner by way of Northport or Glen Arbor. Patience is a virtue under such circumstances." At a time when the freshest news emanated from the area's docks, the two Grand Traverse towns that lay along the Manitou Passage would be the first to know who had won the Presidential race. People gathered at the docks to meet every arriving ship to hear if there was word of how the momentous vote had gone. For those who stood by Lincoln, the Grand Traverse vote by itself was encouraging. In an article titled "Was that Thunder?" the *Herald* said: "The result of the Election on Tuesday far exceeded our most sanguine hopes...We have made a clean sweep of every town." Newly independent Antrim County also voted solidly Republican. The big surprise came out of the tip of Leelanau, a traditional Democratic stronghold. The paper wrote: "Northport, the County Seat, has done nobly. It was conceded, before the election, that the Copperheads would carry it by 25 majority, through the agency of the Indian vote, which went solid against us. We have beaten them by a majority of 11 in a poll of 113 votes – the Republican ticket receiving 62 and the Copperhead 51. Good enough."[401]

Finally, the November 18 *Herald* carried the momentous news – Lincoln had won a second term as President. The great decision of 1864 had been made – the Civil War would continue until its conclusion on the battlefield. As predicted, the news reached the Grand Traverse paper circuitously, brought by "A gentleman who left Chicago on Saturday last and arrived here on Tuesday by way of Glen Arbor." The defeated Democratic candidate apparently had enough of politics and the war, for the same issue of the *Herald* reported: "Gen. McClellan has resigned his commission as Major General in the U.S. Army." McClellan must have been particularly mortified by the soldiers' vote, which weighed more heavily against him than the civilian tally. The soldiers' vote in Michigan gave Lincoln, 9,402; McClellan 2,955"[402] – over a 3 to 1 majority. The compromise position had been aired and rebuked, and now all the vast resources and energies of the North would be focused on ending the prolonged conflict through battle.

In his first speech to Congress following his reelection, President Lincoln addressed the recent Confederate invasions of the United States from Canada, including the St Albans incident. In a section of his address titled "Naval Power on the Lakes" he said: "In view of the insecurity of life in the region adjacent to the Canadian border, by recent assaults and depredations committed by inimical and desperate persons who are harbored there, it has been thought proper to give notice that after the expiration of six months, the period conditionally stipulated in the existing arrangements with Great Britain, the United States must hold themselves at liberty to increase their naval armament upon the lakes, if they shall find that proceeding necessary."[403] A half century old tradition of an unarmed, peaceful border between the United States and Canada remained seriously at risk.

The same week Northern voters reelected Lincoln, the 10th Michigan Cavalry participated in a significant action in East Tennessee, surprising and routing a force under Confederate General John Morgan. Since the war began, Morgan's cavalry had harassed Union armies in Kentucky and Tennessee, and his raids, which included an 1862 foray through Ohio and Indiana in which the 1st Michigan Sharp Shooters were engaged, displayed a mastery of hit and run tactics. But like so many other great Southern generals, by November 1864, his time had run out. An officer in the 10th Michigan Cavalry described his demise: "Morgan, with a force of about 7,000 men, made up of nine pieces of Artillery, two regiments of Infantry and his entire cavalry force, are encamped along the Greenville road in East Tennessee. The Tenth Michigan Cavalry, then in command of Major Newell...is ordered by General Gillam to attack the enemy camp. Marching all night, he dismounts his men at daylight and charges into Morgan's first camp, driving the enemy in hot haste, leaving their breakfast half cooked, and their dead and wounded. Reaching the second camp, the enemy is found in better condition.

"General Gilliam comes up with the Ninth Tennessee Cavalry, orders that regiment to charge with sabers, but the sharp fire from the enemy drives the regiment back...the enemy driving the Ninth advances rapidly, with a large cavalry force, at least a thousand strong, filling the road from fence to fence. The Tenth Michigan opens fire at about half pistol range with carbines, and soon the road is blocked with dead and wounded, men and horses. The enemy confused, hastily falls back, pursued to the woods, but is shelled out and pushes on to Greenville, is again charged on, becomes demoralized, breaks up and flees. Morgan and staff are discovered under shelter of a house, a company of the Thirteenth Tennessee is sent to capture him, he rushes for his horse, but is shot in the attempt by a sergeant of the company."[404] Another American leader fell dead.

Further east, General Sherman's army left Atlanta and began their march across Georgia toward the Atlantic seaboard. Fifty thousand Union troops disappeared into the heart of the Confederacy, foregoing the usual lines of com-munications and supplies that followed armies. Sherman attempted on a grand scale what he had seen Omena's General Grierson accomplish the year before in Mississippi – his army would travel light and live off the land. For a month, re-ports of the Union Army's movement through Georgia came mostly from Con-federate newspapers. The articles described Sherman's progress in the bleakest of terms. Many of the stories depicted a tattered and hungry army being chased by Confederate General Hood's resurrected forces. Grant began to worry that his decision to set Sherman's army free in the Deep South might well end in another northern military debacle.

The names of those chosen in Lincoln's latest draft call were released about the same time as the news of his reelection. The call was extensive and swept Grand Traverse men of all stations into the Union Army. To date, in 1864 alone, Lincoln had asked for over 700,000 more soldiers. The *Herald* wrote of Traverse City: "Our village is full of drafted men who are waiting the arrival of the Provost Marshall and Draft Commissioner from Grand Rapids. They are expected on the *Alleghany*.[405] The next edition of the weekly paper published a list of the men called from Leelanau – 108 in all – one quarter of the total num-ber of the peninsula's citizens who had voted in the last election.

A December article in the *Herald* gave the drafted men a hint of where they may be headed. It said: "Sherman is pursuing his victorious march to the sea board. He has captured Millegeville, the Capital of Georgia, whence the Ander-sonville prisoners are removed, and Augusta, one of the great ordnance depots of the Southern Confederacy. The whole South is in a panic."[406] The liberation of Andersonville Prison, where dozens of Grand Traverse men had been sent, aroused the anger of Sherman's soldiers as they witnessed the living skeletons of their comrades arriving at Union field hospitals. Families throughout the North whose sons, fathers, and husbands were prisoners of war waited anxiously to discover who had survived the brutal death camp.

The *Grand Traverse Herald* reported that the 15th Michigan Infantry, home to dozens of Grand Traverse soldiers, was among "the Michigan troops who have shared the perils and the glory of the march of the immortal Sherman through Georgia."[407] Local representation in the 15th swelled following the lat-est draft call, due in a large part to the success of Sherman in Atlanta. Over 50 Grand Traverse men joined the 15th, including 20 men from the Glen Arbor who enlisted in one day. The 39 year-old barrel maker, John Dorsey, one of Glen Arbor's first white settlers, signed up with the regiment. So did 43 year-old

Union soldiers remove heavy ammunition from Fort McAllister, near Savannah, 1864. *Library of Congress*

John I. Miller of Leland, the Leelanau County Treasurer who helped build the town's first dam and sawmill. Charles Norris, whose brother had died while fighting in Custer's Michigan Cavalry Brigade, also enlisted with the 15th Michigan. Within months, the new recruits were all a thousand miles from home, fighting their way through the heart of the Confederacy with Sherman.

Fear in the North about the fate of Sherman's army turned to joy on December 13, when a dispatch from the General reached a Union gunboat on the Atlantic coast. After describing his army's capture of Fort McAllister near Savannah harbor, Sherman wrote: "The army is in splendid order, and equal to anything. The weather has been fine, good travelling. We reached Savannah three days ago…we have not lost a wagon on the trip, but have gathered in a large supply of negroes, mules, horses, etc., and our teams are in far better condition than when we started.

"We have utterly destroyed over two hundred miles of rails, and consumed stores and provisions that were essential to Lee's and Hood's armies. The quick work made with…the opening of communications with our fleet, and the consequent independence for supplies, dissipates all their boasted threats to head me off and starve the army." Sherman concluded the communication by saying: "I consider Savannah as already gained."[408]

Sherman's March to the Sea consumed the wealth of Georgia as it moved beyond its supply lines, turning foraging into a military science. Railroads, cotton gins, factories, and any other entity judged to aid the war effort were put to the torch. However, the psychological damage to the South caused by a Union Army advancing nearly unopposed through its center was perhaps worse. Many of the Rebel troops detailed to stop the Sherman's army in Georgia deserted. Slaves from hundreds of miles in every direction fled their plantations and joined the advancing blue columns, causing the force to grow as it moved toward the Atlantic coast.

The *Grand Traverse Herald* filled in the specifics of Sherman's lost month in Georgia. It said: "The details of the march of Gen. Sherman are published, and read almost like a romance...The real facts of his expedition as they now transpire convict the rebel press of the most stupendous lying. All their accounts of repulses of his forces, damage inflicted upon our cavalry...and the obstructions placed in the way, were the purest inventions. In utter contempt of any force the enemy could bring against him, he scattered his men over an extent of country nearly sixty miles wide. He fed his men on poultry, sweet potatoes, and the very fat of the land generally. Three of his scouts captured the capitol of the State, the Mayor insisting upon surrendering to them...

"He played most dreadful havoc with the leading lines of Southern railroads...The rails were burned and bent, and the road bed and bridges destroyed. Somewhere between 4,000 and 6,000 negroes were gathered in by the army, and the country was stripped of food, horses, and cattle...and the total casualties of the route less than 1,000 men...Its exposure of the utter hollowness and weakness of the rebellion is most complete."[409]

In early December, a *Herald* article titled "Gloom in Dixie" commented on the state of the South following Lincoln's election to a second term and Sherman's successful March to the Sea. The paper said: "The Richmond correspondent of the *London Times* gives a most discouraging account of the condition of affairs in Dixie. He says Lee's army is almost worn out, while signs of exhaustion are everywhere apparent...This correspondent has hitherto maintained the invincibility of the South."[410] Time was running out for the Confederate States of America.

The same edition of the paper carried news of the continued growth and prosperity along Lake Michigan. During the most destructive four years in the history of war on American soil, the region, anchored by the city of Chicago, experienced its greatest surge in population to date. The *Herald* wrote: "On the first of July, 1837, Chicago contained but four thousand inhabitants…it now contains a population of 169,353, an increase of 31,167 since 1862."[411] The figure amounted to a 55% rise from the 1860 Census figure, making Chicago the fastest growing city in North America. During the same time, the population of Grand Traverse County more than doubled as Homestead Act farmers poured in to stake their claims. The frontier days along Lake Michigan were passing and the region began to adjust to its new role as part of the nation's settled heartland. The next generation of pioneers headed further west toward new opportunities. The *Grand Traverse Herald* reported: "The overland emigration during the past season is estimated at over 150,000 persons. The main body of the emigrants have located at Colorado, Nevada, Utah, California, Idaho and Montana."[412]

On December 15, 1864, news reached the Smith family that son-in-law Payson Wolfe was one of the lucky few who made it out of Andersonville Prison alive. Reverend Smith wrote: "Mail came…1 letter from Payson to Mary dated Dec. 1. He had just arrived on his way from prison as well – expected to get a furlough to come home – we feared we should never see him again." Several days later, an Indian friend delivered a letter from Payson that revealed chilling details of his captivity in Andersonville. Smith wrote: "Pepequa got a letter last night from Payson Dec. 2 in which he says Sa qua on is dead – 1 of our members – also Shako & Kewaquiskum, when he last heard from him, was very sick, probably long ago dead – he is also a member. Payson had been four days without food, had suffered beyond description. It may be - it is quite probable - all the rest of the prisoners are dead. How shocking to contemplate the cruelties of the Southern rebels, only fit to be compared to those who rebelled in heaven."[413]

On December 22, General Sherman sent a telegram to President Lincoln, saying: "I beg to present you as a Christmas gift the city of Savannah, with 150 heavy guns and plenty of heavy ammunition, and also about 25,000 bales of cotton." The two remaining Confederate armies of any strength – those of Generals Lee and Johnston - were now cut off from the Deep South and isolated along the mid-Atlantic seaboard.

For the Smith family of Northport, the tragedy-filled year of 1864 came to a joyful conclusion. Reverend Smith wrote: "Payson arrived about 2 PM a parolled prisoner – was parolled at Savannah & 1100 prisoners took the Steam Ship *Constitution* & were landed at Annapolis. They were furnished a suit of clothes on going on board & another suit when they landed at Annapolis." Although now clothed and well-fed, six months as a prisoner of war had taken a toll on the 1ˢᵗ Michigan Sharp Shooter. Smith recounted the evening's conversation with Wolfe, writing: "He says they suffered terribly while prisoners, going 2 & 3 days and a number of times four days with out eating at all – were robbed of their blankets & overcoats & lived & slept in the open weather, their bed on the ground, their covering the rain – water sometimes 4 inches deep where they had to lie."[414]

Several days later, the extended Smith family again gathered for supper, and the after-dinner conversations between the Reverend and Private Wolfe continued in their gruesome tone. The Northport diarist wrote: "Payson…tells shocking stories of their sufferings while prisoners. He says that when men got so weak they could not keep their rations on their stomachs – would vomit up beans as soon as swallowed. Others would rush up & eat the vomit with greediness & often the boiled rice would be alive with full grown maggots. He has eat it so – was obliged to or would starve."[415]

The final 1864 edition of the *Grand Traverse Herald* reported that a visit of Canada's Attorney General to Washington "led to a satisfactory understanding between the Government and the Provincial authorities in regard both to the mode of dealing with the rebel raiders now in custody and the best means of preventing thieving incursions by land or water with the border States in the future."[416] The torrent of bad tidings that defined 1864 appeared to be easing up.

Among the Civil War letters saved by Northport volunteer Joshua Middleton was an unsigned correspondence written by a soldier of the 26ᵗʰ Michigan Infantry. The writer expressed for many the range of emotions people in the North felt as the tragic year, and the tragic war, approached its end. The unidentified Lakeshore Tiger wrote: "I am sitting to day in my little shelter tent… and thoughts are crowding my mind of the war and its great effects, of the great good, and the many sorrowing hearts its has caused. Oh how many loving wives are there to mourn the loss of a husband! How many fathers and mothers to weep over the dead son. How many orphans by the cruel war. Yes! How many family circles are there in the North to day that have not some loved one to mourn. Alas but very few. Nearly all have someone dear to them who fills the soldiers grave, fallen whilst fighting in the battles of their or his country and now lying as he fell under a mound of earth in the far south. Yet tis sweet to die for ones country.

"I was sorry to hear of the death of Samuel Cole. He adds another to the list of those that have passed from this world whilst serving his country. Absent though he may be, we will never be so ungrateful as to forget the memory of those patriots, heroes, and martyrs whose virtues we will try to imitate and hope for a happy reunion in heaven, yes. Farewell to the Hero in silence to sleep… they have died fighting against cruelty and oppression fighting to save the greatest and only pure republican government in this world. Let their memory ever be green. In a few short months I hope and believe this rebellion will have been quelled, the fearful carnage of the war will be at an end. Peas [Peace] will once again smile on our land; and we will still be the great good and strong nation of the world, then we will come forth from the fire of trial and have proved to the world that American people can and will govern themselves and that our country is indeed the land of the free and the home of brave."[417]

Freedmen among the Richmond ruins. *Library of Congress*

CHAPTER EIGHT

1865
The End is Soon to Come

Private Joshua Middleton's first letter of 1865 revealed his cautious optimism that the Civil War was near its end. The Quaker soldier wrote: "There is a rumor of peace, the rebs are getting in rather a tight fix. They are quarreling amongst themselves now in Richmond. There is a rumor here this morning that Sherman has demanded the surrender of Charleston, how true it is I do not know. But so it must be soon, I think the end is soon to come, hoping it may be so."[418] Reports coming out of the South confirmed Middleton's perception. An article in the first *Grand Traverse Herald* of the year titled "Negroes Conscripted in the Army" said: "The rebel Senate last Saturday went into secret session, and a stormy time was had. The question of at once arming the negroes was brought up, and is believed to have passed by an almost unanimous vote. For several days every able-bodied negro has been quietly seized and hurried off to the camps of instruction."[419] Although Confederate President Jefferson Davis refused to sign the law, his government had conceded that the situation was desperate, for it had previously vowed never to allow blacks to serve. The old order of the South was disintegrating.

During January, George Smith worked on behalf of daughter Mary and her husband Payson Wolfe, who remained in Northport on furlough while recovering from his ordeal in Andersonville Prison. On the 11th, Smith wrote: "Went in sleigh to Manseau's Mill…carried 4 bushels for Mary & 4½ for myself - got it ground and reached home before dark." The next day, "Mary got a letter from Pay Master General, in answer to my letter, containing a check for 32 dollars being Payson's pay for May and June."[420] Though half a year late, Wolfe had at last received his 50 cents a day wages for fighting in the deadliest two months of the American Civil War.

Other Indian war heroes from Grand Traverse benefited from Smith's efforts that winter. The Reverend "looked up the record and made certificates of the marriage of William Mixernasa & Mary Ahimekwasega - so that the widow can draw pay &c of her husband who died a prisoner in Camp Sumpter Ga Oct.24. He is said to have bourn his sufferings with temperance and meekness."[421] In another instance, the preacher helped secure the enlistment bounties, "each to the amount of $250.00," for two Natives serving in the 1st Michigan Sharp Shooters, "1 is John Jacko, 1 John Keen ah nun essi." A few days later, the *Herald* noted that "Members of the Church and Congregation of the Rev. Geo. N. Smith of Northport, Mich., made him a very agreeable visit and on their departure left in his hand money, groceries, &c, in all to the amount of sixty dollars," in recognition of his dedication to the Grand Traverse community.

While the end result of the Civil War was now apparent, the suffering and death of Smith's extended Indian family and friends continued. In an early February article titled "Northport Volunteers," the *Herald* wrote: "Lewis Miller left here on Wednesday morning for Grand Rapids, with three Indian recruits from Northport. Payson Wolf[e], a parolled prisoner who has just been exchanged, accompanied them to join his regiment." Escaping death at Andersonville had earned Wolfe a furlough but not a discharge, and by the end of February he was back in Virginia with the remnants of the 1st Michigan Sharp Shooters. Here Payson was again struck by the scourge of winter camps – disease – the number one killer of soldiers during the Civil War. Smith noted that he received "two letters from Payson at Camp Parole, Annapolis, Md, he has been sick but is better." While Payson survived, one of his Grand Traverse friends was not so lucky. Smith wrote: "1 of the young Indians who went with Payson died after three days sickness."[422]

A February news story named "Michigan Legislature" explored the make-up of the government that had steered the state through the Civil War years. It said: "In the Senate, there are 11 farmers, 10 lawyers, four merchants, one publisher, one lumberman, one painter, one physician, one horticulturalist, and one miscellaneous...Fourteen are natives of New York, two of Michigan, four of Vermont, three of Pennsylvania, two of New Hampshire" and one from Scotland, Virginia, Massachusetts, New Jersey and Maine. "In the House there are 48 farmers, 18 merchants, nine lawyers, six physicians, nine lumbermen...one cooper, one roofer, one carpenter, one banker, and one teacher...Fifty-six are natives of New York, 12 of Vermont, seven of Massachusetts, five of Connecticut, three of Pennsylvania",[423] and two each from Germany, England, and Ohio.

The scarcity of seated legislators born in Michigan bore witness to the quarter century of rapid growth in the state's population, including the decade-long surge in Grand Traverse Country. The vast majority of people settling in Michigan were educated New Englanders who had come by way of the Erie Canal. The eastern political mindset of many Michigan newcomers, as embodied by the *Herald's* nomadic editor Morgan Bates, had helped sharpen the radically progressive edge of the state's Republican Party, which had governed the state since the war's inception.

Michigan's government of farmers and tradesmen spoke of the opportunities available to immigrants entering the western Great Lakes at the time. Many of Michigan's leading citizens and legislators had arrived nearly empty-handed, but were able to rise to their positions through the sweat of their labor. The principles they supported as legislators during the Civil War were not vague notions, but a set of values that had produced tangible benefits for themselves and their fellow citizens.

The willingness of Michigan legislators to legally apply Lincoln's "new birth of freedom" was recorded in the February 1865 *Grand Traverse Herald* article titled "Prompt Action." It read: "The Legislature of this State ratified the action of Congress amending the Constitution of the United States so as to prohibit Slavery, in one hour after the receipt of the official notice…Michigan was the first State to ratify."[424] The action of Congress referred to involved the 13th Amendment to the U.S. Constitution, which abolished slavery throughout the nation. However, the *Herald* did not have all the facts when the paper went to press, for although Michigan attempted to become the first state to ratify the historic document, they had been beaten by Illinois and Rhode Island. By the end of the month, 15 other states had passed the amendment. The new template for the post-war United States was rapidly taking shape, with Michigan quick to embrace the future.

Sherman's army did not rest long after the capture of Savannah and in the New Year began its relentless march toward South Carolina - the first state to attack the national flag. Though now capable of receiving supplies by water along the Atlantic coast, Union soldiers continued to rely principally on forage for sustenance, with the added advantage of keeping what they consumed out of Rebel hands. It soon became clear that Sherman's greatest challenge was not on the battlefield – there was no Confederate army available that was capable of halting the Union advance. The real test was to keep his force from getting bogged down in the rugged Southern terrain. The army often forded rivers, traversed swamps, and cut through dense forests that had never seen a road. Fortunately, many of Sherman's soldiers were from the western Great Lakes states, and their frontier experience had taught them how to overcome obstacles set forth by nature. Locals along the route were awed by the speed at which the Union army moved through their country, applying their skills with saws and axes to create thoroughfares through the previously impenetrable land. The Southerners witnessed for themselves the power of free labor at work. With the slaveholding culture in ashes, it was a way of life they would have to adapt to.

The ugly face of Union vengeance was saved for South Carolina, the Rebel state most soldiers blamed for tearing them away from their homes and families and causing the death of so many of their countrymen. After crossing the state line, Sherman's advance was accompanied by wanton destruction, especially in regards to the trappings of the Old South. Plumes of black smoke marked their progress through the state. The first wave of Union foragers descended on the elegant mansions of the plantations and looted all that was sellable or edible. Some Union soldiers carried in their knapsacks a private stash of plunder. Stragglers and deserters from both armies and bands of runaway slaves roamed the lawless land, completing the devastation. The *Grand Traverse Herald* wrote: "The news from South Carolina is highly encouraging. Gen Sherman writes there is no point of importance in the State that does not lie at his mercy." Another story noted that "Large numbers of runaway slaves are constantly arriving into the Union lines…for the purpose of enlisting in the army." Another icon of the Old South was being laid to waste.

Editor Bates continued to attack the shattering Confederacy and its supporters, rebuffing Lincoln's idea of eventual reconciliation as friends. His report in the March 3 *Herald*, coming from the city where the first shots of the Civil War were fired, brought Bates particular delight. He wrote: "Glorious News! "The Old Flag Waves over Sumter! Charleston and Columbia Evacuated. Gen. Sherman took possession of Columbia, the Capital of South Carolina on the 17th of February, and on the 18th Charleston was evacuated and the Stars and Stripes were displayed over Fort Sumter. The Rebellion is crushed in South Carolina, the nursery and hotbed of Treason."[425] Smith must have read this edition of the *Herald*, for the next day he wrote: "News has arrived confirmed that Charleston was taken the 18 of Feb – nearly destroyed by the rebel army – being blown up & fired by them as they evacuated. Many women & children & Old

Following the April 1861 cannonade on Fort Sumter, the Republican Governor of Wisconsin, Alexander Randall, addressed the state legislature and said, "This war began where Charleston is – it should end where Charleston was." As this 1865 Charleston street scene shows, Governor Randall's wish became a reality. *Library of Congress*

men in distress, many destroyed – all frantic – many mutilated by the explosions. The Flag is again raised over Fort Sumter. This is all terrible but glorious." There was a tremble in Reverend Smith's words for he, unlike Bates, felt no joy when he considered the awful price of victory.

In the winter of 1865, the British press, which during the war often lobbied in support of a Confederate nation, acknowledged that the time for an independent South had passed. The *Herald* published a report on the change in attitude, writing: "The *London Times* concedes at last that we are getting the better of the Rebellion. In an article on Sherman's…recent victories, it admits…that there is no longer any enemy in Secessia capable of opposing our chief armies. The fact that the former should be able to march a distance of three hundred miles through the heart of a hostile country without considerable opposition, carries conviction…that the Confederacy is a hollow shell, which our Generals are on the point of shivering into atoms. The truth at last forces itself upon the unwilling minds of our Foreign enemies, that the days of the Great Conspiracy are numbered, and the success of the Union cause certain. While they may not confess this with their lips, they feel it in their hearts. And they will live, each and all of them, to regret the course they have taken in our quarrel with the South."[426]

In another article, the *Herald* noted: "A British army officer, having traveled extensively in this country, publishes in a London paper the conclusion which he arrived at concerning our resources and ability to carry on the war. He states that he considers the Northern States inexhaustible in men and money, and in traveling over an extent of territory of a thousand miles through the United States, he saw very little to indicate the existence of a great war, and nothing that gave the least sign of the exhaustion of men."[427]

In the Great Lakes region, the possibility of more Confederate raids from across the Canadian border continued to strain relations between the United States and Great Britain. In an article titled "Gunboats for the Great Lakes," the *Herald* wrote: "The Senate has passed the House measure, which has thus become law, to put six fast single gun steamers, for the revenue service, on the lakes. This will make the full number we are entitled to maintain on the lakes by our present treaty with Great Britain. It cannot be done too soon. A million dollars is appropriate therefore."[428] Worries about a naval clash on the lakes raised tensions that a new, international war may follow the disastrous one that was winding down. The *Herald* wrote: "A Toronto paper says the British Government has ordered 30 gunboats, carrying 3,500 trained men, to be sent out from England to the lakes, and that they will probably be there as soon as navigation season opens." Confederates saw the escalation of the American Civil War into an international conflict as one of their few remaining hopes for national survival and worked to keep tensions high along the border with Canada.

As 1865 progressed, the proportion of news in the *Herald* related to the war began to decrease. People were tired of hearing about death and destruction and wanted to put the conflict behind them. In response, the paper renewed its prewar habit of describing Grand Traverse. A March edition cited excerpts from a presentation given before the State Agricultural Society at Lansing, which said: "The Grand Traverse region, already so well and favorable known, embraces a territory almost exclusively adapted to agriculture, and is now being quite rapidly settled. The surprising returns of this region for the last two or three years cannot failed to have arrested attention of every observing citizen; and conclusively demonstrate, that it must soon take rank with the very first agricultural portions of the State. The abundance of its hardwood, (principally beech and maple), its proximity to Lake Michigan, and its noble bay, give more than ordinary value to its lands; and in connection with the existing large demand for wood, cannot fail very materially to aid in the settlement of the country embraced within its limits.

"The settlement at Traverse City, through its enterprising founders, Hannah, Lay & Co, is too well known to need any description here. Its lumber and agricultural interests have already converted it into one of the most important points in the State, and its future growth bids fair to be rapid, and in the character of its population, valuable to the State at large. During the last two years, whole townships lying between Traverse City and Frankfort have been settled and organized." The region's rapid settlement during the Civil War was due largely to the Homestead Act of 1862. The free land the national law offered brought growth and vitality to Grand Traverse even as many of the area's men marched off to fight..

The *Herald* article continued: "Other thriving towns have sprung up in this region, among which are Elk Rapids, Northport, now a port of entry, and Glen Arbor, all of which have received an impetus in their growth from the wood trade with Chicago, and her passing steamers. Four hundred steam boat arrivals are registered at Northport for each of the last three or four years; and during the last year there has been cut and shipped to the Chicago market, by Elk Rapids and Traverse City, upwards of twenty million feet of lumber... Fruit and horticulture are also most successfully carried on, and there is every promise that the northern portion of the State, will soon be found equally productive in these respects with that further south."

Bates must have been delighted to hear that Greeley's bleak assessment of Northern Michigan that ran in the *New York Tribune* a half a decade before had finally been put to rest. However, an excerpt from the speech again revealed a prejudice shared by many Euro-American settlers along the Great Lakes, including the *Herald's* Morgan Bates. It said: "The Indian Reservations...have for a number of years, embarrassed and excluded settlement. Some of the very best lands in the vicinity were thus tied up for a number of years, much to the annoyance of *bona fide* settlers, who seeking their possession, were compelled to turn aside and locate elsewhere. But, as it is now understood, these reservations for the most part, run out in July next, and so the restrictions referred to, bid fair at last to be removed."[429]

It was apparent that the heroic service of Michigan Indians during the Civil War had not persuaded Bates and many of his contemporaries to examine their position concerning Indian treaty rights. Time and again, their opinions regarding Native ownership of land proved inconsistent with their stated philosophy of treating all men equally. In essence, Bates and his like-minded friends considered Euro-American settlement a godsend and branded any obstruction to its progress an "annoyance." When their passion to see the wilderness transformed clashed with the Native rights to their homeland, respect for agreements made in United States treaties fell by the wayside.

For Bates in particular, the consistent Indian vote for Democratic candidates during the Civil War contributed to the editor's disregard for Native positions. Bates equated the Democratic Party to all the evils of slavery and called it the enemy of freedom. In the microcosm of northern Michigan politics, however, the Democratic Party had become a rare power base for Native bands. A number of the region's successful Democratic office holders were Indians, carried in by what was often the unanimous vote of their community. Despite their allegiance to the Democrats, Northern Michigan Indians believed they had proved their loyalty through their hard service in Union blue. But even at a time when reports of Native soldiers' deaths on the battlefields of Virginia and in the prison camps of Georgia streamed back to the region, the hope that Grand Traverse Indians had won a new status by fighting for the Union was being diminished by opinions expressed in the *Grand Traverse Herald*

The newspaper suggested where the energies of the battle-hardened U.S. Army might be directed in the near future now that end of the Civil War was in sight. It said: "Accounts from Colorado Territory represent that Indian outrages on the overland mail route continue. Along portions of the road it appears to be unsafe for a white person to be seen. Mail stations and ranches have been burned, large numbers of horses and cattle run off, many persons, including women and children murdered, and the telegraph and other property destroyed. It is supposed to be the design of the savages to butcher every white person on the road, unless the military be speedily enforced."[430] While the war to emancipate one race in the South wound down, another bent on the destruction of a race of "savages" was shaping up in the West. The future did not bode well for the Grand Traverse Bands or for American Indians in general.

The extreme winter weather in Grand Traverse during the first months of 1864 foreshadowed the worst year of the American Civil War. In 1865, the cold season was considerably more tolerable. The *Herald* wrote: "The winter which passed calmly away on Tuesday, was the most pleasant, even and delightful one we have ever experienced in this climate. Sleighing commenced on the 24th of November and has been uninterrupted good to this present writing, and at no time was it better than on the first of March. The mercury has been down to zero only three days the entire winter…The average range has been from 25 to 35 above."[431] *Herald* readers could hope that the change for the better in the weather reflected the fortunes of war in 1865.

The paper mentioned two Grand Traverse soldiers who came home to visit in March, both bearing the scars of war. One article said: "We understand that Oscar Eaton, of Whitewater, returned home on a furlough, last Saturday. He has been absent from his family two years and a half fighting the battles of his country. Welcome home." During his time gone, Eaton described to *Herald* readers the travails of the 26th Michigan Infantry in Virginia, and on June 3, 1864, he was hit by a Confederate minie ball near Totopotomoy Creek, one of many bloody battles in Grant's Overland Campaign. Eaton, who had seen years of hard service, would survive both the wound and the war - many of his friends in the regiment were not as lucky. A second article read: "Mathew Glendening, of this town, returned home on furlough last Saturday. He was wounded at the Battle of Burgesses Farm on the 27th October and was taken prisoner on the 28th, carried to Richmond and kept three months and eight days, when he was parolled, and returned home on a 30 days furlough."[432] For nearly half his short time in the Union Army, Glendening lay wounded in the Confederate's notorious Libby Prison, but he also had the good fortune to come out of the Civil War alive.

Another soldier, Traverse City's Ora E. Clark, sent a letter to his former employer, Perry Hannah, describing conditions in the part of Alabama where he served. He wrote: "I am in Decatur, Ala., or rather what was Decatur before the rebellion broke out and fire and sword had laid waste this once happy and peaceful land. Decatur was once a nice thriving town of four or five thousand inhabitants, but to-day lies one vast heap of ruins. There are but two or three buildings now standing and those are used for officers headquarters; this is strictly a military post. The country for miles around is laid waste, both houses and fences have been swept away by fire, and the ruin and desolation every where meet the eye of the beholder."[433]

In contrast, the *Grand Traverse Herald* ran an associated article on Hannah's lumbering operation that described an area and an economy that flourished uninterrupted during the Civil War. It said: "Hannah, Lay & Co. have broken up their lumber camps and the men are now engaged in running the logs down the Boardman River. They have cut logs enough the past winter to make fifteen million feet of sawed lumber, which will be manufactured here and shipped to Chicago between the months of May and December. When the present stock of logs is converted into lumber it will make one hundred million feet that they have manufactured at Traverse City within the last twelve years. One unaccustomed to the business can hardly imagine the vast pile of lumber this would make."[434] While cordwood cut from Leelanau's ancient hardwood forests had propelled Northport into the position of lead harbor town in Northern Michigan, it was lumber sawn from stands of Boardman River white pine that was helping build rival Traverse City into its equal. Both Grand Traverse towns were thriving and bore no physical scars from the war, while whole sections of the South lay in ruins.

With Grand Traverse harbors frozen shut until April, articles in the *Herald* from the 'outside' continued to run at least a week behind news in the making. Railroads and telegraphs had brought rapid communication to cities on the Atlantic coast and along the southern Great Lakes, but in the winter of 1865, ice and snow still had the effect of isolating Grand Traverse Country. For this reason, Lincoln's inaugural address of March 4 did not appear in the *Herald* until March 14. In the speech, the President presented his retrospective on the war, saying: "Four years ago, all thoughts were anxiously directed to an impending civil war. All dreaded it; all sought to avoid it…Both parties deprecated war, but one of them would make war rather than let the nation survive, and, the other would accept war rather than let it perish, and the war came. One-eighth of the whole population were colored slaves, not distributed generally over the Union, but localized in the Southern part of it. These slaves constituted a peculiar and powerful interest. All knew that this interest was somehow the cause of the war…

"Neither party expected for the war the magnitude or the duration which it has already attained. Neither anticipated that the cause of the conflict might cease…even before the conflict itself might cease…Both read the same Bible and pray to the same God, each invokes his aid against the other. It may seem strange that any man should dare to take a just God's assistance in wringing their bread from the sweat of other men's faces. But let us judge not, that we not be judged…

"Fondly we do hope, fervently we do pray, that this mighty scourge of war may speedily pass away; yet, if God wills that it continue until all the wealth piled by the bondsman's 250 years of unrequited toil shall be sunk, and every drop of blood drawn with the lash shall be paid by another drawn by the sword, as was said three thousand years ago, so still it must be said that the judgments of the Lord are true and righteous altogether; with malice toward none, and charity for all.

"With firmness in the right, as God gives us to see the right, let us strive on to finish the work we are in, to bind up the nation's wounds, and care for him who shall have borne the battle, and for his widow and his orphans – to do all which may achieve and cherish a just and lasting peace among ourselves and with all nations."[435]

The medical supply boat *Planter* unloads at the General Hospital wharf on the Appomattox River. *Library of Congress*

Many scholars consider April 1865 the most significant month in American history - the culminating act in a play that determined the fate of the United States. During the month, Americans experienced the swings of joy and heart-break on a national scale as rarely felt before or since. On April 1, General Lee sent all the men he could spare from the Richmond defenses to attack Federal positions southwest of the city at a place called Five Forks. The Rebel General desperately hoped for a victory that would revitalize the Confederacy. General George Pickett of Gettysburg fame led the attack of the tattered and half-starved Rebel army, and in a replay of the 1863 battle in Pennsylvania, his charge was repulsed with great loss. Pickett's advance had been beaten back by General Custer's Michigan Cavalry Brigade, which had just arrived after sacking the

Shenandoah Valley. William Novotny of Grand Traverse and the 7th Michigan Cavalry was wounded during the day's fighting.

General Grant knew that Confederate forces defending Richmond were now stretched hopelessly thin and on April 2 he ordered the Union Army to attack two key fortifications along the Petersburg line. By late afternoon, following the type of vicious, close-in combat that had become the hallmark of Virginia battles, the Union Army drove the Rebels from their entrenchments. Lee's soldiers began to withdraw from the Petersburg earthworks they had stubbornly held for ten months. The fall of the Confederate capital was imminent. The *Herald* wrote: "Deep gloom pervades Richmond, and everyone seems to feel the day of reckoning has come."[436] In an 1861 *Herald* article, Bates had correctly predicted: "The whole weight of the struggle is to fall upon Virginia, and her soil is to be the scene of bloody strife." Four years later, many of the most beautiful and productive places in the South's leading state had been reduced to charred ruins, and its army had been decimated.

Confederate President Jefferson Davis was attending Sunday services in Richmond when he received a message from General Lee saying that he could no longer protect the city. The shaken Davis left the church and later fled further south. Throughout the day, Union soldiers saw the distant smoke and the flash of explosions and knew something big was going on behind Rebel lines. The rampant rumor that Lee was giving up on the Petersburg front could be true, but the men had heard this many times before, only to see months of more bloodshed. But now the word was coming down from the highest ranks, and cheers rang out along the trenches as each unit received the news. However, a regiment of skirmishers would have to go out and see if the Confederates had indeed abandoned their positions. As was often the case during the past year of fighting in Virginia, the deadly honor fell to the 1st Michigan Sharp Shooters.

Several hours before dawn on April 3, the remaining Sharp Shooters crawled out of their defenses and made their way toward the Confederate works. For many dreary months, orders to cross the ground they now covered had often been a death sentence. Only the night before, an assault against the same positions resulted in several casualties in the Michigan regiment. Veteran Northport Sharp Shooters Payson Wolfe and Wallace Woolsey again took their places on the thin blue line and raced toward the entrenched Confederates. Each had charged Rebel defenses many times in the last year and escaped uninjured. Both knew there were only so many times you could be so lucky.

The Sharp Shooters broke into a run as they crossed the last hundred yards of open ground. With powder and shot in desperately short supply, the Rebels had the habit of waiting until the last second to release their deadly volleys. The Michigan men could only hope that the minie balls they were sure would come would somehow miss their mark. But in a moment, the dreaded invisible line had been passed, and the Sharp Shooters charged unharmed into the empty earthworks. The Confederates were gone.

The Sharp Shooters realized the way to Petersburg was open before them. The regiment had the chance to be the first to enter the city that for the last ten months had been the impenetrable symbol of Confederate power. What only minutes before had been a resigned charge towards possible death now became a sprint toward glory. As they neared Petersburg, the mayor and several other influential citizens met the Sharp Shooters and surrendered, asking that what little was left standing be spared. A detachment of the riflemen raced toward city hall and hung their flag from its bell tower. The regiment that had suffered so terribly over the last year in Virginia had made its last charge.

The parade of Union soldiers that marched through Petersburg in the hours that followed cheered at the sight of the Sharp Shooter's colors flying over the city and then moved on toward Richmond. The soldiers in the Michigan regiment were posted as guards in Petersburg, and those who survived the hard year of fighting intact began to dream of making it home. The *Grand Traverse Herald* praised the soldiers who had secured Petersburg, writing: "Wherever Michigan regiments are stationed they gain the respect and confidence of the people. We notice that the citizens of Petersburg have petitioned that the brigade containing the 2d Michigan Infantry and 1st Sharpshooters be detailed as Provost guard of the city."[437] The days of fighting for two Michigan regiments were over. Many others had not been so lucky, for in the first three days of April 1865, 20,000 more American soldiers were added to the casualty rolls of the Civil War.

Since the paper's founding, every issue of the *Grand Traverse Herald* had promoted the most radical ideas of the emerging Republican Party. In 1858, discussions about the abolition of slavery and a "new birth of freedom" in the nation made people in Grand Traverse uncomfortable, to say the least. The worldly New Yorker Morgan Bates was ahead of his time when he wrote in the first issue of the *Herald*, "In politics we admit no such word as Neutrality. We hate slavery in all its forms and conditions, and can have no fellowship or compromise with it."

Six years later, Northern armies had destroyed the institution of slavery and much of the South in the process, at the cost of 600,000 lives and counting. The radical Republican values Bates espoused had made it to the mainstream, and Northern Michigan voters now embraced his paper's positions in lopsided numbers. The *Herald's* constant Republican drumbeat, and the fact it had no real competition anywhere in the northern Lower Peninsula, had relentlessly shaped

Ruins around Tredegar Iron Works in Richmond, April 1865. *Library of Congress*

public opinion in Grand Traverse in favor of Lincoln and the war. Bates's efforts on behalf of the Republican cause did not go unnoticed, and in 1868 he was elected Lt. Governor of Michigan.

Union resolve was paying off. The end of the crippling conflict was in sight, and the United States would resume its course with a new set of values. Looking forward to peace, President Lincoln now preached forgiveness, national healing, and reunion with rebellious States under the most favorable terms. Most everyone in Grand Traverse looked forward to an end in the fighting and to the nation being restored. Then, on the afternoon of April 3 – the same day Republican candidates swept the Grand Traverse area elections – Richmond fell to Union forces. Lee's battered Army of Northern Virginia, which had repeatedly repelled superior Union forces from their home state and for the last year fought the mightiest army on earth to a stalemate, had finally cracked under the weight of the Northern war machine. George Smith learned of the victory ten days after the fact on the Northport docks and wrote: "News came tonight that Richmond was taken…we hope it is true."[438]

The next day, the *Grand Traverse Herald* confirmed the news from Richmond. The paper said: "The *Chicago Tribune* of the 4th sends forth these ringing, thrilling utterances: The Rebel citadel has fallen. Richmond is ours! The news sped through the country yesterday on the wings of lightning, and lighted up the nation with a blaze of glory. Four years ago this month the rebellion was inaugurated at Charleston, in the smoke of cannon hurling shot and shell at Fort Sumter. Four years ago this month loyal men vowed eternal war on the traitors who dared to drag the stars and stripes in the dust. Four years ago this month the nation entered into a solemn covenant, never to lay down its arms till the very nest of treason should be reached and crushed. The vow has been fulfilled, the covenant kept…Of all the places hateful to God and man, Richmond has been, for four long years, the most abhorred and detested. Not even Charleston, with all its crimes, has been so odious. Apart from its distinction as the rebel capital, it has so embodied the spirit of secession, its press has been so infuriated and its people so possessed with the devil of rebellion, that no other spot on earth can bear comparison with it for all the distinguishing marks of abomination. Upon it has been centered the animosity of every loyal heart; against it have been directed the most powerful armies of the Union; in its defense have been collected the utmost resources and ability of the Confederacy; around it have fallen thousands of the bravest and best of the land; while in its fate, it may be said that the whole world has felt an absorbing interest.

"Richmond had fallen and a day of jubilee has come to the whole nation. We do well to rejoice, for this is the grandest event that ever happened to us as a people. It makes little difference which way the remnant of Lee's army has gone. If Richmond could not be held, nothing can be. The struggle may continue for a brief period, but it will be a hopeless and feeble contest. The heart has been reached. The rebellion is among the things of the past. From the ashes of the rebel capital will rise a new life to the United States of America. Freedom will henceforth be the crown and glory of the Republic. The golden age of America will date from 3d of April, 1865, when the flag of the Union was restored upon the battlements of Richmond…We have passed through a trial, which no nation before has encountered and survived."[439]

As Morgan Bates had predicted at the outbreak of the Civil War, Virginia paid dearly for its central role in the rebellion, with its people now brought to their knees. The *Herald* wrote: "The people of Virginia are in a very impover-ished condition, and thousands of them continue to be fed by our commissaries, to keep them from starving. Citizens and civil officials are rapidly coming in to take the oath of allegiance at Richmond."[440]

While the *Herald* portrayed the fall of Richmond as a joyful event, George Smith more accurately reflected the mood of the North as it witnessed the final collapse of the Confederacy. He wrote: "We raised the pole and hoisted [the flag] PM in honor of the victory but made no further demonstrations. There is no enthusiasm."[441] For Smith and many others, the length and the cost of the Civil War made it hard to celebrate its end. Almost every family had experienced its misery first hand, and there were still hundreds of thousands of soldiers far

A man stands among the ruins of his home in Richmond, 1865. *Library of Congress*

from home, their fate unknown. It was a terrible time to be fighting on the front, with peace so close, and the reality of going home so near. The potential for death in the war's last hours seemed intolerably cruel. But the dreadful tone of the conflict had been set over four long years, and its deadly closing costs were yet to be paid in full. Grand Traverse soldiers were not spared in the expense.

General Lee made one final attempt to fight his way out of Virginia, attacking the Union Army at a place called Farmville on April 7. The 26th Michigan Infantry was out ahead of the main force, as they had been through most of Virginia's fiercest battles. By now, the Lakeshore Tigers had earned the reputation as "the best skirmish regiment in the corps," an honorable but deadly accolade. During the first week of April in Virginia, with the end of the Civil War in sight, the 26th Michigan lost "in killed and wounded, about sixty, or more than one-fourth of its number present for duty."[442]

In Lee's last assault, George Allen of Traverse City, who had served with Company A of the Lakeshore Tigers since William Voice had been chosen as its sergeant in 1862, was shot in the head and killed instantly. Charles Clark of Northport, the seasoned veteran who still hurt from wounds suffered at Spotsylvania the year before, also died in the April 7 battle. The two Grand Traverse men had the terrible luck of being among the very last of hundreds of thousands of American soldiers who died in Virginia during the Civil War. By the end of the day, aided by their sacrifice, Union forces had finally trapped Lee's fabled army in a no-win situation at Appomattox, leaving him only one alternative.

On the same day the *Herald* hit the streets with the news of the fall of Richmond, boats brought even better news to the Northport docks. Smith wrote: "Lee surrendered his army to Gen Grant last Sabbath. He had evacuated Richmond but could not get away. Sheridan had captured 18,000 of his men." Navigation season had burst into full swing and the news of Lee's surrender was only five days old when it reached the suddenly busy harbor. General Grant announced the historic event in a telegram to E.M. Stanton, Secretary of War, which read: "General Lee surrendered the army of Northern Virginia this afternoon upon the terms proposed by myself."

The defeated General Lee had chosen to surrender rather than prolong the struggle through guerilla warfare. Throughout the Virginia countryside, Rebel soldiers followed their commander's wishes and laid down their arms. Lee, whose revered leadership had nearly carried the Confederacy to independence through military victory, had in defeat taken a great step toward national unity and healing. In the meantime, however, there were many fresh wounds in the making as the final death notices worked their way back home, and one devastating scene left to be played in the national tragedy.

The last functioning Southern army, some 40,000 men strong, was still loose in the Carolinas under command of Sherman's long-time adversary, General Joseph E. Johnston. Linking up with Johnston had been Lee's goal when he was ultimately cornered in Virginia. Sherman's force, which included a total of five Michigan infantry regiments, was now chasing the battered Rebels through North Carolina and closing in on Raleigh, one of the last Confederate state capitals still in the South's possession. When the capital fell into Union hands on April 14, General Johnston saw the futility of any more bloodshed and contacted Sherman about terms of surrender. It would have been a joyous day in the North if President Lincoln had not chosen to see a play at Ford's Theatre that evening.

On the morning of April 20, Northport's Reverend Smith wrote: "Very hard thunder showers through last night, more water fell I think, than I ever knew in the same time. The country seemed to be flooded." The same morning, Catherine Miller of Leland mailed a letter to her husband John Miller, the former Leelanau County Treasurer who was then fighting in North Carolina with the 15th Michigan Infantry. Catherine's words confirmed Smith's report on the weather and spoke of conditions in Grand Traverse from the perspective of a war-weary mother. Her letter, dated April 20, 1865, said: "Dear and beloved husband:

"I will send you these few lines to let you know we are pretty well…the children health is well and I wish your health would be the same as theirs. The grapes is beginning to grow nice and the bud on the peach tree are coming out a little. We had a thunder storm last night…rane all night…we got a five quart pan full of water under the stove pipe so you can guess how much it did rane.

"If you could hear our little John read and spell and say his prayers you would be glad. Now I begin to think that you will come back, the news is so good at present. I have told the children that you was coming home pretty soon and they commenced to jump and sing and you would stay here all the time and they was so glad. We have not had a boat yet. It is very lonesome. The place has not been so poor as it is now. Most every body is without meet or flower or butter or lard. My best wishes to you Dearest Husband, our respect to you and Napolian. I remane your wife for life, Catherine Miller."

The news of the fall of Richmond allowed Catherine Miller to "begin to think" that her husband John would soon return alive to Leland. From her choice of words it was clear that she was aware that many other Grand Traverse wives and mothers had not been so fortunate. Though the strains of war were making life tough back in Leland, for the moment the signs of spring and good news from the front let her hope that the bleak time may soon be over. For the first time since her husband left for the war the previous fall, Catherine Miller felt optimistic about the future. She would have shuddered to hear that the "Napolian" to whom she sent her respects – the 15th Michigan Infantry soldier Napoleon Paulus of Leland – had been wounded in North Carolina on April 12, 1865. But there was much worse news to come later that day.

Catherine Miller's letter also addressed the Grand Traverse region's continuing dependence on water for its connection to the outside world. While the *Herald* reported that navigation season had been open for two weeks, the big, steam powered ships had yet to stop at Leland, prolonging the isolation of winter in the Lake Michigan town. However, Catherine Miller, and the whole of Grand Traverse Country, would once again be reminded that during the Civil War, the news carried on the Great Lakes water highway was often a cause of immense sorrow.

On the afternoon of April 20th, Reverend Smith wrote: "The *City of Madison* came 1 PM Rose's Dock…it brought Chicago papers of the 18th. President Lincoln, the Benefactor of mankind, is dead, shot by a copperhead. The ball entered the back of his head at the base of the skull & passed through the frontal bone of the right eye. It is the most awful calamity to every loyal heart. He was shot in Ford's Theatre 1/2 past 9 last Friday eve by J. Wilkes a Tragedian, an aider and abettor of Jeff Davis. Sec Seward & Son were near killed, perhaps will die, by Surrat."[443] The next day, Smith continued: "Spent great part of the day reading details of President Lincoln's death." Among his sources was the latest edition of the *Grand Traverse Herald*, which ran a piece titled "The Nation in Mourning. *President Lincoln Assassinated.*" It said: "Dexter and Noble's vessel arrived in Elk Rapids on Tuesday morning bringing the terrible news of the assassination of President Lincoln…In the midst of our rejoicing over the surrender of Lee and his army, we are stricken down with a grief too deep for utterance. A nation is in mourning for its honored and beloved chief."

While Lincoln had pushed for a gentle and forgiving reunion with the defeated Confederacy, his assassination turned many against the idea, including Morgan Bates. The enraged editor continued: "Treason has done its worst; but when the heart and brain recover from the stunning effect of this terrible blow all Rebeldom may look for stern retribution. This foul murder will be avenged. The Northern heart is fired. Every loyal man is a "Lincoln Avenger.""

The Southern Rebels and their Northern aiders and abettors are treacherous in everything and can be trusted in nothing. Their parole of honor is a rope of sand." A few days later, Reverend Smith wrote: "The nation is greatly agitated & afflicted in the death of our beloved President." The same week, Union quartermaster John Boizard sent a letter to his wife in Glen Arbor describing the reaction in Lincoln's home state: "The whole country is placed in solemnity. All buildings in the City of Chicago are decorated with Crape. Old men weep in the streets, men appear to be infuriated with the dastardly act. J. Wilkes Booth, the actor, is supposed to be the murdered."[444] The hope for a benign national reunion had died along with Lincoln.

The lead editorial of the April 28 *Grand Traverse Herald* continued with the theme of vengeance over reconciliation. This time editor Bates printed a sermon by his twin brother and noted orator Reverend Merritt Bates, who said: "The murder of the President...will give a shock to the whole civilized world. If it was instigated by the Rebels of the South, it was the most short-sighted madness and folly, as well as the most horrid wickedness, of which they could have been guilty. If it was the result of a plot formed by northern traitors, as we strongly suspect it was, it will recoil upon them with a force that will crush them to pumice. History does not record a fouler, meaner act. Our grief is so profound and our indignation so intense, that we hardly dare to write upon the subject... To all who have shared in the infernal plot, whether Southern Rebels or Northern traitors, we would say, in the name of every loyal man, beware. If you are discovered, a fearful retribution awaits you."[445]

Reverend Merritt Bates did not hesitate to portray Lincoln as a divine instrument, a man sent from above to guide the nation in crisis. He had, after all, risen from obscurity to take on the Presidency just as the nation disintegrated. For four years, he suffered at the hands of his critics, his generals, and from the weight of the death and destruction the Civil War had brought. Yet Lincoln was able to elevate the conflict to a battle between good and evil, and cleanse the nation of its original sin of slavery. In addition, the President had been shot on Good Friday, only five days after completing his earthly mission of leading a newly-defined nation to victory. Ironically, the instant beatification of Lincoln in death belied the fact that only a half year before, his reelection was very much in doubt.

Reverend Bates continued: "But why was not the arm of the assassin paralyzed before the pistol could be fired? We believe there is a Power which could have done this. More, we believe that four years of the life of the President was preserved amidst imminent and constant peril, by a special Providence. "Every man," says one, "is immortal till his work is done."[446] Reverend Smith's Sunday sermon in Northport also focused on Lincoln's assassination. He wrote: "I preached in reference to the death of the President…it was a solemn time – tears were freely shed."

Another April 28 article in the *Herald* revealed the breadth of emotion sweeping the North. The paper wrote: "The *Terre Haute Express* says that a Mrs. Dunbar of that city said on Monday that she was glad of President Lincoln's death and were she near his grave would take pleasure in dancing on it. This was more than the loyal women of the neighborhood could bear, and accordingly on Tuesday a dozen or more went to her house and forced her to take in hand a flag draped in mourning and proceed up town shouting at intervals, "Hurrah for the Union." The ladies formed in line, and as the novel procession passed through the principal streets, no little commotion was caused. The ladies were allowed to proceed without let or hinderance, and the universal verdict was, "served her right."

On May 3, John Boizard wrote his wife in Glen Arbor: "Booth, the Murderer, has been killed by a Sergeant of New York Cavalry. They fired the barn, arrested his accomplice, and exterminated the Murderer. President Lincoln's remains will arrive here sometime on Monday, and all business will cease…Gen'l Johnston has surrendered all the forces of Georgia and South Carolina, and there is another Army (Rebel) west of the Mississippi which will have to give up."

Before the assassination of Lincoln, the momentous news carried in the May 5 *Herald* of the surrender of the last sizeable Confederate army would have brought great joy to the North. Now the story was masked in the sadness brought on by the Lincoln assassination. The paper said: "The official bulletin from the War Department brings the intelligence from Gen. Grant of Johnston's surrender to Sherman under the same terms that Lee received." However, the enraged Northern public was no longer in the mood for reconciliation, and they rebuked the friendly terms Sherman offered the Rebels. The *Herald* wrote: "A new and somewhat startling development comes from Sherman's army, indicating that Gen. Sherman had opened and consummated negotiations of armistice with Johnson, on terms which seemed to have received a decided negative from the President and Cabinet. The official terms will be found in our dispatches. They are modeled after those which Grant gave to Lee, but are much more liberal in their provisions, and admit of a greater latitude in construction. They would have scarcely met the approval of the loyal people two weeks ago, and now their condemnation will be sharp and decisive."[447] General Sherman, who was hated throughout the South for his March to the Sea, now found himself a villain in the North for being generous toward the vanquished Rebels - a position Lincoln himself had promoted before his assassination.

The *Herald* continued: "Gen. Grant, upon reaching Raleigh, notified Johnston that the armistice between himself and Sherman was annulled, and gave him until Wednesday last to surrender or fight. Johnston replied that he would surrender if Jeff Davis and other rebel leaders might leave the country. As Gen. Grant had previously informed him that his jurisdiction did not extend to civil matters, of course this condition was strictly gratuitous, and not to be entertained for an instant. The surrender embraces all the rebel forces from…North Carolina and Georgia…East of the Mississippi River the rebellion is dead."[448]

The Lincoln assassination again focused national attention on the United States border with Canada. In an article titled "A Gigantic Conspiracy," the *Herald* recounted an article in the *New York Times* which "urges strongly that the nest of rebel traitors in Canada…should be broken up." The paper said: "There is very little room to doubt that the assassination of President Lincoln was but one incident of a conspiracy which they devised and set in motion." If there was any provable link between the Lincoln assassination and Confederates based in Canada, given the agitated state of the North, an armed invasion of Canada may well have occurred. No such link was found, but the Confederate hijacking of the propeller *Philo Parsons* on Lake Erie in 1864 underscored the need for a modern naval vessel to represent United States interests on the Great Lakes. An article in the *Grand Traverse Herald* titled "New Gun Boat for the Lakes" said: "The *Buffalo Commercial Advertiser* learns that…a shipbuilder of Brooklyn…is preparing to commence the construction there of a new gunboat for the Government."[449] The ship was a Lincoln legacy, part of his plan to win the war on all fronts. Should the enemy again attempt to cause trouble on the Great Lakes, they would be met with the newest in naval weaponry developed during the Civil War. Fortunately, there were no more Rebel incursions from Canada, and in time peace along the international border again prevailed.

Another *Herald* story described the reaction to Lincoln's murder by the 10th Michigan Cavalry, the regiment with a large contingent of Grand Traverse volunteers now serving in Tennessee. The paper said: "A letter from the 10th Michigan cavalry, stationed near Knoxville, speaks of the sorrow the troops felt upon hearing of the death of President Lincoln. There were sixty minute guns fired at sunrise, with half hour guns till sunset. A private of the regiment named Kenedy was arrested and sent to military prison, for saying he was glad the President was dead, and that he had prayed for it for some time. Previous to his arrest the boys went to his cabin, and pulled it down, nearly burying him in the ruins."

Although the 10th Michigan Cavalry had seen nearly continuous fighting over the last year, the final line of the article pointed to the fact that it was the scourge of disease, not combat, that struck the regiment the hardest. It said: "A new recruit, Franklin H. Mosher, Company I, died in hospital on the 15th of chill fever."[450] It is possible to trace the 10th Michigan's movements through the border states of Kentucky and Tennessee by noting the places where Grand Traverse soldiers died of various ailments. Volunteer J.H. Turner of Traverse City died in January 1864 when an epidemic swept through their training camp in Kentucky. The lives of David Phelps and Sgt. William Morgan came to an end in Knoxville in March and May respectively. Elliot Wright of Leelanau died at Strawberry Plains in June, while David Beebee of Antrim was struck down by illness in Knoxville the day before Christmas, 1864. By the war's end six months later, the 10th Michigan Cavalry had lost a total of 31 men to combat and 240 to disease.

One last disaster awaited Michigan troops making their way home in April 1865. In an article headlined "Blowing up of a Steamer on the Mississippi – 1,300 or 1,400 Lives Lost," the *Herald* documented another terrible turn of events in the saga of Union soldiers recently freed from Southern prisons. The paper said: "The steamer *Sultana*, from New Orleans the evening of [April]

Soldiers crowd the decks of the *Sultana* on April 26, 1865, the day before she exploded on the Mississippi River near Memphis, resulting in the worst maritime accident in American history. *Library of Congress*

21st, arrived at Vicksburg with her boilers leaking badly. She remained there for thirty hours, repairing, and took on 1,996 Union soldiers and 35 officers, lately released from Cahawba and Andersonville prisons. She arrived at Memphis last evening. After cooling, she proceeded. At 3 in the morning, when seven miles up, she blew up, immediately taking fire and burning to the water's edge. Of 2,156 souls aboard, not more than 750 have been rescued. Five hundred of the rescued are now in hospitals. Two or three hundred, uninjured, are at the Soldier's Home. Captain Marston, of the *Sultana*, is supposed to be lost.

"At 4 o'clock this morning, the river in front of Memphis was covered with soldiers struggling for life. Many were badly scalded. Boats immediately went to their rescue, and are still engaged in picking them up. General Washburn immediately organized a board of officers to investigate the matter. They are now at work doing so."[451]

The investigation found that the *Sultana* was carrying more than five times the passengers than she was built for. To add to the danger, her machinery had been pushed to the limit due to the strong spring currents, and a hasty patch had been made to her boiler only days before the explosion. History is unable to give an exact figure of the soldiers lost in the *Sultana* disaster, for the movement of Union prisoners released from Southern camps was neither organized nor well documented, and it is impossible to say how many soldiers longing to get home crowded her decks. However, an estimated 250 Michigan soldiers were aboard the vessel, a number of them survivors of Andersonville. There were still 1st Michigan Sharp Shooters unaccounted for after their release from the Georgia prison, and this latest piece of news carried by the *Herald* must have cut deeply into the hopes of those awaiting word of the fate of a loved one.

In an article the following week titled "Resources of the Country," the *Grand Traverse Herald* wrote: "Now that the tumult of war is over, and thousands of our soldiers will soon be returning to their formal peaceful avocations, a wonderful development of the resources of the country will commence. The manufacturing interests, protected and stimulated by the high tariff, will take a fresh start. The mining business will open with renewed vigor. The agricultural districts all over the country will be more extensively cultivated, and new regions in the West and on the Pacific will give up their latent wealth profusely to the labor and industry of another race of agriculturalists – our disabled veterans. We shall produce henceforth more cotton, tobacco, rice, children, sugar, grain, gold, patriotism, silver, iron, and coal than ever before, and will exhibit, to the wonder of the world, more extraordinary results from our works of peace than ever the grand military and naval resources which war has developed."[452]

Signs of future conflict with Indian nations to the west of the Great Lakes again surfaced just as the fighting between North and South ended. The *Herald* said: "There is some show of a renewal of Indian troubles in Minnesota. A family of four persons named Jewett were murdered in Blue Earth county...the scene of former Indian massacres, by an Indian raiding party."[453] It was a bad time for Indians to resist westward expansion into their homelands, for the Civil War had just trained millions of soldiers in the art of killing. In the decades that followed, cavalry Generals Sheridan and Custer, would lead some of these veterans against the Native peoples of the West in a war of conquest, as the violence of the Civil War moved out onto the plains.

Soon after the surrender of Confederate armies, the Federal government began to dismantle the vast Union war machine. The *Grand Traverse Herald* wrote: "The North Atlantic Squadron has been reduced from 30 to 20 vessels, and the other squadrons are being similarly reduced. Chiefs of bureaus, commandants of navy yards, etc., have been ordered to commence immediately the curtailment of their expenses to the lowest point possible. All resignations of officers tendered are at once accepted, and a large proportion of the force employed is being discharged, and the vessels laid up. There will be no further accumulation of ordnance or other supplies, and contracts for the same are being revoked." Quartermaster John Boizard wrote that the "Government has issued a Grand order to reduce the force of Employees, also stop recruiting for volunteers. Many offices will be dropped as the war is coming down to a point."[454] The most powerful military machine on earth began to contract in light of the hard-won peace.

On May 23 and 24, the victorious armies of Generals Grant and Sherman marched in the Grand Review through the streets of Washington, DC. The two-day event was one of the great displays of military might in all of human history. People throughout the North flocked into the capital city to honor the soldiers, both living and dead, who had sacrificed much for the cause. On May 23, veterans of the brutal Virginia campaigns marched past the reviewing stands. The miles of hardened veterans passing by included the 1st, 20th, and 26th Michigan Infantry Regiments, the 1st, 5th, 6th, and 7th Regiments of the Michigan Cavalry Brigade, and the 1st Michigan Sharp Shooters, and the 1st New York Light Artillery, all with Grand Traverse soldiers in their ranks. The next

Grand Traverse soldiers in the 15th and 26th Michigan Infantry and the 1st Michigan Sharp Shooters, along with the Michigan Cavalry Brigade and other Michigan regiments, joined in the Grand Review in Washington, May 23 and 24, 1865. *Library of Congress*

day, the honor fell to General Sherman's soldiers, including the 15th Michigan Infantry Regiment. It was the last hurrah of the terrible yet nation-defining conflict. For many people in the North, the Grand Review marked the end of the Civil War.

On June 4, the 26th Michigan Infantry was mustered out in Alexandria, Virginia, 13 months after they had marched from that city into the lethal Overland Campaign. In nearly three years of service, 280 of its soldiers had died, including 118 killed or mortally wounded in battle, with 162 more struck down by disease. Over ten percent of the regiment's fatalities were Grand Traverse men. But even this long awaited day of joy was tainted by the sadness of the death of another Lakeshore Tiger. As the survivors of the 26th celebrated the end of their enlistments and packed for the trip home, Henry Budd of Company A, who was still suffering from wounds received in action in May, 1864, died in a New York hospital of disease. He left a wife and nine young children in Northport to mourn his loss. Nearly two months later Reverend Smith wrote: "Word came last night that Mr Budd died of Small pox…on Davis Island Hospital NY Harbor. Mrs Budd is much afflicted."[455]

The *Grand Traverse Herald* praised the resilience the nation displayed now that the war had ended, writing: "The rapidity with which the work of pacification of the South has gone on is marvelous. The world never witnessed anything like it. The historian searches in vain for a parallel of war so gigantic so suddenly arrested as that which from our country has just emerged. Three months ago the Rebellion was powerful. Vast armies confronted our forces in the field. The insurgent capital was defended by an apparently impregnable wall of fire. The Confederate leaders scouted the idea of peace on any other terms than that of the recognition of the independence of the South. The most hopeful of us believed that the war would last at least through the summer, while the Southern country would long after be infested by roving bands of guerillas.

"But what a marvelous change have a few weeks wrought! The war is ended. The insurgent armies have disappeared as if by enchantment. The old Flag floats from every State house and fortress from the James to the Rio Grande. The Rebel capital is once more a Union city. Every vestige of the Rebel Government has been swept away as by the bosom of destruction. The strongholds in which Treason entrenched itself have all been wrested by our gallant armies. The supremacy of the Government had been vindicated over every foot of Southern soil.

"And not only has the power of the rebellion been broken, but its ruins are rapidly disappearing. Not only have the Southern armies melted like ice before the sun, but the fragments into which they crumbled have disappeared. There is an absolute peace in Virginia to-day as there is in New York. Hardly a guerilla band of any importance is known from Maryland to Texas. With the exception of the isolated bodies of desperadoes, whose mission is not so much war as plunder, the South is as outwardly pacific to-day as it was before the Rebellion broke out.

"This result, so much the more gratifying because unexpected, speaks well for the American character. It naturally gravitates toward order. It revolts against anarchy and disorder. It instinctively takes refuge under the shield of established institutions. Demoralized as our Southern brethren have become by Slavery, they scorn to become mere robbers and guerillas, and hasten to avail themselves of the fruits of peace. Satisfied that the rebellion is a failure, they philosophically bow to the force of circumstances, and accept their fate like sensible men."[456]

Joshua Middleton described the "old house" in a July 1865 letter to his sister. Joshua is standing with his family at the far right of the photograph. *Donna Allington Collection*

By July 11, Lakeshore Tiger Joshua Middleton was back in Northport working on his farm. A letter to his sister on this date showed he was trying to leave the horror of war behind. He wrote: "I was very anxious…to help put in all the crops we could. I wanted to see if I could buy me a team of some sort…Cattle are scarce here and men are inclined to war prices yet. If only I knew what such cattle are selling for I could tell where I could do the best. I want a good solid team and such a one is hard to find here.

"We will have a few apples this season and eight tame cherries, if they do not drop off – they were only set out this spring. There will be plenty of berries. Raspberries are just coming in. If you have any garden seed to spare, save it for me…Beman has been chopping east of the house in the Birch, for to make me a meadow. We cut all sorts of wood for Propellers now. They are not so particular as they used to be. We get 87 ½ [cents] for chopping wood."[457] In the correspondence, Middleton spoke of two elements of the Civil War economy in Grand Traverse that faced different futures. The first – the fruit of the cherry tree – would sustain the region in the coming centuries. The second – cordwood fuel – would rapidly decline as near-shore stands of hardwood forest gave way to farms and towns and steam-powered ships changed over to coal.

Middleton and his fellow soldiers resumed their lives in a United States that had put the worst of its demons to rest. The course of the country had been indelibly altered, steered by blood and law closer to its founding principle that "all men are created equal." The Grand Traverse men returning from the war had also been transformed. They had witnessed how the curse of sectional rivalry had nearly devoured the United States. Many had fought in the worst battles in American history and seen friends fall by their sides. They had traveled across vast stretches of the country, mixed in battle with men of different states, marched through hundreds of big cities and small towns, and helped secure the very survival of the nation. All told, nearly three million American soldiers had come to know a United States that lay beyond the comforts of their homes, and their vision of the country now included the faraway places they had experienced. All had been tempered by the fires of battle, and a changed nation and people began to rise from the ashes of the American Civil War.

On July 28, 1865, the remnants of the 1st Michigan Sharp Shooters boarded a train in Washington for their trip home. Their regimental history recorded that during their two years of service, over 280 Sharp Shooters perished - 120 killed in action, 100 of disease, and 60 in Confederate prison camps. The records of Indian casualties in the Sharp Shooters are sketchy, but it appears that the Natives of Company K suffered the worst losses. At least 24 of its soldiers were killed in combat or died in Confederate prisons and more than 30 were wounded. More were victims of disease. All told, very few Indians in Company K made it home to Michigan unscathed.

Two days before the 1st Michigan Sharp Shooters arrived back in Jackson, Reverend Smith wrote: "Louis Muskoquan came yesterday with his family. He was released from Andersonville prison the 26 of March – was on the *Sultana* when she blew up. He seems to have lived thro almost everything, it is wonderful that he is alive."[458] From that day forward Reverend Smith of Northport, and his counterpart Morgan Bates of the *Grand Traverse Herald*, avoided writing about the war, preferring instead to proceed on the nation's new and hard-won course. The Civil War era had come to an end.

MAP AND PHOTOGRAPH INDEX

ENDNOTES

CHAPTER 1: AMERICAN FRONTIERS

1   Arvilla Smith Diary, May 1833.
2   Although called the Northern Canal by Arvilla Smith, the official name was the Champlain Canal.
3   In 1833, the Erie Canal was commonly referred to as the Western Canal.
4   Arvilla Smith Diary, August 1833.
5   *Old Wing Mission,* Robert W. Swierenga and William Van Appledorn, p. 378.
6   Arvilla Smith Diary, 6/12/1836.
7   Arvilla Smith Diary, 10/23/1836.
8   Arvilla Smith Diary, 4/1, 4/13/1839.
9   Arvilla Smith Diary, 5/23, 6/16/1839.
10 George Smith Diary 8/1, 10/6/39.
11 George Smith Diary, 10/13/1839.
12 Arvilla Smith Diary, 12/29/1839.
13 George Smith Diary, 12/22/1839.
14 Northport, on the east coast of the Leelanau Peninsula, is three miles inside Grand Traverse Bay.
15 Arvilla Smith Diary, 3/30/1841.
16 Letter to "Mr Stuart, Sept 1, 1843."
17 Arvilla Smith Diary, 3/29/1844. Arvilla ended her diary soon after this notation.
18 George Smith Diary, 4/3, 2/26, 5/11/1849.
19 George Smith Diary, 5/15/1849.
20 George Smith Diary, 7/25/1849.
21 George Smith Diary, 9/17, 9/27, 9/30/1849. L'Arbor Crouche in Smith's Diary is now spelled L'Arbre Croche.
22 George Smith Diary, 10/6, 10/23/1849.
23 Article 4, Section 2, Clause 3 was removed from the Constitution by the 13th Amendment.
24 *Personal Memoirs of Ulysses S. Grant.,* 1886. Cosimo, Inc., New York, 2007, p. 458.
25 George Smith Diary, 2/5/1850.
26 George Smith Diary, 7/11/1850.
27 George Smith Diary, 11/12/1850.
28 George Smith Diary, 4/12/1851.
29 George Smith Dairy, 4/14/1851.
30 George Smith Diary, 7/3/1851.
31 George Smith, Northport to Rev. Samuel J. Bissell, Twinsburg, Ohio 11/17/1851
32 George Smith Diary, 4/3/1852.
33 George Smith Diary, 7/3/1852.
34 George Smith Diary, 11/30/1852.
35 www.pbs.org/wbgh
36 Millbrook, Millie D. *Twice Told Tales of Michigan and Her Soldiers in The Civil War.* Lansing: Michigan Civil War Centennial Commission, 1966.
37 Douglass, Frederick. *Narrative of the Life of Frederick Douglass, An American Slave.* Boston: Published at the Anti-Slavery Office, 1845.
38 *A History of Northern Michigan and its People,* Perry F. Powers. Lewis Publishing Co., Chicago, 1912. In 1853, the Michigan Legislature passed Act No. 34, which completed the organization of Grand Traverse County. The Act contained the clause: "The county of Leelanau is hereby erected into a township by the name of Leelanau, and the first township meeting shall be held at the home of Peter Dougherty." In effect, unorganized Leelanau County, whose boundaries at the time included all of Benzie County, assumed a township's status within Grand Traverse County.
39 George Smith Diary, 7/1/1854.
40 George Smith Diary, 4/25/1854.
41 George Smith Diary, 5/5/1854.
42 George Smith Diary, 10/7/1854.
43 George Smith Diary, 10/13/1854.
44 George Smith Diary, 3/2, 4/7, 6/13/1854.
45 George Smith Diary, 7/10, 7/15/1854.
46 George Smith used the word 'propellor,' while 'propeller' was the more common spelling.
47 George Smith Diary, 7/15/1854.
48 George Smith Diary, 12/13/1854.
49 George Smith Diary, 5/31/1855.
50 George Smith Diary, 9/11/1855.
51 *Ethnohistorical Report on the Grand Traverse Ottawas.* Dr. Richard White, Michigan State University. pp. 100-102.
52 George Smith Diary, 1/26/1856.
53 George Smith Diary, 2/19, 2/26, 2/29/1856.
54 George Smith Diary, 4/26/1856.
55 George Smith Diary, 6/17/1856. Pine River was then the name of the present day site of Charlevoix.

56   George Smith Diary, 6/23, 6/25/1856.
57   George Smith Diary, 7/20/1856.
58   George Smith Diary, 5/3/1855.
59   George Smith Diary, 7/27/1855.
60   George Smith Diary, 9/22/1855.
61   George Smith Diary, 11/14, 11/18/1856.
62   George Smith Diary, 11/19, 12/19, 2/20/1856.
63   George Smith Diary, 3/2/1857.
64   The name of the Native settlement was spelled in a variety of ways, this is the one George Smith used.
65   George Smith Diary, 5/27/1857.
66   By the early 20th century, the college had been converted to Benzonia Academy with George Catton serving as its headmaster. Here he raised his son Bruce, the Pulitzer Prize winning Civil War author.

CHAPTER 2: SEPARATE PATHS

67   President James Buchanan to Secretary of State Lewis Cass, October 24, 1857.
68   Charles Stuart served as Democratic U.S. Senator from Michigan from 1853 to 1859 and later as a colonel in the Union Army. Zachariah Chandler was a Republican who represented Michigan in the U. S. Senate from 1857-1875.
69   George Smith Diary, 5/6/1858.
70   George Smith Diary, 8/25/1858.
71   George Smith Diary, 9/26, 10/22/1858.
72   *Grand Traverse Herald,* 11/3/1858.
73   *The Traverse Region, p. 63.* H.R. Page, Chicago, 1884.
74   *History of Michigan* by Charles Moore, 1915, as quoted in the 12/10/1858 *Grand Traverse Herald.* Moore stated that "during his early newspaper experience, he [Bates] floated his printing outfit down the Ohio and Mississippi Rivers and established the *New Orleans Picayune.*" Actually it was fellow *New Yorker* reporter George Kendall who founded the *Picayune* in 1837, though Bates apparently delivered the presses.
75   *History of Michigan* by Charles Moore, p. 1128
76   GTH, 11/3/1858.
77   GTH, 5/13/1859.
78   GTH, 5/17/1867.
79   George Smith Diary, 12/3/1858.
80   GTH, 11/19/1858.
81   GTH, 11/19/1858, as compiled from the Ogdensburg *Sentinel.*
82   GTH, 2/11/1859.
83   George Smith Diary, 12/21/1858.
84   GTH, 1/7/1859.
85   GTH, 12/3/1858.
86   Battles with a least 12,000 recorded casualties.
87   GTH, 11/3/1858.
88   GTH, 6/3/1859.

89   GTH, 11/3/1858.
90   GTH, 11/26/1858.
91   GTH, 12/3/1858.
92   GTH, 12/3/1858.
93   GTH, 2/18/1859.
94   GTH, 2/4/1859.
95   GTH, 5/13/1859.
96   GTH, 5/20/1859.
97   GTH, 5/13/1859.
98   GTH, 1/21/1859. This is the only record that identifies today's Lake Leelanau as two different entities - Carp Lake to the north and Traverse Lake to the south.
99   GTH, 2/11/1859.
100   GTH, 2/11/1859.
101   The home of Reverend Peter Dougherty, which still stands today.
102   GTH, 2/18/1859.
103   GTH, 9/23/1859.
104   GTH, 11/15/1859.
105   GTH, 1/7/1859.
106   GTH, 1/7/1859.
107   GTH, 1/7/1859.
108   GTH, 7/14/1859.
109   GTH, 11/25/1859.
110   GTH, 5/20, 5/27/1859.
111   GTH, 9/16/1859.
112   GTH, 12/28/1860.
113   GTH, 4/22/1859.
114   GTH, 4/15/1859.
115   GTH, 4/29/1859.
116   GTH, 12/30/1859.
117   GTH, 12/30/1859.
118   GTH, 6/3/1859.
119   GTH, 9/12/1859 listed but needs correction, no such paper date.
120   GTH, 10/14/1859.
121   George Smith Diary, 11/11/1859.
122   George Smith Diary, 12/2/1859.
123   GTH, 12/23/1859.
124   GTH, 12/23, 12/29/1859.

CHAPTER 3: THE SOUTHERN SCARE-CROW

125   GTH, 1/6/1860.
126   GTH, 1/13/1860.
127   GTH, 1/27/1860.
128   GTH, 2/10/1860.
129   GTH, 2/24/1860.
130   GTH, 6/7/1860.
131   GTH, 3/2/1860.
132   George Smith Diary, 3/3, 4/14/1860.
133   GTH, 11/16/1860.
134   GTH, 6/7/1860.
135   GTH, 6/15/1860.
136   George Smith Diary, 5/23/1863.
137   GTH, 6/15/1860.
138   GTH, 7/6/1860.

139   GTH, 8/17/1860.
140   GTH, 5/35, 6/1, 8/24/1860.
141   George Smith Diary, 8/8/1860.
142   GTH, 6/1/1860.
143   GTH, 5/25/1860.
144   GTH, 6/1/1860 from the 5/18/1860 *Detroit Tribune*.
145   GTH, 9/28/1860.
146   GTH, 9/28/1860.
147   GTH, 8/24/1860.
148   George Smith Diary, 9/6/1860.
149   Hilton, George Woodman. Great Lakes Passenger Steamers, pp. 46-49. Stanford University Press, Stanford, CA, 2002.
150   George Smith Diary, 4/12/1859.
151   GTH, 10/14/1858; 10/4/1859.
152   GTH, 11/16/1860.
153   GTH, 11/30, 11/23/1860.
154   GTH, 12/14/1860.
155   GTH, 11/24, 12/14/1860.

CHAPTER 4: 1861 | CIVIL WAR!

156   GTH, 1/25/1861.
157   George Smith Diary, 3/18/1861.
158   GTH, 3/29/1861.
159   GTH, 3/29/1861.
160   GTH, 6/21/1861.
161   GTH, 4/26/1861.
162   *The Political History of the United States of America During the Great Rebellion*, Edward McPherson. Philp & Solomons, New York, 1864.
163   George Smith Diary, 5/20/1861.
164   GTH, 5/17/1861.
165   GTH, 5/10, 5/31/1861.
166   GTH, 6/7/1861.
167   GTH, 11/16/1861.
168   GTH, 6/7, 6/21/1861.
169   From a reprint of the article in the 9/27/1861 GTH.
170   GTH, 8/9/1861.
171   GTH, 6/21/1861.
172   GTH, 6/21/1861.
173   GTH, 6/14/1861. Reprinted from an article in the *Albany Evening Journal*.
174   The July, 1861 battle is referred to as Manassas or Bull Run, and sometimes both place names.
175   GTH, 9/20/1861.
176   GTH, 8/9/1861.
177   GTH, 9/20/1861.
178   GTH, 11/1/1861. Busteed is the correct spelling.
179   GTH, 10/4/1861.
180   GTH, 10/11/1861.
181   GTH, 9/20/1861; George Smith Diary, 9/16/1861.
182   GTH, 9/27/1861.
183   GTH, 9/20/1861.
184   GTH, 10/18, 11/8/1861.
185   George Smith Diary, 8/26/1861, 10/8/1861.
186   GTH, 2/14/1862.
187   GTH, 11/30/1861.
188   GTH, 12/6/1861. John Brown Sr. received the nickname "Old Ossawatamie" in recognition of the place he killed a number of pro-slavery farmers in Kansas in 1856.

CHAPTER 5: 1862 | GONE TO WAR

189   *Boizard Letters*, Empire Historical Society.
190   GTH, 1/3/1862.
191   GTH, 1/3/1862.
192   George Smith Diary, 1/20/1862; GTH, 1/3/62. Reprinted from an article in the *Albany Journal*.
193   GTH, 1/10/1862.
194   GTH, 1/24/1862.
195   GTH, 6/13/1862.
196   GTH, 2/28/1862.
197   GTH, 3/7/1862.
198   GTH, 3/21/1862.
199   GTH, 3/21/1862.
200   *Michigan in the War*, John Robertson, p. 583, and *Mackinac*, Mackinac State Historic Parks, p. 46-8.
201   GTH, 4/4/1862. From a letter signed Geo. B. McClellan, Fairfax Court House, March 14, 1862.
202   *Personal Memoirs of Ulysses S. Grant*, p. 132.
203   *Personal Memoirs of Ulysses S. Grant*, p. 135.
204   GTH, 5/2/1862.
205   *Personal Memoirs of Ulysses S. Grant*, p. 142-43. Fort Henry was abandoned days before the capture of Fort Donelson.
206   GTH, 5/1862.
207   George Smith Diary, 4/11/1862.
208   GTH, 4/11/1862.
209   GTH, 4/11/1862.
210   George Smith Diary, 5/2/1862.
211   GTH, 6/20/1862.
212   GTH, 6/20/1862.
213   GTH, 5/16/1862.
214   GTH, 6/6/1862.
215   GTH, 5/23/1862.
216   GTH, 6/13/1862.
217   GTH, 7/4/1862.
218   George Smith Diary, 5/16/1863.
219   GTH, 8/15/1862.
220   Letter dated July 20, 1862 as reprinted in the *Grand Traverse Herald*, 8/15/1862.
221   GTH, 8/15/1862.
222   GTH, 8/15/1862.
223   GTH, 8/22/1862.
224   George Smith Diary, 9/4/1862.
225   GTH, 9/19/1862.
226   George Smith Diary, 9/16/1862.

227 George Smith Diary, 9/19/1862.

228 GTH, 10/3/1862.

229 GTH, 10/10/1862.

230 GTH, 10/10/1862.

231 *History of Leelanau Township*, Northport Area Heritage Association.

232 GTH, 11/7/1862.

233 George Smith Diary, 10/24, 10/28/1862.

234 GTH, 10/31/1862.

235 George Smith Diary, 11/4/1862; GTH, 11/7/1862.

236 George Smith Diary, 11/6/1862.

237 George Smith Diary, 11/17, 11/18/1862.

238 GTH, 11/21/1862.

239 GTH, 11/21/1862.

240 *The Inner World of Abraham Lincoln.* Michael Burlingame, p. 105.

241 Reverend Smith Diary, 1/7/1863. The report of Albert Powers' loss of a leg later proved false.

CHAPTER 6: 1863 | WHIP OR GET WHIPPED

242 *Life and Times of Frederick Douglass*, pp. 428-30. Boston, 1892, DeWolfe & Fiske Co.

243 GTH, 1/2/1863.

244 GTH, 1/16/1863.

245 GTH, 2/6/1863.

246 George Smith Diary, 2/1/1863.

247 GTH, 8/14/1863.

248 GTH, 1/2/1863.

249 GTH, 1/30/1863.

250 GTH, 1/23/1863.

251 George Smith Diary, 1/17/1863.

252 *The Traverse Region*, p. 49. H.R. Page, Chicago, 1884.

253 A clerical error made in Lansing on the bill to incorporate Leelanau County in 1863 spelled its name as Leelanaw. The mistake that was not legally corrected until 1896.

254 GTH, 2/27/1863.

255 GTH, 3/20/1863; George Smith Diary, 3/25/1863.

256 GTH, 3/20/1863.

257 GTH, 4/17/1863.

258 GTH, 1/2/1863.

259 From the *Detroit Advertiser and Tribune*, as reprinted in *Grand Traverse Herald*, 3/27/1863.

260 *Personal Memoirs of Ulysses S. Grant*, p. 461.

261 GTH, 3/27/1863.

262 *The Boizard Letters*, 7/6/1863 letter from Harriet Fisher to the Boizards, p. 26. Empire Heritage Group, Empire, MI, 1993.

263 GTH, 5/16/1863.

264 GTH, 4/20/1863, from a W.E. Sykes letter written 2/21/1863.

265 George Smith Diary, 4/17/1863.

266 GTH, 3/13/1863. From a letter written by "J.H. Hollingsworth, Camp of Mercantile

267 George Smith Diary, 3/17/1863.

268 GTH, 4/17/1863.

269 GTH, 4/17/1863.

270 GTH, 6/19/1863. The 6/26/1863 issue of the paper corrects the pioneer's name to Benjamin W. Hall.

271 GTH, 6/26/1863.

272 GTH, 6/26/1863.

273 GTH, 8/7/1863.

274 GTH, 5/8/1863.

275 *Harper's Weekly*, 6/6/1863, p. 358.

276 *Personal Memoirs of Ulysses S. Grant*, p. 192.

277 *Harper's Weekly*, 6/6/1863, p. 354; *The Civil War A Narrative: Fredericksburg to Meridian*, Shelby Foote, 1963. Random House, New York, 1986, p. 34; *Memoirs of William Tecumseh Sherman*, W.T. Sherman, 1875. Copyright Literary Classics of the United States, New York, N.Y., 1990, p. 283; *The Civil War A Narrative: Fredericksburg to Meridian*, Shelby Foote, 1963. First Vintage Books edition, Random House, New York, 1986, p. 334.

278 *History of the Twentieth Michigan – Civil War*, Byron M. Cutcheon. Lansing 1904

279 George Smith Diary, 4/25/1863.

280 Leelanau County Clerk's records, May 9, 1863.

281 *The Boizard Letters*, pp. 26-27, letter from Harriet Fisher to the Boizards dated 7/6/1863; John Fisher to Boizards 11/5/1863. Empire Area Heritage Group, Empire, MI, 1993.

282 GTH, George Smith Diary, 5/2/1863.

283 GTH, 6/12/1863.

284 GTH, 8/7/1863.

285 GTH, 7/10/1863.

286 *These Men Have Seen Hard Service*, p. 58. Raymond Herek, Wayne State University Press, Detroit, 1998. From the *Detroit Advertiser and Tribune*, July 14, 1863.

287 GTH, 6/26/1863.

288 *The Boizard Letters*, pp. 26-27, letter from Harriet Fisher to the Boizards dated 7/6/1863.

289 GTH, 4/24, 7/10/1863.

290 GTH, 7/10/1863.

291 GTH, 7/17/1863.

292 GTH, 6/9/1865.

293 Written by Captain William E. Miller, 3rd Pennsylvania Cavalry, who at a critical moment in the battle led a charge to the aid of Custer, reversing Confederate momentum.

294 GTH, 7/17/1863.

295 National Park Service website

296 GTH, 8/14/1863.

297 Former Presidents John Adams and Thomas Jefferson both died on July 4, 1826, their

Battery, Young's Point, Seven Miles from Vicksburg, February 11, 1863. See *This Republic of Suffering* by Drew Gilpin Faust.

departures separated by four hours and four hundred miles. Exactly fifty years before, on July 4, the two had signed the Declaration of Independence.

298 GTH, 7/17/1863.

299 George Smith Diary, 7/1-7/4/1863.

300 George Smith Diary, 7/10/1863.

301 *The Crooked Tree Indian Legends of Northern Michigan,* John C. Wright, p. 123. John C. Wright, Harbor Springs, 1917. Wright was Garrett Graveraet's nephew, Sophie Bailly was his grandmother.

302 "Indian Legends of Northern Michigan," John C. Wright, pp. 81-89. *Michigan History Magazine,* Michigan Historical Society, Volume II, 1918.

303 Smith Diary, 8/1/1863.

304 Smith Diary, 8/1/1863. In nautical terms, ships headed west out of Buffalo journeyed "up" lake, while those traveling back were going "down," no matter what the compass said. Ships leaving Grand Traverse Country for Chicago, steering directly south, were "upbound."

305 Smith Diary, 8/26/1863.

306 Fernando Wood served a second term as mayor of New York from 1860-1862. When South Carolina seceded from the Union in 1861, Wood, fearing the loss of lucrative profits from cotton shipped through New York harbor, pressed the city council to also secede and form a new state. Though Wood was no longer mayor in at the time of the riots in 1863, he denounced the draft and helped stir up fears among immigrants that freed blacks would take their jobs.

307 GTH, 7/24/1863.

308 *Michigan in the War* by John Robertson, p. 291. W.S. George & Co., Lansing, 1880.

309 *The Boizard Letters,* A letter from Harriet Fisher to the Boizards, 8/26/1863, p. 28; GTH, 7/17/1863.

310 GTH, 9/25/1863.

311 GTH, 5/6/1864; *The Boizard Letters,* p. 27; George Smith Diary, 9/22/1863.

312 George Smith Diary, 9/2, 9/7, 9/10, 9/22/1863.

313 George Smith Diary, 10/5, 12/3/1863.

314 GTH, 7/31, 9/25, 10/30/1863.

315 GTH, 10/16/1863.

316 GTH, 10/30/1863.

317 GTH, 7/24/1863.

318 GTH, 11/20/1863.

319 GTH, 12/4/1863.

320 GTH, 12/11/1863.

CHAPTER 7: 1864 | A FEARFUL TIME

321 George Smith Diary, 1/1-1/10/1864.

322 GTH, 1/22/1864.

323 George Smith Diary, 1/4/1864. The added name, Jacob Haines, was the 6th volunteer Smith referred to.

324 Joshua Middleton, 6/30/1864 letter to his sister from Jarvis Hospital.

325 Joshua Middleton, p. 5, 2/8/1864.

326 Joshua Middleton , letters dated April 1864, written in a camp near the Rapidan River in Virginia.

327 GTH, 4/25/1864.

328 Gen. John Peck, New Berne, North Carolina 2/3/1864, to Major R.S. Davis.

329 George Smith Diary, 2/9/1864.

330 Joshua Middleton, letter dated 4/23/1864.

331 GTH, 2/12/1864.

332 GTH, 1/8/1864.

333 GTH, 3/4/1864.

334 George Smith Diary, 3/20/1864.

335 GTH, 4/8/1864.

336 George Smith Diary, 4/1/1864; GTH, 4/22, 5/6/1864.

337 GTH, 6/17/1864.

338 Michigan Central Railroad.

339 Paul Gravel Letter dated Nashville, April 28, 1864.

340 *Michigan in the War,* Robertson, p. 563.

341 Letter to George Mason, April 1786.

342 Joshua Middleton, letters to his sister "Em," the first undated, the second dated 4/23/1864.

343 Herek, *These Men Have Seen Hard Service,* p. 119.

344 *Personal Memoirs of Ulysses S. Grant,* p. 311.

345 George Smith Diary, May 18, 19, 1864.

346 *Personal Memoirs of Ulysses S. Grant,* p. 310

347 *Personal Memoirs of Ulysses S. Grant,* p. 321.

348 Joshua Middleton, from a letter dated 6/30/1864.

349 Many of the particulars about the service of Grand Traverse soldiers in the Civil War are borrowed from the book *Forest Haven Soldiers* by Leonard J. Overmyer III, with the author's permission. Mr. Overmyer is a Civil War expert whose specialty is the 26th Michigan Infantry.

350 Captain Nelson Ames, *Historical Sketch,* July 3, 1893.

351 Herek, pp. 146-149.

352 *Michigan in the War,* p. 372.

353 GTH, 8/12/1864.

354 Robertson, *Michigan in the War,* p. 294.

355 GTH, 6/17/1864.

356 George Smith Diary, 5/20/1864.

357 GTH, 6/17/1864.

358 George Smith Diary, 5/26, 5/27, 5/31/1864.

359 GTH, 6/24/1864.

360 Joshua Middleton letters, 6/30/1864.

361 *Personal Memoirs of Ulysses S. Grant,* p. 344.

362 GTH, 7/29/1864. Colonel Deland.

363   GTH, 8/12/1864.

364   *Personal Memoirs of Ulysses S. Grant*, p. 353.

365   George Smith Diary, 6/20/1864.

366   George Smith Diary, 6/16/1864.

367   Middleton used the short form of "copperheads," a derogatory reference to anti-war Democrats in the North.

368   George Smith Diary, 6/30/1864 and the GTH, 6/24/1864.

369   Joshua Middleton from Jarvis hospital, Baltimore, 6/30/1864.

370   GTH, 8/12/1864.

371   George Smith Diary, 7/19/1864.

372   George Smith Diary, 7/22/1864.

373   *Memoirs of Ulysses S. Grant*, p. 360.

374   George Smith Diary, 8/3/1864.

375   National Park Service.

376   GTH, 8/12/1864.

377   GTH, 9/16/1864.

378   George Smith Diary, 8/16. 8/17, 8/21, 8/26/1864.

379   George Smith Diary, 8/24/1864.

380   GTH, 9/16/1864.

381   Joshua Middleton letter from Jarvis Hospital, Baltimore, dated 9/4/1864.

382   Joshua Middleton letter from Jarvis Hospital, Baltimore, dated 11/27/1864.

383   *Personal Memoirs of Ulysses S. Grant*, p. 361.

384   GTH, 9/30/1864.

385   George Smith Diary, 9/16/1864.

386   Robertson, *Michigan in the War*, p. 564.

387   GTH, 10/14/1864.

388   GTH, 10/7/1864.

389   GTH, 10/21/1864.

390   The five townships of Leelanau County in 1864 were Leelanau, Bingham, Elmwood, Glen Arbor, and Centreville.

391   George Smith Diary, 10/25/1864.

392   GTH, 10/14/1864.

393   GTH, 9/30/1864.

394   GTH, 12/2/1864; *Michigan in the War*, John Robertson, pp. 312-313.

395   George Smith Diary, 10/29, 10/30, 10/31/1864.

396   George Smith Diary, 11/6/1864.

397   GTH, 11/4/1864.

398   GTH, 11/4/1864.

399   George Smith Diary, 11/17, 11/8/1864.

400   Joshua Middleton, letter dated 11/9/1864.

401   GTH, 11/11/1864.

402   GTH, 11/18/1864.

403   GTH, 12/23/1864.

404   Michigan in the War, p. 566.

405   GTH, 11/25/1864.

406   GTH, 12/9/1864.

407   GTH, 12/23/1864.

408   GTH, 1/6/1865.

409   GTH, 1/6/1865.

410   GTH, 12/2/1864.

411   GTH, 12/2/1864.

412   GTH, 1/6/1865.

413   George Smith Diary, 12/15/1864.

414   George Smith Diary, 12/28/1864.

415   George Smith Diary, 12/30/1864.

416   GTH, 12/28/1865.

417   Joshua Middleton archives, undated, unsigned letter.

CHAPTER 8: 1865 | THE END IS SOON TO COME

418   Joshua Middleton, letter dated 1/15/1865.

419   GTH, 1/6/1865.

420   George Smith Diary, 1/11, 1/12/1865.

421   George Smith Diary, 2/6/1865. Camp Sumpter was the official name of Andersonville Prison.

422   GTH, 2/3/1865; George Smith Diary, 3/26/1865.

423   GTH, 2/17/1865.

424   GTH, 2/17/1865.

425   GTH, 3/3/1865.

426   GTH, 2/17/1865.

427   GTH, 1/20/1865.

428   GTH, 1/13/1865.

429   GTH, 3/10/1865.

430   GTH, 2/10/1865.

431   GTH, 3/3/1865.

432   GTH, 3/3/1865.

433   GTH, 4/21/1865.

434   GTH, 4/7/1865.

435   GTH, 3/17/1865.

436   GTH, 4/7/1865.

437   GTH, 4/28/1865.

438   George Smith Diary, 4/13/1865.

439   GTH, 4/14/1865.

440   GTH, 5/12/1865.

441   George Smith Diary, 4/14/1865.

442   *Michigan in the War*, Robertson, p. 296.

443   George Smith Diary, 4/20/1865.

444   GTH, 4/21/1865; George Smith Diary, 4/27/1865; *The Boizard Letters*, 4/16/1865.

445   GTH, 4/28/1865.

446   GTH, 4/28/1865.

447   GTH, 4/28/1865.

448   GTH, 5/12/1865.

449   GTH, 5/5, 4/21/1865.

450   GTH, 5/5/1865.

451   GTH, 5/5/1865.

452   GTH, 5/12/1865.

453   GTH, 5/12/1865.

454   GTH, 5/12/1865; John Boizard, Chicago, May 3, 1865.

455   George Smith Diary, 7/28/1865.

456   GTH, 6/30/1865.

457   Joshua Middleton, 7/11/1865.

458   George Smith Diary, 7/25/1865.

INDEX